Traveling the **Lewis** & **Clark Trail**
Second Edition

Julie Fanselow

FALCON®
HELENA, MONTANA

A FALCON GUIDE®

Falcon® is continually expanding its list of recreational guidebooks. All books include detailed descriptions, accurate maps, and all the information necessary for enjoyable trips. You can order extra copies of this book and get information and prices for other Falcon books by writing to Falcon Publishing, Inc., P.O. Box 1718, Helena, MT 59624 or calling our toll-free number, 1-800-582-2665. Also, please ask for a free copy of our current catalog. Visit our website at www.Falcon.com, or contact us by e-mail at falcon@falcon.com.

Cover photo by Michael Sample
Cover background: "At Lemhi" by Robert F. Morgan
All interior photos by author unless noted otherwise.

Project Editor: Leeann Drabenstott
Production Editor: Patrick Straub
Maps by Tony Moore
Copyeditor: Shana Harrington
Page Compositor: Marita Martiniak
Cover design by Michael Cutter

Library of Congress Cataloging-in-Publication Data
    Fanselow, Julie
    Traveling the Lewis and Clark Trail/by Julie Fanselow.--2nd ed.
        p. cm.
    Rev. ed. of: The traveler's guide to the Lewis & Clark Trail. c1994.
    ISBN 1-58592-042-8
    1. Lewis and Clark National Historic Trail--Guidebooks. I. Fanselow, Julie. Traveler's guide to the Lewis & Clark Trail. II. Title.

F592.7 .F35 2000
917.804'33-dc21

00-026416

CAUTION

Outdoor recreational activities are by their very nature potentially hazardous. All participants in such activities must assume the responsibility for their own actions and safety. The information contained in this guidebook cannot replace sound judgment and good decision-making skills, which help reduce risk exposure, nor does the scope of this book allow for disclosure of all the potential hazards and risks involved in such activities.

Learn as much as possible about the outdoor recreational activities in which you participate, prepare for the unexpected, and be cautious. The reward will be a safer and more enjoyable experience.

 Text pages printed on recycled paper.

Contents

To the memories of:
Meriwether Lewis (1774–1809)
William Clark (1770–1838)
and Ruth Fanselow (1925–1987)

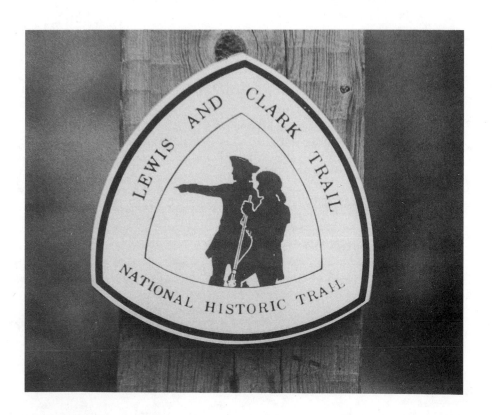

ACKNOWLEDGMENTS

When I began researching this second edition of *Traveling the Lewis & Clark Trail*, I didn't expect I would spend even more time tracing the route than I had the first time around. But that's what happened; I wound up taking my own advice, seeking every opportunity to linger on the trail.

Many people helped. For this edition and the previous one, I am thankful for advice, counsel, and logistical assistance from Jim Becic, Chan Biggs, Victor Bjornberg, Butch Bouvier, Jim Cook and the Clearwater Canoe Company, Larry and Bonnie Cook, Bob Doerk, Pete Donatucci, Lisa Eckert, Larry Epstein, Linda Fee, Sally Freeman, Larry Grantham, Calvin Grinnell, Peter Grubb and Betsy Bowen and the whole ROW team, George Harbaugh, Robin Harbaugh, Linda Hartung, the staff of the Horse Prairie Ranch, Mimi Jackson, Barb Kubik, Chuck Knowles, Terry Korpela, Stan Lawson, Steve Lee, Craig Madsen, Steve Matz, Chuck Mead, Pauline Nez, Harlan and Barb Opdahl, Jim Peterson, Chuck Raddon, Marlin Roth, Carol Ryan, Mark Selvik, Jane Schmoyer Weber, Bob Singer, Wilbur Werner, Mark Wetmore, Richard Williams, and Doug Yunker and his partners at BirdWoman. Dozens of other people at local museums and visitors bureaus also provided valuable information. Thanks to you all.

Leeann Drabenstott and Molly Jay are more than fine editors; they are champions of this book, and I thank them, along with everyone else at Falcon.

Stephen Ambrose did me a big favor when he picked up the first edition of this book while researching his own ode to the Corps of Discovery, *Undaunted Courage*—and later when he told Falcon's Bill Schneider what a help it had been. Professor Ambrose has done more than any one person to generate modern interest in the Lewis and Clark story, and he has my admiration.

Dayton Duncan's *Out West* served as my own inspiration to hit the trail. He, too, has proven an advocate for my work, and I thank him.

My husband, Bruce Whiting, is my partner in all things. My daughter, Natalie Fanselow Whiting—born just after the first edition of this book came out—has begun joining me on some of my own voyages of discovery. My father, Byron Fanselow, is a great friend to me and grandfather to Natalie. I also value the support of Carrol Whiting, who sends me everything the *Billings Gazette* ever prints about Lewis and Clark.

Finally, I hold a special thought for my father-in-law, Ray Whiting, who in the spirit of everyone from Lewis and Clark to Horatio Alger, made his way west to Montana as a young man. He died in 1998, and he is buried near the bluffs of the Yellowstone River where they tumble across the plains to meet the Missouri. His spirit lingers on over this confluence country; it isn't the same visiting eastern Montana without him there.

PREFACE

These days, travelers think little of crossing a continent in a matter of hours. But less than 200 years ago, a small group of Americans undertook a journey so complex and so potentially dangerous that their president and benefactor, Thomas Jefferson, and their fellow citizens half expected they would never return. In less capable hands, the mission surely would have failed. But Meriwether Lewis and William Clark had the intelligence, the bravery, and the generous spirit to see it through.

The trip was the Lewis and Clark Expedition of 1804–1806, and it ranks among the world's greatest journeys of discovery. This guidebook aims to help travelers—both actual and armchair—relive the expedition's excitement and drama. In these pages, you will find details about the major historic sites all along the Lewis and Clark Trail, along with information on modern recreational and scenic attractions, activities, and visitor amenities along the way. In short, this is a guide for people who want to retrace Lewis and Clark's route while finding some adventures of their own.

It is true we can whip across our nation in mere hours or days. But these are journeys of expedience, not experience. Today, we must give ourselves the luxury of taking time to linger and learn, even dawdle and drift.

Few artifacts of the Lewis and Clark journey remain along the route, and in many areas, interpretation is minimal. A trip along the trail today is very much a journey of imagination. But there are many places visitors can well imagine what it was like to be Lewis and Clark, and this book aims to guide you to the best of those places.

MAP LEGEND

Interstate Highway		Outward Bound 1804–1805		....
U.S. Highway		Homeward Bound 1806		- - - - - - - - - - - -
State Highway		Town		O **LEWISTON**
Forest Road		Airport		✈
River or Stream		Point of Interest		▢
Peak	**Mt. Hood** 11,239 ft.	Lewis & Clark Campsites/Landmarks		**Camp Wood**
Boundary		Interpretive Center		
Trail	....	River and Scenic Boat Trips		
		Hiking		
Compass	N W E S	Bicycling		
		Native American Site		
Scale	0 5 10 miles	Equestrian		

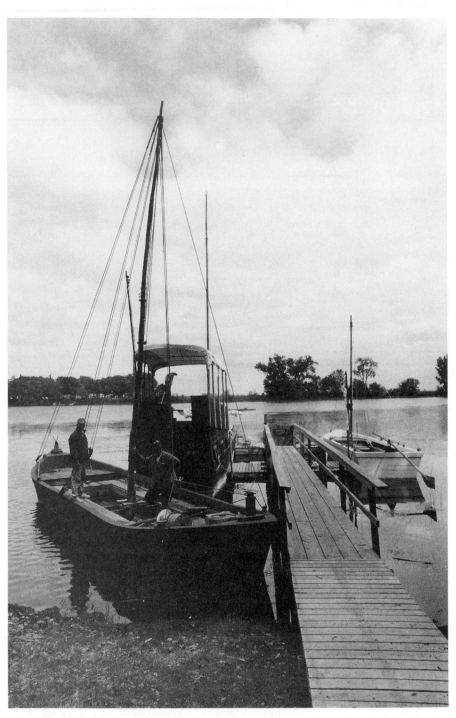

Keelboat and pirogue replicas.

CHAPTER ONE

THE CORPS OF DISCOVERY: A BRIEF HISTORY AND OVERVIEW

From his youth, Thomas Jefferson was fascinated with the West. Not so much the West as he understood it, for even as president he never traveled far from his Virginia home, but the West as he imagined it: a land of mystery and revelation, a land where the United States could stretch its boundaries and grow into a preeminent world power.

In his inaugural address of 1801, Jefferson described America as "kindly separated by nature and a wide ocean from the exterminating havoc of one quarter of the globe, possessing a chosen country with room enough for our descendants to the thousandth and thousandth generation." With these blessings, he asked, "what more is necessary to make us a happy and prosperous people?" Jefferson expected it would take the passing of a full 40 generations just to explore the whole of the United States. Remarkably, it took only four years to chart a large measure of the continent.

For years, Europeans and Americans believed that by following the Missouri River to its headwaters, they would discover a Northwest Passage to the Pacific Ocean. French, British, and Spanish explorers had long tried to prove this theory, and when the United States was born in 1776, the contest for domination of the Western frontier became a four-way race.

The power struggle continued for another quarter-century, with the young American nation siding first with one European power, then another. Ultimately, France's desire to limit English influence in North America made possible the United States' acquisition of the Northwest via the Louisiana Purchase. For $15 million—less than four cents an acre—the United States bought more than 800,000 square miles of land.

The Louisiana Purchase had an incalculable effect on the future of the United States. With its boundaries set by the Missouri and Mississippi river drainages, the deal doubled the country's area, giving the young nation access to a wealth of valuable natural resources. Assessing the agreement's impact, noted historian Bernard DeVoto wrote: "There is no aspect of national life, no part of our social and political structure, and no subsequent event in the course of our history that it has not affected." And what a bargain it proved to be: even by the time the interest was paid, the Louisiana Purchase cost America a total of just $23 million.

The Louisiana Purchase is often viewed as the event that precipitated the Lewis and Clark Expedition, but plans for the trek were already well under way by the time the deal was signed. In fact, Jefferson had long wished for an expe-

1

Bronze relief depicting signing of the Louisiana Purchase, Missouri State Capitol grounds, Jefferson City.

dition and started laying groundwork for the mission in the fall of 1802. At that time, he asked the Spanish minister, the Marques de Casa Yrujo, whether Spain would object if the United States sent a small party to explore the Missouri River to seek the Northwest Passage. (Spain was to transfer the land in question to France under an 1800 treaty, but the move hadn't yet taken place.) Yrujo wrote back that he saw no need for the exploration since the European powers had already sought and disproved the notion of a Northwest Passage. Yrujo also warned Jefferson that Spanish authorities would be notified if he proceeded with the idea.

Undaunted, Jefferson sent a secret message to Congress in January 1803. He asked for an appropriation of $2,500 for an expedition to seek the source of the Missouri River and, upon finding it, follow the best course westward to the Pacific Ocean, "for the purpose of extending the external commerce of the United States."

Jefferson had hired Meriwether Lewis as his private secretary, at least in part with an eye to the possible expedition. As DeVoto wrote in his edition of the Lewis and Clark journals, "Lewis was a family friend, but Jefferson had many friends better qualified by background and education to be secretary to the President. He was however, uniquely qualified for a project which Jefferson had cherished for many years, the exploration of the Missouri River and the lands west of its source." In his letter offering employment to Lewis, Jefferson wrote, "Your knowledge of the Western country, of the army and all its interests and relations have rendered it desirable for public as well as private purposes that you should be engaged in that office."

Lewis was born August 18, 1774, just a few miles from Jefferson's home in Virginia, the second of three children of plantation owners William and Lucy Meriwether Lewis. His father died when Meriwether was just five years old. Lucy soon married again, and the family moved to Georgia. Early on, Meriwether showed great intellect, but much moodiness, too.

By age 13, Meriwether was sent back to Virginia to continue his education and learn how to run the plantation, which was still in his family. After his stepfather, John Marks, died in the early 1790s, young Meriwether traveled to Georgia to bring the rest of his family back to Virginia. Soon after, he joined the Army. He had served six years and risen to the rank of captain by the time Jefferson sought his help in Washington, D.C. Lewis, just 26 years old when he received the job offer of secretary in March 1801, readily agreed. A year and a half later, he was working at Jefferson's behest to draw up plans for the Western expedition.

Congress approved the appropriation in February 1803. Secretary of War Henry Dearborn officially authorized the mission in July 1803. Preparations for the journey went into high gear as Lewis gathered supplies and ordered a keelboat built. He traveled to Philadelphia for a crash course in all kinds of scientific disciplines. He learned from Andrew Ellicott how to take celestial observations. Dr. Benjamin Rush, along with helping plan the expedition's scientific and cultural goals, instructed Lewis in rudimentary medicine.

Originally, Lewis was to select a second-in-command from the party's ranks after the expedition had gotten under way. But as preparations progressed, Jefferson and Lewis—aware of the trip's significance—decided it might be best to select Lewis's right-hand man before the journey started. The man they chose was William Clark, under whose command Lewis had served seven years earlier.

Clark was born August 1, 1770, in Virginia, the younger brother of George Rogers Clark (who became a hero in the Revolutionary War). William followed in his family's military footsteps, and by 1795 was put in command of an elite company of riflemen at Fort Greenville, Ohio. It was there he met Meriwether Lewis, and the men quickly became friends. William soon left the Army to take care of his older brother, George Rogers, who was battling alcoholism and debt in Indiana. But he and Lewis stayed in touch by mail and visits.

On June 19, 1803, Lewis wrote to Clark, told him of the mission, and said, "If therefore there is anything … in this enterprise, which would induce you to participate with me in its fatigues, its dangers, and its honors, believe me there is no man on earth with whom I should feel equal pleasure in sharing them with as yourself." He further noted that Jefferson would promise Clark—who had resigned as a lieutenant—a full captain's commission and all the attendant benefits. "Your situation will in all respects be precisely such as my own," Lewis concluded.

Weeks went by with no word from Clark. Jefferson and Lewis prepared to ask Lt. Moses Hooke, their second choice, if he would accept the role. But Clark's reply finally came on July 29. "My friend I do assure you no man lives with whom I would prefer to undertake such a trip as yourself," Clark wrote to Lewis, thus ending any thoughts of what history might have come to call the "Lewis and Hooke Expedition."

The co-leaders set about the task of choosing the men to accompany them. In Lewis's words, they looked for "good hunters, stout, healthy, unmarried, accustomed to the woods and capable of bearing bodily fatigue in a pretty considerable degree." Some members of the expedition were recruited for special skills they possessed: Lewis wanted Patrick Gass along as a carpenter and boatbuilder, for example. Gass had grown up in western Pennsylvania and into manhood with the young nation, ever moving west with the frontier, and he turned out to be one of the most interesting members of the expedition.

George Drouillard was selected as an interpreter and hunter, and the importance of his latter task can't be underestimated: it took four deer and an elk or one deer and a buffalo to feed the entire group for 24 hours. John Shields, a relative of Daniel Boone, hired on as gunsmith, and Clark later wrote: "The party owes much to the ingenuity of this man by whom their guns are repaired when they get out of order, which is very often."

One recruit had no say in the matter. Ben York, a Clark family slave, had been William Clark's constant companion since early childhood and there was no question he would accompany Clark on the trip west. York became the first black man to join a military expedition, cross the Continental Divide, and reach the Pacific Ocean. He was a large, strong, and good-natured man. The Indians considered York "great medicine," and would travel long distances to see and touch him.

The recruits sensed they were embarking on a journey of great importance. On April 8, 1804, John Ordway wrote: "Honored parents: I am now on an expedition to the westward with Captain Lewis and Captain Clark to the western ocean. This party consists of 25 picked men, and I am so happy as to be one of them." Even Seaman, Lewis's Newfoundland dog, proved a valuable member of the expedition. He retrieved game and, with his barking, alerted the party to the presence of grizzly bears and buffalo.

Many of us spend hours agonizing over what belongings to take on a two-week vacation, so it is hard to imagine what it might be like trying to pack for a trip of undetermined length. The food alone weighed seven tons. Other items selected included a blacksmith's forge, mill for grinding corn, carpenters' tools and axes, surveying and navigational instruments, medical supplies, cooking utensils, an iron boat frame, 52 lead canisters weighing 420 pounds for sealing 175 pounds of gunpowder, six kegs—or 30 gallons—of brandy, and canvas for tarpaulins.

Congress's $2,500 appropriation purchased the following: mathematical instruments, $217; provisions, $224; materials for portable packs, $55; pay for hunters, guides, and interpreters, $300; pay for members' moving expenses, $100; weapons, $81; camp equipment, $255; medical supplies, $55; boats, $430; and $87 for contingencies. The largest single budget item, $696, paid for Indian presents. That amount purchased 47.5 yards of red flannel, 12 dozen pocket mirrors, 73 bunches of beads, 2,800 fishhooks, and 4,600 needles.

Even back then, the federal government occasionally had a tough time living within its means. Although only $2,500 was originally allocated, the corps carried a letter of credit from Jefferson, and actual expenditures wound up totaling about $38,000. Still, few people would dispute the investment was worth it. Aside from strengthening American claims to the West, the expedition had an immeasurable impact on scientific, anthropological, and geographic knowledge.

The Corps of Discovery—a nickname given to the expedition by Jefferson—finally left Camp Wood, Illinois, on May 14, 1804. The men returned on September 23, 1806, two years, four months, and 10 days after they had departed. In the interim, they lived one of the greatest examples of exploration and cooperation the United States—or the world, for that matter—has ever seen ... a trip we shall examine in much greater detail as we follow the corps' progress west.

Stepping back in time with a visit to the Lewis and Clark Center at St. Charles, Missouri.

CHAPTER TWO

HOW TO USE THIS BOOK

$\mathcal{B}$y the time its travels were completed, the Lewis and Clark Expedition had logged more than 7,500 miles paddling, hiking, and riding across the continent and back.

Obviously, it would be difficult to duplicate such a journey today. But it is possible to take a great Western vacation focusing on the Lewis and Clark Trail. What's more, the historical aspects of a Lewis and Clark vacation can easily be combined with your favorite leisure activities, be they camping, canoeing, sightseeing, fishing, golf, hiking, or just plain taking it easy.

There are two ways to travel. Some travelers would like to see the whole trail in one trip, and it's possible to retrace the route in your vehicle in just under two weeks using the itinerary below. But many people would rather take their time discovering the route, covering one section one year and another the next.

SUGGESTED ITINERARIES

The following is a suggested Lewis and Clark trip designed to fit within a two-week vacation period. The main itinerary is for travelers who prefer sightseeing and visiting historical sites. In-depth alternatives are offered for adventure-oriented travelers or others seeking to spend more time in fewer places.

DAY 1: THE ST. LOUIS/ST. CHARLES AREA, MISSOURI.

Start with a visit to the **Lewis and Clark State Memorial** on the banks of the Mississippi River in Illinois (just off Illinois Highway 3 south of Alton). Next, tour the **Museum of Westward Expansion** and **Gateway Arch**; **William Clark's grave** in St. Louis's Bellefontaine Cemetery; and the **Lewis and Clark Center** in St. Charles. Overnight in St. Charles.

Approximate driving time/distance: Not applicable; all sites in St. Louis metropolitan area.

DAY 2: ST. CHARLES, MISSOURI, TO KANSAS CITY, MISSOURI.

Drive west along the Missouri River. Possible stops include the Daniel Boone Home; the German-style town of Hermann; **Jefferson City**, where a relief on the Capitol Grounds depicts the signing of the Louisiana Purchase; **Arrow Rock**;

and **Fort Osage**, a trading post Clark helped build after the expedition. Missouri 94 and 100 parallel the river from St. Charles to Jefferson City. From there, follow U.S. Highway 63 to Columbia; Interstate 70 to Boonville; Missouri 41 through Arrow Rock to Marshall; and U.S. Highway 65 and U.S. Highway 24 to Fort Osage and the Kansas City area. Overnight in Kansas City.

Approximate driving time/distance: Six hours, 275 miles.

In-depth alternative: Spend a few hours—or days—bicycling or hiking along the Katy Trail. For Lewis and Clark buffs, the best stretches are those closest to the Missouri River, such as the portion near Rocheport in central Missouri. Overnight in a riverside town or drive on to the Kansas City area.

DAY 3: KANSAS CITY, MISSOURI, TO SIOUX CITY, IOWA.

Travel north on Interstate 29 to the Omaha/Council Bluffs area, possibly stopping for side trips to **Lewis and Clark State Park** (northwest of Kansas City on Missouri 45) and nearby **Atchison, Kansas,** where the expedition spent July 4, 1804. Continue on to Council Bluffs, Iowa, via I-29 and visit the Western Historic Trails Center and the **Lewis & Clark Monument Park** on the bluffs overlooking the Missouri. Cross into Omaha, Nebraska, and visit the Joslyn Art Museum to see its Karl Bodmer collection or **Fort Atkinson State Park.** Take either U.S. Highway 75 or I-29 to Onawa, Iowa, where a replica of the Corps of Discovery's keelboat is on display at Iowa's **Lewis and Clark State Park.** Continue north to Sioux City and see the **Sergeant Floyd Monument.** Overnight in Sioux City.

Approximate driving time/distance: Seven hours, 340 miles.

DAY 4: SIOUX CITY, IOWA, TO PIERRE, SOUTH DAKOTA.

Take I-29 north to Vermillion, South Dakota, and visit **Spirit Mound.** (Mound may be seen from South Dakota 19; ask permission to hike to its top.) Next, see the **Lewis and Clark Visitor Center** at Gavins Point Dam west of Yankton, South Dakota. Have lunch in one of the many nearby park areas. Take South Dakota 46 and South Dakota 50 to Platte, then South Dakota 45 to Interstate 90. Follow the interstate to Chamberlain; then take SD 50 and South Dakota 34 north and west to Pierre. Visit **Farm Island State Recreation Area** and the **Teton Council Site.** Overnight in Pierre.

Approximate driving time/distance: Seven hours, 325 miles.

In-depth alternative: Rent a canoe or book a guided trip and paddle the free-flowing stretches of the Missouri River near Ponca State Park or Niobrara State Park.

Day 5: Pierre, South Dakota, to Bismarck/Mandan, North Dakota.

Drive north to Mobridge on U.S. Highway 83 and 12. Visit the **Sacagawea and Sitting Bull monuments** west of town, and continue north on South Dakota 1806, which changes to North Dakota 24 at the border. Follow ND 24 and North Dakota 6 north to **Fort Abraham Lincoln State Park** and visit its On-A-Slant Indian Village. If time permits, take a cruise on the Lewis and Clark riverboat. Overnight in Bismarck or Mandan.

Approximate driving time/distance: 4.5 hours, 225 miles.

Day 6: Bismarck/Mandan, North Dakota, to Williston, North Dakota.

Take US 83 north to Washburn. Visit the **North Dakota Lewis and Clark Interpretive Center** and **Fort Mandan** replica; then take North Dakota 200 to the **Knife River Indian Village National Historic Site.** North Dakota 200 loops back to US 83. Drive north to North Dakota 37. Follow ND 37 and North Dakota 1804 north of **Lake Sakakawea,** stopping for a picnic lunch at one of the parks en route. Overnight at Williston.

Approximate driving time/distance: 5.5 hours, 260 miles.

In-depth alternatives: Take a canoe trip near Washburn, either on your own or with a local outfitter. Book a trip on a wagon train retracing Lewis and Clark's route, or arrange for a personal tour of tribal lands from a local historian.

Day 7: Williston, North Dakota, to Fort Benton, Montana.

Start the day with a visit to the Missouri-Yellowstone confluence and nearby **Fort Union National Historic Site.** Take U.S. Highway 2 across northern Montana to Havre, and then follow U.S. Highway 87 south to **Fort Benton.** Explore Fort Benton's riverfront. Overnight in Fort Benton or Great Falls.

Approximate driving time/distance: Seven hours, 385 miles (to Fort Benton); 420 miles (to Great Falls).

In-depth alternative: Plan a multi-day trip on the Wild and Scenic Upper Missouri downriver from Fort Benton.

Day 8: Fort Benton, Montana, to Dillon, Montana.

Take US 87 from Fort Benton to Great Falls. Visit the **Great Falls of the Missouri** and the **Lewis and Clark National Historic Trail Interpretive Center.** Drive south on Interstate 15 to Exit 209, and take the **Gates of the Mountains** boat tour. If time permits, visit the Montana Historical Society in Helena; then drive southeast on U. S. Highway 287 to Three Forks and Missouri Headwaters State Park. From Three Forks, take Montana 2, 55, and 41 to Dillon, watching for **Beaverhead Rock** en route. Overnight in Dillon.

Approximate driving time/distance: Five hours, 250 miles (from Great Falls).

In-depth alternative: Take a naturalist-led boat trip on the Jefferson River near the Missouri headwaters.

DAY 9: DILLON, MONTANA, TO MISSOULA, MONTANA.

Visit Clark's Lookout in Dillon and the **Camp Fortunate Overlook** at Clark Canyon Reservoir southwest of town. Continue over **Lemhi Pass,** following the directions given in chapter 7. (This road may not be suitable for large RVs or vehicles towing trailers; check locally for current road conditions.) Pick up Idaho 28 at Tendoy, Idaho, and continue north to Salmon. Follow U.S. Highway 93 over **Lost Trail Pass** and down to **Ross' Hole** and the Bitterroot Valley. Stop in Lolo, site of **Traveler's Rest.** Overnight in Missoula.

Approximate driving time/distance: Five hours, 200 miles.

In-depth alternatives: Stay a few days at a guest ranch near Lemhi Pass, or spend some time rafting the Salmon River—the river Lewis and Clark could not conquer.

DAY 10: MISSOULA, MONTANA, TO LEWISTON, IDAHO.

Retrace U.S. Highway 93 south to Lolo and take U.S. Highway 12 west to Lewiston, Idaho, allowing plenty of time for the 108-mile stretch between Lolo Pass and Kamiah, Idaho. Possible stops include the **Lolo Pass Visitor Center** (closed for renovations in 2000–2001), Powell Ranger Station (the site of **"Colt Killed Creek"**) and—if your vehicle has high clearance—part of the rugged **Lolo Motorway,** which traces the Lewis and Clark route more closely than US 12 does. (See precautions and directions in chapter 7 and inquire locally for road conditions.) If time permits, also visit the Nez Perce National Historic Park sites at Kamiah, Weippe, Orofino, and Spalding. Overnight in Lewiston.

Approximate driving time/distance: Five hours, 225 miles (allow more time for exploration of the Lolo Motorway).

In-depth alternatives: Take a horse–packing or mountain-biking trip over the Lolo Trail, or book a canoe voyage on the Clearwater River.

DAY 11: LEWISTON, IDAHO, TO THE DALLES, OREGON.

Drive west of Lewiston/Clarkston on U.S. Highway 12, stopping briefly at the **Lewis and Clark Timeline** in Clarkston and **Lewis and Clark Trail State Park** near Dayton. Pick up Washington 124 at Waitsburg, and continue west to **Sacajawea State Park** near Pasco. Reconnect with US 12 and follow it to U.S. Highway 730 across the Oregon border. Visit **Hat Rock,** named by Captain Clark. From Umatilla, Oregon, take either Washington 14 or I-84 (via Interstate 82) west to The Dalles, Oregon, gateway to the Columbia Gorge. Overnight in The Dalles.

Approximate driving time/distance: 5.5 hours, 270 miles.

DAY 12: THE DALLES, OREGON, TO THE PACIFIC OCEAN.

Cross the Columbia River and continue west on Washington 14. Stop at **Beacon Rock,** named by the expedition. Hike to the top or drive to the state park lookout/picnic area. Other activities might include a visit to Bonneville Dam or the Lewis and Clark cruise on the sternwheeler *Columbia Gorge* at Cascade Locks. From the Portland/Vancouver area, proceed west to the ocean via one of the routes described in chapter 8 (U.S. Highway 26 from Portland is fastest). Overnight on the coast.

Approximate driving time/distance: 3.5 hours, 180 miles (using U.S. Highway 26 to coast).

In-depth alternative: Go kayaking on the Lower Columbia near Skamokawa, Washington.

DAY 13: ON THE PACIFIC COAST, OREGON/WASHINGTON.

Visit **Fort Canby State Park** and its Lewis and Clark Interpretive Center on Washington's Cape Disappointment. Return to Oregon and visit **Fort Clatsop National Memorial,** the **Saltworks,** and **Ecola State Park.**

Approximate driving time/distance: About 35 miles; sites all located on the Pacific Coast.

In-depth alternative: Hike over Tillamook Head, either as a day trip or as an overnight backpacking expedition.

The main 13-day itinerary is tailored to fit into a two-week vacation, which, including weekends, typically encompasses 16 days. But most people will need to factor in several travel days at each end of the trip to drive from home to St. Louis, and from Astoria back home. Add a few more days to your vacation, if possible, or see a part of the trail this time, saving the remainder for another year. Another option might be flying to St. Louis, renting a vehicle, driving the trail to Oregon, and flying home from there.

WHEN TO GO

Much of the Lewis and Clark Trail lies in the High Plains and mountains of the West, where weather is typically unpredictable and often extreme. The best period for travel is mid-July through mid-September. Fortunately, the trail has plenty of indoor interpretive centers and attractions to help travelers pass the time should inclement weather strike.

Modern explorers may want to plan their trip to coincide with one of the annual Lewis and Clark festivals held along the trail. The biggest include those in St. Charles, Missouri (third weekend of May); Onawa, Iowa (second weekend in June); Great Falls, Montana (late June); and Yankton, South Dakota (late August). A complete listing of known festivals can be found at the end of the book.

TOURING WITH A GROUP—OR ON YOUR OWN?

When the first edition of this book first came out in 1994, very few package tour operators had Lewis and Clark offerings. That has changed; many top tour companies now lead travelers to trail highlights, and more are joining the field every year. Guided tours are the priciest way to travel the Lewis and Clark route, but most everything—from meals to lodgings to interpretation—is included. Here's a sampling:

American Spirit Rail Tours (formerly Montana Rockies Rail Tours) has a seven-day combination rail-motorcoach tour, "In the Path of Lewis and Clark," covering Montana, Idaho, and Oregon with a focus on Native American encounters along the way. American Spirit Rail Tours, 1055 Baldy Park Avenue, Sandpoint, Idaho 83864; (800) 519-7245; www.keokee.com/railtour.

History America Tours, in conjunction with The History Channel, has a "Lewis and Clark in the Shadows of the Rockies" tour. Typically offered in August, the tour visits major sites in Montana and Idaho, including the seldom seen Two Medicine Fight Site area and a bit of the Lolo Trail. Gary Moulton, editor of the Lewis and Clark journals, was scheduled to be along as historian guide for several years starting in 2000. History America Tours, P.O. Box 797687, Dallas, Texas 75379; (800) 628-8542; www.historyamerica.com.

Lindblad Special Expeditions runs annual trips up the Columbia and Snake rivers. Titled "In the Wake of Lewis and Clark," the one-week trips sail on a 70-passenger vessel and typically take place in late spring and early fall. Special Expeditions Inc., 720 Fifth Avenue, New York, New York 10019; (800) 397-3348; www.expeditions.com.

Gavins Point Visitor Center on Lewis and Clark Lake, Nebraska.

Off the Beaten Path offers a small-group journey, "In the Footsteps of Lewis and Clark through Montana." No more than 18 people travel on these tours, which travel in a minibus with an expert guide. Highlights include a canoe trip on the Jefferson River and a stay at the Horse Prairie Ranch near Lemhi Pass. Off the Beaten Path, 27 East Main Street, Bozeman, Montana 59715; (800) 445-2995; www.offbeatenpath.com.

Rocky Mountain Discovery Tours has three Lewis and Clark–oriented motorcoach tours—an 8-day Rocky Mountains tour, an 11-day trip that travels from Montana to the Pacific Ocean, and a 17-day journey along the entire expedition route from St. Louis to the Pacific. Rocky Mountain Discovery Tours, PMB 520, 248A North Higgins Avenue, Missoula, Montana 59802; (888) 400-0048; www.rmdt.com. In addition to these offerings, many companies offer small-group, adventure-oriented trips focused on river running, horseback rides, hiking, or a combination of these activities. Because adventure trips tend to center on a specific area, I list them in the chapters as we work our way west. Bear in mind these trips are not just for hard-core adventurers; most are fully accessible to people with little or no experience in wilderness settings. They're excellent alternatives for people who would like an interpreted, outdoors-oriented trip.

I have established a website, www.lewis-and-clark.org, featuring updated trail information and news of activities and events along the route—information that might surface once this book goes to print. In addition, I am available to help travelers pick a guided trip or plan custom itineraries for vacations along the Lewis and Clark Trail. For details, visit www.guidebookwriters.com and follow the links to the Lewis and Clark Trail, or write to Julie Fanselow, P.O. Box 1593, Twin Falls, Idaho 83303-1593.

HOW TO TRAVEL

There are two schools of thought on how to drive across America. Some folks like to take the major, limited-access highways and get where they are going as fast and as soon as possible. Others prefer the scenery and slower pace of secondary roads.

After thousands of miles spent researching American historic trails, I've come to the conclusion that it's best to mix secondary roads and major highways. I take secondary highways and backroads most of the time, but every once in a while—when I get tired of dodging farm machinery and watching for dogs and children by the roadside, or if I need to make a little time, having dawdled a little too long—I get on an interstate.

But remember: the joy of discovery most often comes far from the interstates and large cities, and that is what a modern-day journey along the Lewis and Clark Trail is all about. You won't see many chic boutiques, trendy restaurants, or tourist traps along this route. What you will find is land, water, wind, mountains—and people who stubbornly find ways to live where life isn't too easy.

Of the 7,500 miles traveled by Lewis and Clark, nearly 6,000 miles were traveled on water. For that reason, modern explorers should attempt to include at least one (and preferably more) river trips on their own journey. Many scheduled pleasure boat rides—such as those at Bismarck, North Dakota; the Gates of the Mountains near Helena, Montana; and the sternwheeler *Columbia Gorge* at Cascade Locks, Oregon—last just a few hours and are easily worked into most travel itineraries. Others, notably excursions on Montana's Wild and Scenic Missouri River, require at least a full day and can take up to a week. However much time you can give to river exploration will be time well spent.

In many cases, two or more roads parallel the waterways followed by Lewis and Clark. When planning a trip, write in advance to the state transportation departments and request free highway maps and state visitors guides (see addresses near the end of this chapter). Use a highlighter pen and, with the help of this book and the visitors guides, map out the route that looks most interesting.

Most of the areas described in this book are easily accessible with any passenger car or truck in good working condition. In a few locations, however, it is wise to inquire locally before setting out. Roads can be closed part of the year, and some roads, notably Lemhi Pass and the Lolo Motorway, are not suitable for RVs or vehicles towing large trailers. It's also smart to outfit your vehicle with the following: dashboard compass, working odometer, full-size spare tire and jack, gasoline can, shovel, axe, and a basic emergency kit including flashers. Once on the road, pay attention to the gas gauge: it's a long way between filling stations in many parts of the West.

WHERE TO STAY, WHAT TO EAT

The Lewis and Clark Trail primarily runs through small-town and rural America. Lodging options are limited along a few stretches, so it pays to do some advance planning. The trip outlined above recommends overnight stops in places where motels and campgrounds are fairly plentiful.

Because of its distance from urban America, a Lewis and Clark Trail vacation is quite affordable. Larger cities along the route typically offer a mixture of chain motels and mom-and-pop inns. Smaller towns usually have at least one locally owned motel. These can be a great bargain, often less than $40 a night for a double. Reservations are a good idea in some areas, especially the Oregon/Washington coast and Montana's larger towns. In general, however, finding a room before 6 P.M. or 7 P.M. shouldn't pose much trouble. If you plan to arrive later, call ahead to save a room. If you're really into budget travel, you'll find Hostelling International-American Youth Hostel facilities in several cities along the trail, including St. Louis; Portland and Seaside, Oregon; and Chinook, Washington. Beds at all but Chinook can be reserved in advance by calling (800) 909-4776. Dorm-style accommodations at hostels typically run only $10 to $15 per person per night; private rooms are sometimes available for a slightly higher price.

Consider camping along at least part of the trail. Aside from being economical, camping affords a better taste of what travel was like for the Corps of Discovery—after all, Lewis and Clark and company sure didn't have their choice of motels in 1804. Camping options range from RV parks to primitive, pick-your-own sites in the national forests. You might even choose to sleep in a tepee or fire lookout.

Quite a few small towns along the Lewis and Clark route have municipal parks that offer free or very-low-cost camping to tourists passing through. Many are well posted at the entrances to town. As much as possible, I've noted the presence of these parks throughout the text of this book.

Travelers who want to slow down and spend a few days in one place may want to look into a stay at a Western-style guest ranch or bed-and-breakfast inn. Accommodations of these sorts abound along the Lewis and Clark route. Be aware, however, that many may require a minimum stay of anywhere from two nights to a week. Rates at guest ranches can be high—up to several hundred dollars a day per person—but remember they usually include all meals and

TREADING LIGHTLY

The United States will soon mark the bicentennial of the Lewis and Clark Expedition. Interest in the Corps of Discovery has risen exponentially in recent years, and while many people are content to follow the explorers' route from their armchairs, others are eager to see at least part of the route for themselves. This has put added pressure on the trail, particularly the stretches that remain much the same as the explorers found them. In some cases, sites are sacred to Native Americans, who lived in these places long before the explorers' arrival. Some portions of the trail are ecologically threatened; many simply will not survive unless visitors take care to tread gently. That's why, especially over the coming few years, it's important for trail visitors to learn about and practice low-impact recreation.

Here are a few guidelines for treading lightly along the trail:

- Pack out all garbage.

- Check locally for travel and fire restrictions.

- Leave cultural artifacts and interpretive signs undisturbed.

- Get permission before walking or driving on private land.

- Keep noise to a minimum and be respectful of other travelers.

- In heavily used areas, concentrate activities in areas already impacted by previous use. Stay on established trails; use existing campsites away from water, main trails, and other campers; use existing fire rings but only build fires if wood is abundant and if regulations allow wood fires; pack out all human waste or bury it in a hole at least 200 feet from surface water; and leave a clean camp for others.

- In lightly used areas, disperse impact to minimize damage to any one site. Travel in a small group. When no trails are available, spread out or follow routes over such durable surfaces as sand, exposed bedrock, or gravel. Move camp nightly, if possible. If a fire is necessary, build it in a fire pan. Disperse human waste away from water sources, or—if human discovery is likely——bury it in a hole. When you leave, try to disguise any signs of your camp by ruffling trampled-down grass and picking up even the smallest pieces of litter.

It's critically important that we preserve the Lewis and Clark Trail's wildest places for generations to come. To learn more about minimum-impact outdoor recreation, consult *Leave No Trace* by Will Harmon (Falcon), a quick-reference guidebook packed with practical information on this topic. ▲

activities. Travelers can save money by packing a cooler full of sandwiches, drinks, and snacks. But part of the fun of traveling is eating in restaurants at least once in a while. When the time comes, consider sampling some regional cuisine: catfish in Missouri, buffalo burgers on the Great Plains, huckleberry pie in western Montana and Idaho, and seafood in the Northwest. Keep an eye open for farmers' markets, too; most towns of at least a few thousand people have them during summer and fall, often on Saturday mornings. They're a great place to pick up fresh produce and get local information.

Each of the travel chapters ends with a list of lodging options, campgrounds, and restaurants for areas along the trail. The chapters and the listings follow Lewis and Clark's route generally from east to west (with a few variations for the homeward-bound trips). In most cases, establishments mentioned are simply representative of those available in each town; listing in this book does not imply endorsement of any kind. Hotel, motel, and bed-and-breakfast rates listed are generally for double occupancy during the summer travel season and are accurate as of 1999. The text lists direct numbers to each lodging, including toll-free numbers when available, but the following chainwide toll-free reservation numbers may come in handy, too: Best Western, (800) 528-1234; Budget Host, (800) 283-4678; Clarion Inns (800) 252-7466; Comfort Inns, (800) 228-5150; Days Inn, (800) 329-7466; Hilton Hotels, (800) 445-8667; Holiday Inns, (800) 465-4329; Quality Inns, (800) 228-5151; Sleep Inns, (800) 753-3746; Travelodge, (800) 367-2250.

More complete lists of hotels, motels, campgrounds, and restaurants are available from state and local tourism bureaus. State tourism offices are listed later in this chapter, and many local offices are noted throughout the book.

WHAT TO PACK

Bearing in mind that Western weather can be unpredictable and fast changing, even in midsummer, it's best to be prepared with a variety of clothing. On hot days, lightweight, light-colored clothing will be most comfortable. But pack a sweater, jacket, and rain gear for when the weather turns cold or wet. Sneakers or walking shoes are best for touring historic sites, but toss in a pair of lightweight hiking boots and sport sandals. Casual clothing is appropriate everywhere along the trail. Don't forget a swimsuit, sun block, and wide-brimmed hat.

Campers should make sure their gear is waterproof and able to stand up to high winds. A ground cloth and extra tent stakes are good ideas. Other camp essentials include a simple tool kit with a hammer, axe, and pocketknife; a reliable camp stove and fuel (wood campfires are prohibited in some locations); cooking and eating utensils; a can opener; insect repellent; a bucket for hauling water and washing dishes; biodegradable dish soap; rope (for clothesline and other uses); first-aid and snakebite kits; a camp lantern and flashlight; matches; trash bags (along with separate space for recyclables); and a bag for dirty laundry.

Travelers hoping to preserve their trip in pictures should include a wide-angle lens and polarizing filter for the high, wide horizons and beautiful skies. Binoculars might come in handy, as will books and travel games. And don't forget a good atlas or state highway maps—the maps in this book are general and should always be used in conjunction with a more detailed local highway map.

TRAVELING WITH KIDS

To children, all of life is an adventure, with new discoveries made every day. Seen from this perspective, a trip along the Lewis and Clark Trail makes an ideal family vacation. It's interesting, educational, informal, and can easily be combined with a more traditional Western vacation, say, to Yellowstone National Park or the Oregon coast. Moreover, it is an economical vacation choice, since most historic sites are free or cheap, and since nearly all of Lewis and Clark's route lies far from expensive big cities and traditional tourist attractions.

Still, it's always a challenge to keep kids happy and occupied. Here are a few ideas on how to do it. Have them keep a journal like Lewis and Clark did, describing their trip in words and pictures. (Journaling is a great way to develop writing skills, and this is a grand time to start.) Although long-winded recitations from the captains' journals may prove ponderous to young ears, look for short passages to read at picnic stops or around the campfire. Or buy a children's-book version of the Lewis and Clark story, and let your kids read along as they go.

Plan a Lewis and Clark scavenger hunt, making a list of items the kids can look for along the way. Such "treasures" might include a keelboat, dugout canoe, Indian earth lodge, river, animals, and statues of Lewis, Clark, Sacagawea, York, and Lewis's dog, Seaman. You might want to provide an inexpensive camera so your child can take photos as the discoveries are made. President Jefferson asked Lewis and Clark to describe and, where possible, get samples of the flora and fauna they encountered along their way. Your children can do the same thing on a smaller scale. Young naturalists might enjoy a small bug-catching box, sketch pad, or leaf and wildflower press.

If you're camping, consider packing along a separate tent for the children (if they're old enough). Most kids love having a tent of their own, and it will give the grown-ups some rest and privacy, too. Kids also enjoy having a bit of their own money to spend on vacation. Help them learn financial responsibility and decision-making by giving each child a special trip allowance. Make sure they know this money should cover any souvenirs or extras they want to buy, and that it should last the whole trip.

WHAT TO READ

Many travelers will want to read more about Lewis and Clark before, during, or after tracing the captains' route of discovery. For maximum enjoyment, get a copy of the Lewis and Clark journals and read along to learn what the voyagers found as they crossed the continent. The complete journals are published in several multi-volume editions (with Gary E. Moulton of the University of Nebraska the editor of the most recent, definitive set), but a one-volume abridgement will suit the vacation traveler's purposes just fine. Many people believe Bernard DeVoto's version is the best, though Moulton's own one-volume abridgement may be out by the time you read this, too. (Moulton's work corrected some mistakes made in the earlier journals on which DeVoto relied.)

One of my favorite books about Lewis and Clark is Dayton Duncan's *Out West: An American Journey*. I first read this wonderful book upon its publication in 1987, and it accompanied me on my own explorations of the route while researching this guidebook. Duncan traced the explorers' route on his own in a camper van. In clean and thoughtful prose, his book weaves history with modern-day observations about life in the western United States. It is a gem.

Other books that might be of interest include *Undaunted Courage: Meriwether Lewis, Thomas Jefferson, and the Opening of the American West*, by Stephen Ambrose; *Lewis and Clark Historic Places*, compiled by Roy E. Appleman and recently reprinted by the Jefferson National Parks Association; *The Way to the Western Sea*, by David Lavender; *Lewis & Clark: Pioneering Naturalists*, by Paul Cutright; *Passage of Discovery: The American Rivers Guide to the Missouri River of Lewis and Clark*, by Daniel Botkin; *River-Horse*, by William Least Heat-Moon, which traces the author's voyage along Lewis and Clark's water route; *Voyages of Discovery: Essays on the Lewis and Clark Expedition*, edited by James Ronda; *Lewis and Clark: Partners in Discovery*, by John Bakeless; and *Lewis and Clark: Voyage of Discovery*, by Dan Murphy and David Muench.

There are many others. In fact, don't be surprised if, during the course of your Lewis and Clark explorations, you find yourself wanting to read everything you can about the captains and the expedition. "Once you get interested, you become a buff, and there's constant controversy about why they did this, how they did this, what did that look like, what were they wearing," says Butch Bouvier, a Lewis and Clark aficionado from western Iowa. "It's constant. It's exciting."

TENDING THE TRAIL

Since it is a federally designated National Historic Trail, the 3,700-mile Lewis and Clark route is administered by the National Park Service in cooperation with other federal, state, and local agencies; the Lewis and Clark Trail Heritage Foundation and other private organizations; and private landowners along the route. Together, they work to identify, preserve, and interpret sites important to the expedition. The Park Service publishes and distributes a general information brochure and map of the trail. It's widely available along the route, or you can request a copy by writing to Lewis and Clark National Historic Trail, 1709 Jackson Street, Omaha, Nebraska 68102, or by sending an e-mail to Midori_Raymore@nps.gov.

People interested in learning more about the Corps of Discovery and trail preservation may want to join the Lewis and Clark Trail Heritage Foundation. This not-for-profit organization holds an annual convention with seminars, field trips, and social activities each August. The foundation publishes *We Proceeded On*, a scholarly yet entertaining quarterly journal dedicated to the Lewis and Clark Expedition and related topics. Many members also take part in local and state chapter activities. For information, write the Lewis and Clark Trail Heritage Foundation, P.O. Box 3434, Great Falls, Montana 59403, or access the group's website at www.lewisandclark.org.

The Lewis & Clark Bicentennial Council is the main organization preparing for the 200th anniversary commemoration of the Corps of Discovery. For more information on the national effort, or to find a bicentennial group near you, contact the National Lewis & Clark Bicentennial Council, P.O. Box 9550, Seattle, Washington 98109-0550. Its website is at www.lewisandclark200.org.

American Rivers is the nation's foremost river conservation organization. One of its main initiatives is the "Voyage to Recovery" effort aimed at revitalizing the Missouri River before the Lewis and Clark Bicentennial. For more information on American Rivers and its work, call (202) 347-7550; write American Rivers, 1025 Vermont Avenue N.W., Suite 720, Washington, D.C. 20005; or see the website at www.americanrivers.org.

State Tourism Offices

Illinois Bureau of Tourism
State of Illinois Center
100 W. Randolph St.
Chicago, IL 60601
(800) 223-0121
www.enjoyillinois.com

Missouri Division of Tourism
Truman Office Building
P.O. Box 1055
Jefferson City, MO 65102
(800) 877-1234
www.missouritourism.org

Kansas Travel & Tourism Division
700 S.W. Harrison, Suite 1300
Topeka, KS 66603
(800) 252-6727
www.kansascommerce.com

Iowa Division of Tourism
200 East Grand Ave.
Des Moines, IA 50309
(800) 345-4692
www.traveliowa.com

Nebraska Tourism Office
P.O. Box 98907
Lincoln, NE 68509-8907
(800) 228-4307
www.visitnebraska.org

South Dakota Department of Tourism
711 East Wells Ave.
Pierre, SD 57501
(800) 732-5682
www.state.sd.us./tourism/

North Dakota Tourism
604 East Blvd.
Bismarck, ND 58505
(800) 435-5663
www.ndtourism.com

Travel Montana
1424 9th Avenue
P.O. Box 200533
Helena, MT 59620-0533
(800) 847-4868
www.visitmt.com

Idaho Travel Council
700 W. State St., 2nd Floor
Boise, ID 83720
(800) 847-4843
www.visitid.org

Washington State Tourism Division
P.O. Box 42500
Olympia, WA 98504
(800) 544-1800
www.tourism.wa.gov

Oregon Tourism Division
775 Summer St. N.E.
Salem, OR 97310
(800) 547-7842
www.traveloregon.com

A NOTE ON SPELLING

Modern readers always wonder how Lewis and Clark, who were certainly among the smartest people of their day, could be such terrible spellers. Their journals contained, for example, 27 different spellings of Sioux and 24 different versions of Charbonneau, the French interpreter who joined the party during its 1804–1805 winter stay in North Dakota. And proper names weren't the only object of such mangling; Lewis, Clark, and their men had a way of garbling even simple words.

The reality was that in the early nineteenth century, even the most learned Americans used wildly irregular spellings. Noah Webster, who published his pioneering dictionaries in the late 1700s and early 1800s, advocated such variants as "wimmen," "groop," and "bilt." Many historians insist on preserving the captains' misspellings in journal quotes. I appreciate the argument behind such preservation, but for the sake of readability, I have rendered all journal quotes into modern, standard English. In the case of the Indian woman who accompanied the expedition, I use the spelling 'Sacagawea,' generally considered to be most accurate, unless a different spelling is used in a proper name (as in North Dakota's Lake Sakakawea or Washington's Sacajawea State Park).

IS THIS BOOK OUT OF DATE?

All across the United States, communities and organizations are getting ready to mark the 200th anniversary of the Lewis and Clark Expedition during its bicentennial of 2004–2006. New attractions and activities celebrating the Lewis and Clark legacy are planned nearly everywhere along the route. Some may be in place by the time you read this book, and we'd like to know about them. Other things may change, too. Restaurants and motels may open, close, or take new names, and visitor attractions may alter operating schedules.

If you find an error, omission, or change, please write Julie Fanselow in care of Falcon Publishing, P.O. Box 1718, Helena, Montana 59624. You can also submit information on the website at www.lewis-and-clark.org. Either way, we will use your input in future editions of *Traveling the Lewis & Clark Trail.*

Thanks, and happy travels!

CHAPTER THREE

ILLINOIS, MISSOURI, AND KANSAS

I set out at 4 o'clock P.M., in the presence of many of the neighboring inhabitants, and proceeded on under a gentle breeze up the Missouri.

—William Clark, May 14, 1804,
upon leaving Camp Wood.

CAMP WOOD

*O*ur journey begins at a monument on the banks of the Mississippi River. There, surrounded by a gauntlet of rocks, sits a ring of substantial stone pillars commemorating the start of the Lewis and Clark Expedition.

The actual site of Camp Wood has long since disappeared, swallowed up by urban development, industrialization, and the shifting channels of the Mississippi, Missouri, and Wood rivers. Historians believe the camp sat about 3 miles northwest of the monument, an area dredged by oil companies operating in the vicinity. The approximate location is about 2.5 miles north of the present north bank of the Missouri River at its mouth.

But it was in this general area that the expedition planned and trained for its mission. The party camped here from December 12, 1803, through May 14, 1804, mostly under the command of Clark, who whipped the corps into a disciplined band while Lewis gathered supplies and information elsewhere in the St. Louis area.

Lewis and Clark weren't the first white visitors in the vicinity. Jacques Marquette and Louis Joliet discovered the confluence in 1673, and other early European explorers followed. Their impressions of the site blended horror and delight. Describing a thicket of dead trees clogging the river, Marquette wrote he "had seen nothing more dreadful." But Father Pierre Francois de Charlevoix called it "the finest confluence in the world. The two rivers are much the same breadth, each about half a league; but the Missouri is by far the most rapid, and seems to enter the Mississippi like a conqueror."

Strictly speaking, the Lewis and Clark expedition didn't begin at Camp Wood at all, but in Pittsburgh, Pennsylvania, where Lewis picked up the keelboat he had ordered built for the voyage. The boat was supposed to be ready July 20, 1803, but when Lewis arrived, he found it nowhere near completion. The boatbuilder hired for the task had a penchant for drink, and it was all Lewis could do to keep the man at his task. The boat was finally finished August 31. It

measured 55 feet in length, was 8 feet wide at its center, and could carry about 10 tons of cargo. Just four hours after the boat's completion, Lewis set out down the Ohio River with at least 11 other men, including several expedition recruits, and a single pirogue, or dugout canoe.

It wasn't easy going. The Ohio was unusually low that year, and the crew frequently had to unload the keelboat cargo to get the craft past shallows, riffles, and other obstructions in the channel. The party stopped in Wheeling, West Virginia, to get additional supplies and a second pirogue.

The Corps of Discovery.

After more stops in Marietta and Cincinnati, Ohio, and Big Bone Lick, Kentucky, Lewis reached the Falls of the Ohio near Louisville, Kentucky, in mid-October 1803. Here, he was finally reunited face to face with his friend Clark. The party spent nearly two weeks in the area, during which Lewis and Clark had long conversations with Clark's older brother, George Rogers Clark, who knew much about the personalities and places on the frontier. When the corps left Clarksville, as the family settlement near Louisville was called, it included the two leaders; Clark's slave, York; and several of the men who would make up the permanent party: William Bratton, John Colter, Joseph and Reuben Field, Charles Floyd, George Gibson, Nathaniel Pryor, George Shannon, and John Shields. Colter of Virginia and Shannon of Ohio had come downriver with Lewis; the rest joined up near the Falls of the Ohio.

From Clarksville, the expedition made good time. At Fort Massac in Illinois, the captains recruited George Drouillard, Joseph Whitehouse, and John Newman. Moving up the Mississippi River at last, the corps passed Fort Kaskaskia and Cahokia, Illinois. (The latter is the site of notable Indian mounds that Clark and recruit John Collins later returned to explore on a field trip from Camp Wood.) The expedition reached the Camp Wood site on December 12. Originally, Lewis had hoped to be 200 or 300 miles up the Missouri River before making the first winter camp. But the lateness of the season, combined with the fact the territory up the Missouri had not yet been transferred to the United States, meant the journey's official start would have to wait until spring.

With winter camp established, Lewis and Clark wasted little time starting final preparations for their mission. Lewis had initially thought the expedition would include 10 to 12 men, but the Ohio River cruise had convinced the leaders that at least twice that many would be needed to propel the boats, hunt, interpret, manage supplies, and ward off any Indian attacks. So throughout the winter, Clark continued to recruit, often as Lewis attended to last-minute matters in St. Louis.

Once enlisted, the high-spirited young soldiers had to be trained. At first, discipline was quite a problem. Drinking and fighting were rampant, and there also were instances of insubordination, refusal to stand guard, theft of government property, and men going AWOL. Roy E. Appleman, author of the National Park Service's account of the expedition, wrote, "At one time or another, practically all the men in camp engaged in some wrongdoing. Yet some of the rowdiest and most undisciplined, such as (John) Colter and Reuben Field, were later to number among the most reliable in the command." Clark used a mixture of punishment and incentive to handle the men, and discipline had improved greatly by the time the corps left Camp Wood.

Over the winter, the party also made numerous refinements to the keelboat to promote more efficient loading. Lockers were built to protect supplies, with lids that could be lifted to serve as defensive breastworks in the event of attack. Clark also outfitted both the keelboats and the pirogues with weapons including a small cannon (for the keelboat) and swivel guns.

Shortly before the expedition's departure, Clark received some bad news: the War Department had denied his commission as captain in the Corps of Engineers. In a letter including Clark's commission as a second lieutenant in the Corps of Artillerists, Lewis explained to his friend that in the peacetime Army, officer vacancies were scarce, and the Corps of Artillerists position was all that was available. But as he had promised earlier, Lewis swore to Clark that—in his mind, if not that of the government—Clark was his co-captain. It was a secret kept safely between the friends for the duration of the two-and-a-half-year mission.

By 2003, Camp Wood's "Site 1," as it's now known, will be the scene of a major new interpretive center planned by the state of Illinois. For now, here's how to get to the existing Illinois Lewis and Clark monument: Take Illinois 3 north of its intersection with Interstate 270 (the major beltway around St. Louis), and turn left on New Poag Road, 3 miles from I-270. Watch for signs pointing the way.

The road leads west, past a diversion-canal bayou where locals pass the time angling for catfish. At the end of the road, the state of Illinois erected 11 stone pillars, one for each of the states Lewis and Clark passed through on their journey. A plaque on each pillar details a key incident in the expedition's travels.

The monument site is quiet aside from the waves that sometimes break as boats chug by. For now, there are no visitor amenities, nothing to do but stand and contemplate. But if you're in the area, the monument is worth a visit, as are the nearby attractions of St. Louis and St. Charles, if for no other reason than to help place the expedition, its duties, and its goals in perspective.

Illinois 3 is also known as The Great River Road. A few miles upriver from the monument sits Alton, Illinois, a city well-known for riverboat gambling and an antiques district. Both are located near the riverfront area. The seventh and final Lincoln-Douglas presidential debate was held at the intersection of Broadway and Market streets here in 1858. Bridge fanciers will want a look at Clark Bridge, the striking cable stay suspension span over the Mississippi River here. The Clark Bridge also is the route to U.S. Highway 67 and Missouri 94. Although these highways roughly parallel the Missouri River, most travelers will want to move west via St. Louis (see below).

Alton's Spencer T. Olin Community Golf Course, designed by Arnold Palmer, is considered among the best public courses in the metropolitan St. Louis area. The Piasa Bird, located on a limestone bluff along Illinois 100, re-creates the flying-monster pictograph discovered in 1673 by Pere Marquette. Illinois 100 also parallels a 20-mile bike trail between Alton and Pere Marquette State Park, one of Illinois' largest and most popular. Call (800) 258-6645 or stop by the Alton visitor center (kitty-corner to the Alton Belle Casino parking lot) for more information on activities and events in southwestern Illinois.

To proceed west via St. Louis, retrace Illinois 3 south to Interstate 270. Just over the Mississippi River, the state of Missouri runs a comprehensive statewide visitor center at the Riverview Drive exit. Head 2 miles north on Riverview from the welcome center turnoff to reach the new Columbia Bottom Conservation Area, with its view of the confluence of the Mississippi and Missouri rivers. Or turn south for the most direct route to the St. Louis riverfront. After a few miles Riverview Drive bears left into Hall Street. When Hall Street dead-ends at a "T," turn right and watch for the signs for Interstate 70 East. Get on the freeway and watch for the Riverfront/Arch exit.

ST. LOUIS

At the time of the Lewis and Clark Expedition, St. Louis was a mere 40 years old but already on its way to becoming one of the most important cities in the United States. Its location made St. Louis the ideal hub of transportation, exploration, mercantile activity, and culture. Consequently, the city attracted everyone from fur traders to scientists, military agents to missionaries. It was here Captain Lewis gathered much of the intelligence essential to the expedition's success, as well as where he witnessed the March 9–10, 1804, ceremonies

The Gateway Arch in St. Louis, Missouri.

marking the transfer of Upper Louisiana from France to Spain and from Spain to the United States.

Any visit to St. Louis should begin at the Jefferson National Expansion Memorial, best known for its graceful stainless-steel centerpiece, the 630-foot Gateway Arch. The Arch is America's tallest monument, topping the 555-foot Washington Monument and the 305-foot Statue of Liberty. It is a marvel of engineering and design.

The Museum of Westward Expansion beneath the Arch celebrates the vision of Thomas Jefferson and offers one of the nation's best overviews of why the Lewis and Clark Expedition took place. Exhibits are arranged in a wagon-wheel fashion, with each decade radiating off a hub. In the center stands a life-size statue of Jefferson, who stood 6-foot-3. He is seen gazing out toward an ocean mural on the far wall, and strategic lighting ensures Jefferson's shadow is cast in all directions, just as his influence looms formidably even today.

Central to the museum's Lewis and Clark interpretation are the large, floor-to-ceiling photographs of sites along the expedition route. These beautiful images serve as a backdrop for everything else on display. Smaller photos show plants and animals seen by the corps, and a map of the Louisiana Purchase illustrates how that event nearly doubled the size of the United States.

Other exhibits pay tribute to later great American explorers, from the Oregon Trail pioneers to Charles Lindbergh and the Apollo astronauts. A newer feature of the museum features an "animatronic" representation of Captain Clark as he appeared in 1832, by then Superintendent of Indian Affairs, explaining why early explorers gave peace medals to the Native Americans they met. The museum also offers fine interpretive programs, including talks by rangers who sometimes discuss the Lewis and Clark Expedition. And no visit would be complete without a ride to the top of the Arch. After a four-minute ride up the monument's innards in a pod-like tram car, the visitor is treated to outstanding views reaching 30 miles both east and west on a clear day.

The museum is open from 8 A.M. to 10 P.M. Memorial Day through Labor Day and 9 A.M. to 6 P.M. the rest of the year. Admission to the Arch tram and museum is $6 per person age 17 and up, $4 for students ages 13 through 16, and $2.50 for children ages 3 through 12. Also worthwhile are movies in the Arch Odyssey Theatre, with its four-story screen, and another theater showcasing the "Monument to the Dream" documentary, which describes the building of the Arch. (Each showing carries an additional charge.) There may be a wait of an hour or more to take the tram, so buy your tickets as soon as you arrive, and then enjoy the museum and other activities. All facilities are closed Thanksgiving, Christmas, and New Year's Day. For more information, call (314) 425-4465 or see the Gateway Arch website at www.nps.gov/jeff/arch-home. The Jefferson National Expansion Memorial also includes an expansive park surrounding the Arch and the Old Courthouse. The latter features exhibits on early St. Louis,

William Clark's grave at Bellefontaine Cemetery, St. Louis, Missouri.

ST. LOUIS TRAVEL TIPS

Lambert–St. Louis International Airport (STL) is served by most major and Midwest regional airlines. The airport will be undergoing a major expansion starting in 2001. Rental cars are available from numerous companies. The Amtrak station is at 550 South 16th Street, and the Greyhound terminal is at 1450 North 13th Street.

St. Louis's MetroLink light-rail system is an easy way to get around town. Although parking is plentiful and fairly cheap at the riverfront, savvy travelers will hop the MetroLink at Laclede's Landing to explore other area sites such as Union Station and Forest Park. It's also possible to take the train from several convenient stops near the airport and Interstate 70 (though you'll want to leave early if it's the night of a Cardinals home game, when the park-and-ride lots are jammed). Look for a MetroLink route map at your hotel, or call (314) 231-2345 from 6 A.M. to 8 P.M. weekdays or 8 A.M. to 5 P.M. weekends.

including a diorama showing the transfer of the Louisiana Territory.

Although Lewis spent the most time in St. Louis the winter before the expedition, it was Clark who eventually made the city his home. After the expedition, Clark owned several buildings—none still standing—in the general vicinity of what is now the Gateway Arch. These included various Clark residences; his museum of Indian curiosities (an early St. Louis tourist attraction); and storehouses and offices he used in dealing with the Indians. Late in life, Clark lived mainly at his farm on Bellefontaine Road about 3.5 miles north of the city, but he died at the downtown home of his son, Meriwether Lewis Clark.

Clark is buried at the mammoth Bellefontaine Cemetery, 5 miles north of downtown on Florissant Avenue. The grave is situated on an elaborate stone plaza featuring an obelisk and bust of the explorer, along with a buffalo's head and gargoyle. Clark is described here as a "soldier, explorer, statesman and patriot. His life is written in the history of his country." No one would dispute that. Some may, however, question the Biblical quote also prominently displayed: "Behold, the Lord thy God hath set the land before thee. Go up and possess it." Certainly, that was what Lewis and Clark did. But these captains, along with their boss the president, envisioned a United States where the Native Americans and the more recently arrived whites could exist in harmony. The notion that the continent was somehow ours to plunder with no thought given to consequence came largely after the time of Jefferson, Lewis, and Clark.

To find the grave from the Florissant entrance, take Willow Avenue to Vine Avenue, bear left then right onto Althea Avenue, then left onto Aspen Avenue. Aspen runs into Meadow Avenue, where the Clark family plot is located. Better yet, stop at the office for a map to Clark's grave and a look at a chart of the Clark family tree, with branches hailing from St. Louis, Louisville, and Michigan. Guided tours are available by appointment. The cemetery is open to visitors from 8 A.M. to 5 P.M. daily.

TOURING ST. LOUIS

As the largest city along the Lewis and Clark route, St. Louis offers a full menu of urban attractions. Once you've seen the Arch, take time to explore the bustling riverfront area. Visitors can choose from a scenic riverboat cruise, casino gambling, a Cardinals game at Busch Stadium, or explorations of the shops, restaurants, and nightlife of Laclede's Landing, the restored historic area just north of the Arch.

South of the Arch, the Soulard area thrives on live musical entertainment, with more than 30 restaurants and pubs, many offering jazz and blues. Soulard is also home to the Anheuser-Busch Brewery, where free tours (complete with product samples) are offered Monday through Saturday. Union Station, west of the riverfront along Market Street, has been transformed from a train station to a major shopping, dining, and entertainment destination.

The Grand Center area west of downtown is home to many cultural and architectural landmarks, including Powell Symphony Hall and the Fox Theatre; the EarthWays Home, an 1893 Victorian structure that now serves as a showcase for environmentally sustainable living; and the Samuel Cupples House, with its Romanesque design and Trusheim Art Glass Collection. Ask at area businesses for a copy of the neighborhood walking tour brochure.

The Missouri Historical Society in Forest Park plans a major Lewis and Clark exhibition to commemorate the bicentennial. Billed as a reunion of expedition artifacts and documents not seen together since 1806, the exhibition will be on view here for several months in 2004 before traveling around the nation. Call (314) 746-4599 for more information. Other Forest Park attractions include the St. Louis Zoo, with more than 3,400 animals; the Muny, an outdoor performing arts center; and the St. Louis Art Museum. The St. Louis Science Center, in an impressive building straddling Interstate 64 adjacent to the park, has great shows in its Omnimax Theater and McDonnell Planetarium. Forest Park also offers bicycle rentals, bike/jog/walk paths, fishing, boating, skating, golf courses, and tennis courts.

Six Flags Over Mid-America, one of the nation's biggest amusement parks, is located about 30 miles southwest of downtown, near the Allenton exit off Interstate 44. Raging Rivers, a water park, is in Grafton, Illinois. For more information about St. Louis–area attractions, call the convention and visitors commission at (800) 247-9791 or write to 10 South Broadway, Suite 1000, St. Louis, Missouri 63102.▲

ST. CHARLES

Although Camp Wood can rightfully be called the expedition's starting point, St. Charles was where final preparations were made, last-minute supplies obtained, and the boatload readjusted. Moreover, as we have seen, the expedition was shy one captain upon its arrival in St. Charles May 16, 1804. Lewis caught up to the corps May 20, and they formally got under way the next day.

In his journal, Clark described St. Charles in this way: "This village is about one mile in length, contains about 100 houses and about 450 inhabitants, chiefly French. Those people appear poor, polite, and harmonious." Founded in 1769 as a fur-trading post by Louis Blanchette, a French-Canadian hunter, St. Charles was the first permanent white settlement on the Missouri River. Early white inhabitants called the area Les Petites Cotes ("The Little Hills") because of the surrounding terrain.

After the United States took over the Louisiana Territory, St. Charles's influence grew. Its location near the confluence of the Mississippi and Missouri rivers made it an ideal outfitting port for land and water routes to the West. The city also was the eastern terminus of the Boonslick Road, which led to the Boone brothers' salt works in Howard County. St. Charles served as Missouri's first state capital from 1821 to 1826.

The Lewis and Clark Center at 701 Riverside Drive features down-home exhibits on the expedition. Its centerpiece is a second-floor diorama by artist Evangeline Groth that traces the corps' journey to the Pacific Ocean. Other displays tell why some of the expedition's supporting characters—Sacagawea, Pierre Cruzatte, Ben York, and Lewis's dog, Seaman—were so important to the venture's success. Reproductions of items used by the expedition are also on view. Another display notes that the last-minute purchases made in St. Charles included tin cups, knives, "and all the tobacco in town."

The center has a trading post and offers a variety of classes and programs for school and youth groups. It also sells a handy booklet telling about Lewis and Clark in St. Charles, complete with a map that pinpoints sites known to the expedition. The center is open daily (except major holidays) from 10:30 A.M. to 4:30 P.M. Admission is $1 for adults and 50 cents for children ages 3 through 17. For more information, call (636) 947-3199.

After visiting the center, take some time to explore St. Charles's South Main Street historic district, with its cobblestone streets and charming little parks. (Self-guided walking tour brochures are available at most businesses.) The building at 719 South Main Street, now Karen's River Cabin, was built in the 1790s and stood when Lewis and Clark were in town. On the riverfront, the Goldenrod Showboat presents Broadway-style dinner theater shows. Nearby, an enclosed pavilion showcases the work of the Discovery Expedition of St. Charles, a project through which Lewis and Clark buffs plan to authentically re-create

Lewis and Clark's trip on the Ohio, Mississippi, and Missouri rivers in keelboat and pirogue replicas. The group is raising funds and looking for people to take part in the journey. For more information or to request enlistment papers, write the Discovery Expedition of St. Charles, 314 South Main Street, St. Charles, Missouri 63301, or send a fax to (636) 925-1759.

The Lewis and Clark Rendezvous, staged the third weekend each May, includes a reenactment of the corps' 1804 encampment. Other activities include a parade, crafts and foods of the period, a fife and drum corps muster, and military reenactment groups demonstrating eighteenth- and nineteenth-century drill tactics.

St. Charles serves as a major access point to the Katy Trail, one of America's most unusual state parks. See the Katy Trail section later in this chapter for more information. This may also be the honeymoon capital of the Lewis and Clark Trail, with several wedding chapels and many bed-and-breakfast inns ready to serve romantic couples. For more information on things to see and do in St. Charles, stop by the visitors bureau at 230 South Main Street, or call (800) 366-2427.

THE SHAKEDOWN CRUISE

Interstate 70 cuts a wide, straight swath across Missouri, allowing motorists to traverse the state in about four hours. But travelers who stay on I-70 miss some of the most beautiful hill country and the quaintest small towns in the Midwest . . . reason enough to consider following the meandering Missouri River and the route of Lewis and Clark across at least part of the Show-Me State. Good roads parallel the river on both sides to Jefferson City—Missouri 94 to the north and Missouri 100 to the south. Drive these for a while until you grow tired of the relentless roller coaster hills and curves; then return to I-70 to make up some time. It's worth noting that, unlike most states, Missouri marks many of its secondary roads with letters, not numerals—a system started in 1932.

  Start southwest from St. Charles on MO 94 and see suburban St. Louis disappear in your rear-view mirror as the road becomes a panorama of wildlife areas, wineries, and access points to the Katy Trail, the longest rails-to-trails conversion in the United States. Once the site of one of the world's largest munitions plants, the Weldon Spring area is now laced with fishing ponds (with boat rentals and bait available at Busch Lodge off of Missouri Highway D) and trails, including two named for our heroes. Past the junction with MO D, watch on your left for the Lewis and Clark trailhead parking lot. The 8.2-mile Lewis Trail takes about five hours to hike, while the 5.3-mile Clark Trail takes about three hours. A few miles farther west, the rugged Lost Valley Trail is open to both hiking and mountain biking.

This is also Daniel Boone country, where the famous American frontiersman spent the last two decades of his life, from about 1799 through 1820. In other words, the aging pioneer was living here when Lewis and Clark trekked through the area in 1804 and again in 1806, but no record exists of an encounter between the parties. For an in-depth look at Boone's life, visit the Daniel Boone Home on Missouri Highway F near Defiance. One of Missouri's most popular attractions, the dwelling was completed in 1810 and still houses many Boone family heirlooms. The grounds also include "The Judgment Tree," a large elm under which Boone settled disputes between white men and local Indians. Other important Boone family sites in Missouri include Daniel's grave at Marthasville and the Boone's Lick State Historic Site north of Boonville.

More important for our explorations, this country also served as the shakedown cruise section for the Lewis and Clark Expedition, the area where the men became intimate with the river on which they would do most of their traveling over the next couple of years. Of the 7,500-plus miles covered by Lewis and Clark, roughly three-quarters of them were on the Missouri River. Rising in southwest Montana where the Madison, Gallatin, and Jefferson rivers join, the river drains one-sixth of the land in the contiguous United States. Hundreds of rivers and creeks join the Missouri over its 2,315-mile course to the Mississippi.

For tens of thousands of years, the Missouri was free and wild. But as the nation expanded, the demand for hydroelectric power and desire for flood control resulted in one of history's largest public works efforts, the Pick-Sloan Project of the 1940s and 1950s, which created six huge dams in the Dakotas and Montana. Combined with dredging and channelization farther downriver, the dams changed the Missouri into a river far different from the one Lewis and Clark saw.

Indeed, the Missouri of 1804 was considered to be the most unruly river in America, and it didn't take the corps long to find out why. Keelboats were pulled along by hand with a 1,000-foot line called a cordelle tied to the mast. The keelboat often had to be towed against a strong current, and it typically took at least 20 men to cordelle a keelboat along most sections of the Missouri. At times, sandbars made cordeling impossible. In those instances, the boat would be poled or even rowed upstream. A small mast sail was sometimes used if winds were favorable, yet snags were another constant hazard. Blistering summer heat, thundering rainstorms, mosquitoes, gnats, and ticks made matters still more difficult all across Missouri and onto the Plains.

The expedition had other matters to address as well. Jefferson had compiled a long list of duties and objectives, chief among them keeping journals. Along with noting latitude, longitude, and landmarks, the captains were to record extensive details of any Indian nations encountered; "the soil and face of the country, its growth and vegetable productions, especially those not of the U.S."; animals; minerals, "volcanic appearances"; and climate.

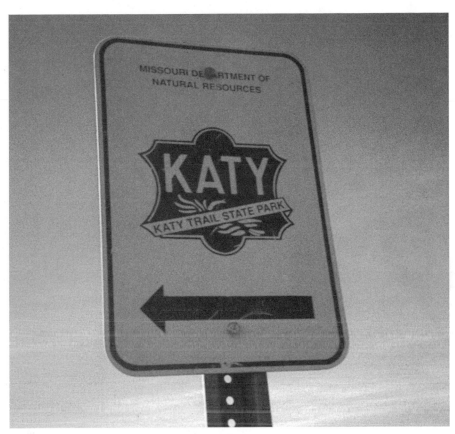

Bike or walk close to the river on the Katy Trail.

Both Lewis and Clark kept journals, and their versions of the trip are the best known today. But other expedition members contributed written accounts, too. Joseph Whitehouse's was one of the most detailed; Clark frequently fed him information in the hope that if the captains' journals were lost, another comprehensive account might survive. Others who kept journals were Patrick Gass, Nathaniel Pryor, Charles Floyd, and John Ordway. Gass, perhaps the most unlikely journal writer, was the first to hit print. He'd had only 19 days of schooling, but he wrote faithfully during the expedition, and his work, edited afterward by a schoolteacher, came out in 1807—the first book to be published about the expedition.

Mapmaking was another of the expedition's primary duties. In an 1805 letter, Jefferson wrote, "The work we are now doing is, I trust, done for posterity in such a way that they need not repeat it. We shall delineate with correctness the great arteries of this great country. Those who come after us will extend the ramifications as they become acquainted with them and fill up the canvas we begin."

Clark did most of the mapmaking. Using simple navigational instruments and his own estimates, he measured the length and direction of each bend of the rivers and the distance they had traveled, scribbling these courses and distances next to his sketch maps. In most instances, his "guesstimates" were remarkably accurate. Clark's maps recorded a wealth of other information, too, including campsites, creeks and rivers, Indian villages, and bad rapids.

And as instructed, the captains made note of the plants and animals they encountered. More than 120 animals and 170 plant species, many new to science, were described in the journals. Consequently, two entire plant categories—Lewisia and Clarkia—were named after the explorers, and their names also were freely assigned to landmarks and natural features across the land. When the corps members published their work, readers were fascinated to hear for the first time of such beasts as grizzly bears, bighorn sheep, and pronghorn antelope.

With all these duties, it would seem Lewis and Clark had scant time for adventure. But barely under way, Lewis had a close brush with death on May 23, 1804. On that day, the captains stopped to explore an area known as Tavern Cave, located east of present-day Washington, Missouri. "The challenge was too much for Lewis," David Lavender wrote in his book *The Way to the Western Sea*. "While Clark was adding his name to the register inside the cavern, Meriwether found a break in the precipice, ascended it, and began working his way along the edge. A foothold crumbled. He slid and bounced downward about 20 feet. Just short of disaster, Clark wrote in his journal, 'He saved himself by the assistance of his knife,' driving it wildly one assumes, into some crevice that held. Just how he extricated himself from the dizzy perch does not appear."

Tavern Cave is about 2 miles north down the railroad tracks from the village of St. Albans, an upscale housing and golf development. St. Albans is located off of Missouri Highway T, which makes a hilly loop north of MO 100, the main road east of Washington (on the opposite side of the river from MO 94, with a crossing via Missouri 47 at Dutzow). Several interpretive markers stand in front of the village's Chesterfield Day School, but hiking to the cave itself isn't recommended since it's on private land and accessible only by walking the railroad tracks. The state of Missouri may improve access to the cave by the time the bicentennial begins; check locally for updates. For now, it's not really worth backtracking to St. Albans unless you really want to sneak a peek at the lifestyles of Missouri's rich and famous.

Washington is a town of about 10,000 people with a good selection of interesting shops and restaurants and a mile-long riverfront park. Lewis and Clark camped in the vicinity two days after the episode at Tavern Cave. From

Washington, continue west on MO 100 or MO 94, through Missouri's scenic and hilly wine country. New Haven and Hermann are two other communities worth exploring on the MO 100 side.

First settled around 1805, New Haven was originally called Miller's Landing for pioneer Philip Miller. The Missouri-Pacific Railroad reached here in 1855, and the present town was laid out and renamed the next year. Today's New Haven begins up on MO 100 and tumbles down the river bluffs to a pleasant landing district with an antiques mall, a year-round Christmas store, a 1930s movie theater, and dining. A stairclimb from the downtown district leads to a viewpoint.

John Colter, one of the most famous members of the Lewis and Clark Expedition, settled a few miles east of New Haven in 1810. After the expedition, Colter went on to great fame as the first white man to discover what is now Yellowstone Park. He was probably buried in the New Haven area, although the location is uncertain. His grave was likely never marked and may have disappeared when the local river bluffs were reshaped to construct a levee—one of a handful that was able to withstand the floods that wracked the Midwest during the summer of 1993.

Hermann, sometimes called Little Germany, is reminiscent of Rhine Valley towns with its distinctive architecture. White settlers had arrived in the area by the early 1800s, and a town historical marker notes how the returning Lewis and Clark Expedition "joyfully hailed the sight of cows along the riverbank here."

Hermann was founded by the German Settlement Society of Philadelphia in 1836 as a place where German customs and language could be preserved "amid the benefits of America." The town was laid out on part of an 11,300-acre parcel purchased by Society agent George F. Bayer for $15,612. The society disbanded in 1839, but a steady stream of Germans continued to arrive for years afterward.

The year 1843 was a momentous one in Hermann history. That year, many newly arriving German emigrants died when a steamboat exploded. In 1843, Hermann also became the fourth town to serve as seat of Gasconade County—a title it retains today. The present courthouse was built in 1898. At one point, the town also boasted a German-language newspaper known for its anti-slavery views and a German school. River shipping and winemaking became big industries.

Hermann is a fairly touristy place, but one can understand why city slickers from St. Louis and Kansas City might want to head here for a weekend. Wine and beer tasting are big activities; fortunately, there are also plenty of accommodations available for anyone who samples a bit too much.

Hermann has a nice campground in its city park, with spots designed for tents as well as RVs. In addition to restrooms with showers, the park also has plenty of picnic tables, tennis courts, great playground equipment, and a pool.

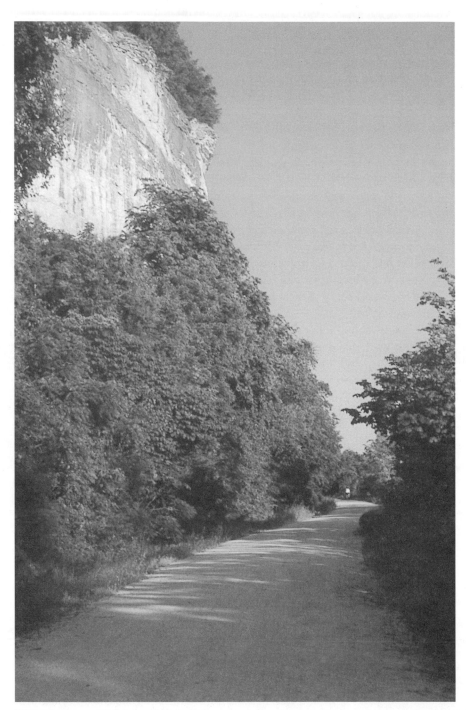

Katy Trail near Rocheport, Missouri.

Check the weather report before pitching a tent here, however: signs warn visitors the area is subject to flash flooding.

Cross the Missouri again at Hermann and proceed west on MO 94 (or I-70, 13 miles north via Missouri 19) to Jefferson City. The highlight here is a bronze relief on the state Capitol grounds depicting the signing of the Louisiana Purchase. Robert R. Livingston (seated) and James Monroe are seen witnessing French Marquis Francois de Barbois Marbois signing the purchase agreement, one of the most momentous events in American history. With their pen strokes, these men nearly doubled the size of the United States.

Other sights on the Capitol grounds include several lovely fountains and an imposing statue of President Jefferson. The Capitol itself hasn't had the greatest luck. First built in 1826, it was destroyed by fire in 1837. The second building, started that year, burned in 1911 after being struck by lightning. The present Capitol was built in 1918.

Inside, the Missouri Museum features historical and contemporary displays. Thomas Hart Benton's mural, "A Social History of the State of Missouri," is painted on all four walls of the House Lounge, located on the west wing of the third floor. The statehouse is open and free tours are available daily except Easter, Thanksgiving, Christmas, and New Year's Day.

Jefferson City's other attractions include the Jefferson Landing State Historic Site, with several buildings dating from the 1830s to the 1850s; the Governor's Garden, where outdoor drama is sometimes held; and the Runge Nature Center at 2901 West Truman Boulevard, featuring a large aquarium and hands-on nature exhibits. July is a big month for celebrations: a large Fourth of July party featuring fireworks shot off from a Missouri River barge; the annual Old Car Roundup set each mid-July downtown; and the Cole County Fair, held the last week of the month.

From Jefferson City, the traveler once again has a choice of routes. U.S. Highway 63 provides speedy access to Columbia and I-70 to the north, while Missouri 179 takes a more leisurely approach, reaching the interstate west of Columbia. MO 179 stays somewhat closer to the river; a popular attraction en route is Croy's River Hills Farm at Marion. Lewis and Clark camped nearby on June 4, 1804, and the farm now features a zoo, trail, gift and snack shops, and pick-your-own produce.

Columbia sits several miles from the Missouri, but what it may lack in location, it more than makes up in culture and recreation. Columbia is home to the main University of Missouri campus, Columbia College, and Stephens College, which together add some 27,000 students to Columbia's population of about 70,000. Campus highlights include the Francis Quadrangle at MU, where six ionic columns are all that remain of Academic Hall, destroyed by fire in 1892; Stephens College's Firestone Baars Chapel, designed by Eero Saarinen, the same

THE KATY TRAIL

  In 1986, the Missouri-Kansas-Texas (MKT) Railroad decided to end operations on a trans-Missouri route from near St. Charles to Sedalia. The decision paved the way for creation of the Katy Trail, at 185 miles the longest biking, hiking, and handicapped-use rails-to-trails project in the United States. ("Katy" is the popular abbreviation for MKT.)

The Katy Trail parallels the Missouri River across much of eastern Missouri, affording Lewis and Clark buffs an opportunity to see the river "trail" up close in several areas. Scenic wonders abound. Lewis and Clark noted the limestone bluffs south of Rocheport (on U.S. Highway 40 west of Columbia), known as the Manitou (or Moniteau) Bluffs for the Indian word for Great Spirit. These bluffs once had many pictographs, which Clark noted in his journal entry of June 7, 1804: "A short distance above the mouth of a creek is several curious paintings and carving on the projecting rock of limestone inlaid with white, red and blue flint of a very good quality...." To see the area now known as Lewis and Clark Cave, ride east 4 miles from the Rocheport trailhead. The cave itself is full of bats and is off-limits to exploration, but this is a lovely riverside ride that's among the Katy Trail's nicest stretches.

Katy Trail users wheel or walk past an array of wildflowers, and the trail's location along the Missouri River Flyway means migrating bird and waterfowl sightings are common. But the Katy Trail experience also means visits to small Missouri towns far from the interstate highways, where a slower way of life is still savored. If you can, come in fall when it's cooler and much of the route is ablaze in color. But no matter what the season, anyone who enjoys easy cycling or hiking through pastoral settings should plan to spend at least a day on the Katy Trail.

Katy Trail State Park was designed for bicyclists and hikers. Wheelchairs are welcome, too, but other motorized vehicles (except official and emergency vehicles) are prohibited. Users should stay on the trail, as the areas immediately outside trail boundaries are often on private property. Pets should be kept on a leash.

Businesses catering to cyclists and hikers are springing up all along the route. Bike rentals are widely available, starting at about $5 an hour or $20 a day for a standard bike—more for tandems, recumbent bikes, and high-performance models. The listing below is but a sample; for detailed information on the route, its history, and amenities along the way, check out *The Complete Katy Trail Guidebook* by Brett Dufur, widely available along the route.

The Touring Cyclist, with locations in St. Charles (636-949-9630; www.tcyclist.com) and Augusta (636-482-4038) rents bicycles and runs an annual Katy Trail end-to-end tour. This ride, covering 30 to 50 miles a day, usually takes place mid-September.

Scenic Cycles in Marthasville (636-433-2909; www.scenic-cycles.com) has bike rentals at similar prices to The Touring Cyclist. Scenic Cycles can also outfit you for an extended Katy Trail trek, with everything from pickup at the airport in St. Louis to lodging arrangements along the trail.

Steamboat Junction (573) 236-4664) near Bluffton is one of several bed-and-breakfast inns right along the Katy Trail. Camping is available, too, as is a refreshment stand for cyclists just passing by.

Trailside Café & Bike Rental (573) 698-2702) in Rocheport is the closest bike shop to the portion of trail nearest Lewis and

Clark Cave, described above. Before or after your ride, stop in for a barbecue beef sandwich or homemade baked goods. **Katy O'Neil**, a "bed-and-bikefest" nearby, features a hot tub and accommodations in a converted boxcar.

For more information on the Katy Trail, contact the Missouri Department of Natural Resources, P.O. Box 176, Jefferson City, Missouri 65102, or call (800) 334-6946.▲

architect responsible for the Arch in St. Louis; and the Chinese Pavilion at Columbia College.

Cultural attractions include the Shelter Insurance Gardens, where concerts are staged at 7 P.M. each Sunday during June and July; Maplewood Barn Theatre, where outdoor dramas are presented in a converted barn Memorial Day through Labor Day; and a variety of art galleries. (Columbia College is considered one of the nation's top fine and commercial art schools; its gallery is located on North 10th Street.) Recreational possibilities range from swimming, golf, and tennis to cycling on the nearby Katy Trail. Columbia Mall at Stadium and Bernadette streets is the city's largest, but Columbia also has a thriving downtown district centered near Providence Road and East Broadway. For more information on area attractions, call (573) 875-1231.

ARROW ROCK AND FORT OSAGE

Boonville, located near I-70 and Missouri 87, is one of the oldest towns in central Missouri and has more than 400 buildings on the National Register of Historic Places. The town has a good selection of food and lodging, along with brown-bag concerts in the summer, the Missouri River Festival of the Arts in August, and daily tours of the historic districts.

From Boonville, the river flows west then north to Arrow Rock, long a major stopping point for people headed west. Lewis and Clark reached the area June 9, 1804, and Clark noted "several small channels running out of the river below a bluff and prairie (called the Prairie of Arrows)." Even at that time, the area had already received its name.

In the mid–nineteenth century, many emigrants passed through the area on

Arrow Rock, Missouri.

their way to the western trailheads leading to Santa Fe, Oregon, and California. The town's population peaked around 1860 but dropped off after the Civil War and the decline of traffic on the nearby Missouri River.

Today, Arrow Rock looks much like it did in the mid-1800s. An interpretive center (open 10 A.M. to 4 P.M. Monday through Saturday and noon to 6 P.M. Sunday) explains the town's history, and visitors can see the past up close by walking through town. Historic buildings include the Old Tavern (dating to 1834) and a home occupied by famed frontier artist George Caleb Bingham from 1837 to 1845.

About two dozen merchants and innkeepers are doing their best to keep Arrow Rock alive, and the town enjoys thriving tourism, especially in the summer and fall. Major events include an arts festival the third weekend of May and a crafts festival the second weekend each October. The Lyceum Theatre presents a half-dozen different dramas each summer, with performances usually set Wednesday through Sunday evenings. The town has several bed-and-breakfasts, and camping is available at Arrow Rock State Park.

Arrow Rock State Historic Site is located 17 miles from Boonville and 15 miles from Marshall. To get there, take I-70 Exit 98 to Missouri 41. For more information, call (816) 837-3330.

From Arrow Rock, it's a short drive to one of the most extraordinary natural

locations along the lower Missouri River. The 1993 floods created a side channel, or chute, in an area known as Lisbon Bottoms. Instead of sealing off the
chute as it normally would, the Army Corps of Engineers has allowed the river
to take its natural course, or nearly so. (Although engineers have erected a rock
wall at the north end of the chute, it notched this barrier to allow the river to
continue flowing through, while still maintaining the main channel for barge
traffic.) The result: Lisbon Bottoms and adjacent Jameson Island comprise one
of the only stretches south of Sioux City, Iowa, where visitors can see a Missouri
River which resembles the waterway seen by Lewis and Clark.

Lisbon Bottoms and Jameson Island are now designated part of the Big
Muddy National Fish and Wildlife Refuge. Eventually, river advocates hope
to establish many free-flowing areas like this all along the Lower Missouri.
Lisbon Bottoms is located down river from Glasgow, which is 19 winding
miles north of Boonville via Missouri 87. There's a boat ramp at Glasgow
for people who would like to travel down river to Lisbon Bottoms. Small
crafts like canoes or kayaks can usually negotiate the chute through the
notch at its north end, though it's smart to call the refuge office at (573)
876-1826 to assess river conditions before setting out. Larger boats could
run up the chute from its south end. You can also get a view from the
riverbanks by following MO 87 then Highways Z, 328, and 319 to the nearly

abandoned community of Lisbon. The vista is actually best a bit south of Lisbon; look for signs announcing the wildlife refuge in this area.

From Arrow Rock, continue northwest on MO 41 to Marshall, the seat of Saline County and gateway to Van Meter State Park, an area featuring ancient Indian burial sites and ceremonial mounds (12 miles northwest on MO 41 and 122). At Marshall, pick up US 65 going west; it turns into U.S. Highway 24 at the small crossroads of Waverly.

US 24 proceeds west through an area filled with orchards offering everything from asparagus to blackberries to Christmas trees, depending on the season. The rural vistas blend with picturesque small-town scenes: young men working on a souped-up yellow car, complete with painted red flames streaking across its side, and older folks porch sitting into the twilight. Sweetly scented fruit blossoms replace diesel fumes, and a hawk may be spotted soaring above the trees. Best of all: almost no billboards. These roads have character.

Many small towns along the Lewis and Clark route have annual summer festivals or community picnics, usually advertised with signs posted near the village limits. If you happen to be in the right place at the right time, by all means stop and investigate. Anticipate a good meal, friendly conversation, and maybe some sightseeing tips, too.

Lexington, Missouri, was settled in 1822 by former residents of Lexington, Kentucky. The town became a busy river port and was the site of a three-day Civil War battle won by the Confederates. The battlefield is now a state historic site, and a cannonball fired during the September 1861 event may still be seen lodged in a column at the courthouse.

Lewis and Clark reached the present site of Fort Osage in late June 1804 and named it Fort Point, noting its suitability for a military installation. In 1808, Clark returned to supervise the construction of a fortified trading post to sway the Indians from Spanish and British influence. Fort Osage was operated by the government until 1822 and played an active and important part in the earliest development of the Louisiana Territory.

Interest in Fort Osage was revitalized during Missouri's statehood centennial in the 1920s. Restoration started in 1941 and was completed in 1962. To get to the site, take US 24 to Buckner; then turn north on Sibley Street (Missouri Highway BB). Directional signs point the rest of the way to the park.

Fort Osage was run by George Sibley, and he seemed to enjoy his post, noting in his diary: "I am very comfortably fixed." A household inventory done in 1813 included a cherry dining table, ten Windsor chairs, a walnut cupboard, and brass candlesticks. In his diary, Sibley noted his typical daily meals: coffee and unbuttered toast for breakfast; beef, pork, or venison and potatoes for midday dinner; and a dish of tea and milk and hominy for supper. "Frequently, we are honored with an Osage chief or war captain to dine or sup with us," he added, "and very often are favored with the company of the princesses and young

Fort Osage, Missouri.

ladies of rank, decked out in all the finery of beads, red ribbons and vermillion, silver ornaments and scarlet blankets."

Start your visit with a walk through the museum, which outlines the post's operations. A showcase displays items recovered during archaeological excavations at the site, including building materials, tools, household furnishings, and personal items. There's also an exhibit detailing the history of the U.S. Army at Fort Osage.

Next, stroll the grounds and visit some of the restored buildings. Authentically attired living history interpreters are frequently on hand to describe what life was like during Fort Osage's heyday. Reproductions of trade-era goods including tin wear, beads, buttons, tin whistles, lanterns, and more are available for purchase in the factory.

Fort Osage stages several special events each year, including the Spring Flint Knap-In (held in mid-May), Independence Day festivities on the Fourth of July, Children's Day in early August, a rendezvous and trade fair in early September, and a Christmas Frontier Open House in early December. An annual calendar of events is published each March. To request a copy, call (816) 795-8200 ext. 1260.

The Fort Osage admission fee is $3 for adults and $2 for youth and seniors; children under five are admitted free. The site is open from 9 A.M. to 4:30 P.M.

KANSAS CITY–AREA ATTRACTIONS

Lewis and Clark didn't spend a lot of time in what is now Kansas City. They reached the area on June 26, 1804, camping near the confluence of the Missouri and Kansas rivers, and returned on September 15, 1806, just days before arriving back in St. Louis. Kansas City's tribute to the Corps of Discovery rests on a bluff at 8th and Jefferson, at a small park known as Lewis and Clark Point.

A small plaque notes that, on the homeward journey, the captains stood on this point and noted its "perfect command of the river" before proceeding to shoot an elk and gather custard apples, or paw-paws, for that day's respite. Bicentennial plans call for a new Lewis and Clark sculpture in Kansas City, as well as further development in the riverfront area. The riverfront already is home to the Arabia Steamboat Museum, featuring more than 200 tons of treasure from the sunken vessel, and an open-air City Market.

History buffs may also want to pay a visit to Kansas City's suburban neighbor to the east, Independence. The town served as a primary jumping-off spot for the Oregon Trail, the California Trail, and the Santa Fe Trail. All are described in detail at the National Frontier Trails Center, 318 West Pacific Avenue, which recently added a major exhibit called "Blazing the Way West: From Lewis and Clark to Fur Traders and Trappers." The center is open 9 A.M. to 4:30 P.M. Monday through Saturday and 12:30 P.M. to 4:30 P.M. Sunday. Call (816) 325-7575 for more information.

Every Labor Day Weekend, Independence stages Santa-Cali-Gon Days, a festival marking the city's role as "Queen City of the Trails." Independence was also the hometown of President Harry S. Truman, and tours are available at several important sites, including the Truman Library and the home at 219 North Delaware Street, where Harry and Bess lived from their marriage in 1919 to his death in 1972.

With its fine architecture, broad boulevards, and European-style gardens and fountains, Kansas City often surprises visitors who expect little more than an overgrown cow town. In fact, Kansas City is one of the Midwest's largest and most progressive metropolitan areas. Get oriented at Kansas City's visitor center, located at Exit 9 just off Interstate 70 in view of the massive Harry S. Truman Sports Complex, where baseball's Royals and football's Chiefs enjoy separate stadiums capable of seating a total of 118,000 fans.

Sports-crazy Kansas City doesn't limit itself to spectator events. The city hosts an abundance of recreational activities, including golf, swimming, horseback riding, boating, hiking, and tennis. Much of the activity centers around 1,772-acre Swope Park. Worlds of Fun and Oceans of Fun, two popular theme parks, are located 13 miles north of Kansas City on Interstate 435.

Culture plays an equally strong role in Kansas City. The Nelson-Atkins Museum of Art (45th and Oak streets) includes 58 galleries and the largest collection of Henry Moore sculptures in the United States. Kansas City was home to artist Thomas Hart Benton, whose home may be toured at 3616 Belleview Avenue. Kansas City is world famous for its jazz scene, now documented at the Kansas City Jazz Museum at 1616 East 18th Street and still going strong at clubs all around town.

Top shopping areas include Westport, where Kansas City began and where westward-bound emigrants frequently outfitted themselves for their trips, and Country Club Plaza, the first planned shopping center in the United States.

Antiques fans flock to 45th Street and State Line Road, a district with more than 50 antique, arts, and crafts dealers. Crown Center just south of downtown is yet another place to shop, eat, and party.

For more information on Kansas City, write the Convention and Visitors Bureau of Greater Kansas City at 1100 Main Street, Suite 2550, Kansas City, Missouri 64105, or call (800) 767-7700.▲

Wednesday through Sunday mid-April through mid-November and weekends only the rest of the year. Stop at the visitor center to buy tickets before proceeding onto the actual fort reconstruction.

Picnic grounds are available both at Fort Osage and at nearby Hayes Park, which also has a playground. A honey farm and several orchards in the vicinity welcome visitors.

LEWIS AND CLARK STATE PARK (MISSOURI) AND WESTON BEND STATE PARK

From Kansas City, take Interstate 29/U.S. Highway 71 north to Missouri 45 (Exit 5), the route closest to the Missouri River. Lewis and Clark camped in the vicinity of Leavenworth, Kansas, on July 1, 1804, and September 13, 1806. Leavenworth is also known as the first incorporated town in the Kansas Territory and as site of Fort Leavenworth, an outpost traversed by branches of the Oregon and Santa Fe trails in the mid-1800s. The town remains a major military community, and the Frontier Army Museum at the post offers a bit of Lewis and Clark interpretation including a handsome mural of the White Cliffs section of the Missouri River in Montana. Leavenworth also is home to one of the most famous prisons in the United States.

A short ways upriver back on the Missouri side, the Show-Me State has two good riverside state parks, both accessible off of MO 45. Weston Bend State Park mostly occupies the bluffs high above the Missouri River. A scenic overlook offers a fine vantage point for sunsets. Farther north on MO 45, Lewis and Clark State Park ranks as one of Missouri's smaller state parks. Nevertheless, it is blessed with the presence of a sandy beach and a 365-acre lake popular for fishing, swimming, boating, and waterskiing.

Lewis and Clark Point. The confluence of the Missouri and Kansas rivers in Kansas City, Missouri.

Sugar Lake—called Gosling Lake by Lewis and Clark—is a good example of an oxbow lake, a phenomenon seen up and down the banks of the Missouri River. Oxbow lakes are formed by abandoned flood plain meanders. A thousand or more years ago, the river meandered over a wide valley creating vast wetlands. Constant riverbed erosion during flooding deepened the main channel, gradually isolating bends or oxbows. Eventually, the oxbows lost all but flood-level contact with the river, creating shallow lakes. Modern-day flood-control measures continue to isolate these oxbow lakes.

Lewis and Clark State Park has a 70-site campground, with facilities that include hot showers, a laundry room, dump station, and playground. Sugar Lake is known for its bass, bluegill, channel catfish, carp, and buffalo fish. For more information, call (816) 579-5564.

The town of Weston was a thriving port town from its founding in 1837 until a flood moved the Missouri River a mile away in the late nineteenth century. Weston went through some tough times, its 1853 population of 5,000 dropping to 1,000 by 1890. But in recent years, Weston has made a new name for itself through historic preservation and a charming little downtown shopping district.

Weston is also noted for its excellent limestone springs. Lewis and Clark paused to enjoy the water in 1804, and by the 1830s, the springs were a popular

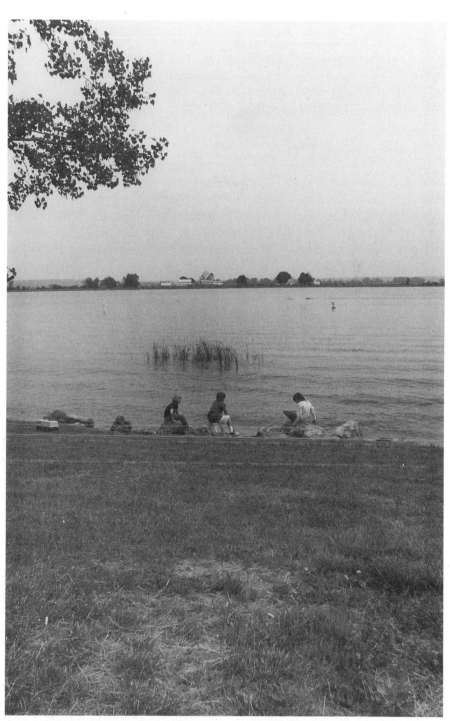

Lewis and Clark State Park, Missouri.

stopping place for wagons heading west. One of those who stopped was Benjamin J. Holladay, who settled in the area in 1838. Realizing that the limestone water, free of acid and iron, was perfect for making whisky, Holladay opened a distillery in 1856. The McCormick Distilling Company, as it is known today, is still in operation and offers free tours daily March through November.

INDEPENDENCE CREEK (KANSAS)

From Lewis and Clark State Park, it's a short drive to Atchison, Kansas, where the Corps of Discovery spent the first of three Fourth of Julys on their two-and-a-half-year trip. The town of Atchison marks the occasion at Independence Park on the city's riverfront. A sign there reads: "The Lewis and Clark Expedition passed this area on July 4, 1804. They camped north of here at the mouth of a creek which they named Independence Creek, in honor of the day. They celebrated 'by an evening gun and an additional gill of whisky to the men.'" Clark, in his journal, remarked that "as we approached this place the prairie had a most beautiful appearance, hills and valleys interspersed with copses of timber gave a pleasing diversity of the scenery."

Atchison is also noted for its Victorian-era architecture. Eighteen structures built during the late 1800s (including the birthplace of pioneering aviatrix

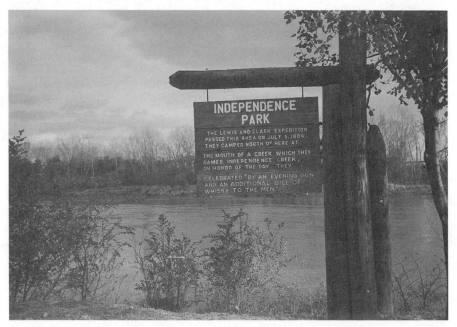

Riverfront at Atchison, Kansas.　　　　PHOTO BY LYNN HOFFMAN

Amelia Earhart) are featured in a 2.4-mile walking/driving tour. Stop by the Santa Fe Depot Visitor Center and Museum, 200 South 10th Street, for a brochure.

The International Forest of Friendship is another popular attraction, honoring people from all over the world who have contributed to aviation and space travel. The park's centerpiece is a tree grown from a sycamore seed taken to the moon on Apollo 14. Atchison has a community theater, outdoor downtown shopping mall, hiking trails, and more than 25 city lakes. For more information, call (800) 234-1854.

From Atchison, cross the Missouri River back to Missouri and follow U.S.

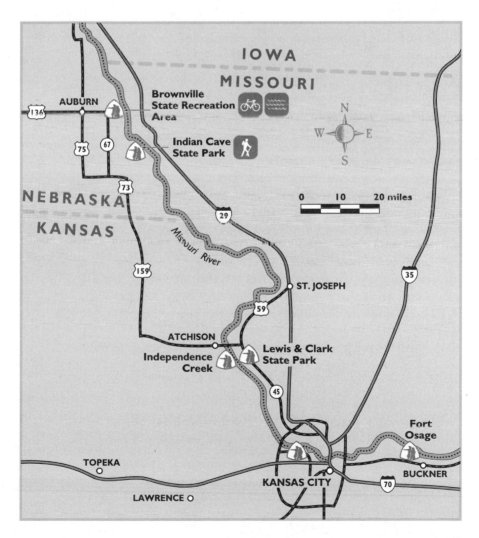

Highway 59 to St. Joseph, where the Pony Express was headquartered during its brief existence in 1860–1861. Two main sites interpret the "lightning mail" system: the Patee House Museum at 12th and Penn and the Pony Express Museum at 914 Penn Street. Other popular museums include the St. Joseph Museum at 11th and Charles and the Albrecht-Kemper Museum of Art at 2818 Frederick Boulevard. Get back on Interstate 29 (via Interstate 229 out of St. Joseph) to head north into Iowa.

Alternatively, head north from Atchison on Kansas 7 or US 73. These scenic routes run north into Nebraska, traversing the Sac, Fox, and Iowa Indian reservations and a lot of pretty prairie country.

LODGING

Rates are for double occupancy during summer season as of 1999 and are subject to change.

ALTON, ILLINOIS

Comfort Inn, (618) 465-9999, 11 Crossroads Ct. $60–$70.

Holiday Inn, (618) 462-1220, IL 3 at IL 140. $85–$95.

Super 8 Motel, (618) 465-8885, 1800 Homer Adams Pwy. $60–$65.

GREATER ST. LOUIS/ST. CHARLES, MISSOURI

Adams Mark St. Louis, (314) 241-7400, 4th & Chestnut Sts. $150–$200.

Baymont Inn, (636) 946-6936, 1425 S. 5th St. (St. Charles). $75–$85.

Best Inns of America, (618) 397-3300, I-64 and IL 157 (Caseyville, Illinois). $56–$68.

Boone's Lick Trail Bed & Breakfast, (636) 947-7000, 1000 S. Main St. (St. Charles). $85–$160.

Drury Inn Convention Center, (314) 231-8100, 711 N. Broadway. $85–$115.

Hampton Inn—St. Louis Airport, (314) 427-3400, I-70 Exit 236. $85–$100.

Holiday Inn—Forest Park, (314) 645-0700, 5915 Wilson Ave. $80–$155.

Hostelling International—The Huckleberry Finn Youth Hostel, (314) 241-0076, 1904—08 S. 12th St.

Lococo House II Bed & Breakfast, 1309 N. 5th (St. Charles), (636) 946-0619. $75–$85.

Travelodge at the Airport, (314) 890-9000, 9645 Natural Bridge Rd. $50–$70.

WASHINGTON, MISSOURI

Lewis and Clark Inn, (636) 239-0111, 500 Hwy. 100 E. $45–$63.

Schwegmann House Bed & Breakfast Inn, (800) 949-2262, 438 W. Front St. $75–$150.

DEFIANCE, MISSOURI

Parsons House Bed & Breakfast, (800) 355-6878, on the Katy Trail. $75–$95.

HERMANN, MISSOURI

Captain Wohlt Inn Bed & Breakfast, (573) 486-3357, 123 E. Third St. $65–$125.
Hermann Motel, (573) 486-3131, 112 E. 10th St. $40–$65.

BLUFFTON, MISSOURI

Steamboat Junction Bed & Breakfast, (573) 236-4664, on the Katy Trail. $40–$70.

JEFFERSON CITY, MISSOURI

Best Western Inn, (573) 635-4175, 1937 Christy Dr. $55–$65.
Hotel DeVille, (573) 636-5231, 319 W. Miller St. $60–$70.
Ramada Inn, (573) 635-7171, 1510 Jefferson St. $70–$80.

COLUMBIA, MISSOURI

Best Western Columbia Inn, (800) 362-3185, 3100 I-70 Dr. S.E. $55–$75.
Drury Inn, (573) 445-1800, 1000 Knipp St. $75–$85.
Eastwood Motel, (573) 443-8793, 2518 Business Loop 70E. $38–$45.
Red Roof Inn, (573) 442-0145, 201 E. Texas Ave. $46–$61.

ROCHEPORT, MISSOURI

School House Bed & Breakfast, (573) 698-2022, 504 3rd St. $95–$155.
Katy O'Neil Bed & Bikefest, (573) 698-2453, 101 Lewis St., on the Katy Trail. $25–$95.

NEW FRANKLIN, MISSOURI

Rivercene Bed-and-Breakfast, (660) 848-2497, 127 County Rd. 463. $85–$140.

BOONVILLE, MISSOURI

Comfort Inn, (660) 882-5317, I-70 Exit 101. $60–$70.
The Homestead Motel, (660) 882-6568, MO 5. $25–$30.
Morgan Street Repose Bed & Breakfast, (660) 882-7195, 607 E. Morgan St. $75–$95.

ARROW ROCK, MISSOURI

Borgman's Bed & Breakfast, (660) 837-3350. $55–$60.
Down Over Inn Bed & Breakfast, (660) 837-3268. $65–$95.
Westward Trail Bed & Breakfast, (660) 837-3335. $65.

LEXINGTON, MISSOURI

Lexington Inn, (660) 259-4641, US 24 and MO 13. $45–$55.

GREATER KANSAS CITY, MISSOURI/KANSAS

American Inn, (800) 905-6343, 4141 S. Noland Rd. (Independence). $40–$50.
Best Western Seville Plaza, (816) 561-9600, 4309 Main St. $80–$110.
Budget Host Inn, (816) 373-7500, 15014 E. Hwy. 40 (Independence). $40–$45.
Holiday Inn Citi Centre, (816) 471-1333, 1215 Wyandotte St. $100–$120.
Hyatt Regency Crown Center, (816) 421-1234, 2345 McGee. $205–$275.

Quarterage Hotel, (800) 942-4233, 560 Westport Rd. $90–$110.

Sleep Inn, (816) 224-1199, I-70 Exit 20 (Blue Springs). $65–$75.

Woodstock Inn Bed & Breakfast (816) 833-2233, 1212 W. Lexington Ave. (Independence). $65–$95.

LEAVENWORTH, KANSAS

Prairie Queen Bed & Breakfast, (913) 758-1959, 221 Arch St. $75–$110.

WESTON, MISSOURI

Apple Creek Bed & Breakfast, (816) 640-5724, 908 Washington. $75–$85.

Benner House Bed & Breakfast, (816) 640-2616, 645 Main St. $85–$90.

Inn at Weston Landing, (816) 386-5788, 526 Welt. $75–$100.

ATCHISON, KANSAS

Atchison Motor Inn, (913) 367-7000, US 73 and US 59. $36.

Comfort Inn, (913) 367-7666, 509 S. 9th St. $45–$60.

ST. JOSEPH, MISSOURI

Days Inn, (816) 279-1671, I-29 Exit 47. $50–$70.

Drury Inn, (816) 364-4700, I-29 Exit 47. $70–$80.

Pony Express Motor Inn, (816) 233-3194, I-29 Exit 47. $30–$50.

ROCK PORT, MISSOURI

Rock Port Inn, (660) 744-6282, I-29 Exit 110. $40–$50.

CAMPING

GREATER ST. LOUIS, MISSOURI/ILLINOIS

Babler Memorial State Park, (636) 458-3813, 20 miles west via MO 100 and MO 109.

North Greater St. Louis KOA, (618) 931-5160, 3157 West Chain of Rocks Rd. (Granite City, Illinois).

St. Louis RV Park, (800) 878-3330, 900 N. Jefferson Ave. (downtown).

ST. CHARLES, MISSOURI

Sundermeier RV Park, (636) 940-0111, 111 Transit St.

HERMANN, MISSOURI

Hermann City Park, (573) 486-5953, junction of MO 19 and 100.

BLUFFTON, MISSOURI

Steamboat Junction, (573) 236-4664, on the Katy Trail.

COLUMBIA, MISSOURI

Finger Lakes State Park, (573) 443-5315, 10 miles north via US 63.

NEW FRANKLIN, MISSOURI

Katy Roundhouse, (660) 848-2232, 1893 Katy Drive.

ARROW ROCK, MISSOURI

Arrow Rock State Historic Site, (660) 837-3330.

MARSHALL, MISSOURI

Van Meter State Park, (660) 886-7537, 12 miles northwest of Marshall.

GREATER KANSAS CITY, MISSOURI/KANSAS

Basswood Country RV Resort, (816) 858-5556, 15880 Interurban Rd. (Platte City).
Kansas City East KOA, (816) 690-6660, I-70 Exit 28 (Oak Grove).
Trailside Campers Inn of K.C., (816) 229-2267, I-70 Exit 24 (Grain Valley).

WESTON, MISSOURI

Weston Bend State Park, (816) 640-5443, MO 45.

RUSHVILLE, MISSOURI

Lewis and Clark State Park, (816) 579-5564, MO 45.

ATCHISON, KANSAS

Atchison State Fishing Lake, (913) 367-7811, north on KS 7.
Warnock Lake, (913) 367-4179, City of Atchison.

ST. JOSEPH, MISSOURI

Walnut Grove Campground, (816) 233-1974, I-29 Exit 53.

ROCK PORT, MISSOURI

KOA—Rock Port, (660) 711-5105, I-29 Exit 110.

RESTAURANTS

ALTON, ILLINOIS

Café La Rose, (618) 463-2711, 300 Alby (in the Old Post Office Mall). Soups, sandwiches, and desserts at lunch.
Historic Midtown Restaurant, (618) 465-1321, 7th & Central Ave. Homestyle cooking, open since 1876.
Ralph's, (618) 465-3230, 219 W 3rd. Casual fine dining.
Tony's Restaurant and Lounge, (618) 462-8384, 312 Piasa. Steaks, chops, and Italian specialties.

GREATER ST. LOUIS/ST. CHARLES, MISSOURI

Café Beignet, (636) 947-3000, 515 S Main St. (St. Charles). Breakfast and lunch in historic building.
Cardwell's, (314) 726-5055, 8100 Maryland Ave. (Clayton; also in Frotenac). Creative upscale food.

Imo's Pizza, (314) 644-5480, 1000 Hampton, near Forest Park. Local favorite, with many locations.

Jake's Steaks, (314) 621-8184, 708 N. 2nd St. Steaks with a Southwestern flair.

Lewis and Clark's, (636) 947-3334, 217 S. Main (St. Charles). Contemporary menu, open-air dining on upper floors.

Norton's Café, (314) 436-0828, 808 Geyer. Cajun and Creole specialties.

Station Casino St. Charles, (636) 949-7777. The Feast Buffet and The Broiler fine dining.

Trainwreck Landing, (314) 436-1006, 720 N. 1st St. Ostrich burgers, sweet potato fries, other unusual pub fare.

WASHINGTON, MISSOURI

American Bounty Restaurant, (636) 390-2150, 430 W. Front St. Casual fine dining with river view.

Char-Tony's Ristorante, (636) 239-2111, 1116 W. Front St. Local favorite for steaks, seafood, pasta.

Creamery Hill Café/Basket Case Deli, (636) 239-7127, 323-A W. 5th St. Deli by day, fine dining at night.

NEW HAVEN, MISSOURI

Raymond's of New Haven, (573) 237-7100. Front St. Upscale dining.

HERMANN, MISSOURI

Vintage 1847 Restaurant, (573) 486-3479, at Stone Hill Winery. Casual dining with scenic hilltop view.

JEFFERSON CITY, MISSOURI

Das Stein Haus, (573) 634-3869, 1436 Southridge Dr. German food.

Madison's Cafe, (573) 634-2988, 216 Madison. Casual dining featuring homemade pastas.

COLUMBIA, MISSOURI

Blue Cactus Café, (573) 443-2583, 3915 S. Providence. Southwestern specialties.

Boone Tavern & Restaurant, (573) 442-5123, 811 E. Walnut. Outdoor dining, Sunday brunch.

Flat Branch Pub & Brewing, (573) 499-0400, 115 S. 5th St. Handcrafted beer and full restaurant menu.

Jack's Gourmet Restaurant, (573) 449-3927, 1903 I-70 Business Loop 70E. Dinner club featuring steak and seafood.

Shakespeare's Pizza, (573) 449-2454, 225 S. 9th St. Local favorite.

ROCHEPORT, MISSOURI

Abigail's, (573) 698-3000, 100 E. 1st St. Lunch and dinner Wednesday to Sunday.

Les Bourgeois Winegarden & Bistro, (573) 698-2300. Blufftop dining overlooking Missouri River.

ARROW ROCK, MISSOURI

Arrow Rock Ice Cream Emporium, (660) 837-3337. Sandwiches, desserts.

The Evergreen Restaurant, (660) 837-3251, MO 41. Fine dining in restored 1840s home. Call for reservations.

GREATER KANSAS CITY, MISSOURI/KANSAS

Corner Restaurant, (816) 931-6630, 4059 Broadway. Westport's favorite breakfast spot.

Gates Barbecue, (816) 753-0828, 3201 Main and five other locations. Often voted KC's best.

Milano, (816) 426-1130, 2450 Grand Ave. in Crown Center. Casual Italian dining.

Ophelia's, (816) 461-4525, 201 N. Main (Independence). Fine dining.

River Market Brewing Co., (816) 471-6300, 500 Walnut. Pizza and pub fare.

Stanford & Sons, (816) 561-7454, 504 Westport Rd. Fun dining in one of KC's oldest buildings.

Stephenson's Apple Farm Restaurant, (816) 373-5400, I-70 Exit 14 (Independence). Country atmosphere.

Truman's Steaks & Spirits, (816) 468-0620, 511 N.W. Barry Rd. (off US 169).

WESTON, MISSOURI

America Bowman Restaurant, (816) 640-5235, 520 Welt. Traditional Irish dishes.

ATCHISON, KANSAS

The River House, (913) 367-3330, 101 Commercial St. Casual fine dining with a river view.

Paolucci Restaurant and Lounge, (913) 367-6105, 113 S. 3rd St. Italian-American cuisine.

ST. JOSEPH, MISSOURI

Frederick Inn Steak House, (816) 364-5151, 1627 Frederick Ave. Casual dining.

Sunset Grill, (816) 364-6500, 4012 River Rd. Pasta, seafood, steaks.

ROCK PORT, MISSOURI

Trail's End Restaurant, (816) 744-6389, I-29 Exit 110. Open 24 hours.

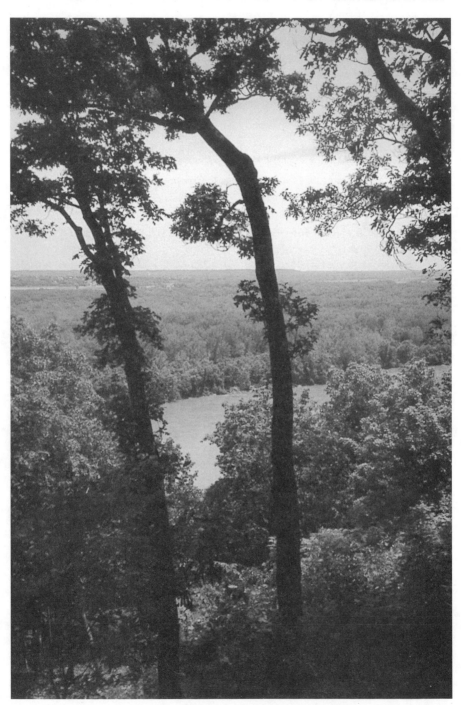

The Missouri River from Indian Cave State Park, Nebraska.

CHAPTER FOUR

NEBRASKA, IOWA, AND SOUTH DAKOTA

This scenery already rich pleasing and beautiful was still farther heightened by immense herds of buffalo, deer, elk, and antelopes which we saw in every direction feeding on the hills and plains. I do not think I exaggerate when I estimate the number of buffalo which could be (comprehended) at one view to amount to 3,000.

—Meriwether Lewis, September 17, 1804,
near present-day Chamberlain, South Dakota.

INDIAN CAVE STATE PARK/BROWNVILLE STATE RECREATION AREA

Summer on the Missouri River can be an unpredictable time, as the Corps of Discovery learned in July 1804. One day, the men would be in danger of sunstroke. The next, they'd be shivering through a thunderstorm. Clark described a typically atypical summer day, July 14, like this: "Some hard showers of rain this morning prevented our starting out until 7 o'clock. At half past seven, the atmosphere became suddenly darkened by a black and dismal-looking cloud . . . in this situation the storm which passed over an open plain from the northeast struck the (our) boat on the starboard quarter, and would have thrown her up on the sand island dashed to pieces in an instant, had not the party leaped out on the leeward side and kept her off with the assistance of the anchor and cable until the storm was over. . . . In this situation we continued about 40 minutes when the storm suddenly ceased and the river became instantaneously as smooth as glass."

  The episode Clark described took place near present-day Indian Cave State Park in southeast Nebraska. This heavily wooded park offers a smorgasbord of pursuits, with something to interest everyone. Twenty miles of trails wind through the park, with many backpacking campsites and nine Adirondack-style shelters with three sides and a roof. These are first-come, first-serve. Other activities include RV camping, guided hour-long horseback rides, weekend living history programs, bison

Meriwether Lewis Museum of Missouri River History at Brownville, Nebraska.

barbecues, and boat rides. There's a fine Missouri River view from the park's scenic overlook. The park is especially stunning in fall, when the trees blaze with color. Indian Cave State Park is east of Nebraska 67 via Nebraska South 64 East north of Shubert. For more information, call (402) 883-2575.

Moving upriver, the corps approached present-day Brownville, Nebraska. Brownville has a population of only about 150 people, but it frequently has several times that many visitors. Many come to trace the past at Brownville State Recreation Area. A historical marker at the site notes that on July 15, 1804, Lewis and Clark camped south of here on the northeast side of the river after traveling about 10 miles. The next morning, the keelboat caught on a snag in the river; despite the delay, the corps made 20 miles that day. Clearly, the men were becoming expert boatmen.

The recreation area's centerpiece is the Meriwether Lewis Museum of Missouri River History and the *Meriwether Lewis*, a steam-powered U.S. Army Corps of Engineers vessel that is drydocked within sight of the river. In its heyday, the *Meriwether Lewis* helped stabilize the Missouri for navigation starting in the 1930s. The boat remains pretty much as it was during its active career, and anyone who served on a similar craft would find it especially interesting. Tours are available, and there are plenty of exhibits including a Missouri River Rat Hall of Fame and a former cabin filled with Lewis and Clark lore. Admission is $1 for adults and 50 cents for kids ages 6 through 12. (Younger children are admitted free.) Hours are 10 A.M. to 5 P.M. daily June through August, with the same hours but on weekends only May and September.

Brownville State Recreation Area has a pleasant primitive campground in a grove of trees not far from the steamboat. (Some sites even command views of the old vessel through the trees.) There are only 14 sites, and they tend to go quickly. The *Spirit of Brownville* paddlewheeler offers two-hour cruises from the park at 3 P.M. Saturday and Sunday mid-June through mid-August, plus dinner cruises and trips to Indian Cave State Park. Call (402) 825-6441 for rates and information.

Brownville was settled in 1854, making it one of Nebraska's oldest communities. It's an interesting little town with its own concert hall and something happening almost every weekend all summer long, from the big flea market Memorial Day Weekend to repertory theater. The Brownville Methodist Church, oldest of its kind in Nebraska, still holds services every Sunday. Another local landmark, the Muir House, has a third-floor observatory. Several other fascinating buildings may be seen in the town's historic district, an area roughly bounded by First, Seventh, Nemaha, and Richard streets.

Missouri River at Brownville.

Brownville is also a trailhead for the Steamboat Trace, a 21-mile rails-to-trails conversion. From Brownville, the trail travels north through Peru and on to Minersville, a point southeast of Nebraska City. Along the way, riders and hikers can see swallow nests along cliffs that were described in the Lewis and Clark journals. Thurman's Bike & Sports at 1104 3rd Corso (three blocks south of Main Street) in Nebraska City can provide a rental bike and transportation to and from the trailhead for $25 per person, which includes use of a cell phone. Bike rentals without the shuttle also are available for $12 per half-day and $15 for a full day. For more information, call (402) 873-7509.

From Brownville, travelers can cross the Missouri to access Interstate 29. Or continue west on U.S. Highway 136 to Auburn, known as southeast Nebraska's antiques capital with about 30 dealers. From Auburn, U.S. Highway 75 heads north through the southeastern corner of the Cornhusker State, with lush, rolling green hills and prosperous-looking farms. Twenty-five miles north of Auburn, the highway reaches Nebraska City. This area is especially lovely in springtime when the apple trees are decked out in blossoms. Nebraska City's attractions include Arbor Lodge State Historical Park and the Morton Orchard and Tree Farm, both of which commemorate the life of J. Sterling Morton, the founder of Arbor Day. Lewis and Clark camped July 18–19, 1804, near what is now Riverview Marina State Recreation Area, a Missouri River access point just north of Nebraska City. A Lewis and Clark interpretive center is planned for the Nebraska City area, with an opening expected sometime before the expedition's bicentennial commemoration.

OMAHA, COUNCIL BLUFFS, AND FORT ATKINSON

Lewis and Clark conducted their first council with an Indian tribe at a Nebraska site called Council Bluffs, not to be confused with the Iowa city of the same name. Early in August 1804, the captains met with a group of Oto and Missouri Indians at the site about 15 miles north of downtown Omaha. Fort Atkinson State Historical Park marks the site today, but before heading there, visitors may want to stop to see several points of interest in the Omaha-Council Bluffs area.

The Western Historic Trails Center, located about a half-mile south of I-80 Exit 1-B in Council Bluffs, ranks among the most inventive interpretive sites along the Lewis and Clark Trail. Unusual painted, three-dimensional aluminum sculptures detail the Lewis and Clark Expedition as well as the Mormon, Oregon, and California Trails. A short film in the museum theater contrasts nineteenth-century travel with the road trips of today. Before departing, visitors are asked to later send the center a postcard from their own travels along any of the trails. These are prominently displayed in a two-sided glass case near the entrance, and they're lots of fun to read.

A 0.5-mile path leads to the nearby Missouri River banks. In addition, a 6-mile bike trail leads to Lake Manawa, near the site of the expedition's July 22–26 "White Catfish Camp." (Council Bluffs reenacts this encampment with a living history festival in late July.) The trails center also includes a very good gift shop and Iowa travel information center. Hours are 9 A.M. to 6 P.M. daily from May 1 through September 30, and 9 A.M. to 5 P.M. daily the rest of the year except Thanksgiving, Christmas, and New Year's Day. Admission is free, but donations are welcome. Call (712) 366-4900 for more information.

Next, visit Lewis & Clark Monument Park on the hillside north of Council Bluffs. The stone-plaza monument offers an outstanding view of the Missouri River and Omaha; the city of Council Bluffs is all but obscured by the lush woods cascading down the hillsides. The site is a favorite with red-tailed hawks, which are often seen riding the thermals above the bluffs. It's a splendid place for a picnic, especially at sunset.

To get to the overlook, take North 16th Street and turn right at the sign for Big Lake Park. Drive beneath a railroad trestle into the park and skirt its edges on the road. Past a second railroad trestle, turn left on North 8th Street. After about 0.3 mile, turn left again. The entrance to the park is 0.7 mile up the hill on the left.

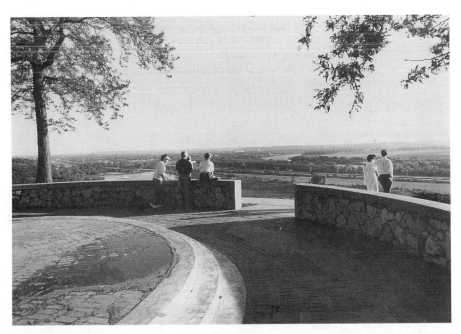

Lewis and Clark overlook, Council Bluffs, Iowa.

Omaha's N.P. Dodge Park also pays tribute to the corps' first encounter with native people. A small plaque in the parking lot near the camping area notes that the expedition camped just across the river. Dodge Park has plenty of big grassy areas for a variety of sports, as well as a bridle trail, horse camping area, boat ramp, and RV dump station. To get to Dodge Park from Council Bluffs, take I-29 north, then Interstate 680 west over the Mormon Bridge, and then follow the signs to the park.

Fort Atkinson is located just east of the town of Fort Calhoun, a few miles north of Omaha along US 75. Archaeological crews from the Nebraska Historical Society conducted digs at the site during the 1950s, hoping to establish the location of the fort's walls, gates, and outbuildings. All records at the fort indicated it was the site of the Indian council. But sometime after 1827, when the fort was decommissioned, the Missouri River shifted course and is now about 3 miles east of the original bluff. Moreover, the face of the land is much different now than nearly 200 years ago, with scrub trees and brush covering the face of the bluffs, and it is impossible to tell exactly where the council was held. Still, one can walk the grounds secure in the knowledge it was near here the first momentous encounter took place.

For a while, it looked like the council was not to be. In late July, camped to the south near the Platte River, Drouillard and Cruzatte went out in search of the Indians, only to learn the Otos had moved onto the plains for their annual buffalo hunt. Dejected, the explorers moved upriver. But just a few days later, Drouillard located a Missouri Indian who said that while most of the Otos were off on the buffalo hunt, a hundred or so Indians were camped nearby. On July 29, the captains sent one of the French boatmen, Liberte, with the Missouri Indian to locate the Indians and invite them to council.

The Corps of Discovery moved upriver, arriving at the bluff July 30. Captains Lewis and Clark walked up the bluff together and marveled at a landscape far different than any they'd yet seen. "This prairie is covered with grass of 10 or 12 inches in height, soil of good quality and at the distance of about a mile still farther back the country rises about 80 or 90 feet higher, and is one continued plain as far as can be seen," Clark wrote. "From the bluff on the second rise immediately above our camp, the most beautiful prospect of the river up and down and the country opposed presented itself which I ever beheld."

Back at camp, the men waited. The Indians finally arrived late on August 2, and the captains suggested they meet the next morning. Lewis, aided by Clark, stayed up late that night writing the first speech he would make to the Indians. It was an important occasion, the first instance in which the party would attempt to fulfill one of the principal orders set forth by President Jefferson. "In all your intercourse with the natives treat them in the most friendly and conciliatory manner which their own conduct will admit," Jefferson wrote. "Allay all jealousies as to the object of your journey, satisfy them of its innocence, make them acquainted with the position, extent, character, peaceable and commercial dispositions of the U.S., of our wish to be neighborly, friendly and useful to them, and of our dispositions to a commercial intercourse with them."

The next day, Lewis told the Otos all that and more. In a long speech, he explained how the Missouri River was now controlled by the United States— the Great Father in Washington—and that, if the Indians honored that sovereignty, there would be good trading for all. The Indians followed with a speech

TOURING OMAHA–COUNCIL BLUFFS

With a population of about 625,000 people, Omaha–Council Bluffs is the last major metropolitan area near the Lewis and Clark Trail until Portland, Oregon. As such, it offers quite a lot in the way of recreation, visitor attractions, culture, and shopping.

The Joslyn Art Museum, 2200 Dodge Street, is one of the Midwest's best. Housed in a marble Art Deco building, the Joslyn's collections include works from ancient Greece and Egypt and from the European masters. It may be best known, however, for its outstanding collection of art depicting the American West, especially the work of Swiss artist Karl Bodmer.

Bodmer's work is of great interest to Lewis and Clark buffs chiefly for its depiction of the Upper Missouri, a region the artist traversed with his boss, Alexander Phillip Maximilian, Prince of Wied, on the steamboat *Yellow Stone*, in the 1830s. Bodmer's paintings depict in image much of what Lewis and Clark noted in their journals 30 years earlier. He also is known for his many beautiful Indian portraits.

The Henry Doorly Zoo, another popular Omaha attraction, is located at Deer Park Boulevard and South 10th Street. Zoo highlights include a huge open-air aviary and the Lied Jungle, stocked with rainforest plants, animals, birds, and fish from Asia, Africa, and South America. A children's petting zoo, aquarium, educational center, and steam train ride are also among the exhibits and activities.

Omaha is at its liveliest in the Old Market area, which is centered around Howard and 11th streets downtown. The area throngs with people every evening after work and on the weekends. Other sightseeing possibilities in Omaha include Father Flanagan's Boys Town, 2 miles west of Interstate 680 on U.S. Highway 6; the Omaha Children's Museum, packed with hands-on activities at 500 South 20th Street; horse racing at Ak-Sar-Ben May through August; and the Great Plains Black Museum, 2213 Lake Street Omaha, was also the site of the Mormons' winter headquarters as they moved west during the mid-1840s. A center commemorating the trek is located at 3215 State Street.

Council Bluffs has several riverboat casinos and greyhound racing. Other Bluffs attractions include the RailsWest Railroad Museum at 16th Avenue and South Main Street; the Golden Spike Monument at South 16th Street and 9th Avenue; and the Grenville M. Dodge Home at 605 3rd Street, erected in 1869 by the Civil War general and railroad builder.

  The Omaha–Council Bluffs area is starting to build an admirable trails network, most under the umbrella of an organization known as Back to the River. On the Nebraska side, many miles of trails have been built atop flood control levees, including a 10-mile stretch paralleling the Missouri River south of Bellevue. Also in Bellevue, watch for signs on Bellevue Boulevard pointing the way to the Great Marsh, a long-silted backwater that has been dredged. A 2-mile footpath trail from the marsh leads to Hidden Lake. An 11-mile biking/walking trail from downtown Omaha to Dodge Park should be completed by 2001, and there are also plans for a pedestrian crossing between Omaha and Council Bluffs—by water taxi, gondola, bridge, or a combination—by about 2002. For more information on any of these projects, call the Papio–Missouri River Natural Resources District at (402) 444-6222.

Council Bluffs is the northern terminus of the Wabash Trace Nature Trail, a 63-mile route through the Loess (pronounced "Luss") Hills of rural western Iowa, a rare land formation found only here and in China. The trailhead is behind Lewis Central School along U.S. Highway 275 south of Iowa 92 in south Council Bluffs. For more information, call Southwest Iowa Nature Trails at (712) 328-6836.

Annual events in the area include the Renaissance Faire of the Midlands, held the second weekend each June at Iowa Western Community College in Council Bluffs; the Phantasmagoric Arts Festival, held each August in Council Bluffs' Bayliss Park; and the Omaha Summer Arts Festival, also held each June. The Omaha Royals minor-league baseball team plays Pacific Coast League ball at Rosenblatt Stadium, which also is home to the NCAA College World Series each spring. For more information about Omaha, call (800) 332-1819, or stop by the visitor center near I-80's 13th Street exit. To learn more about Council Bluffs, stop by the visitor center at the RailsWest Museum, or call (712) 325-1000. ◢

of their own, "promising to pursue the advice and directions given them that they were happy to find that they had fathers which might be depended on," Clark wrote. The speeches were accompanied by gifts to the Otos, and by a demonstration of the corps' airgun, an example of new American technology that never failed to amaze the natives. It is true the captains were disappointed that they were unable to meet with the main chiefs of the Otos and Missouris. On the other hand, this first encounter with the Indians had gone smoothly. All in all, the council had to be considered a success.

Fort Atkinson's visitor center has a videotape on the Louisiana Purchase and Lewis and Clark Expedition that can be shown on request. Another video details the fort's military history. Fort Atkinson served as an important outpost for frontier exploration and trapping until it was abandoned in 1827, replaced by Fort Leavenworth, which was better situated to protect traffic on the Santa Fe Trail.

A walking trail leads from the visitor center to the fort's reconstruction. The fort consisted of a rectangular formation of one-story barracks built from horizontal logs. The barracks opened out upon an enclosed parade ground. Other buildings included a large council house for negotiating with the Indians, a gristmill, a schoolhouse, and a brick kiln.

Fort Atkinson's visitor center is normally open daily Memorial Day Weekend

Omaha's Eppley Airfield (OMA) is served by American, ComAir, Continental, Delta, Frontier, Southwest, Midwest Express, Northwest, TWA, and United airlines. Rental cars are available from all major companies. Omaha is on Amtrak's Chicago–to–West Coast California Zephyr line, with the station at 1003 South 9th Street. Long-distance bus service is available from Greyhound at 1601 Jackson Street in Omaha.

Metro Area Transit runs extensive bus service in Omaha and a handful of routes in Council Bluffs. For schedule information, call (402) 341-0800.

through Labor Day Weekend from 9 A.M. to 5 P.M. During late April, May, September, and October, the visitor center is open weekends from 10 A.M. to 5 P.M. Living history days take place the first weekend of every month May through October. For more information, call (402) 468-5611.

Fort Calhoun is a tiny town of small, neat houses, and a few home-style restaurants. In addition to Fort Atkinson, Fort Calhoun is home to the Washington County Historical Museum. Three miles east of town, check out the hiking and biking trails and canoe access at Boyer Chute National Wildlife Refuge. Another short drive north, you'll reach DeSoto National Wildlife Refuge, noted for great fishing and an exhibit on the wreck of the steamboat *Bertrand* in 1865. From the Omaha–Council Bluffs area, travel north on US 75 (in Nebraska) or I-29 (in Iowa) to Onawa, Iowa, home of the Hawkeye State's version of Lewis and Clark State Park.

LEWIS AND CLARK STATE PARK (IOWA)

Although it is located along the Corps of Discovery's route, nothing really remarkable happened at Iowa's Lewis and Clark State Park. The expedition camped in the vicinity on August 10, 1804, on the far side near the present-day KOA campground. The site is worth a visit, however, because it is home to a full-scale replica of the expedition's keelboat, as well as its two pirogues.

The keelboat replica was designed and constructed by a group called the Friends of Discovery under the supervision of Butch Bouvier, a local woodwright, history aficionado, and boat buff. To create the replica, Bouvier used both William Clark's drawings of the keelboat and his own research into early-nineteenth-century boat building. Its hull was launched in 1987, and its deck, mast, sidewall lockers, and cabins were added later. Bouvier also built a small model of the boat that now sits in the park superintendent's office.

Today, the full-scale boats are maintained by volunteers. In fact, visitors who stop by the park early in the season may find the "Friends" on the scene, doing maintenance on the project. The boats are usually on view from mid-May through August. The best time to visit, however, may be during the Lewis and

Butch Bouvier and Les Peary with a keelboat replica at Lewis and Clark State Park near Onawa, Iowa.

Clark Festival the second weekend each June. Events include music and dancing, historical presentations, a buffalo burger feed, a black powder shoot, an art show, a fire-starting contest, and more. Over the next few years, Lewis and Clark State Park hopes to build a visitor center to shelter and interpret the boats year-round.

Like its Missouri neighbor, Iowa's Lewis and Clark State Park rests on the shore of an oxbow lake. Blue Lake was part of the river in 1804 and now serves as nucleus of a state park that offers a campground with boat access, a beach, and good fishing opportunities. Picnic areas and hiking trails make the park a nice spot for day use, too. For more information, call (712) 423-2829.

The town of Onawa is just east of the park. It boasts what is supposed to be the widest Main Street in America, a claim to fame celebrated the third Saturday in each June with an old-fashioned dance, car show, and "cruise." Onawa also lures visitors with Casino Omaha, a 24-hour gaming emporium stocked with hundreds of slot machines and a variety of tables.

BLACKBIRD HILL

From Onawa, cross the toll bridge over the Missouri River into Nebraska and rejoin US 75 at Decatur. Somewhere between here and Macy, 10 miles to the north, is Blackbird Hill, grave of the chief of the Omahas.

After the meeting at Council Bluffs, the Corps of Discovery once again started up the Missouri. It wasn't long before one of the privates, Moses Reed, requested permission to go back and retrieve a knife he said he'd left at the council site. Soon, however, it became apparent Reed had deserted, the second man to do so in one week. Liberte, sent earlier to call the Otos to council, had also disappeared.

The captains sent a four-man search party to bring the deserters back. Meanwhile, the main party moved farther upriver in hopes of meeting the Omahas. On August 11, 1804, they came upon a mound about 300 feet high, marked at the top with a post. It was Blackbird's grave. Lewis, Clark, and 10 of their men decided to climb up, have a look, and pay their respects—even if Blackbird was the sort of man who won tribute out of fear, not admiration. For a brief time, the Omahas had enjoyed great power under Blackbird. He frequently used arsenic to poison his rivals, and by this and other means, he and his tribe waged a war of terror over any party trying to pass through their country. But Blackbird's reign was cut short when a smallpox epidemic swept through the Omaha village, reducing its population from 700 to no more than 300.

In Blackbird's day, and in the time of Lewis and Clark, Blackbird Hill offered a commanding view up and down about 70 miles of the Missouri River. These days, timber growth has obscured what once was a fine view, and the site

View of Missouri River from Blackbird Hill wayside, Decatur, Nebraska.

on the Omaha Indian Reservation is off-limits to the general public. But a road wayside area about 3.5 miles southeast of the actual site provides a similar hilltop view of the Missouri, along with interpretation of Omaha history. The overlook is situated along US 75 about 2.5 miles north of Decatur.

The Omahas' earliest known home was the Ohio River Valley. Like Lewis and Clark after them, the Omaha people knew how tough it was to battle the Missouri upstream, and their name means "against the current." By 1700, the tribe had migrated to the Blood Run site about 100 miles north of the Blackbird Hill area, and moved several more times around the vicinity before building their "Big Village" about 20 miles north of Blackbird Hill in 1775. Creation of this village (called Tonwontongathon in the Omaha language) coincided with Blackbird's rise to power.

A shelter at the site recreates the look of an Omaha earthlodge, although, at just 30 feet in diameter, it would have been considered small. Many lodges spanned up to 60 feet in diameter, able to accommodate large families and their horses. The exhibit notes how two men of the Lewis and Clark Expedition—Pierre Cruzatte and Francois Labiche—were sons of Omaha mothers and thus began the tribe's long history of U.S. military service.

The Corps of Discovery located the main Omaha village August 14 and hoped for a council, but again, the village was nearly deserted. Finally, on

August 17, the search party returned with Reed in tow, accompanied by three Indian chiefs who had been traveling with Reed and who hoped to make peace with the Omahas. Liberte, for his part, had been caught but got away.

Found guilty of desertion the next day, Reed was sentenced to run four times through a gauntlet of his peers, who beat him with willow switches. This shocked the visiting Indian chiefs, who "petitioned for pardon of this man," Clark wrote. But after the captains explained the necessity for such punishment, "they were all satisfied with the propriety of the sentence," Clark added. Afterward, the mood turned merrier as everyone celebrated Captain Lewis's 30th birthday with an extra measure of whisky and dancing.

Continue north on US 75 through some very pretty hill country. The Omaha Nation runs a bingo and casino hall located south of Macy, and the town is the site of the annual Omaha powwow the weekend nearest the full moon of August. Winnebago, 10 miles to the north, serves as headquarters for the Winnebago Indian Reservation. Its powwow takes place the last full weekend in July. Dakota City, just south of South Sioux City, Nebraska, has an aptly named park at Cottonwood Cove, with riverside picnic tables and a boat launch amid the tall trees.

SERGEANT FLOYD MONUMENT

It seems almost unbelievable that during more than two-and-a-half years in the wilderness, facing everything from grizzly bears to rattlesnakes to extreme weather, only one member of the Lewis and Clark Expedition died. The Sergeant Floyd Monument in Sioux City pays tribute to that man.

The Omahas never returned to their village during the corps' brief respite there, so a council was held with the visiting Oto and Missouri chiefs on August 19. "We showed them many curiosities and the airgun which they were much astonished at," Clark wrote. But by the end of the day, the captains' attention had turned to Sergeant Charles Floyd, who was clearly very ill with what the captains believed was a bilious colic. "We attempt to relieve him without success as yet, he gets worse and we are much alarmed at his situation," Clark wrote. Modern doctors and historians believe Floyd actually suffered from an infected appendix—an ailment no doctor of the time could have cured.

On the morning of August 20, 1804, the corps proceeded upriver as usual. But by noon, Floyd had taken a turn for the worse. The party halted to prepare a warm bath for their colleague. But before it was ready, Floyd turned to Clark and said, "I'm going away. I want you to write a letter." Those were the sergeant's last words.

The corps saw another riverside bluff a mile or so away and decided it would be a fitting final resting place for their comrade. Floyd was wrapped in a blanket

View from the Sergeant Floyd Monument at Sioux City, Iowa.

and carried to the hilltop. "We buried him with all the honors of war, and fixed a cedar post at his head with his name, title and day of the month and year," Clark wrote. "Captain Lewis read the funeral service over him." The bluff on which Floyd was buried was named after him, as was a small stream in the vicinity.

Over the next few decades, Sergeant Floyd's grave became something of a nineteenth-century tourist attraction. The corps visited on its way home in 1806; later visitors probably included artists George Catlin and John Audubon and Prince Maximilian. According to Roy Appleman, author of a National Park Service guide to Lewis and Clark sites, an 1857 flood swept away part of the bluff, reportedly exposing some of poor Floyd's bones. The remains were rescued and reburied about 200 yards back from the face of the bluff in an unmarked grave—but that site was nearly forgotten when dirt from railroad construction was dumped nearby. Finally in 1900, the current 100-foot concrete obelisk was erected and Floyd's remains once again interred. The monument was dedicated in 1901, the first site ever to be registered as an official National Historic Landmark.

To visit the site, travel 0.5 mile east and 0.5 mile north of I-29 Exit 143. A plaque on the monument reads: "In commemoration of the Louisiana Purchase made during the administration of Thomas Jefferson, third president of the

United States, April 3, 1803; of its successful exploration by the heroic members of the Lewis and Clark Expedition; of the valor of the American soldier; and of the enterprise, courage and fortitude of the American pioneer, to whom these great states west of the Mississippi River owe their secure foundation."

Below the monument, a rock wall provides a panoramic overlook. Today's view, dominated by highways and railroad tracks, isn't especially scenic, but an interpretive panel points out several spots of historic note, including the approximate site of Floyd's death and the mouth of the Floyd River, where Lewis and Clark camped after the burial.

The sergeant's memory is preserved elsewhere in and around Sioux City, too. Floyd Boulevard is one of the town's main thoroughfares, and a small town south of Sioux City is named Sergeant Bluff. Most prominent, however, is the Sergeant Floyd Riverboat Museum and Welcome Center. The dry-docked *Sergeant Floyd*, once a diesel inspection boat, plied the Missouri River for 50 years as flagship of the U.S. Army Corps of Engineers construction fleet. The boat now serves as a museum focusing on Missouri River history, but it also includes memorabilia from the Lewis and Clark Expedition. Travel information and gifts are also available. The center is located at 1000 Larson Park Road (Exit 149 off of I-29). Hours are 8 A.M. to 6 P.M. Monday through Saturday and 10 A.M. to 6 P.M. Sunday from May through September.

The Sergeant Floyd Riverboat Museum and Welcome Center, Sioux City, Iowa.

Off-season, the center is open 9 A.M. to 5 P.M. Monday through Saturday and noon to 5 P.M. Sunday.

Baseball fans may want to take in a game of the minor-league Sioux City Explorers, who play at Lewis and Clark Park on the city's south side. The Sioux City Public Museum, located in a former mansion at 2901 Jackson Street, includes displays on anthropology, archaeology, natural history, science, and military memorabilia. The Sioux City Art Center at 225 Nebraska Street offers changing exhibits of contemporary artwork from the Upper Midwest. Sioux City's big annual festival, Rivercade, is held in late July. For more information on area events and attractions, stop by the welcome center or call (800) 593-2228.

From Sioux City, continue north on I-29 to Vermillion, South Dakota, home of Spirit Mound. Somewhere near the town of Elk Point, the Corps of Discovery chose Patrick Gass to replace Charles Floyd as sergeant. A marker in the town's park commemorates that event.

Spirit Mound

At their meetings with the Oto Indians, the explorers heard a story they found foolish and fascinating at the same time. "In a northerly direction from the mouth of this creek in an immense plain a high hill is situated, and appears of a conic form, and by the different nations of Indians in this quarter is supposed to be the residence of devils," Clark wrote on August 24, 1804, as the party approached present-day Vermillion, South Dakota. "They are in human form with remarkable large heads, and about 18 inches high, that they are very watchful and armed with sharp arrows with which they can kill at a great distance; they are said to kill all persons who are so hardy as to attempt to approach the hill. . . . So much do the Omaha, Sioux, Otos and other neighboring nations believe this fable, that no consideration is sufficient to induce them to approach the hill."

At first, the captains decided to sail on by the trail leading to Spirit Mound. But they reconsidered and, as David Lavender wrote in *The Way to the Western Sea*, "curiosity and conscience got the best of them. Just suppose such creatures did exist and they left the discovery to someone else?"

So Lewis, Clark, and nine other men made the trip on August 25. It was an oppressively hot day, and it took nearly three hours to reach the landmark. Lewis's dog, Seaman, collapsed on the way; he was almost joined by his master, who two days earlier had mildly poisoned himself while tasting the minerals of a bluff the party had encountered near Sioux City. But they finally made it and were rewarded, not by death, but by an inspiring view of the surrounding plains. Clark described it thus: "From the top of this mound we beheld a most beautiful landscape; numerous herds of buffalo were seen feeding in various directions; the Plain to the north-northwest and northeast extends without interruption as far as can be seen."

Spirit Mound near Vermillion, South Dakota.

The explorers concluded it must have been the swirl of birds and insects on the mound that produced the Indian legends—that, and the fact the mound did stand out quite remarkably from the surrounding landscape. They soon retreated to the Vermillion River where, hungry and thirsty, they found water and a variety of delicious fruits including grapes, plums, and currants.

Spirit Mound is still visible today, located on private land west of South Dakota 19, about 8 miles north of Vermillion. An interpretive sign is placed in view of the mound, but the landmark is well worth a closer look, mainly because it is one of just a few places along the Lewis and Clark Trail that today's traveler can know with certainty he or she is standing in the exact spot the explorers stood. To get permission, stop at the farmhouse at the site, or call in advance. Tim and Paula Seep at (605) 624-0083 live at the site; Paula also runs a delightful small gift and plant shop, Victorian West. If you can't reach the Seeps, try Ernest and Doris Schmidt, who own most of the land at the site. Their number is (605) 624-5388. Take care to close all gates, and keep your pets on a short leash.

The view from atop Spirit Mound is indeed beautiful. In recent years, the landmark has become a focus of preservation efforts, particularly since the site now abuts a feedlot that is steadily eroding the bluff. Both the state and federal governments are now working toward acquiring the land and restoring it to its

1804 condition. For more information, contact the Spirit Mound Trust, P.O. Box 603, Vermillion, South Dakota 57069.

Vermillion is a pleasant college town of about 10,000 people. The South Dakota state legislature named Vermillion the site of the university in 1862, but classes weren't held until 20 years later. Vermillion was originally located closer to the river, but a big flood in 1881 forced the town to move atop the bluffs.

The local Lions club has established a public campground right along the business route on the edge of town; in addition to RV space, the park offers lots of shade trees and a playground for kids. Another park, Prentice Park, has a swimming pool with a water slide and a Frisbee golf course. Vermillion's cultural attractions are centered on the University of South Dakota campus and include the Shrine to Music Museum, home to more than 6,000 rare and antique instruments, and the W. H. Over State Museum. From Vermillion, it's about a half-hour drive to Yankton on South Dakota 50.

RIVERS AND LAKES: THE NEBRASKA–SOUTH DAKOTA BORDER

Two stretches of river along the Nebraska–South Dakota border still bear some resemblance to the river seen by Lewis and Clark. The river flows free from below Gavins Point Dam to near Sioux City and again from the mouth of the Niobrara River to Fort Randall Dam. Snags, sandbars, islands, eroding banks, and a merrily meandering channel all still exist in this area.

Public river access points are available at several places along these stretches. Nebraska ramps include those at Niobrara, Cedar County northeast of Wynot, and Ponca State Park. In South Dakota, public ramps can be found at Riverside Park in Yankton and Clay County Park near Vermillion. If you don't have a craft of your own, consider renting a canoe or two from Missouri River Tours, an outfitter based on the river north of Wynot, Nebraska. Marlin Roth (pronounced "Roath") grew up on the Mighty Mo and is one of the area's best boatmen. He can advise visitors on where to paddle, and he runs a shuttle service for patrons who need help getting their boats back to headquarters. Prices start at just $5 for a quick paddle around Roth's camp and an adjacent backwater to $40 for full-day rentals. Roth also runs guided river tours in his motorized "johnny boat," custom-made to maneuver easily through the wild Missouri's shallow sections. (The boat can accommodate about four people. Call for prices.) Just downriver from Roth's headquarters, boaters can see chalk bluffs mentioned in the Lewis and Clark journals and float past several campsites used by the corps during their passages through here in August 1804 and September 1806. Nearby Goat Island is a favorite place for primitive camping.

Missouri River bluffs near Wynot, Nebraska.

For more information, call Roth at (402) 985-2216 or write Missouri River Tours, P.O. Box 121, Belden, Nebraska 68717.

Upriver from Gavins Point Dam, the Missouri becomes Lewis and Clark Lake. The expedition camped from August 28 to September 1, 1804, on the bottomlands below Calumet Bluff on the Nebraska side and held a council with the friendly Yankton Sioux. (Pierre Dorion, who had joined the expedition on June 12, provided interpretation.) Today, the area's shores teem with one campground, beach, and boat ramp after another. Most of the 2 million or so annual visitors have recreation on their minds, but it's also possible to find a healthy dose of history, notably at the Lewis & Clark Visitor Center, located on the Nebraska side of the river.

The center sits atop Calumet Bluff, and its focus is on the history of the Missouri River. This is a great stop for kids, who can pull a rope to hear a steamboat whistle, try their hand at spinning a pilot wheel, examine natural specimens with a magnifying glass, or just pull up a big floor pillow and read awhile. Other exhibits share the story of the U.S. Army Corps of Engineers, which helped build everything from the Panama Canal to the six main stem dams of the Pick-Sloan project. Together, these dams—Gavins Point, Fort Randall, Big Bend, Oahe, Garrison, and Fort Peck—make up the nation's largest dam system, with storage capacity of about 22.5 trillion gallons. Gavins Point

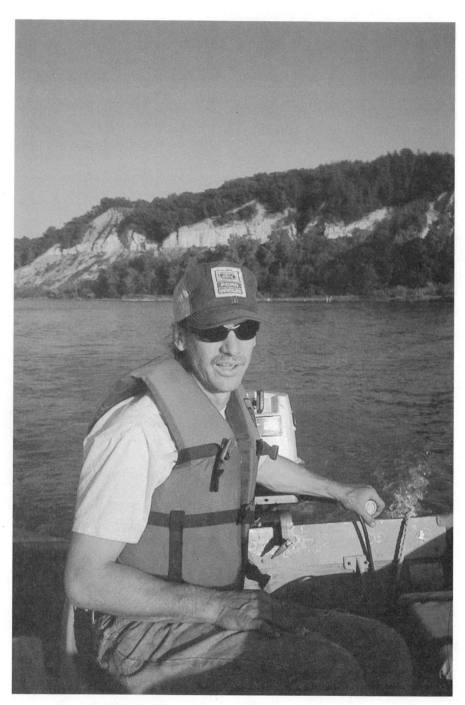

Missouri River boatman Marlin Roth.

Dam was completed in 1957, and if all its spillway gates opened wide at once, the total flow would be 4.5 million gallons a second—enough to cover a football field in 14 feet of water in one second.

Slide presentations are shown daily, and tours of the dam are also available daily through the summer and by appointment the rest of the year. The visitor center is open seven days a week from 8 A.M. to 6 P.M. weekdays and 10 A.M. to 6 P.M. weekends from Memorial Day through Labor Day. Hours vary the rest of the year. For more information, call (402) 667-7873 ext. 3246. Picnic tables and several hiking trails are available outside on the bluff.

There are probably a thousand or more campsites surrounding Lewis and Clark Lake, but since they manage to fill up fast on many summer weekends, it's important to stake a place early. The campgrounds all look quite inviting, but in wet years, they can be abuzz with annoying gnats and small black flies. The usual insect repellents seem to have little power over these cursed critters, but local park personnel say a dab of vanilla extract may ward them off for a while. Try that, or play it safe and find a motel room in Yankton.

Other than the insect swarms, this is a splendid area, flanked by heavily treed, rolling hills. A nature foot trail in the Gavins Unit of South Dakota's Lewis and Clark State Recreation Area leads to a commanding view of the Missouri River bluffs. An interpretive shelter imparts information on the expedition's travels through the area.

Lewis and Clark Lake on the Nebraska–South Dakota border.

Yankton, South Dakota, is a good-sized town with many hotels and restaurants. Many businesses cater to vacationers, but local people clearly enjoy the abundant recreation access, too. A popular bike path stretches from Yankton 8 miles out to the Lewis and Clark state recreation areas. Most of the trail is fairly flat, aside from a formidable hill just west of town. Lewis and Clark Marina just west of Gavins Point Dam (on the Nebraska side) rents and services boats for do-it-yourself sailors. Cottonwood Corral west of Yankton on South Dakota 52 also rents canoes and bicycles. The Yankton area's biggest annual events include Riverboat Days and a Lewis & Clark Festival, typically held one weekend after the other in late August.

It's a half-day's drive from Yankton to Pierre—South Dakota's capital and site of Lewis and Clark's fearsome confrontation with the Teton Sioux. Cross-country travelers in a hurry will probably want to make a beeline for Pierre via U.S. Highway 81, Interstate 90, and U.S. Highway 83. Dawdlers, on the other hand, will relish some time on Nebraska 12. Crofton, the Nebraska town nearest Gavins Point Dam, has a few restaurants and hotels and a nine-hole golf course with a view of the lake. Campers are welcome to spend one night free in Crofton's city park. Longer stays cost $2 per night, with a limit of seven days.

Wynot, the Missouri River Tours base noted above, is a 16-mile drive east of Crofton. Newcastle, 32 miles east of Crofton, is best known as home of the Ionia Volcano. Clark reported here that the bluff felt hot to the touch, and later fur traders frequently noticed dense smoke and fire in the vicinity. In 1839, J. N. Nicollet tried to prove the phenomenon was not of volcanic origin, theorizing that the decomposition of beds of iron pyrites in contact with water resulted in a heat capable of igniting other combustible materials. Still, volcano stories persisted, spurred on by an earthquake in 1877. The next year, a flood undermined the bluff and nearly wiped out the town of Ionia. Volcano tales sputtered out soon after, and around 1900, scientists finally learned the heat was generated by the oxidation of shale. Ponca State Park, about 14 miles east of Newcastle, has good camping, cabins, swimming, and picnicking, along with a Missouri River overlook with a bit of Lewis and Clark interpretation and a boat launch.

It's a 30-mile drive west of Crofton to Niobrara State Park, one of Nebraska's best. Here's another grand opportunity to take a guided Missouri River trip, with rafting excursions typically offered twice daily in summer, except on Tuesday and Wednesday. The two-and-a-half-hour trips include plenty of historic and nature interpretation. Cost is $12 for anyone 12 and up and $10 for children ages 6 to 12. No children under 6 are allowed. If the floats aren't running when you visit, take a hike down to the mouth of the Niobrara River. Find the Cramer interpretive shelter, with its brief outline of area history including Lewis and Clark lore; then locate the graveled foot trail leading down to the bottomlands. A pedestrian bridge crosses the Niobrara, finally about to meet the Missouri after its long run across Nebraska's northern tier.

Other activities at Niobrara State Park include trail rides, Saturday-evening buffalo stew cookouts, good fishing, and bicycling. The park accommodations are superb, with several hilltop cabins overlooking the rivers and a big swimming pool nearby.

From Niobrara, there are several ways to cross the river back into South Dakota. The newly built Chief Standing Bear Memorial Bridge spans the river east of town, linking Nebraska 14 and South Dakota 37. An interpretive area on the South Dakota side explains how the expedition, returning downriver in September 1806, met a group of Yankton Sioux whom they'd encountered two years before. Realizing they were old friends, the parties exchanged news and smoked pipes together before Lewis and Clark resumed their homeward journey. From the rest area, SD 37 heads north about 20 miles to meet state SD 50 at Tyndall.

Alternatively, travelers can continue west on NE 12 to U.S. Highway 281, which leads across Fort Randall Dam then winds north to I-90 west of Mitchell, South Dakota. Right over the border, pause a few minutes to see the former site of Fort Randall, built in 1856 as a military outpost. Fort Randall Dam impounds 101-mile-long Lake Francis Case. The Fort Randall Casino and Hotel deals up gambling, entertainment, and dining twenty-four hours a day, 10 miles west of Wagner on South Dakota 46. The Snake Creek Recreation area, 14 miles west of Platte on South Dakota 44, is another major access to Lake Francis Case.

You can always tell when you're close to a major hydropower dam, which, near the Missouri River in the Dakotas, is just about everywhere. Huge high-tension electrical power poles dot the landscape, ready to carry electricity across the heartland. Dayton Duncan thought they looked like "giant kachina dolls, totems of the triumph and power of science." They also seem to resemble a company of robots transfixed on the high plains, arms outstretched, their huge and powerful legs cemented to the ground.

In the expedition's day, however, it was nature that commanded the men's attention. Paul Cutright, in his book *Lewis and Clark: Pioneering Naturalists*, called the 20 days the expedition spent between the Niobrara and Teton rivers the trip's most exciting period of zoological discovery. They saw pronghorn antelope, bison, wolves, magpies, coyotes, jackrabbits, and the curious "barking squirrels," better known today as prairie dogs. The latter was especially elusive. Private John Shields killed the first one, which was cooked for dinner, but finding another sample to send back to President Jefferson proved quite difficult. "Having no further luck with their guns, they resorted to digging," Cutright wrote. "After going down six feet and finding the runways seemed bottomless, they gave that up and tried flooding. This became a full-scale operation, with all members of the corps participating except a guard left with the boats. They spent a major portion of the day carrying water from the river and pouring it into the subterranean passageways. Though they persisted until nightfall, they succeeded in capturing only one, flushing it out alive. Clark had better luck a few days later. 'I killed four,' he reported, 'with a view to have their skins stuffed.'"

Somewhere near Platte, South Dakota, Private George Shannon finally reunited with the rest of the Corps of Discovery on September 11, 1804. Shannon, the youngest member of the group but one of its most expert woodsmen, had gotten separated from the rest of the men about two weeks before; he thought he'd fallen behind, but he actually was far ahead.

Interstate 90 meets the Missouri River at Chamberlain, known for its walleye fishing and pheasant hunting. The U.S. Army Corps of Engineers runs a nice campground near downtown at American Creek, a waterway named by Lewis and Clark in mid-September 1804. Akta Lakota Museum on the grounds of St. Joseph's Indian School exhibits traditional Yankton and Teton Sioux beadwork, quillwork, tools, and weaponry. The Crow Creek and Lower Brule Indian reservations are nearby, offering bison herd tours and other opportunities to experience Native American culture. For more information on travel through South Dakota's Indian reservations, call the Alliance of Tribal Tourism Advocates at (605) 245-2327.

From Chamberlain, follow SD 50 north to South Dakota 34, which leads west past the Big Bend of the Missouri to Pierre.

PIERRE AND THE TETON COUNCIL SITE

The expedition had a close call on the night of September 20–21, 1804, while camped in the vicinity of what is now West Bend State Recreation Area. "At half past one o'clock this morning the sand bar on which we were camped began to undermine and give way which alarmed the sergeant on guard," Clark wrote. "The motion of the boat awakened me; I got up and by the light of the moon observed that the sand had given away both above and below our camp and was falling in fast. I ordered all hands on as quick as possible and pushed off, we had pushed off but a few minutes before the bank under which the boat and pirogues lay gave way, which would certainly have sunk both pirogues."

This was an unnerving episode, but even more troubling events were yet to come. The expedition entered what is now the Pierre area on September 23, camping near present-day Antelope Creek. That evening, three Sioux boys swam to the camp and told the explorers that two Teton Sioux villages were not far upriver. "We gave those boys two carrots of tobacco to carry to their chiefs, with directions to tell them that we would speak to them tomorrow," Clark wrote.

On the 24th, Lewis and Clark somewhat nervously prepared for their meeting with the Teton Sioux—a tribe other Indians had mentioned with much fear and loathing. The explorers knew the Sioux were now dominating the area; even

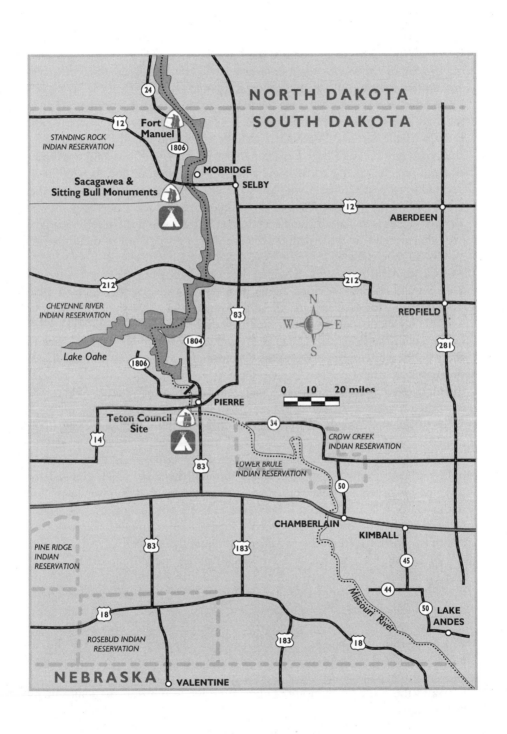

Jefferson had told them that "on that nation, we wish most particularly to make a favorable impression." The boats moved 13 miles to the mouth of the Bad River, which the explorers renamed the Teton River, perhaps in hopes of placating the Sioux. (It is once again known today as the Bad River.) Several chiefs arrived that evening, and arrangements were made for a council the next day.

The meeting took place at noon on the 25th on a sandbar in the mouth of the Bad River. Three Teton Sioux chiefs—Black Buffalo, The Partisan, and Buffalo Medicine—were on hand. But both sides soon found they were barely able to communicate: Pierre Dorion had stayed back with the Yankton Sioux, and no one else in the corps knew enough Sioux to translate. It was finally decided to employ Cruzatte, who knew Omaha, to translate through a member of that tribe made prisoner by the Sioux. Almost immediately, the Sioux showed signs of greediness, laughing and sneering at the gifts given them. They said the explorers must either trade with the Sioux alone or give up one of their pirogues and its cargo in tribute.

The captains attempted to lighten the mood by rowing the chiefs out to the keelboat and staging the usual airgun demonstration, accompanied by a measure of whisky for each Indian. The airgun failed to impress the Sioux, and the whisky only made matters worse: the chiefs pretended to be drunk and started falling about the deck. Exasperated, the captains shipped the Indians back to shore on the white pirogue. But as the boat reached the sand, one Indian hugged the mast and others grabbed its mooring rope—a signal they intended to seize the pirogue by force. The Partisan again told Clark the explorers would not be permitted to pass farther upriver.

At that, the captains' moods changed from wariness to anger. Clark brandished his sword, and Lewis swiftly loaded the keelboat's swivel guns and ordered the crew to man their rifles. The Indians, in turn, strung their bows and pulled arrows from their quivers. Black Buffalo, the main chief, grabbed the towrope and ordered his warriors to let go, but repeated that the river was closed to the whites. Clark stood in the water, sure he could not chance a retreat. But he ordered his men to row the pirogue to the keelboat, pick up reinforcements, and return to shore. Together, they finally faced down the Sioux.

Incredibly, the captains agreed to Black Buffalo and Buffalo Medicine's request that they, along with two other Sioux, be permitted to spend the night on the keelboat. No one slept well that night. On the 26th, the boats traveled upriver to the second and larger Sioux village. Here, the whites were treated with deference: Lewis and Clark were even carried to the village aloft on a buffalo robe. Much entertainment and feasting followed over the next two days, but the explorers remained wary, particularly since the Sioux continued to insist they be allowed to sleep on the keelboat, and because several Omaha prisoners warned Cruzatte the Sioux were simply biding time while plotting the white mens' destruction.

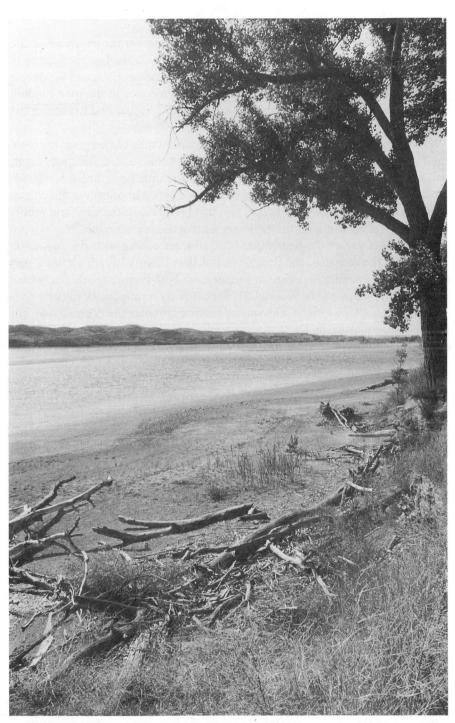

Missouri River near the Teton Council Site, South Dakota.

Hearing that news, the captains decided to leave on the morning of the 28th. But before they could cast off, Sioux warriors again grabbed the keelboat's cable. Black Buffalo, on the keelboat and expecting a ride upriver, said his people demanded more tobacco. Disgusted, Clark tossed tobacco to the men holding the cable and grabbed the rope away from them. The Sioux tried to reclaim the rope, but the boats made a clean getaway.

"The four-day ordeal was over," Roy Appleman wrote. "Against weaker men, the Tetons would have triumphed. Only sleepless vigilance, excellent judgment, and bold determination had saved the day. For the time being at least, the two captains had gained much prestige and established U.S. authority over this stretch of the Missouri. . . . The news spread rapidly up and down the river and promised a peaceful welcome for the explorers among the upriver tribes."

The exact site of the September 25, 1804, encounter with the Sioux has been lost in the mouth of the Bad River, but Fort Pierre's Lilly Park has a sign marking the approximate location. Situated on Fort Pierre's south side where the Bad River meets the Missouri, Lilly Park is fairly scruffy looking, but it does offer camping for $6 a night. The second Sioux encounter site is unmarked, but it probably took place on the west river bank about 4 miles north of Fort Pierre and 2 miles south of Oahe Dam. A county road leading along the river offers access at several points. Below Oahe Dam, the Missouri again looks much as it did in the early 1800s.

Another site associated with the expedition is Farm Island State Park, located just east of Pierre on SD 34. Expedition member John Colter is said to have hunted here just before the encounter with the Sioux, who may have stolen his horse. Later, other members of the expedition may have stopped on the island to pick up game Colter had shot.

The state park was actually on the island until the completion of Big Bend Dam downriver at Fort Thompson. That dam created Lake Sharpe, and park officials feared it would inundate the island, so they moved the park's buildings and campground to the mainland. One feature remained unmoved, however. Today, a simple monument marking Lewis and Clark's visit is no longer accessible, situated as it is in a slough, swamped by reeds and cattails. Park staff say canoeists or other boaters may be able to find it, but the plaque on the monument was stolen several years ago. A photo of the monument remains on display at the park visitor center.

Farm Island is still well worth visiting for its good camping, fishing, boating, and swimming. The island itself has returned to a near-wilderness state, most of it accessible only on foot. A park naturalist conducts guided interpretive hikes in summer. Walkers, joggers, and bird watchers favor the trail in the warmer months, while cross-country skiers find its flat terrain ideal for easy winter outings.

The town of Pierre itself is named for Pierre Chouteau, but the name is

South Dakota State Capitol, Pierre.

pronounced "Peer"—no one seems to know why. Fort Teton, built at the present site of the town of Fort Pierre, was established in 1817 and is credited with being the state's first continuous settlement. But the white man's history at Pierre dates back before those days, and even before the time of Lewis and Clark. In 1743, Chevalier and Louis La Verendrye, two explorers from French Canada, planted a lead plate on a hill in what is now Fort Pierre, claiming the region for the King of France. Like Lewis and Clark 60 years after them, the Verendryes were looking for a route to the Pacific Ocean. They'd come down the Missouri River and traveled as far west as the Black Hills before returning to present-day central South Dakota.

The plate was covered with rocks and remained hidden for 170 years. In 1913, three students from Fort Pierre High School found the plate. A monument was built to the Verendryes, and Gutzon Borglum—sculptor of Mount Rushmore—was the keynote speaker at its dedication in 1933. The Verendrye Plate was a top historical find since it provided a key to early white exploration of the region.

The plate is now on display at the South Dakota Cultural Center, located near the Capitol grounds in Pierre. Built for the state centennial in 1989, the 63,000-square-foot building is completely underground, reminiscent of Arikara earthlodges that used to dot the Missouri River valley. The center's symbol is the

SOUTH DAKOTA ON THE BEATEN PATH

For a state with well under a million people and an off-the-beaten-path location, South Dakota does a remarkably good job promoting itself. Visitors following the Lewis and Clark Trail will be mostly immune to the relentless public relations campaign that is Interstate 90, but as long as you're in the area, you may want to check out some of South Dakota's myriad claims to fame—some dubious, others divine.

The closest big-name attraction to our route is the Corn Palace in Mitchell, a Moorish-inspired monument to agriculture at 6th and Main streets. Built in 1892, the palace is decorated inside and out with thousands of bushels of native corn, grains, and grasses. It's also the site or the inspiration for all of Mitchell's big annual events: the Corn Palace Stampede Rodeo in late July, and the Corn Palace Festival and Corn Palace Polka Festival, both in mid- to late September.

Heading west on I-90, Badlands National Park is accessible via Exits 131 (Cactus Flat) and 110 (Wall). The Badlands are known for their raw, rugged landscape and some of the world's finest fossil beds, formed about 37 million years ago during the Oligocene epoch. Backcountry adventure abounds, with the Castle Trail particularly acclaimed for its varied prairie topography and wealth of wildlife, including pronghorn antelope, bison, badgers, coyotes, and prairie dogs.

For a quick look at the Badlands, drive the 40-mile loop road (South Dakota 240) between Cactus Flat and Wall. Primitive camping is available, as are cabins at the Sioux-run Cedar Pass Lodge, located south of Cactus Flat. The White River Visitor Center, on the Pine Ridge Reservation in the park's South Unit, features displays and programs on Sioux history. For a very different look at South Dakota, visit the Pine Ridge Indian Reservation south of the Badlands. This was the site of the 1890 Wounded Knee Massacre, where more than 350 Indians were killed by federal troops.

West of the Badlands, the traveler enters the famous Black Hills region. Wind Cave National Park, adjacent to Custer State Park on South Dakota 87, offers daily subterranean tours during the summer. The excursions range from short candlelight walks to more strenuous spelunking missions. Jewel Cave National Monument, 14 miles west of Custer, South Dakota, on U.S. Highway 16A, is one of the longest caves in the world. It, too, offers tours, as do a number of privately held caves scattered throughout the area. Custer State Park is known for its 18-mile wildlife loop drive and abundant recreation.

The Black Hills were named by the Lakota Sioux for the dark appearance of their coniferous forests. The Sioux considered the land sacred, and their rights to it were assured in a treaty signed in 1868. But the U.S. government broke the pact during the gold rush of the late 1870s. In recent years, the Supreme Court offered the Sioux $200 million as compensation for loss of their lands, but the Sioux were not interested. They want only the land.

Today's Black Hills are heavily commercialized, but their beauty remains mostly intact. Check with the USDA Forest Service office in Custer for maps and information on the area's many scenic byways (and for restrictions on motor homes and trailers, which may have trouble negotiating the region's roads).

Mount Rushmore is probably the best-known Black Hills attraction. Created under the direction of Gutzon Borglum, it features the 60-foot-high heads of presidents George Washington, Thomas Jefferson, Abraham Lincoln, and Theodore Roosevelt, all bathed in floodlights each night at dusk.

The Crazy Horse Memorial near Custer was started in 1947 by sculptor Korczak Ziolkowski to honor Chief Crazy Horse and the Native Americans. When completed, it will measure 563 feet high and 641 long, which would make it the largest statue in the world. It, too, is lit nightly at dusk.

Although gambling continues to proliferate throughout the United States, western South Dakota still draws crowds to its small gaming towns, perhaps because visitors feel a bit wilder when they gamble in the West. After all, it was in Deadwood that Bill Hickok was shot in the back while playing poker in 1876. He's buried alongside Calamity Jane (who claimed she was his secret bride) in Mt. Moriah Cemetery overlooking the city.

Nearby, the town of Lead (rhymes with "greed") is famous for its Homestake Gold Mine, largest in the Western Hemisphere. And in early August, Sturgis attracts hordes of Harley enthusiasts for the Black Hills Motorcycle Classic. Spearfish is home to the Black Hills Passion Play, presented Sunday, Tuesday, and Thursday from June through August. For more information on South Dakota, write the state Department of Tourism, Capital Lake Plaza, Pierre, South Dakota 57501, or call (800) 843-1930, or (800) 952-2217 in South Dakota. ▲

Sioux Horse Effigy, occasionally on loan to other museums nationwide; it's also the symbol seen on South Dakota historical highway markers statewide.

  Pierre has a delightful waterfront area, Steamboat Park, with a trail that loops around a causeway to La Framboise Island. The island is a natural area where only foot traffic is permitted; it's also an occasional gathering place for peaceful demonstrations by Lakota people and their sympathizers seeking to protest past and present mistreatment. (In summer 1999, a local motel employee warned me off walking to the island because of such a demonstration. That, of course, made me want to visit all the more.) Pedal & Paddle at 411 South Pierre Street rents bikes for $25 for 24 hours (no shorter rentals available), as well as kayaks at $25 a day for a single and $35 a day for a double. The shop is only two blocks from the waterfront, with wheeled carts available to tote your boat to the river.

Fans of Dayton Duncan's *Out West* will no doubt want to make a pilgrimage to the D&E Cafe at 115 West Dakota in Pierre, where Duncan chowed down dinner for less than $4 and $2 for breakfast, including newspaper and tip. Prices have risen a bit since Duncan's mid-1980s visit, but the D&E is still one heck of a deal. Other places worth a stop in Pierre include the beautiful State Capitol grounds and the South Dakota Discovery Center and Aquarium. For more information on Pierre, call (800) 962-2034.

Thirty-one miles northwest of Fort Pierre off of South Dakota 1806, the Triple U Buffalo Ranch was the setting for the film *Dances With Wolves*. Formerly known as the Houck Ranch, Triple U offers tours to help visitors see the shaggy beasts, as well as sites where the filmmaking took place. You'll also find a bed-and-breakfast, a gift shop, and camping, as well as hunting packages. For more information or to reserve a trip, call (605) 567-3624. Also north of Pierre, Cowan Ranch offers summertime trail-ride suppers overlooking the Missouri River. Call (605) 945-1812 or (605) 224-5796 for more information.

THE LAKE OAHE REGION

Travelers who haven't realized it already will probably note north of Pierre that South Dakota has devised an ingenious way of marking state routes closest to the Lewis and Clark Trail. The road on the east side of the Missouri River is South Dakota 1804 (for the year the corps first passed through), and the one on the west side is South Dakota 1806 (named for the year the expedition returned). North Dakota continues this system, but no other states have adopted it. It's important to note that neither of the routes proceeds in a continuous fashion along the river; each frequently sputters out near the shores of Lake Oahe. The quickest way north is US 83 to Selby, then U.S. Highway 12 to Mobridge.

North-central South Dakota is dominated by Lake Oahe, the massive manmade body of water created by Oahe Dam and the largest of the four Missouri River reservoirs in South Dakota. President John F. Kennedy dedicated the rolled-earth dam north of Pierre in 1963. It is 245 feet high, 9,300 feet long, and backs up a lake capable of storing some 23.5 million acre-feet of water. "Oahe" is a Sioux word meaning "foundation" or "a place to stand on."

Lake Oahe offers 2,250 miles of shoreline, and 39 separate recreation areas dot its length from Pierre to Bismarck, North Dakota. Some of them—including those at Okobojo Point, Little Bend, Sutton Bay, Whitlock Bay, Swan Creek, and Indian Creek—are in the vicinity of campsites used by Lewis and Clark. Primitive camping is available at nearly all the sites, and about half have boat ramps. Lake Oahe is known for excellent walleye fishing, with nearly half a million caught each year.

Onida is one of a handful of towns right along US 83. It has a park with a pool and playground on the southeast side of town; a free parking area (with no facilities) just south of town is best suited for self-contained RVs.

View of Lake Oahe at Mobridge, South Dakota.

Gettysburg was settled by Civil War veterans in 1883. It is home to the Dakota Sunset Museum at 207 West Commercial Avenue, open after noons daily between Memorial Day and Labor Day. In addition to exhibits of items used by Gettysburg-area pioneers, the museum displays a replica of the Medicine Rock, a huge boulder held sacred by the Sioux. The tribe looked on the rock as an oracle, often praying there for advice and for the safety of their children. The original boulder is now submerged under Lake Oahe, one of many sacred sites in the Dakotas flooded by the Pick-Sloan project dams.

Located 5 miles east of US 83, Gettysburg has golf, tennis, and swimming facilities, along with free camping in its city park. Gettysburg is also gateway to the popular East and West Whitlock Bay recreation areas on Lake Oahe. West Whitlock State Recreation Area was once a popular Mandan and Arikara campsite, and a replica Arikara earthlodge may be seen—though it is not as impressive as similar dwellings at Fort Abraham Lincoln State Park and Knife River Indian Villages Historic Site in North Dakota.

Selby is at the intersection of US 83 and US 12, and it's here the traveler can turn west for Mobridge. Campers are welcome to stay free at Selby's park near the end of Dakota Street.

It was in this vicinity near the North Dakota border that the expedition was greeted by the Arikara Indians and enjoyed an encounter far different from that

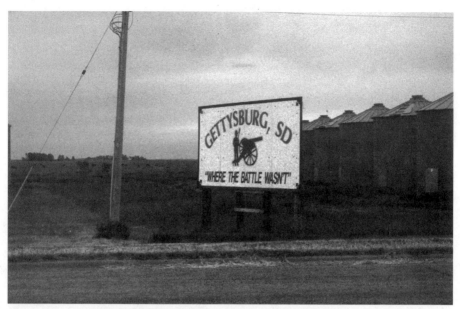

Civil War veterans settled the town of Gettysburg, South Dakota.

with the Teton Sioux. They stayed several days, held a council, and traded gifts with the natives. For the first time on the expedition, some of the men apparently took their hosts up on what Clark termed a "curious custom . . . to give handsome squaws to those whom they wish to show some acknowledgements to." The Indians, for their part, were especially fascinated with York, the first black man they had ever seen. "Those Indians were much astonished at my servant," Clark wrote. "All flocked around him and examined him top to toe."

With about 4,000 people, Mobridge serves as the "big town" for north-central South Dakota. The community reportedly got its name when somebody wired that the Missouri River had been bridged, or "Mobridged," for short. Mobridge is known for its walleye and pike fishing, sailboarding, and the annual Sitting Bull Stampede Rodeo July 2–4. The Klein Museum on US 12 displays prairie and Indian artifacts and items from local history.

Aside from the lake recreation, Mobridge's big draw is the Sitting Bull Monument on a ridge west of Lake Oahe. To get there, take US 12 west out of Mobridge; then turn left on SD 1806 and drive south 4 miles. You really can't miss it: just look for a billboard nearly as big as the monument itself.

 South Dakotans claim this is the burial place of Sitting Bull, the great Sioux leader killed in the area in 1890. He was originally buried at Fort Yates, North Dakota, just over the border, but Mobridgers maintain the body was moved to its "rightful" place in 1953. Many in North Dakota disagree, however; they say the South Dakotans got the wrong bones. In any case, a second Sitting Bull gravesite may be seen south of the town of Fort Yates, North Dakota. The Mobridge monument is a 7-ton granite bust carved by Korczak Ziolkowski, the same sculptor who started the Crazy Horse carving near Custer, South Dakota.

Mobridge's Sitting Bull site is also notable for its monument to Sacagawea, the Shoshone woman who would join the Lewis and Clark Expedition during its 1804–1805 winter stay in North Dakota. Although some people feel Sacagawea lived to be an old woman in Wyoming, most historians agree she actually passed away at a young age and was buried at Fort Manuel, a Missouri Fur Company trading post. On December 20, 1812, a clerk who compiled the daily journal of events at the fort wrote, "This evening the wife of Charbonneau, a Snake squaw, died of a putrid fever. She was . . . the best woman in the fort, aged about 25 years." Fort Manuel was probably located near what is now the west shore of Lake Oahe a few miles south of the North Dakota border. There is no interpretation of the site, but we will learn much more about Sacagawea as we follow Lewis and Clark west.

Nearby, the Grand River Casino & Resort offers gaming, food, and lodging from the Standing Rock Sioux Tribe. From here, it's about a two-hour drive north to the Bismarck-Mandan area.

LODGING

Rates are for double occupancy during summer season as of 1999 and are subject to change.

BROWNVILLE, NEBRASKA

Thompson House Bed & Breakfast, (402) 825-6551, 5th and College St. No children under 12.

AUBURN, NEBRASKA

Auburn Inn, (402) 274-3193, 517 J St. $45–$60.

NEBRASKA CITY, NEBRASKA

Apple Inn, (800) 659-4446, 502 S. 11th. $44–$50.
Days Inn, (402) 873-6656, 1715 S. 11th. $42–$50.

GREATER OMAHA, NEBRASKA/COUNCIL BLUFFS, IOWA

American Family Inn, (402) 291-0804, 1110 Fort Crook Rd. (Bellevue). $45–$55.
Ameristar Casino Hotel, (712) 328-8888, I-29 Exit 52 (Council Bluffs). $90 and up.
Baymont Inn, (402) 592-5200, 10760 M St. (Omaha). $55–$75.
Embassy Suites, (402) 346-9000, 555 S. 10th St. (Omaha). $160–$190.
Heartland Inn, (877) 334-3277, I-80 Exit 5 (Council Bluffs). $58–$65.

Redick Tower Hotel, (402) 342-1500, 1504 Harney St. (Omaha). $90 and up.

Sleep Inn, (402) 342-2525, 2525 Abbott Dr. (Omaha). $55–$70.

ONAWA, IOWA

Super 8 Motel, (712) 423-2101, I-29 Exit 112. $50–$60.

SIOUX CITY, IOWA

Best Western City Centre, (712) 277-1550, 130 Nebraska St. $80.

Fairfield Inn, (712) 276-5600, 4716 Southern Hills Dr. $80–$90.

Hilton Sioux City, (712) 277-4101, 707 4th St. $80–$110.

Marina Inn, (402) 494-4000, 4th and B St. (South Sioux City, Nebraska). $80–$110.

Park Plaza Motel, (402) 494-2021, 1201 1st Ave. (South Sioux City, Nebraska). $45–$50.

Riverboat Inn, (800) 238-6146, 701 Gordon Dr. $60–$70.

VERMILLION, SOUTH DAKOTA

Comfort Inn, (605) 624-8333, 701 W. Cherry St. $55–$70.

Goebel House Bed & Breakfast, (605) 624-6691, 102 Franklin St. $65

YANKTON, SOUTH DAKOTA

Best Western Kelly Inn, (605) 665-2906, E. SD 50. $80–$90.

Days Inn, (605) 665-8717, 2410 Broadway Ave. $55–$60.

Gavins Point Bed & Breakfast, (605) 668-0691, 252 Gavins Point Rd. $70–$80.

Lewis & Clark Resort, (605) 665-2680, at Lewis & Clark Lake Rec. Area. $75–$80.

Midway Gulch Cabins and Vacation Homes, (605) 668-9574. $50 and up.

Mulberry Inn Bed & Breakfast, (605) 665-7116, 512 Mulberry St. $37–$60.

CROFTON, NEBRASKA

Argo Hotel Bed & Breakfast, (800) 607-2746, $45–$125.

NIOBRARA, NEBRASKA

Hilltop Lodge, (402) 857-3611. $35–$45.

TYNDALL, SOUTH DAKOTA

Tyndall Shady Rest Motel, (605) 589-3980, three blocks off SD 50. $35–$50.

PICKSTOWN, SOUTH DAKOTA

Fort Randall Inn, (800) 340-7801.

GEDDES, SOUTH DAKOTA

The Barn Bed & Breakfast, (605) 337-2483. $55–$65.

PLATTE, SOUTH DAKOTA

Dakota Country Inn, (605) 337-2607, SD 44. $50.

Kings Inn, (605) 337-3385, SD 44. $30–$70.

CHAMBERLAIN, SOUTH DAKOTA

Alewel's Lake Shore Motel, (605) 734-5566, 115 N. River St. $40–$50.

Cedar Shore Resort, (888) 697-6363, I-90 Exit 260. $90–$120.

Oasis Inn, (605) 734-6061, I-90 Exit 260. $70–$90.

PIERRE/FORT PIERRE, SOUTH DAKOTA

Best Western Ramkota Inn Rivercentre, (605) 224-6877, 920 W. Sioux. $70–$80.

Budget Host State Motel, (605) 224-5896, 640 N. Euclid. $40–$50.

Fort Pierre Motel, (605) 223-3111, 211 S. First St. $40–$45.

Governor's Inn, (605) 224-4200, 700 W. Sioux. $55–$105.

River Place Inn Bed & Breakfast, (605) 224-8589, 109 River Place. $65–$100.

Spring Creek Resort, (605) 224-8336, 10 miles north of Oahe Dam on SD 1804. $55.

ONIDA, SOUTH DAKOTA

Wheatland Inn, (605) 258-2341, 200 S. Main St. $25–$55

GETTYSBURG, SOUTH DAKOTA

Bob's Resort, (605) 765-2500, west of town at Lake Oahe. $65–$110.

Harer Lodge Bed & Breakfast, (605) 765-2167, 12 miles north. $50–$85.

South Whitlock Resort, (605) 765-9762, 14 miles west at Lake Oahe.

Trail Motel, (605) 765-2482, 211 E. Garfield. $30–$45.

MOBRIDGE, SOUTH DAKOTA

East Side Motel and Cabins, (605) 845-7867, 510 E. 7th Ave. $30–$40.

MoRest Motel, (605) 845-3668, 706 W. Grand Crossing. $45–$50.

Wrangler Motor Inn, (605) 845-3641, US 12. $55–$70.

CAMPING

BROWNVILLE, NEBRASKA

Brownville State Recreation Area, 0.5 mile southeast of town. Primitive sites.

Indian Cave State Park, (402) 883-2575, 9 miles south on NE 67, then 5 miles east.

NEBRASKA CITY, NEBRASKA

Riverview Marina State Recreation Area, northeast of town on US 73/75 and NE 2. Primitive sites.

GREATER OMAHA, NEBRASKA/COUNCIL BLUFFS, IOWA

Bluffs Run Casino RV Park, (712) 323-2500, I-29/I-80 Exit 1B (Council Bluffs).

N.P. Dodge Park, (402) 444-4673, I-680 30th St. exit, follow signs.

Lake Manawa State Park, (712) 336-0220, south of Council Bluffs on IA 192.

ONAWA, IOWA

Interchange RV Campground, (712) 423-1387, from junction of I-29 and IA 175, go one block east on IA 175, then one block south to campground.

KOA-Onawa, (712) 423-1633, 1 mile west from I-29 on IA 175, then 1.5 miles north on county road.

Lewis and Clark State Park, (712) 423-2829, 1 mile west from I-29 on IA 175, then 1 mile north on IA 324.

SIOUX CITY, IOWA

KOA–North Sioux City, (605) 232-4519, on west side of I-29 between Exits 2 and 4 (North Sioux City, South Dakota).

Scenic Park, (402) 494-7535, 4th & D Sts. (South Sioux City, Nebraska).

Stone State Park, (712) 255-4698, 5 miles north of I-29 on IA 12.

YANKTON, SOUTH DAKOTA

Lewis and Clark Lake/Corps of Engineers, (605) 667-7873, west of town on SD 52.

Lewis and Clark State Recreation Area (Nebraska), northwest of Crofton on Lewis and Clark Lake.

Lewis and Clark State Recreation Area (South Dakota), (605) 668-2985, west of town on SD 52.

PONCA, NEBRASKA

Ponca State Park, (402) 755-2284, 2 miles north of NE 12.

NIOBRARA, NEBRASKA

Niobrara State Park, (402) 857-3373, west on NE 12.

CHAMBERLAIN, SOUTH DAKOTA

American Creek Campground, (605) 734-6772, 2 miles north of I-90 Exit 263 on Lake Francis Case.

Cedar Shore Campground, (605) 734-5273, I-90 Exit 260.

Familyland Campground, (605) 734-6959, I-90 Exit 260.

PIERRE, SOUTH DAKOTA

Downstream Area/Missouri River, (605) 224-5862, north of Pierre below Oahe Dam on Lake Oahe.

Farm Island State Recreation Area, (605) 224-5605, 4 miles east on SD 34.

West Bend State Recreation Area, (605) 875-3220, 26 miles east and 9 miles south on SD 34.

GETTYSBURG, SOUTH DAKOTA

Gettysburg City Park, (605) 765-2264.

River Edge Campsite, 10 miles west of US 83 on US 212.

South Whitlock Resort, (605) 765-9762, 8 miles west of US 83 on US 212.

West Whitlock State Recreation Area, (605) 765-9410, 13 miles west of US 83 on US 212, then 9 miles north.

Selby, South Dakota

Lake Hiddenwood State Park, (605) 649-7876, 2 miles east, then 3 miles north on US 12/83.

Mobridge, South Dakota

Indian Creek, (605) 224-5862, 2 miles east on US 12, then 1 mile south, on Lake Oahe.

Indian Memorial, 3 miles west on US 12, on Lake Oahe.

Kountry Kamping and Kabins, (605) 845-2267, north of town on US 12.

Restaurants

Brownville, Nebraska

Riverview Restaurant, (402) 825-3011, US 136. Full menu and keno lounge.

Auburn, Nebraska

Darling's Cafe, (402) 274-4125, 520 J St. Fish, prime rib, Sunday buffet.

Korner Kitchen, (402) 274-3015, "one block east of the stoplight." Weekend breakfast buffet.

The Wheeler Inn, (402) 274-3681, 1905 J St. Steaks, seafood, salad bar.

Nebraska City, Nebraska

Embers Steak House, (402) 873-6416, junction of US 75 and NE 2. American cuisine with children's menu.

Greater Omaha, Nebraska/Council Bluffs, Iowa

Ameristar Casino, (712) 328-8888, I-29 Nebraska Ave. Exit (Council Bluffs). Four restaurants.

Bohemian Café, (402) 342-9838, 1406 S. 13th St. (Omaha). Czech specialties.

Charlie's on the Lake, (402) 894-9411, 144th and F Sts. (Omaha). Fresh seafood daily.

Dazy Maze, (402) 346-9342, 521 S. 13th St. (Omaha). Vegetarian café.

Falling Water Grille, (402) 346-9000, in the Embassy Suites. Creative continental dining.

McKenna's, (402) 393-7427, 7425 Pacific St. Barbecue and live blues music, children's menu.

Romeo's Mexican Food and Pizza, (712) 323-0042, 19th and Broadway (Council Bluffs).

Tish's, (712) 323-5456, 1115 S. 35th St. (Council Bluffs).

Upstream Brewing Company, (402) 344-0200, 11th and Jackson Sts. in Old Market. New American pub food.

Onawa, Iowa

Casino Omaha Buffet, (712) 423-3700.

SIOUX CITY, IOWA

Bluestem, (712) 279-8060, 1012 4th St. Modern cuisine in historic setting.

Garfield's Restaurant & Pub, (712) 276-6505, 4400 Sergeant Rd. At the Southern Hills Mall.

Green Gables, (712) 258-4246, 1800 Pierce St. Longtime family-owned restaurant.

Horizon Family Restaurant, (712) 255-1658, 1220 Tri-View Ave. (I-29 Hamilton Exit). Open 24 hours, breakfast anytime.

Jerry's Rib House, (712) 233-3026, at the Sioux City Gateway Airport.

VERMILLION, SOUTH DAKOTA

Chae's, (605) 624-2294, 8 W. Main St. Korean, Chinese, and American food.

Recuerdo de Mexico, (605) 624-6445, 112 E. Main St. Mexican food.

Silver Dollar Saloon and Eatery, (605) 624-4830, 1216 E. Cherry St.

Whimp's, (605) 624-9973, Burbank (southeast of town). Steaks.

MECKLING, SOUTH DAKOTA

Toby's Lounge, (605) 624-9905, SD 50. Broasted chicken, shrimp, and fish.

YANKTON, SOUTH DAKOTA

The Coffee House & 3rd St. Deli, (605) 668-9575, 300 W. 3rd St.

The Fillin' Station, (605) 665-1438, 1208 Broadway. Prime rib, pasta, seafood.

JoDean's Steakhouse & Lounge, (605) 665-9884, US 81. Wide menu, Sunday brunch.

Olivia's Fine Cuisine, (605) 665-3308, 302 W. 3rd.

Quarry Steak House, (605) 665-4337, SD 52 near the lake. Prime rib and nightly specials.

CROFTON, NEBRASKA

Argo Hotel Steakhouse, (402) 388-2400. Downtown Crofton.

Bogner's Steakhouse, (402) 388-4626, US 12 and Nebraska 121.

PLATTE, SOUTH DAKOTA

The Barrister, (605) 337-2580, 311 Main St. Dinner Monday through Saturday.

GEDDES, SOUTH DAKOTA

Mom's Kitchen, (605) 337-2131, 3rd and Main. Home cooking and good pie.

CHAMBERLAIN, SOUTH DAKOTA

Al's Oasis, (605) 734-6054, I-90 Exit 260. Truck-stop cafe.

Bridges Bar & Grille, (605) 734-6376. At Cedar Shore Resort.

Casey Cafe, (605) 734-6530, Welcome West Plaza at I-90 Exit 263. Homemade soups, pies, specials.

Rainbow Cafe, (605) 734-5481, Main St. in downtown Chamberlain. Home cooking.

Pierre, South Dakota

Chances Are Brewpub, (605) 224-0848, 347 S. Pierre St. Southwestern and continental fare.

Chikadily's Restaurant, (605) 224-7183, 808 W. Sioux (next to the bridge). Open 24 hours.

D&E Cafe, (605) 224-7200, 115 W. Dakota. Home cooking.

Kozy Korner Family Restaurant, (605) 224-9547, 217 E. Dakota. Specialties include soups and cream pies.

Pizza Ranch, (605) 223-9114, next to the bridge in Fort Pierre.

Onida, South Dakota

Fireside Restaurant & Lounge, (605) 258-2377, US 83.

Gettysburg, South Dakota

Bob's Steakhouse, (605) 765-2500, at the Lake Oahe bridge. Charbroiled steaks.

Mobridge, South Dakota

Captain's Table Dining Room, (605) 845-3641. At the Wrangler Motor Inn.

Dakota Country Restaurant, (605) 845-7495, 122 W. Grand Crossing.

The Wheel Family Restaurant, (605) 845-7474, 820 W. Grand Crossing. View of Lake Oahe.

Sacagawea Statue on the North Dakota State Capitol grounds, Bismarck.

CHAPTER FIVE

NORTH DAKOTA AND EASTERN MONTANA

About 5 o'clock this evening one of the wives of Charbonneau (Sacagawea) was delivered of a fine boy.

—Meriwether Lewis, February 11, 1805,
Fort Mandan, North Dakota.

FORT ABRAHAM LINCOLN STATE PARK

*T*he Lewis and Clark Expedition entered North Dakota on October 14, 1804, and returned to the present North Dakota–South Dakota border 22 months later, en route home from the Pacific. All told, the corps spent a total of 212 days in North Dakota. And since the party made its first winter camp there, Lewis and Clark and their men ended up staying longer in North Dakota than in any other state through which they passed.

Fort Yates, headquarters of the Standing Rock Indian Reservation, is the first town travelers see along North Dakota 1806. There really is a "standing rock" on a pedestal near the Missouri River/Lake Oahe shore, and a plaque explains how the reservation got its name: "A famous sacred stone which many years ago came into possession of the Sioux. According to Dakota legend, it is a body of a young Indian woman with her child on her back who were left in camp when she refused to accompany the tribe as they moved south. When others were sent back to find her, she was found to have turned to stone. This stone is held in reverence by the Sioux and is placed here overlooking the waters in the empire once held by the mighty Sioux Nation."

The corps' camp of October 15, 1804, is in the middle of Lake Oahe, just northeast of Fort Yates. During the day, the corps saw many Indians on both sides of the river and stopped to eat and trade with about 30 Arikaras. Once camped, Lewis and Clark visited a nearby Arikara village. They scouted the area for a possible wintering location, but finding wood and game scarce, decided to press farther north. We shall do the same; it is about an hour's drive from Fort Yates to Fort Abraham Lincoln State Park, located just south of the town of Mandan. Note that North Dakota 24 swings off to the west about 20 miles north of Fort Yates, but ND 1806 hugs the Missouri River and proceeds north to the park. Few amenities are available along this scenic route, but watch for the Standing Rock Sioux Tribe's Prairie Knights complex, among the region's most deluxe tribal resorts. Standing on a hillside above the plains, Prairie Knights has everything from fine lodging and dining to a Lake Oahe marina and plenty of gaming action, not to mention one of the only gas stations on ND 1806 between Mobridge and Mandan.

The corps camped in the vicinity of what was later Fort Abraham Lincoln on October 20, 1804, and August 18, 1806. During the 1804 visit, Clark wrote: "Camped on the leeward side above a bluff containing coal of an inferior quality. This bank is immediately above the old (deserted) village of the Mandans." Clark marveled at the abundant game he saw, noting that he personally killed three deer and watched gangs of bison and wolves. Although the Mandans had abandoned the villages here by the time the expedition arrived, the park is well worth a stop for its excellent interpretation. The highlight is On A Slant Village, with its earthlodge replicas. The village, sacred to the Mandan people, received its name from the sloping ground on which it was situated. The village included about 7 or 8 acres of land, and a 1937 survey of the site found ruins of 75 earthlodges.

Studies of tree rings in the area indicate the village was occupied from about 1650 to 1750. After that, the Mandan population was reduced by a smallpox epidemic and pressure from other marauding tribes. In 1804, as Clark noted, the village was in ruins and the tribe had moved about 60 miles upriver to the Knife River Villages. The Mandan moved into North Dakota from the south, and other ruins are present from the South Dakota line north to the Fort Berthold Indian Reservation, where the Mandan's descendants live today.

The village's earthlodge replicas are typical of those used by the Mandans before they were forced onto the reservation. Twenty to 40 feet in diameter, the earthlodges were owned and primarily built by the tribe's women, with some help from the men. The lodges' main supports were 10 to 15 feet high and made of logs from nearby trees. Over the framework, the Indians placed a thick mat of willows followed by a layer of grass and thick layer of earth. A well-constructed earthlodge would last about 10 years.

Visitors can walk inside several of the structures. Interpretive panels describe lifestyle, legends, and ceremonies. One lodge shows how such a dwelling may have been furnished, complete with an adult's bed, a small replica of a sweat lodge, and a horse stall.

The Ark of the Lone Man, centrally located in the village, is a special point of interest. According to Mandan legend, the Lone Man saved the Indian nation from a great flood by building a palisade around the village. The ark, a symbolic shrine, became a site for religious ceremonies. A red cedar post represents the lone man, and a circular willow band marks the high water of the flood.

The park's visitor center has interpretation of Lewis and Clark's travels through the area, with a replica elk hide journal, peace medal, and espontoon such as that Lewis carried. Mandan culture is well represented, too, by artifacts ranging from pieces of decorated pottery to projectile points. Other exhibits explain the area's heritage of fur trade, railroading, homesteading, and the military. There's also a boxful of dried medicinal plants. Each specimen includes a drawing of the plant in its native state and possible uses.

Fort Abraham Lincoln itself was in operation from 1872 through 1891, providing protection for railroad workers and survey parties, as well as settlements that sprung up in the area. The infantry soldiers stationed at the post

The Lewis and Clark *riverboat at Bismarck, North Dakota.*

found they were no match for the Sioux, who were excellent horsemen. In response, Congress authorized the addition of a cavalry post, and Lieutenant Colonel George Armstrong Custer arrived with the Seventh Cavalry in the autumn of 1873. From here, Custer led expeditions into the Black Hills. When he discovered gold amid the sacred Sioux lands, it marked the beginning of the end for the Sioux way of life.

Tensions rose between the whites and the Indians. Ultimately, it was from Fort Abraham Lincoln that Custer led his troops to the Battle of the Little Big Horn, where he and 265 others were killed by Sioux and Cheyenne warriors led by Sitting Bull and Crazy Horse. Military-oriented exhibits explain the events leading up to the battle, and the trading post offers an excellent selection of the many books written about Custer.

Fort Abraham Lincoln was abandoned in 1891. Most of its original structures were torn down by 1900, with wood from the site reportedly used to construct many buildings in the Bismarck-Mandan area. But several buildings have been reconstructed, including Custer's home. Special events held each year usually include Frontier Army Days (third weekend in June), a Nu'Eta Corn & Buffalo Festival (first full weekend of August), Fur Traders Rendezvous (second weekend of August), and Custer Christmas (second weekend of December). During the Lewis and Clark bicentennial years, the park will probably have a commemoration of the corps' visit on October 20.

Mandan earthlodge replica at Fort Abraham Lincoln State Park, North Dakota.

Fort Abraham Lincoln State Park is open daily from 8 A.M. to dusk all year. The interpretive facilities are open daily from 9 A.M. to 7 P.M. from Memorial Day through Labor Day. Other hours are as follows: 1 to 5 P.M. the last two weekends of April; daily from 9 A.M. to 5 P.M. May 1 to Memorial Day; daily from 9 A.M. to 5 P.M. from the day after Labor Day through September 30; and daily from 1 to 5 P.M. through the month of October. Visits can also be made by appointment from November 1 through April 15, except the Custer Christmas weekend, when the fort is open to all.

During the summer months, the Fort Lincoln trolley runs along the Heart and Missouri rivers between the Third Street Station in Mandan and the state park. You can even get here on bike or on foot; a paved trail runs about 5 miles from Main Street in Mandan to the park.

Park admission is $3 per vehicle, with a separate charge for admission to the Custer House and a guided tour of the cavalry post. A modern campground has nearly 100 sites and river access. For more information, call (701) 663-1464 or (701) 663-9571.

West River Teamsters, based in Mandan, has plans now through 2006 for annual Lewis and Clark Bicentennial wagon train expeditions from Fort Abraham Lincoln to Fort Bismarck. While this blurs the lines a bit historically—wagon trains had nothing to do with the Corps of Discovery—it still sounds like a fun

TOURING BISMARCK/MANDAN

Bismarck/Mandan is one of North Dakota's more populous areas, with about 65,000 people calling the two cities home. Bismarck is also the state capital, and several points of interest are found at the capitol complex. The capitol itself is unusual among statehouses: it looks more like an office building than a seat of government. The 19-story Art Deco–inspired building is nicknamed the "skyscraper of the prairies." A statue of Sacagawea—or "Sakakawea," as she is known in North Dakota—stands nearby. This statue is set to be replicated and included in Statuary Hall in the U.S. Capitol in Washington, D.C., probably by 2001.

The North Dakota Heritage Center also makes its home on the capitol grounds. A large main gallery traces the evolution of human and natural history in North Dakota. Exhibits include a mounted grizzly bear, along with this journal entry from Sergeant Gass: "These bears are very numerous in this part of the country and very dangerous as they will attack a man at every opportunity." Amateur ornithologists will love the extensive displays on North Dakota's birds of wetlands, woodlands, and prairie. There's something for everyone here, from a special section called Dakota Kids for the youngsters to an abundance of nostalgia for the older folks. Hours are 8 A.M. to 5 P.M. Monday through Friday, 9 A.M. to 5 P.M. Saturday, and 11 A.M. to 5 P.M. Sunday. The museum is closed Easter, Thanksgiving, Christmas, and New Year's Day.

 Bismarck has about 25 miles of public trails, including a path along the Missouri River from the Dakota Zoo area north to Pioneer Park. Look in the local phone book's green pages for a map. Dakota Cyclery at 1606 East Main Avenue rents bikes; call (701) 222-1218 for details. Rates are $6 an hour, $15 for a half day, or $25 for a full day.

 The *Lewis and Clark* riverboat, an all-weather cruise vessel, has sailings most afternoons and evenings Memorial Day through Labor Day. Call (701) 255-4233 for times, special events, and other information. Matah Adventures Canoe Rental & Guide Service in Mandan can help do-it-yourselfers get out on the water in the Bismarck-Mandan area. Call (701) 663-0054 for information.

The Bismarck area has a fair number of art galleries for a community of moderate size. Among the most notable are Five Nations Arts, specializing in Native American arts and crafts at 401 West Main Street in Mandan; the Heritage Center museum store; and Bismarck Art and Galleries Association at 422 East Front Avenue in Bismarck. Other attractions include the Dakota Zoo, plenty of golf courses, and several annual powwows. For more information on Bismarck/Mandan, call (701) 222-4308.

way to follow the captains' path across central North Dakota. The five-day treks, set in late July each year, cost $650 in 2000. (A $175 per-day rate is available for people who want to ride a day or two. Family rates are offered as well.) Fees include all meals, guide service, entertainment, and interpretation along the way. For more information, call Ray Hoff at (701) 597-3871, or write West River Teamsters, 411 West Main Street, Mandan, North Dakota 58554.

From Bismarck/Mandan, U.S. Highway 83 continues north to Washburn, 40 miles away. North Dakota 1804 is a good scenic alternative along the Missouri River much of the way. Double Ditch Indian Village State Historic Site lies along this route about 12 miles north of Bismarck. Lewis and Clark camped in this vicinity on October 22, 1804.

FORT MANDAN

As the expedition moved north through the Dakotas, the need to find a place to spend the winter became acute. Beginning in late October 1804, the journal entries mention bitter winds and snow. On October 26, roughly 1,600 miles from Camp Wood, the Corps of Discovery reached the new villages established by the Mandans, Minitaris (later known as Hidatsa), and Amahamis.

About 4,400 people lived in five separate villages. They greeted the white men warmly, and the captains quickly decided this would be a good place to spend the winter months. After several days of searching, a suitable spot was found for a fort. It was there, on the Missouri's east bank about 6 miles below the mouth of Knife River, that Fort Mandan was built.

Construction started November 2, using cottonwood logs cut nearby. Two sides of the V-shaped fort held four rooms each to house the men and their belongings. Each room was 14 feet square, 7 feet high, and equipped with a fireplace. The third side was blockaded by "amazing long pickets." The men occupied the still-unfinished buildings November 16, and the two captains moved into their quarters four days later. The party at that point numbered about 45.

The expedition spent a long winter in a variety of pursuits, chief among them finding enough food. Trade with the Indians brought corn, squash, and berries. Meat was obtained by daily hunting parties. Game was abundant, but many of the animals were in such poor shape during the colder months that only the choicest parts—such as buffalo tongue, heart, and liver—could be used. There

Fort Mandan replica near Washburn, North Dakota.

were many wolves in the area, and harvested animals left overnight without protection were often found completely devoured by the time the men returned to retrieve the game.

They also found themselves expending much energy to stay warm: in his journal entry of December 8, Clark reported several cases of frostbitten feet and, in the case of York, a frostbitten male organ. On December 12, he wrote, "We do not think it prudent to turn out to hunt in such cold weather," and on December 13, more of the same: "The thermometer stands this morning at 20 below zero, a fine day." In all, the temperature dipped below zero, once as low as minus 48 degrees F, on 40 days during the corps' stay.

Despite the bitter cold, a steady stream of visitors came to the fort all winter long. The captains spent many hours talking with the Mandans, mostly seeking to learn as much as they could about the tribes and the country still to come, but also eager to cement relations for future trading. Lewis, Clark, and company were far from the first white men to arrive in this area. Traders, mostly French, had been operating in the area for perhaps a half-century or more, and the captains conferred with some of them during their stay. It was also here the men met Charbonneau and Sacagawea, who were to become among the most famous members of the party.

Lewis and Clark had just hired an interpreter, Rene Jessaume, who had moved into Fort Mandan with his wife and child. When Charbonneau offered his services, the captains said they had no need for him. But Charbonneau wouldn't take no for an answer. He finally sold the captains on the idea by promising that Sacagawea could help the expedition communicate with—and perhaps obtain horses from—her people, the Shoshone, once the party reached the Rocky Mountains.

No one knows whether Sacagawea had much say in the matter. Just a few years before, at about age 12, she had been kidnapped near present-day Three Forks, Montana. She later was either sold to or won by Charbonneau and now, just 16 or 17 years old, was about to give birth to her first child. But despite her youth, Sacagawea more than earned her place in history over the next two years as an indispensable member of the expedition, and one of its most controversial.

Much of the controversy surrounds just how to spell and say her name: there are three predominant versions. Scholars generally agree on the spelling—Sacagawea—used throughout this book, pronouncing it "Sah-CAH-ga-we-a." But the spelling Sacajawea, pronounced "Sah-cah-ja-WE-a," is probably more popular and widespread, especially in the Pacific Northwest. The third version is the one used most often in the Dakotas: Sakakawea, pronounced "Sa-KAH-ka-we-a."

In addition, Sacagawea is frequently—but erroneously—viewed as the expedition's guide, a myth perpetuated by several books written in the early twentieth century. Although she didn't exactly guide the expedition, Sacagawea's assistance proved invaluable when the party reached the Great Divide of western Montana and Idaho. Here, Sacagawea was able to identify landmarks and serve as an intermediary when—in an unbelievable coincidence—the corps came upon the Shoshone village led by Chief Cameahwait, Sacagawea's long-lost brother. Sacagawea helped the expedition in other ways, too: since a war party would not travel with a woman and a baby, she and her baby, Jean Baptiste—or Pomp, as Captain Clark nicknamed him—served as signals of the Corps' peaceful intentions. She also gathered plants and herbs for food and medicine.

Washburn is 38 miles north of Bismarck via US 83. The town celebrates its trail heritage each June with the Lewis and Clark Days, which include a parade, buffalo barbecue, reenactments, lectures, and demonstrations. Nearby Cross Ranch State Park is one of North Dakota's nicest, with its scenic riverside location. Cross Ranch and an adjacent 6,000-acre nature preserve have more than 15 miles of hiking trails, which become cross-country ski routes in winter. Fishing and camping are among the park's other attractions. For a nice lodging alternative, call the state park reservations line at (800) 807-4723 and ask about reserving Cross Ranch's handsome Centennial Cabin.

For a long time, Fort Mandan was the least-interpreted major site along the Lewis and Clark Trail. This was fully remedied by the 1997 opening of the North Dakota Lewis and Clark Interpretive Center at Washburn. In a few short years, this facility has scored several impressive interpretive coups. It is one of

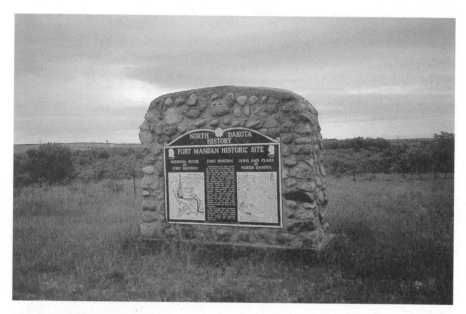

Fort Mandan historic marker.

only a handful of museums anywhere to house a complete set of prints by Karl Bodmer, the Swiss artist who documented life along the Missouri River in the mid-1830s. (The originals, you'll recall, are at the Joslyn Art Museum in Omaha.) It also has had displays of two original documents from the Lewis and Clark Expedition: President Jefferson's letter of instructions to the corps, and the letter Meriwether Lewis sent back to Washington, D.C., after the explorers' Fort Mandan winter.

The permanent exhibits include a good overview of the expedition, with special attention paid to the Fort Mandan winter of 1804–1805 and Native American artifacts representing nearly every tribe the explorers encountered on the way west. Visitors can try on a buffalo robe or a weighted cradle board much like that Sacagawea used to carry her baby. You also learn that the corps members routinely ate 5 to 7 pounds of meat per man per day, and that axes made by John Shields during the Mandan winter were quickly traded around the West. (On the corps' 1806 return trip, John Ordway reported seeing a Fort Mandan ax at a Nez Perce village 900 miles away.)

Here, too, is fine commentary on several questions that vex history students—why, for example, the corps ran into such trouble with the Teton Sioux in South Dakota when their dealings with tribes elsewhere went so well. As one exhibit explains, the Teton Sioux chief Partisan was offended because he had received fewer gifts than his rival chief, Black Buffalo. This incident demonstrated how the

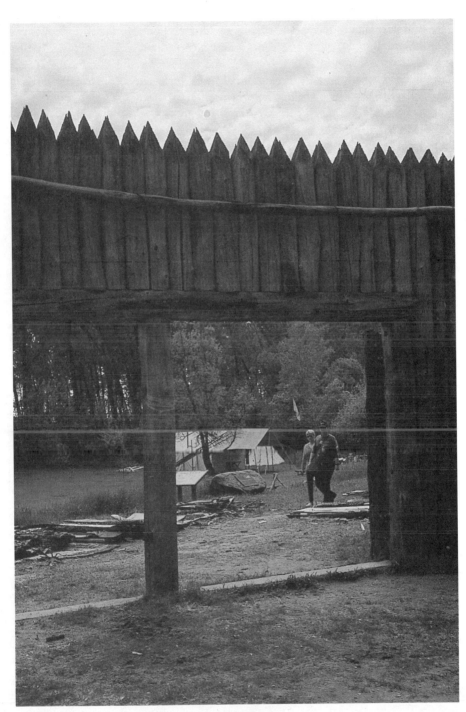

Fort Mandan replica near Washburn, North Dakota.

captains never really understood tribal ways and methods of leadership. Lewis and Clark wanted to deal with one leader whose word would be law among the tribe, but Indian leaders didn't work that way. The chiefs' power "lay in their ability to persuade others to follow," the exhibit notes. "They needed time to hold councils and talk until the group reached an agreement."

On Saturday mornings in the summer, school-age children are welcome to take part in the center's Lewis and Clark Explorer's Club. Free with admission, the club allows young visitors to pursue an activity that their nineteenth-century counterparts may have enjoyed. Past sessions have included doll making, basket weaving, and making "dream catchers." Adults are welcome to participate too.

The center is located at the junction of US 83 and North Dakota 200A. From Memorial Day through Labor Day, it is open daily from 9 A.M. to 7 P.M. Central Time; the rest of the year, hours are 9 A.M. to 5 P.M. Admission is $2 for adults and $1 for students (kindergarten through college); members of the North Dakota Lewis and Clark Bicentennial Foundation, which operates the center, are admitted free. For more information, call (701) 462-8535.

After you've seen the center, plan a trip to the nearby reconstructed Fort Mandan site less than 2 miles away. The replica, approximately 10 miles downstream from the original fort site, was built in the 1970s by local volunteers. It's now run under the auspices of the state bicentennial foundation, which is adding onsite interpretation and living history. This is also a good place to enjoy a

Landing a voyageur canoe at the BirdWoman camp near Washburn, North Dakota.

In the BirdWoman camp near Washburn, North Dakota.

picnic near the banks of the Missouri. Kids will enjoy the trading post, where souvenir offerings include string-your-own trade-bead necklaces. The fort is open all year, weather permitting. It's staffed from 9 A.M. to 5 P.M. Memorial Day through Labor Day.

Since Lewis and Clark wintered here, you may wonder whether you might spend a frosty night at Fort Mandan, too. In general, no camping is allowed at Fort Mandan any time of year, but you might be able to tag along with a rendezvous group that sometimes plans winter visits. Contact the interpretive center in Washburn if you're interested in that sort of thing—and if you don't mind wind chills that regularly plunge to 20 degrees F below zero or colder.

Fort Mandan was the site of the corps' first Christmas on the trail, and the captains reported their crew spent the day "merrily disposed." "We fired the swivels at daybreak and each man fired one round," wrote Sergeant Ordway. "Our officers gave the party a drink of (rum). We had the best to eat that could be had, and continued firing, dancing, and frolicking during the whole day. The savages did not trouble us as we had requested them not to come as it was a great medicine day with us. We enjoyed a merry Christmas during the day and evening until 9 o'clock—all in peace and quietness."

On February 11, as Lewis noted, Sacagawea gave birth to her son, Jean Baptiste, the newest member of the Lewis and Clark Expedition. "It is worthy of remark that this was the first child which this woman had borne, and as is common in such cases her labor was tedious and the pain violent," Lewis wrote. Jessaume, the interpreter, suggested to Lewis that a small portion of rattlesnake's rattle "never failed to produce the desired effect, that of hastening the birth of the child." Lewis just happened to have a rattle in his possession and gave it to Jessaume. "Whether this medicine was truly the cause or not I shall not undertake to determine, but I was informed that she had not taken it more than 10 minutes before she brought forth."

CANOEING THE MISSOURI

The Missouri River flows free from Garrison Dam to south of Bismarck. Here in the vicinity of Washburn, as on the Nebraska–South Dakota border and again in Montana, modern visitors get a rare chance to float a river that still appears much as it did 200 years ago.

BirdWoman Missouri River Adventures is a family-run company that offers canoe trips in its 26-foot-long voyageur canoe and camp stays on riverside land that the Yunker family has lived on since 1945. Named for Sacagawea, the trips aren't strictly Lewis and Clark themed, but a historical hybrid incorporating lore from the North Woods voyageurs and the buckskinner era.

Up to eight people can sign on for the excursions, which can last from two hours to two days, with prices starting at $30 per person. (Children float half-price.) The trips take place on the same stretch of river where Lewis and Clark spent their long Dakota winter. The setting is splendid, but it's the family's small details that make these trips memorable. Meals are served on china, with cloth napkins and silverware. Becky Yunker Salveson and her children are all talented musicians, and they sometimes play at the nightly campfire. Guests can borrow traditional river clothing to wear on their journey if they choose, and the crew even packs ponchos in the canoe in case of rain.

If you have the chance, be sure to stay in BirdWoman's tipi village, which is probably within a few hundred feet of where Lewis and Clark camped October 25, 1805, shortly before they decided to remain in the area for the winter. Three 18-foot-diameter Sioux-style tipis are comfortably furnished with air beds and quilts for up to six people. Sage bundles hang above the door to keep the spirits happy and provide a fragrant welcome. For more information on BirdWoman River Adventures, call (701) 462-3367.

Another Washburn business, Lewis & Clark Canoe and Kayak Rentals, operates out of the Lewis & Clark Café in town. For $30 per day ($25 per kayak), you can paddle in the vicinity of Knife River Indian Village, Fort Mandan, and Cross Ranch State Park. Shuttle service is available for a minimum $10 extra, and box lunches can be included on request. Guided trips may be arranged, too. For more information or a reservation, call (701) 462-3668 or (701) 462-8635 and ask for Dave or Tammy Peyer.▲

Becky Yunker Salveson and her daughters play at the BirdWoman campfire.

On April 7, 1805, the keelboat and 11 men were sent back downriver under the command of Corporal Richard Warfington and accompanied by a vast array of specimens for President Jefferson. Items shipped back included Indian artifacts, 60 plant specimens, many animal skins and skeletons, and four living magpies. Later that same day, the captains and the remainder of the party resumed the upriver trip in six newly built canoes and the two old pirogues.

KNIFE RIVER INDIAN VILLAGES

From Washburn, it's a short drive west on ND 200A to the Knife River Indian Villages Historic Site, near the small town of Stanton. This site, administered by the National Park Service, offers another haunting hint at what life was like in the area when Lewis and Clark arrived.

Start with a stop at the visitor center, where a short film—shown on request—sets the scene by featuring the words of Buffalo-Bird Woman, one of the last Hidatsa to know the old ways. "Sometimes at evening I sit looking out on the big Missouri. The sun sets and dusk steals over the water," she says. "In the shadows, I seem again to see our Indian village with smoke curling upward from the earth lodges. . . . And in the river's roar, I hear the yells of the warrior, the laughter of little children as of old. It is but an old woman's dream. . . . Again

I see but shadows and hear only the roar of the river and tears come into my eyes. Our Indian life, I know, is gone forever."

Gone, perhaps, but not forgotten. A trail from the visitor center winds past what once was the Awatixa Xi'e, or Lower Hidatsa Site. When the earthlodges collapsed, they left circular mounds of earth around hardened, saucer-like floors, surprisingly close together. The Hidatsa had plenty of room to spread out, so the depressions' proximity suggests the village was quite close-knit, perhaps to offer protection from raiding tribes. About 60 earthlodge depressions are plainly visible from the air.

The Awatixa abandoned this village sometime around 1780 after a small-

Knife River.

pox epidemic, but later returned to build a similar village closer to the Knife River. This later village is where Lewis and Clark encountered the Hidatsa Indians when the expedition arrived late in 1804, and it was where Charbonneau and Sacagawea were camped.

Here, the trail dips down to the Knife River. If a civilization can be known by its trash, this is where visitors get an even more intimate glimpse at the village. Molehill-like mounds 2 to 4 feet high near the village edge are middens, or garbage heaps, allowing researchers to reconstruct a 3,000-year archaeological profile of the area. Behind the visitor center, a 40-foot-diameter full-scale earthlodge has been constructed. Its furnishings include an impressive reproduction buffalo robe like the one once worn by Four Bears, a Mandan chief. Tours of the earth lodge are offered daily May through September. You can take a virtual tour of the earth lodge at the park's website, http://www.nps.gov/knri.

Knife River Indian Villages Historic Site is on Mountain Time. Hours are from 7:30 A.M. to 6 P.M. in the summer and daily from 8 A.M. to 4:30 P.M. the rest of the year. It's closed Thanksgiving, Christmas, and New Year's Day. Admission is free, although donations are welcome. Call (701) 745-3309 for more information. The park is the site of the Northern Plains Indian Culture Fest held the fourth weekend each July. Ten miles farther north was the Big Hidatsa village, which also is part of the national monument and open to visitors.

MEDORA AND THEODORE ROOSEVELT NATIONAL PARK

When he first ventured out to North Dakota's Badlands in 1883, Theodore Roosevelt was a sickly young New York State legislator who hoped some time hunting in the Wild West might cure his body and spirit. Like so many before him—and since—Roosevelt fell madly in love with the region and proceeded to spend several years living and ranching in the Dakotas in the mid-1880s before returning to public service as a Spanish-American War hero and, ultimately, as president.

The wealthy French Marquis deMores liked North Dakota, too, so much so he founded a town on the frontier and named it for his bride, Medora von Hoffman. Within a few years, he had established a brickyard, packing plant, stage line, Catholic church, and several stores and saloons.

Today, the town of Medora serves as the southern gateway to Theodore Roosevelt National Park, and, together, they are North Dakota's most popular summer vacation destinations. Location hasn't hurt: The town and park sit right along Interstate 94 in the state's south-west corner. Although this is a bit off the Lewis and Clark Trail, it would be easy enough to detour west on I-94 from Bismarck, visit the Medora area and both the south and north units of Roosevelt National Park, then pick up the Corps of Discovery's route at Williston. North Dakota's "Rough Rider" country may also be a viable stop for travelers who return east on Interstates 90/94. This route also traverses Captain Clark's homeward journey along the Yellowstone River, a trip examined later in this chapter.

Medora is a very small town totally oriented to tourism. Attractions are numerous, ranging from the Medora Musical, performed nightly during the summer at the new Burning Hills Amphitheatre, to the Chateau de Mores State Historic Site, where the marquis's 28-room mansion includes many original furnishings and family possessions. The Medora Doll House claims to have a thousand dolls and antique toys from the eighteenth through twentieth centuries, and the Museum of the Badlands displays exhibits on Native Americans, wildlife, early fur trading, and the pioneer days.

Roosevelt was the best advertisement for one of the area's favorite pursuits: horseback riding. "There are few sensations I prefer to that of galloping over these rolling limitless prairies or winding my way among the barren fantastic and grimly picturesque deserts of the so-called Badlands," he wrote. Medora Stables offers trail rides ranging from one to three hours long from its headquarters on the east side of town (near the Bad Lands Motel), as does Peaceful Valley Ranch, 7 miles north of town in the national park. Mountain biking is huge here, too, with rentals available in town. Check at the park visitor center for information.

Theodore Roosevelt National Park encompasses more than 70,000 acres in its two major units and at Roosevelt's Elkhorn Ranch, about 35 miles north of Medora. Huge herds of roaming American bison are a major attraction in both the south and north units, and pronghorn antelope, mule deer, elk, bobcats, and coyotes are among the other resident animals. Each unit has a designated scenic drive, a 36-mile loop in the south and a 14-mile route in the north, as well as hiking and nature trails. Early mornings or late afternoons are the best time to see the park's legendary colored plateaus, bluffs, and buttes. If you're in the area and have time for just a brief stop, try the Painted Canyon Visitor Center 7 miles east of Medora on I-94.

The park is open all year, although weather conditions generally close some roads during the winter. Campgrounds are situated in both units, and backcountry camping is also available, by permit.

For more information on Theodore Roosevelt National Park, call (701) 623-4466 (South Unit) or (701) 842-2333 (North Unit). For more information on Medora, call the Medora Chamber of Commerce at (701) 623-4910.▲

Stanton is a tiny town with very basic visitor services and an Indian display at the courthouse. Many local people work in nearby Beulah, home of the huge Great Plains Synfuels, where lignite coal is turned into natural gas, or at similar plants in this energy-rich region.

About 40 miles west, near the town of Golden Valley, the Knife River runs through the land of Ron and Lois Wanner, proprietors of Knife River Ranch Vacations. This laid-back, off-the-beaten-path place is an undiscovered treasure where guests can ride horseback, canoe, mountain bike, or just laze in the lodge. It's not a fancy place, but the Wanners are fine hosts. Best of all, with cabins starting at about $55 for two people and reasonably priced activities and meals on request, this is a ranch experience to suit nearly any budget. For more information, write Knife River Ranch, RR1 Box 21A, Golden Valley, North Dakota 58541; call (701) 983-4290; or see the website at www.kniferiverranch.com.

Lake Sakakawea Country

Lake Sakakawea, like Lake Oahe, is one of the nation's largest manmade lakes, 178 miles long with a storage capacity of 24.6 million acre-feet and 1,600 miles of shoreline. The lake is the product of Garrison Dam, another of the six Pick-Sloan projects on the Missouri River. Built by the U.S. Army Corps of Engineers at a cost of $294 million from 1947 through 1954, Garrison is the third-largest earth-filled dam in the United States, after Fort Peck and Oahe. It is 210 feet high and 11,300 feet long. Engineers used 1.5 million cubic yards of concrete in its construction, enough to build a two-lane road 400 miles long.

Despite the superlatives, Lake Sakakawea is relatively easy to break down to a more manageable size, especially along its more accessible northern shores. Secluded bays lure anglers with champion-size walleye, northern pike, small-mouth bass, sauger, chinook salmon, and striped bass. Several state parks, though popular, leave the visitor plenty of room to breathe. North Dakota is one of the smallest Western states in total land area—69,299 square miles—but that's still nearly twice the size of Indiana and more than 14 times the size of Connecticut.

From Stanton, ND 200A (soon ND 200) winds north before turning east at Pick City. Riverdale, 4 miles east, is the headquarters for Garrison Dam. Here in the power plant lobby, visitors can see displays on the dam, along with a 100-square-foot mural of Sacagawea and Pomp, painted by Clarence Cuts the Rope, a Hidatsa Indian. Lake Sakakawea State Park is also nearby, with 300 campsites, several rental cabins, and some of the lake's best salmon fishing.

From Riverdale, drive another 9 miles east to US 83, which heads north, cutting between Lake Sakakawea and the much smaller Audubon Lake. North of the lakes, turn west on North Dakota 37, which, combined with ND 1804, leads all the way to Williston, a distance of about 150 miles. Fort Stevenson State Park is near Garrison, with attractions including a prairie dog town, a 105-site campground, and abundant walleye fishing.

The expedition had its share of exciting and dangerous events in this area. On April 13, 1805, the white pirogue—the boat carrying most of the party's

Lake Sakakawea from Crow Flies High Butte near New Town, North Dakota.

valuables, not to mention the two captains, Sacagawea, Charbonneau, and their son—was suddenly struck by a squall of wind and nearly capsized near the mouth of what is now called Van Hook Arm. On the next day, Lewis wrote they had attained "the highest point to which any white man had ever ascended" on the Missouri, "except for two Frenchmen (one of whom Lapage was now with us) who having lost their way had straggled a few miles farther though to what place precisely I could not learn."

This same day, April 14, the expedition reached the area of Crow Flies High Butte and camped in the vicinity of Bear Den Bay. The winter had hit this area hard: Clark killed a "meager" buffalo bull, and Lewis shot an elk near Indian Creek, so poor it was unfit for use. But they also saw signs of spring: geese nesting in the trees, magpies, black-tailed prairie dogs, and at least two bears.

Parshall, located just off ND 37 before it turns west to New Town, is home to the noted Paul Broste Rock Museum, which displays rocks, fossils, and a large collection of hand-cut rock spheres. New Town is a good place to stop for fuel and food, since few services are available on ND 1804 for the next 75 miles or so. From New Town, drive about 2.25 miles west to a small interpretive area that tells the story of *Pe-Ri-Tska-Wa-Ku-Re* ("Crow Flies High"), a Hidatsa chief who was a leader on the Fort Berthold Indian Reservation. He lived at Like A Fishhook village until a disagreement with another chief led Crow Flies High and his followers to leave.

About 1870, Crow Flies High and his band of some 140 Hidatsa settled around Fort Buford near Williston, using that area as a winter base camp and ranging back into what is now the Lake Sakakawea area during the summers. For almost 25 years, Crow Flies High and his band were self-sustaining, living without government rations. They were forced back on the reservation in 1894, and the chief died of pneumonia in 1900.

The view from Crow Flies High Butte is beautiful. But the butte itself is also worth a look. Cross the Four Bears Bridge, 0.8 mile long, and look back. Nearby, the Three Affiliated Tribes of the Mandan, Hidatsa, and Arikara operate a museum, casino, and lodge. Several powwows are held each summer on the Fort Berthold Indian Reservation, including Twin Buttes, third weekend in June; White Shield, second weekend in July; Mandaree, third weekend in July; and New Town, second weekend in August.

The Three Tribes Museum is definitely worth a look. This is one of a very few places exhibiting an actual Lewis and Clark Expedition peace medal—not a reproduction. There's also an abundance of beautiful bead and porcupine quillwork, some of it more than 100 years old, and an amazing dress decorated with elk teeth. The museum is open daily April through October from 10 A.M. to 6 P.M. Central Time, though it usually closes over the lunch hour from about noon to 1. Admission is $3 for adults, $2 for seniors 60 and over and students ages 13 to 18, and free for children 12 and under. For more information, phone (701) 627-4477.

Calvin Grinnell, a tribal historian and member of the Fort Berthold Lewis and Clark Bicentennial Committee, is able to do guided tours of the area from a native perspective. He offers primitive camping on his land at Saddle Butte, a Lewis and Clark–era landmark. With enough advance notice, he can arrange for tribal dancers and even a sweat ceremony. Call Grinnell at the museum or at (701) 627-4663 to get more information.

It was near here on their return trip that Lewis and Clark reunited on August 12, 1806, after separate explorations along the Missouri (Lewis) and Yellowstone (Clark) rivers. One day earlier, Lewis had been seriously injured when nearsighted Private Cruzatte mistook the captain's buckskin-clad legs for an elk and shot him through both thighs. "The wounds bled considerably but I was happy to find that it touched neither bone nor artery," Lewis wrote. And the next day, "At 1 P.M. I overtook Captain Clark and party and had the pleasure of finding them all well. As writing in my present situation is extremely painful to me I shall desist until I recover and leave to my friend Captain C. the continuation of our journal."

Although just 19 miles from the town of Williston, Lewis and Clark State Park is rarely crowded. The park features rugged Badlands scenery and a nature trail that winds through one of the largest intact native prairies in the North Dakota state parks system. Camping, fishing, and boating are other popular activities.

Williston has only about 13,500 people, but in this country, that's a good-sized town. The traveler will find plenty in the way of motels, restaurants, and shopping, along with several pleasant parks. The Upper Missouri Valley Fair is held just north of town in late June, and the local Frontier Museum's displays include a schoolhouse, medical offices, and a pioneer store. Williston is also the gateway to the North Unit of Theodore Roosevelt State Park (take U.S. Highway 85 south through Watford City), and to the Fort Union and Fort Buford historic sites, which we shall look at in the next section of this chapter. The Lewis and Clark Trail Museum in the small town of Alexander (also located south on US 85) is housed in a 1914 school building, with one room dedicated to a scale model of the explorers' winter camp at Fort Mandan. It's open daily in the summer.

Williston is a stop on Amtrak's Empire Builder line, which runs from Chicago to Portland and Seattle. Starting by 2001 and through the Lewis and Clark bicentennial, Amtrak plans to have historical interpreters on some of its peak-season Empire Builder runs to help relate stories from the Corps of Discovery. The interpreters will probably be on the trains from Minot, North Dakota, through the end of the line in Portland.

THE MISSOURI–YELLOWSTONE CONFLUENCE

The Corps of Discovery's excitement grew as they neared the confluence of the Missouri and the Yellowstone, the Missouri's major tributary. The Yellowstone was finally glimpsed on April 25, 1805, by Lewis and four other men walking overland from the Missouri. "When we had proceeded on about 4 miles, I ascended the hills from whence I had a most pleasing view of the country, particularly of the wide and fertile valleys formed by the Yellowstone and Missouri rivers, which occasionally unmasked by the wood on their borders disclose their meanderings for many miles in their passage through these delightful tracts of country," he wrote. "I determined to camp on the bank of the Yellowstone River which made its appearance about 2 miles south of me. The whole face of the country was covered with herds of buffalo, elk, and antelopes; deer are also abundant, but keep themselves more concealed in the woodland. The buffalo, elk, and antelope are so gentle that we pass near them while feeding without appearing to excite any alarm among them; and when we attract their attention, they frequently approach us more nearly to discover what we are, and in some cases pursue us a considerable distance apparently with that view." True to his word, Lewis and his party did camp on the Yellowstone that night, about 2 miles south of its confluence with the Missouri.

Fort Union on the North Dakota–Montana border.

Visitors watch a blacksmith working at Fort Union.

The next day, Lewis walked to the confluence. En route, he heard several shots, "which announced to me the arrival of the party with Captain Clark . . . after I completed my observations in the evening I walked down and joined the party at their encampment on the point of land formed by the junction of the rivers; found them all in good health, and much pleased at having arrived at this long-wished-for spot, and in order to add in some measure to the general pleasure which seemed to pervade our little community, we ordered a dram to be issued to each person; this soon produced the fiddle, and they spent the evening with much hilarity, singing & dancing, and seemed as perfectly as to forget their past toils, as they appeared regardless of those to come."

As they had at the spots that would become Fort Osage and Fort Atkinson, Lewis and Clark thought this confluence would be, as Clark put it, "a handsome situation" for a military or trading post. The explorers noted the river banks here had a gravel base and were situated well above flood level. Cottonwood and ash trees were available for construction. The site provided a broad vista, which would prevent approaching Indians from being concealed—and which would let the Indians see any trading post from quite a distance. On his return trip in 1806, Lewis surveyed and charted the land near the confluence.

Several years went by before anyone took advantage of the idea, but in 1828, John Jacob Astor's American Fur Company built Fort Union. Under the supervision of Kenneth McKenzie, the fort's first bourgeois (or superintendent), the new fort became a beacon on the Plains. Indians came to trade: first beaver skins; then tanned buffalo robes, elk, antelope, wolf, otter, hedgehog, and even mice. With these, the natives could obtain metal goods, tools, blankets, food, and more. The Assiniboine, Crow, Cree, Gros Ventre, Mandan, Hidatsa, Arikara, Blackfoot, and Hunkpapa Sioux all trekked to Fort Union. Famous white visitors also came to see Fort Union: George Catlin, Prince Maximilian and Karl Bodmer, John Audubon, Jim Bridger, and Father Pierre De Smet were among those who visited the post in its heyday. During those peak years, the fort employed up to 100 people, including clerks, hunters, craftsmen, herders, and traders. It was always a busy place.

Busy, that is, until about the time of the Civil War. By then, smallpox, white westward expansion, and tensions with the Sioux had altered life on the Plains. In 1864, General Alfred Sully described Fort Union as "an old dilapidated affair, almost falling to pieces." Fort Union's era was almost over, but another era—that of Fort Buford—was about to begin.

Fort Union was located 2 miles from the confluence, but Fort Buford, the new infantry post established in 1866, was built overlooking the river junction. The post eventually housed six companies of infantry and cavalry and served as a vital link in American military strategy of the mid- to late-nineteenth century. It was here that Sitting Bull surrendered in 1881; here, too, where Chief Joseph of the Nez Perce was imprisoned after his Montana capture just 42 miles from freedom at the Canadian border. Fort Buford remained in use until 1895, when widespread white settlement of the area made it no longer necessary.

For many decades, Fort Union and Fort Buford were mostly forgotten, but the sites have seen a dramatic upturn in interest and visitation in recent years. Fort Union National Historic Site was a grassy plain when the National Park Service acquired the land in 1966; today, much of the fort has been reconstructed, including the fabulous bourgeois house. Daily tours, living history demonstrations, and special interpretive programs are planned throughout the summer, including the annual Fort Union Trading Post Rendezvous typically held the third weekend of June. The fort is open daily from 8 A.M. to 8 P.M. Central Time, Memorial Day through Labor Day, and 9 A.M. to 5:30 P.M. the rest of the year except Thanksgiving, Christmas, and New Year's Day. Admission is by donation. For more information, call (701) 572-9083.

Fort Buford State Historic Site is located just a few miles east of Fort Union. The old field officers' quarters now house a museum that tells the fort's history, and a stone powder magazine and military cemetery are among the other fort remnants still standing. The site is open annually from mid-May through mid-September, from 8 A.M. to 5 P.M. daily with off-season tours offered by appointment. Admission is $4. A picnic area is nearby. Call (701) 572-9034 for more information.

Montana River Ranch Country Inn near Bainville, Montana, is a bed-and-breakfast lodge and outfitting business on the banks of the Missouri near Fort Union. The Harmon family offers half-day ($275 per person) and full-day ($350 per person) float trips; the latter passes Fort Union and continues to the Yellowstone confluence. Prices includes meals and lodging, and family rates are available. Canoe rentals are also available at $50 per day. For more information, call (877) 277-4084; write HC 58 Box 9, Bainville, Montana 59212; or see the website at www.montanariverranch.com.

The Missouri and Yellowstone rivers meet almost smack-dab on the North Dakota–Montana border. From here, Lewis and Clark Trail travelers have several options for proceeding west: retracing Clark's homeward journey along the Yellowstone River, crossing Montana's most remote country south of the Missouri River, or taking the northern route across the Hi-Line.

HOMEWARD BOUND: CLARK ON THE YELLOWSTONE RIVER

When Lewis and Clark reached the Pacific, their trip was only half over, geographically speaking. And as much country as they'd covered heading west, the captains knew there was much they'd been unable to explore. So even before they left Fort Clatsop, their second winter camp, Lewis and Clark had decided they'd split up near what is now Missoula, Montana, and take separate routes back to the Missouri-Yellowstone confluence.

Clark chose the southerly route, traveling through the Big Hole, over Bozeman Pass, and onto the Yellowstone River—the section we will follow here. This route has little in the way of Lewis and Clark interpretation except for one very notable exception: it was along the Yellowstone, east of present-day Billings, that Clark carved his name at Pompeys Pillar. To this day, it is the only remaining documented physical evidence of the expedition. For that reason, this particular side trip—though long—is well worth the traveler's time if it can be included in the itinerary.

Anyone who lives in the East or Upper Midwest may want to make this trip, as Clark did, on their own way home. (In that event, it will be necessary to read this particular section backward.) But the side trip may also be done while heading west by detouring from Fort Union to Interstate 94 (via Montana 200 and 16), then on to Pompeys Pillar near Billings. From there, the traveler could continue on into Billings and take U.S. Highway 87 north, resuming the corps' westward trek at Great Falls or Fort Benton. Most of the country along the Missouri River west of Fort Peck Dam is inaccessible by motor vehicle, anyway, so this detour, although about 100 miles longer than the alternatives, remains an option. What's a hundred miles in Montana, anyway?

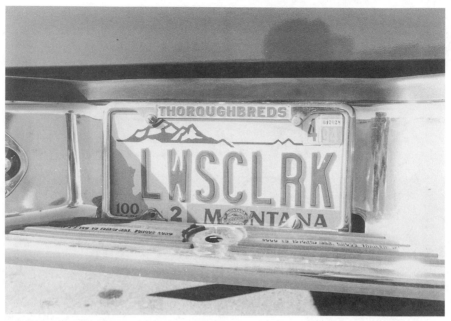

A Lewis and Clark buff's license plate.

Eastern Montana has a reputation as desolate, barren country. The region's topography certainly differs from the mountainous west, and sheer size and the vast distance between highway exits may be the reason some folks consider it monotonous. But eastern Montana has its own raw beauty and plenty of recreational and historical diversions, too.

Sidney, Montana, is the major town along the lower Yellowstone Valley. Long an agricultural center, Sidney enjoyed an oil boom in the late 1970s and early 1980s. Things have calmed down since then, but much of the energy-driven development may still be seen in the new stores and restaurants of this friendly town.

Sidney's pride is the Mon-Dak Heritage Center, a bright, airy museum with changing art exhibits and a fascinating walk-through streetscape on its lower level. One painting, "Lewis and Clark Arriving at the Confluence," by Barbara Schaffner, remains on permanent display near the museum entrance. Other exhibits include fossils, dinosaur bones, a gun collection, and numerous photographs.

From Sidney, follow the Yellowstone Valley down MT 16 to Glendive. (If you're in the mood to fish, try your luck at catching the boneless, bottom-dwelling paddlefish, a species unique to this part of the country. You'll need a state license and a copy of the fishing regulations.) Glendive is the gateway to Makoshika State Park, 3 miles south of town in the badlands. Sightseeing, rock hunting, and hiking are popular activities at Makoshika, and the area has also yielded some major dinosaur fossil finds. Glendive also marks the entrance to I-94.

The next major town, Miles City, is 75 miles west on I-94. Nestled at the mouth of the Tongue River, Miles City relishes its image as a cowboy's town. But this is also a commercial center for southeast Montana, and there are plenty of modern-day visitor amenities. The Miles City Jaycee Bucking Horse Sale, held the third weekend of May, is one of the biggest of its kind: rodeo folks from many states visit to see and buy some of the wildest broncs this side of Dodge. The Range Riders Museum and historic Montana Bar at 612 Main Street are among Miles City's other attractions. The city park on the west side of town is an excellent place to take a break from the road, with a big playground and squirrels that will eat out of your hand.

Although home to only about 2,500 people, Forsyth is notable for some interesting architecture, especially the Rosebud County Courthouse, a Classical Revival building with a copper dome, murals, and stained glass. It dates from 1911.

The Little Big Horn Battlefield National Monument is accessible via Exit 49 from I-94. Follow Montana 47 30 miles south to I-90, then another 15 miles to the battlefield. It was here General George Armstrong Custer and the Seventh Cavalry made their last stand against the Sioux and Northern Cheyenne.

And finally, at long last, Pompeys Pillar National Landmark is found at Exit 23 on I-94. A historical marker and large version of the familiar Lewis and Clark trail sign help point the way.

Clark and his party arrived here July 25, 1806. Looking up at the monolith 200 feet high and 400 paces in circumference, he pronounced it "a remarkable rock" and named it Pompys Tower for Sacagawea's son, who by then was 17 months old and much attached to Clark. (The affection was mutual).

Approaching the pillar, the visitor can't help but feel a real sense of excitement. Here is one of the few sites where little imagination is required: Captain Clark's signature is right there, plainly visible behind the protective glass casing. Looking at the signature, many visitors wonder: Was Clark that tall? Did someone boost him up to make his mark? Actually, the bluff around the signature has eroded since 1806.

After viewing the signature, continue on to the viewpoint on the pillar's west edge. It's a bit of a climb, but hikers are richly rewarded with a sublime view. Clark likely stood on this exact spot, and it is fun to imagine what the surrounding land may have looked like in his day. No interstate, no neatly plowed rectangles of farmland, no houses, no cars. But some things haven't changed much, chief among them the sprawling horizons and the wild, free-flowing Yellowstone, one of the only great Western rivers still unfettered by dams. Clark found two piles of stones placed by Indians at the summit, along with many animals and designs carved on the steep rock faces.

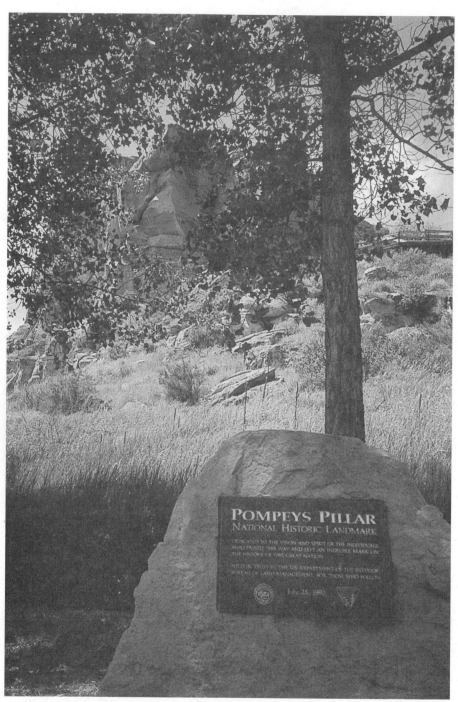

Not averse to graffiti, Clark etched his name on this towering rock (background).

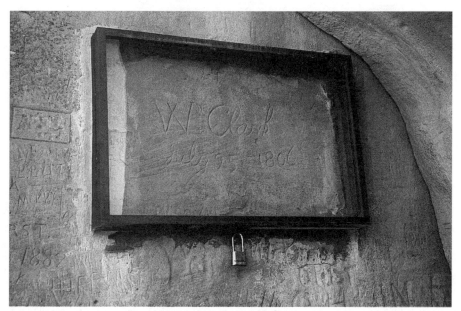

William Clark's signature at Pompeys Pillar near Billings, Montana.

Pompeys Pillar's development as a visitor attraction is something of a recent phenomenon. Montana's first historic marker was a protective grid over the signature, placed by the Northern Pacific Railroad in 1882. The grid did the job, but it also made viewing quite difficult. Some 70 years later, Don C. Foote, the landowner, replaced the grid with bulletproof glass. Ultimately, the Footes sold the site to the Bureau of Land Management, and the site was finally dedicated as a National Historic Landmark in 1992. The name Pompeys Pillar was first seen upon the publication of the Lewis and Clark journals in 1814.

Several plaques sit at the base of the pillar, among them one dedicating the site to "the vision and spirit of the individuals who passed this way and left an indelible mark on the history of this great nation." The site also includes a riverside picnic area, rest rooms, and a small visitor center. Several dugout canoe replicas are also on display, the product of a Lewis and Clark float reenactment a few years back. Anyone unable to climb to Clark's signature will find a replica of his autograph inside the small visitor center.

Pompeys Pillar is accessible all the time. The interpretive staff is there from 8 A.M. to 8 P.M. Memorial Day Weekend through Labor Day Weekend, and from 8 A.M. to 4:30 P.M. weekdays the rest of the year. Admission during staffed hours is $3 per vehicle. For more information, call (406) 875-2233 or (406) 238-1540.

The Yellowstone River is the last free-flowing waterway in Montana. The section near Billings is a good float for canoeists, though you need to watch out for log jams and other snags along the way. Every year on the July Sunday closest to Clark's visit, local boaters celebrate with a Clark Day float to Pompeys Pillar. The event is actually two separate floats—a paddle of 30 miles or so from Billings for experienced canoeists and a shorter, safer stretch for "anything that floats." For the date and more details on this year's event, call Pompeys Pillar.

Voyageur canoes are all the rage on the rivers of Lewis and Clark now, but Thomas R. White of Billings has been plying the Yellowstone in his 22-foot craft for nearly a decade now. He can take up to eight people on his one-day "Voyage of the Bird Woman" trips through the Pompeys Pillar area. En route, he often serenades passengers with such traditional river songs as "Shenandoah." Cost is $100 per person, including lunch; family rates are available. For more information, call (406) 652-7561 or write Voyagers of the Roche Jaune, c/o Thomas White, 2416 Golden Boulevard, Billings, Montana 59102.

Fun Adventures, based in Billings, also plans to offer guided canoe trips on the Yellowstone ranging from three hours to two days, with a special trip planned for each year's Clark Day event. Costs vary; for more information or reservations, call (888) 618-4386 or (406) 254-7180.

From Pompeys Pillar, it's just about a half-hour's drive to Billings, the biggest city in Montana with about 82,000 people. Fun Adventures, mentioned above, offers a 90-minute trolley tour featuring city highlights and history. Stops include the Billings historic district, Yellowstone Country Museum, and Black Otter Trail on the rimrocks. The trolley leaves at 7 P.M. Tuesday and Thursday from the Billings Chamber of Commerce headquarters near I-90, Exit 450. Cost is $10 per person, or $5 for children 10 and under. Fun Adventures also leads downtown historic walking tours at 9 A.M. Tuesday and Thursday (cost is $5 per person) and tours to Pompeys Pillar and Pictograph Caves (cost is $34 per person) daily from April 15 to October 1. Reservations are necessary for all activities. Call (888) 618-4386 or (406) 254-7180.

People touring on their own will find an array of interesting sites. The Peter Yegen Jr. Yellowstone Country Museum displays a variety of Indian, pioneer, and cowboy artifacts at Billings Logan International Airport, while the Western Heritage Center (2822 Montana Avenue) features changing exhibits on the region's history and culture. Oscar's Dreamland, 5 miles southwest of town on Wise Lane, has one of the world's largest collections of historic farm machinery, and the Yellowstone Art Center (located in the original county jail at 401 North 27th Street) focuses on contemporary Western works.

For spur-of-the-moment recreation, Billings has a good selection of parks, including Riverfront Park right along the Yellowstone and Lake Elmo, north of town in Billings Heights. The Mustangs, a Cincinnati Reds farm team, play

June through August at Cobb Field on North 27th Street. Major shopping areas include downtown Billings, with specialty shops and a factory outlet mall, and the West End, home of the Rimrock Mall, Billings' largest, with about 90 stores. Stop by the Billings Chamber of Commerce for more local information or call (800) 735-2635.

From Billings, the traveler can either head north on US 87 toward Great Falls and Fort Benton to pick up the westward trek or follow Captain Clark's route in reverse along I-90 all the way to Three Forks—another major junction for the expedition. Highlights of this latter option might include the following:

• **Park City (Exit 426).** It was near here where Clark and his party actually started their Yellowstone River trip, after following the waterway for some distance overland. Near what is now called the Buffalo Mirage Access, Clark finally found some trees suitable for canoe building. The state-run access area offers camping, fishing, boat ramps, and picnic tables. Traveling on I-90, take the Park City exit and follow the signs 13 miles to the site.

• **Big Timber (Exit 377).** Another Yellowstone River access point, although the major attraction here is probably Big Timber Waterslide, a water-park complex

Montana Centennial Trail Drive Statue at the Billings visitor center.

with a half-dozen large waterslides, Olympic-size swimming pool, bumper boats, and more.

• **Livingston (Exit 322) and Bozeman (Exit 309).** It was between these two towns—helped by Sacagawea, who knew the area from girlhood—that the Clark party crossed Bozeman Pass and descended to the Yellowstone Valley. Both cities are major recreation areas and gateways to Yellowstone National Park (see the side trip near the end of chapter 6).

The Gallatin County Pioneer Museum at 317 West Main Street in Bozeman recently received a large collection of books, atlases, and other materials related to Lewis and Clark. The donation was from Don Nell, a past president of the Lewis and Clark Trail Heritage Foundation. There's also a statue of Sacagawea and Pomp by Bozeman's visitor center on North 7th Avenue.

• **Three Forks (Exit 278).** On their 1804 westward trip, Lewis and Clark finally discovered the Missouri River headwaters here. (See the Three Forks of the Missouri section in chapter 6 for a complete description of the area.) Eastbound in 1806, the Clark party split up at the Three Forks, with Sergeant Ordway and nine others pushing down the Missouri to rendezvous with Captain Lewis, and Clark and 12 others continuing overland to the Yellowstone.

THE HI-LINE

Now we return to Fort Buford for travelers who want to follow the corps' westward journey up the Missouri.

Past the Missouri-Yellowstone confluence, it becomes difficult to trace Lewis and Clark's route by land. Two motor routes parallel the Missouri, but neither very closely. Backroads provide access to the river, but these offer little more than a few miles of riverbank driving. The traveler's best bet is to hightail it for Fort Benton, where—if your schedule permits—outfitters can help you backtrack a ways on a stretch of water that closely resembles the waterway Lewis and Clark experienced—the Upper Missouri National Wild and Scenic River.

But first, we must get across a huge chunk of northeast Montana, a land so vast that high school sports teams frequently must travel all day to reach their opponents. The two major routes across this part of the state are U.S. Highway 2 and Montana 200/US 87. Often called the Hi-Line, after the Great Northern Railway route it paralleled, US 2 is the more popular and practical of the two.

Urged on by Great Falls founder Paris Gibson and copper baron Marcus Daly, rail magnate James Hill decided northern Montana was ripe for settling. Towns like Glasgow, Zurich, Havre, and Malta were named in hopes of appealing to would-be European immigrants; in some instances, Great Northern employees reportedly spun the globe, closed their eyes, and jabbed their finger at

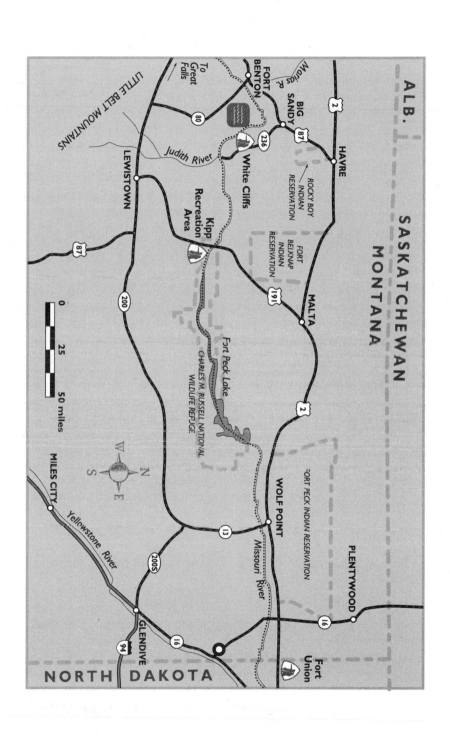

the whirring sphere. Whatever town they hit, that was the new settlement's name.

Many emigrants arrived between 1910 and 1918, eager to claim their land and start farming. For a while, the homesteaders flourished; wet weather and World War I led to inflated grain prices. But a long drought set in about 1918, and many settlers left just as soon as they'd come. These days, however, northeastern Montanans generally do well with wheat, often planted in strips to help control wind erosion.

It's some 350 miles from the North Dakota border to Fort Benton, way too much ground to cover thoroughly when Lewis and Clark lore is the primary objective. So let's take a brief look at highlights of the Hi-Line:

• When folks think of Montana, many think about cowboys, and several outfitters around the state offer honest-to-goodness cattle-drive vacations. Gene and Marsha Foss of Culbertson, Montana, offer several drives each summer. The five-day rides, priced in 2000 at $1,150, are geared to people with all levels of riding experience, and the Fosses have guided people from as far away as Hong Kong and Switzerland. For more information, write Gene Foss, HC 69 Box 97, Culbertson, Montana 59218, or call (406) 787-5559.

• It was somewhere here along the Missouri that the Corps of Discovery had its first encounter with a grizzly bear. The date was April 29, 1805. "I walked on shore with one man. About 8 A.M. we fell in with two brown or yellow bear, both of which we wounded. One of them made his escape, the other after my firing on him pursued me 70 or 80 yards, but fortunately had been so badly wounded that he was unable to pursue me so closely as to prevent my charging my gun; we again repeated our fire and killed him," Lewis wrote.

• Coming from the North Dakota border, Wolf Point is the first major town along the Hi-Line. Wolf Point pays tribute to our heroes at Lewis and Clark Memorial Park, situated several miles east of town on the Missouri River. The town's major event is the Wolf Point Stampede, Montana's oldest rodeo and one of its best. A shared celebration of cowboy and Indian culture, the event takes place the second weekend of July.

• Nashua and Glasgow, less than an hour west of Wolf Point, are the jumping-off spots for Fort Peck Dam, largest and westernmost of the Pick-Sloan Plan impoundments. The earth-filled dam is more than 21,000 feet long, 3,500 feet wide at its base, and 250 feet high. The dam created Fort Peck Lake, with a storage capacity of 19 million acre-feet of water and a surface area of 249,000 acres. The lake stretches about 150 miles west, more than the distance spanned between Pittsburgh and Cleveland, while its total shoreline—nearly 1,600 miles— is longer than that of California.

American white pelicans on the Missouri River.

In addition to Fort Peck the dam, and Fort Peck the lake, there's Fort Peck the town. Built by the U.S. Army Corps of Engineers to house some of the many thousands who worked on the dam, Fort Peck still boasts some interesting architecture, including the COE office, the Fort Peck Hotel, and the popular Fort Peck Theatre, which presents live shows each summer.

• Glasgow's Valley County Pioneer Museum, just west of town, is one of Montana's better small-town museums. It has several Lewis and Clark exhibits; one tells how Lewis and Clark came to name the Milk River, which the Indians had earlier called "The River Which Scolds at All Others." The expedition reached this largest and most important northern tributary of the Missouri on May 8, 1805. "The water of this river possesses a peculiar whiteness, being about the color of a cup of tea with the admixture of a tablespoonful of milk," Lewis wrote. "From the color of its water we called it Milk River."

• Western Montana is full of hot springs, but they're something of a rarity in the state's eastern reaches. Sleeping Buffalo Hot Springs Resort near Saco was named for a group of glacial boulders near the Milk River that, from a distance, resemble a herd of sleeping buffalo. These were held sacred by the Indians, with one rock in particular thought to be the leader. Indians sacrificed possessions at this rock, now part of a roadside monument at the hot springs turnoff. Facilities at the resort include several pools, a water slide, golf course, restaurant, and lodging.

• Malta sits at the terminus of U.S. Highway 191, the best land route to James Kipp Recreation Area, one of the most popular and accessible spots in the Charles M. Russell National Wildlife Refuge, second largest in the continental United States at 1.2 million acres. Located just east of the designated Upper Missouri National Wild and Scenic River, Kipp Recreation Area is a frequent take-out point for longer river trips through the corridor. Lewis and Clark spent nearly two weeks within the CMR's boundaries on their way west in 1805. Today, you can still see much of what they saw: bighorn sheep, pronghorn, deer, elk, and coyotes—everything except grizzly bears and wolves, which now live only in sections of western Montana.

Big as it is, the CMR is difficult to access. The 20-mile CMR Auto Tour Route begins north of the Fred Robinson Bridge, which crosses the Missouri River on Montana 191 about 70 miles southwest of Malta. The Missouri Breaks National Back Country Byway, an 81-mile loop, leaves from just south of the Fred Robinson Bridge. For either route, get a good local map, exercise caution, and don't even think of exploring the area's back roads if rain is threatening—the terrain quickly becomes an impassable gumbo when wet.

• Fort Belknap is the headquarters for the Gros Ventre and Assiniboine Tribes of Montana, with a combined enrollment of about 4,000 people. Together, the tribes offer guided tours of a 10,000-acre tribal bison reserve each day between May 1 through September 30. For more information or to reserve a tour, call (406) 353-2205, or stop in the visitor center just south of the corner of US 2 and Montana 66. Not far west near Chinook, Chief Joseph of the Nez Perce surrendered on October 5, 1877, with his eloquent "I will fight no more forever..." speech. The site is marked at the Bear's Paw/Chief Joseph Battlefield 16 miles south of US 2. If you're in the area in summer, consider attending Milk River Indian Days (the fourth weekend in July) or the Rocky Boy's Powwow (the first weekend of August). The Rocky Boy's Reservation, home to about 2,500 Chippewa-Cree people, is centered near the town of Box Elder on US 87.

• Havre is the most populous town on the Hi-Line, home of Northern Montana College, and jumping-off spot for Fort Benton, Great Falls, and the rest of the Lewis and Clark route. If you have time, stop by the H. Earl Clack Museum in Havre's Lions Park, where exhibits include some excellent photos of Native American sites and a piece of the Berlin Wall. The park also offers reasonably priced RV and tent sites, as well as tours of nearby Fort Assiniboine and an area buffalo jump. The museum is open 8 A.M. to 8 P.M. May 15 through

September 15. Beaver Creek Park, one of the largest county-run parks in the nation, is south of Havre.

Another alternate route across east-central Montana runs about 400 miles from the Dakota border to Fort Benton, following MT 200 (from Sidney to Grass Range), US 87 (from Grass Range to Stanford via Lewistown), and Montana 80 (from Stanford to Fort Benton). This is big, wild country, where a dot on the map doesn't necessarily indicate much. As W. C. McRae and Judy Jewell point out in their *Montana Handbook*, "Between Sidney and Lewistown—a distance of almost 300 miles—Highway 200 passes through only three towns with gas pumps; their combined population approaches 1,500 people. As it connects up these remote enclaves of humanity, Highway 200 intersects a part of Montana often called the Big Lonely. Unpopulated, marginally productive, and often starkly beautiful, this is one of the last vast frontiers left in Montana."

Lewistown is the biggest and most interesting town along this route. Nestled in a valley amid the Judith, Moccasin, and Big Snowy Mountains, this city of about 6,400 was named not for Meriwether Lewis but for an Army officer who established a fort nearby in the 1870s. Lewistown has a handsome downtown area with interesting architecture, notably the Fergus County Courthouse. The Central Montana Museum, in the same building as the chamber of commerce at 408 N.E. Main Street, exhibits pioneer and Indian artifacts.

The Lewistown area's most popular attraction is probably the Charlie Russell Chew-Choo dinner train, which takes a 56-mile, three-and-a-half-hour round trip between Kingston (about 10 miles northwest of Lewistown) and Denton. The train runs every Saturday night from the last weekend in May through the end of September, with a per-person cost of $75 including a prime rib dinner. The train also makes special runs during the mid-August Montana Cowboy Poetry Festival and for the winter holidays. For reservations, call Main Connection Travel in Lewistown at (406) 538-2527.

LODGING

*Denotes towns along Clark's 1806 homeward route.

Rates are for double occupancy during summer season as of 1999 and are subject to change.

FORT YATES, NORTH DAKOTA

Prairie Knights Lodge, (701) 258-7000, 46 miles south of Mandan on ND 1806. $65–$120.

BISMARCK/MANDAN, NORTH DAKOTA

Best Western Seven Seas Inn, (701) 663-7401, 2611 Old Red Trail (Mandan). $65.
Bismarck Motor Hotel, (701) 223-2474, 2301 E. Main St. $33.

Expressway Inn, (800) 456-6388, 200 E. Bismarck Expressway. $40–$50.
Radisson Inn Bismarck, (701) 258-7700 or (800) 333-3333, 800 S. 3rd St. $60 and up.
Select Inn, (800) 641-1000, 1505 Interchange Ave. $38–$48.

WASHBURN, NORTH DAKOTA

ScotWood Motel, (701) 462-8191, 1323 Frontage Rd. $37.

GARRISON, NORTH DAKOTA

Garrison Motel, (701) 463-2858, 0.25 mile east on ND 37. $44.

Indian Hills Resort, (701) 743-4122, ND 1804 west of Garrison on Good Bear Bay. Cabins and condos for rent.

PARSHALL, NORTH DAKOTA

Parshall Motor Inn, (701) 862-3127, N. Main St. $37.

NEW TOWN, NORTH DAKOTA

Cottage Inn, (701) 627-4217, Main St. $35–$40.
4 Bears Lodge, (800) 294-5454, 4 miles west over bridge. $55.
Sunset Motel, (701) 627-3316, ND 23 E.
West Dakota Inn, (701) 627-3721, ND 23 E. $40.

WILLISTON, NORTH DAKOTA

Airport International Inn, (701) 774-0241, US 2 and US 85 N. $42.
El Rancho Motor Hotel, (701) 572-6321, 1623 2nd Ave. W. $41.
Select Inn, (800) 641-1000, 213 35th St. $36.
Super 8 Lodge, (800) 800-8000, 2324 2nd Ave. W. $48.
Travel Host, (701) 774-0041, 3801 2nd Ave. W. $36.

*SIDNEY, MONTANA

Lone Tree Inn, (406) 482-4520, 900 S. Central. $40.
Park Plaza Motel, (406) 482-1520, 601 S. Central. $32.
Richland Motor Inn, (406) 482-6400, 1200 S. Central. $57.

*GLENDIVE, MONTANA

Best Western Jordan Inn, (406) 365-5655, 222 N. Kendrick. $62–$70.
Budget Host Riverside Inn, (406) 377-2349, I-94 and MT 16. $38.
El Centro Motel, (406) 365-5211, 112 S. Kendrick Ave. $32.

*MILES CITY, MONTANA

Budget Host Custer's Inn, (406) 232-5170, 1209 S. Haynes Ave. $40.
Days Inn, (406) 232-3550, 1006 S. Haynes Ave. $38–$48.
Holiday Inn Express, (406) 232-1000, 1720 S. Haynes Ave. $70–$75.

*FORSYTH, MONTANA

Best Western Sundowner Inn, (406) 356-2115, 1018 Front St. $65–$75.
Restwel Motel, (406) 356-2771, 810 Front St. $38.

*BILLINGS, MONTANA

The Billings Inn, (800) 231-7782, 880 N. 29th St. $53–$60.
Hilltop Inn, (800) 878-9282, 1116 N. 28th St. $54–$60.
Radisson Northern Hotel, (406) 245-5121, 19 N. 28th St. $90.
Ramada Limited, (800) 272-6232, 1345 Mullowney Ln. $60–$70.
Sheraton Billings Hotel, (406) 252-7400, 27 N. 27th St. $90–$100.

*COLUMBUS, MONTANA

Riverside Guest Cabins, (406) 322-5066, 44 W. Pike Ave. $45.
Super 8, (406) 322-4101, 602 8th Ave. N. $50–$65.

*BIG TIMBER, MONTANA

C. M. Russell Lodge, (406) 932-5244, I-90 Exit 367. $45–$55.

*LIVINGSTON, MONTANA

Budget Host Parkway Motel, (406) 222-3840, 1124 W. Park. $55–$60.
Del Mar Motel, (406) 222-3120, I-90 business loop. $50–$70.
Murray Hotel, (406) 222-1350, 201 W. Park St. $60 and up.
The River Inn, (406) 222-2429, 4950 US 89. $60–$90.

*BOZEMAN, MONTANA

The Bozeman Inn, (406) 587-3176, 1235 N. 7th Ave. $65–$70.
Gallatin Gateway Inn, (406) 763-4672, 12 miles southwest on US 19. $105–$160.
Holiday Inn, (106) 507-4561, 5 Daxter Ln. $90–$100.
Howlers Inn Bed & Breakfast, (888) 469-5377, east of Bozeman off I-90. $80–$110. On-premise wolf preserve.
Lewis and Clark Motel, (406) 586-3341, 824 W. Main St. $70.
Royal 7 Motel, (406) 587-3103, 310 N. 7th Ave. $40–$46.
Torch & Toes Bed & Breakfast, (800) 446-2138, 309 S. Third Ave. $80–$90.

BAINVILLE, MONTANA

Montana River Ranch Country Inn, (406) 769-2127. $120.

CULBERTSON, MONTANA

Diamond Willow Inn, (406) 787-6218, US 2. $40.
Kings Inn, (406) 787-6277, 408 6th St. E. $36–$48.

WOLF POINT, MONTANA

Big Sky Motel, (406) 653-2300, US 2 E. $35–$40.
Homestead Inn, (800) 231-0986, 101 US 2 E. $38–$43.
Sherman Motor Inn, (800) 952-1100, 200 E. Main. $40–$45.

GLASGOW, MONTANA

Campbell Lodge, (406) 228-9328, 534 3rd Ave. S. $35–$40.
Cottonwood Inn, (800) 321-8213, US 2 E. $56–$62.
La Casa Motel, (406) 228-9311, 238 1st Ave. N. $33–$38.

MALTA, MONTANA

Edgewater Inn, (800) 821-7475 (in state) or (406) 654-1302, 101 US 2 W. $50.
Maltana Motel, (406) 654-2610, 138 S. 1st Ave. $40–$44.

CHINOOK, MONTANA

Chinook Motor Inn, (406) 357-2248, 100 Indiana Ave. $52.

HAVRE, MONTANA

El Toro Inn, (406) 265-5414, 521 1st St. $45–$50.
Super 8, (406) 265-1411, 1901 US 2. $48–$55.
TownHouse Inn, (406) 265-6711, 601 W. 1st St. $60.

LEWISTOWN, MONTANA

B&B Motel, (406) 538-5496, 520 E. Main St. $45.
Pheasant Tales Bed & Bistro, (406) 538-7880. $78.
Yogo Inn, (800) 860-9646, 211 E. Main St. $60–$80.

Missouri River south of Culbertson, Montana.

CAMPING

BISMARCK/MANDAN, NORTH DAKOTA

Bismarck KOA, (701) 222-2662, 3720 Centennial Rd.

Colonial Motel and Campground, (701) 663-9824, 4631 Memorial Hwy. (Mandan).

Fort Abraham Lincoln State Park, (701) 663-9571, south of Mandan on ND 1806.

Hillcrest Acres Campground, (701) 255-4334, from East Bismarck Expressway, 1.25 miles east on Old Hwy. 10.

Mandan Camping Area, (701) 667-3280, four blocks west of ND 1806 on Third St. (Mandan).

WASHBURN, NORTH DAKOTA

Fort Mandan Historical Site, (701) 462-8129, west of town.

City Park, free overnight camping.

PICK CITY, NORTH DAKOTA

Lake Sakakawea State Park, (701) 487-3315.

GARRISON, NORTH DAKOTA

Fort Stevenson State Park, (701) 337 5576, 3 miles south.

Indian Hills Resort, (701) 463-2102, 31 miles west.

WILLISTON, NORTH DAKOTA

Buffalo Trails Campground, (701) 572-3206, 4 miles north via US 2 and US 85.

Lewis and Clark State Park, (701) 859-3071; 16 miles east on ND 1804.

Lund's Landing, (701) 568-3474, 24 miles east on ND 1804.

*GLENDIVE, MONTANA

Green Valley Campground, (406) 365-4156, I-94 Exit 212.

Glendive Campground, (406) 365-6721, I-94 Exit 215.

Makoshika State Park, (406) 365-8596, 2 miles southeast on Snyder Ave.

*MILES CITY, MONTANA

KOA–Miles City, (406) 232-3991, I-94 Exit 135.

*BILLINGS, MONTANA

Big Sky Campground, (406) 259-4110, 5516 Laurel Rd.

Billings Metro KOA, (406) 252-3104, 3087 Garden Ave.

Garden Avenue RV Park, (406) 259-0878, I-90 Exit 450.

*LAUREL, MONTANA

Pelican RV Park, (406) 259-8211, 3444 S. Frontage Rd.

*COLUMBUS, MONTANA

Itch-Ke-Pe Park, (406) 322-5313, on south edge of town.

*BIG TIMBER, MONTANA

KOA–Big Timber, (406) 932-6569, I-90 Exit 377.

*LIVINGSTON, MONTANA

Big Spur Campground, (406) 222-7600, 10.5 miles south on US 89.
KOA–Paradise Valley, (406) 222-0992, 10 miles south on US 89.
Livingston Inn & Campground, (406) 222-1122, I-90 Exit 333.

*BOZEMAN, MONTANA

Bear Canyon Campground, (406) 587-1575, I-90 at Bear Canyon Rd.
Bozeman Hot Springs KOA, (406) 587-3030, 81123 Gallatin Rd. (US 191).
Lexley Acres, (406) 388-6095, I-90 Exit 298 (Belgrade).
Manhattan Camper Court, (406) 284-6930, I-90 Exit 288 (Manhattan).
Sunrise Campground, (406) 587-4797, I-90 Exit 309.

CULBERTSON, MONTANA

Bicentennial Park, south side of town. Free camping with RV hookups.

WOLF POINT, MONTANA

R.B.W. Campground, (406) 525-3740, 7 miles east on US 2.
Rancho Motel & Campground, (406) 653-1940, 1.25 miles west on US 2.

GLASGOW, MONTANA

Shady Rest RV Park, (800) 422-8954, US 2 and Lasar Dr.
Trails West Trailer Park & Campground, (406) 228-2778, 1.5 miles west on US 2 at Skylark Rd.

MALTA, MONTANA

Edgewater Campground, (800) 821-7475, US 2 W.

HAVRE, MONTANA

Beaver Creek Park, (406) 395-4565, south of Havre via 5th Ave.
Earl Clack Museum & Campground, (406) 265-9913, in Lions Park on US 2.
Evergreen Campground, (406) 265-8228, south of town on US 87.
Fresno Reservoir, west of Havre on US 2.
Havre RV Park, (406) 265-8861, 1300 1st St.
KOA of Havre, (406) 265-9722, 9 miles east on US 2.

LEWISTOWN, MONTANA

Mountain Acres RV Park & Campground, (406) 538-7591, north on US 191.
No tents.

RESTAURANTS

FORT YATES, NORTH DAKOTA

Feast of the Rock Buffet at Prairie Knights Casino, (800) 425-8277, 46 miles south of Mandan on Highway 1806.

BISMARCK/MANDAN, NORTH DAKOTA

Captain Meriwether's Landing, (701) 224-0455, at the Lewis and Clark Riverboat Landing. Dining by the river.

The Drumstick, (701) 223-8449, 307 N. Third. Open 24 hours except Sundays and holidays.

Little Cottage Cafe, (701) 223-4949, 2513 E. Main. Homemade soups, pies, and pastries.

Paradiso, (701) 224-1111, 2620 State St. Mexican dining.

Peacock Alley Bar & Grill, (701) 255-7917, 422 E. Main St. Dining downtown in a historic setting.

Seasons Cafe, (701) 258-7700 ext. 1850, 800 S. Third St. (in the Radisson Inn Bismarck). Featuring regional American specialties.

WASHBURN, NORTH DAKOTA

Dakota Farms, (701) 462-8175, US 83 bypass. Wide menu with daily specials.

COLEHARBOR, NORTH DAKOTA

83 Cafe, (701) 442-3294, US 83.

GARRISON, NORTH DAKOTA

Lake Road Restaurant, (701) 463-2569, ND 37. Breakfast all day, sack lunches to go.

Stone Inn Supper Club & Lounge, (701) 337-5590, ND 37 E. Nightly specials, prime rib Fridays and Saturdays.

NEW TOWN, NORTH DAKOTA

Main Lanes & Café, (701) 627-4494, 204 Main St. Home-cooked meals.

Scenic 23 Supper Club & Lounge, (701) 627-9494, east of town on ND 23. Steakhouse.

WILLISTON, NORTH DAKOTA

Gramma Sharon's, US 2 and US 85. Open 24 hours at the Conoco Truck Stop.

Lund's Landing Restaurant, (701) 568-3474, 24 miles east on ND 1804. Pan-fried walleye and juneberry pie.

Trapper's Kettle, (701) 774-2831, north on US 2 and US 85. Informal American dining.

*SIDNEY, MONTANA

New China Restaurant, (406) 482-6188, 821 S. Central Ave.

South 40 Restaurant, (406) 482-4999, 207 2nd Ave. N.W. Wide menu including entrees, burgers, soup and salad bar.

*GLENDIVE, MONTANA

Twilite Dining & Lounge, (406) 365-8705, 209 N. Merrill. Prime rib, steak, chicken, and seafood.

*MILES CITY, MONTANA

Flying J Restaurant, (406) 232-4121, I-90 Baker Exit. Truck-stop eatery open 24 hours a day.

*FORSYTH, MONTANA

Blue Spruce Cafe, (406) 356-7955, 109 S. 10th Ave. Specializing in homegrown beef.

Speedway Diner, (406) 356-7987, 811 Main. Daily specials, homemade pies, salad bar.

*BILLINGS, MONTANA

The Cattle Company, (406) 656-9090, in the Rimrock Mall. Steaks, prime rib, seafood, salads.

Dos Machos, (406) 652-2020, 300 24th St. W. Mexican-American food.

George Henry's Restaurant, (406) 245-4570, 404 N. 30th St. Food made from scratch in early American atmosphere.

Jake's, (406) 259-9375, 2701 1st Ave. N. Steaks, ribs, seafood.

The Rex, (406) 245-7477, 2401 Montana Ave. Steaks, pasta, seafood.

*LAUREL, MONTANA

Little Big Men Pizza, (406) 628-8241, 220 First Ave S. Pizza and more.

*COLUMBUS, MONTANA

Apple Village Cafe, (406) 322-5939, I-90 Exit 408. Sunday brunch, salad bar.

*BIG TIMBER, MONTANA

Country Pride, (406) 932-4419, I-90 Exit 367. Family dining.

Prospector Pizza Plus, (406) 932-4846, 121 McLeod St. Pizza, sandwiches, salad, ribs.

*LIVINGSTON, MONTANA

Livingston Bar & Grille, (406) 222-7909, 130 N. Main. Montana trout, beef, and buffalo burgers.

Martin's Café, (406) 222-2110, 108 W. Park St. Locally popular home cooking.

*BOZEMAN, MONTANA

John Bozeman's Bistro, (406) 587-4100, 125 W. Main. Great American food, generous portions.

Spanish Peaks Brewery and Italian Cafe, (406) 585-2996, 120 N. 19th. Microbrewery/restaurant featuring brick-oven pizza, pasta, and seafood.

Western Cafe, (406) 587-0436, 443 E. Main. Down-home diner with famous cinnamon rolls.

CULBERTSON, MONTANA

M & M's Place, (406) 787-5362, 14 E. Sixth. Family restaurant.

Wild West Diner, (406) 787-5374, 20 E. Sixth.

WOLF POINT, MONTANA

Pat's Pizza and Family Restaurant, (406) 653-2577, US 2. Pizza, subs, and more.

Sherman Motor Inn, (406) 653-1100, 200 E. Main. Wide menu.

GLASGOW, MONTANA

Johnnie Cafe, (406) 228-4222, 433 First Ave. Open 24 hours.

Sam's Supper Club, (406) 228-4614, 307 First Ave. N. Here's the beef.

MALTA, MONTANA

Hitchin' Post, (406) 654-1882, US 2. Western home cooking.

Westside Restaurant, (406) 654-1555, US 2 W. Wide menu.

HAVRE, MONTANA

Andy's Supper Club and Lounge, (406) 265-9963, 658 1st St. W.

4B's Restaurant & Black Angus Supper Club, (406) 265-9721, 604 W. 1st St. Open 24 hours with wide menu.

Iron Horse Pancake House, (406) 265 7891, 335 1st St.

LEWISTOWN, MONTANA

Empire Café, (406) 538-9912, 214 W. Main St. Family dining. Open early for breakfast.

The Whole Famdamily, (406) 538-5161, 206 W. Main St. Homemade sandwiches, salads, soups.

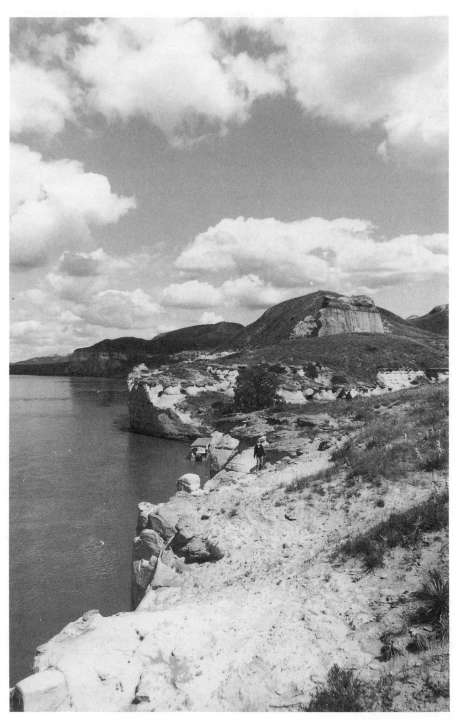

Upper Missouri National Wild and Scenic River.

CHAPTER SIX

CENTRAL MONTANA

The hills and river cliffs which we passed today exhibit a most romantic appearance . . . it seemed as if those scenes of visionary enchantment would never have an end.

—Meriwether Lewis, May 31, 1805,
on the Upper Missouri River.

UPPER MISSOURI NATIONAL WILD AND SCENIC RIVER

*T*he country around Montana's Upper Missouri National Wild and Scenic River looks like a blank spot on many maps, but it is far from barren. And with its slow pace and near total lack of modern intrusions, these Missouri Breaks—as the region is called—are an excellent place to get a feel for what the Lewis and Clark Expedition really saw and experienced on its journey.

Some travelers may even want to build their whole Lewis and Clark vacation around Central Montana, arguably the most important region along the trail. A paddle trip offers views of the river that are all but impossible to experience otherwise. A river trip is just about the only way to see the White Cliffs section, for example. Someone with a four-wheel-drive vehicle could drive down to a few isolated spots on the river but would be unable to get a broad picture of the terrain. A multi-day Upper Missouri river trip, preceded or followed by an exploration of the Great Falls area, would make memories for a lifetime. But even travelers who are trying to trace the entire route over two weeks will find a short river sojourn well worthwhile. After an overview of this area's history, we'll look at options for seeing it firsthand.

The Lewis and Clark Expedition had its share of excitement during its ascent of the Upper Missouri. May 14 was a particularly eventful day, starting with another bear encounter. Six men in the two rear dugout canoes spied a sleeping grizzly—an easy catch, they figured. But this bear proved a beast to kill. Shot first by four of the men, then by the two others, the wounds only enraged the animal, and he gave chase to the hunters. "In this manner he pursued two of them separately so close that they were obliged to throw aside their guns and pouches and throw themselves into the river," Lewis wrote. When the bear finally succumbed, "they then took him on shore and butchered him when they found eight balls had passed through him in different directions."

Later that day, the party experienced another near mishap with the boats. As with the incident in North Dakota, Charbonneau—surely one of the world's worst boatmen—was at the helm of the usually stable and steadfast white pirogue. "In this pirogue were embarked our papers, instruments, books, medicine, a great part of our merchandise and in short almost every article indispensably necessary to further the views, or insure the success of the enterprise in which we are now launched to the distance of 2,200 miles," Lewis wrote. "Suffice it to say, the pirogue was under sail when a sudden squall of wind struck her obliquely and turned her considerably. The steersman alarmed, instead of putting her before the wind lifted her up into it." Confused, Charbonneau wailed at his misfortune until Cruzatte threatened to "shoot him instantly if he did not take hold of the rudder and do his duty," Lewis recalled. "The waves by this time were running very high but the fortitude, resolution and good conduct of Cruzatte saved her. He ordered two of the men to throw out the water with some kettles that fortunately were convenient, while himself and two others rowed her ashore, where she arrived scarcely above the water." In the next day's journal installment, Lewis also gave credit to Sacagawea, who calmly sat in the back of the pirogue and caught most of the boat's light articles just before they washed overboard. Because of her actions, little of real value was lost.

On May 26, Lewis climbed the river bluffs, "which I found sufficiently fatiguing. On arriving to the summit (of) one of the highest points in the neighborhood I thought myself well repaid for my labor; as from this point I beheld the Rocky Mountains for the first time . . . These mountains were covered with snow, and the sun shone on it in such manner as to give me the most plain and satisfactory view. While I viewed these mountains, I felt a secret pleasure in finding myself so near the head of the heretofore conceived boundless Missouri, but when I reflected on the difficulties which this snowy barrier would most probably throw in my way to the Pacific and the sufferings and hardships of myself and party in them, it in some measure counterbalanced the joy I had felt in the first moments in which I gazed on them; but as I have always held it a crime to anticipate evils I will believe it a good comfortable road until I am compelled to believe differently."

Lewis's philosophizing makes for compelling reading 200 years later. Alas, the mountains he saw probably weren't the Rockies . . . he was still too far away. He had likely either spied the Bear Paw Mountains near Havre or the Big or Little Belt mountains south of Great Falls.

On May 28 Lewis and Clark camped near what is now known as Judith Landing, today a major access point to the Missouri River. Many boat trips take out here, and primitive camping is available. There's even a small store selling basic supplies—the only one on the Wild and Scenic stretch beyond the Virgelle

Exploring the rugged landscape of unusual rock formations above the Missouri River, Montana.

Mercantile. The Power Norris Bridge spans the river at Judith Landing, with Montana 236 leading north to Big Sandy and south to Lewistown.

Judith Landing takes its name from the river that runs into the Missouri at the site. At first, Lewis and Clark named it the Big Horn. The next day, however, Clark renamed it the Judith River for his girlfriend in Virginia. Actually, Clark didn't know the young woman all that well: her real name was Julia Hancock, and her friends called her Judy. Nevertheless, she must have been touched by his tribute, for they later were married.

Lewis and Clark had seen tens of thousands of buffalo by the time they reached this area, but the shaggy beasts were to play prominent roles in their journals over the next few days. On May 29, Lewis wrote, "Last night we were all alarmed by a large buffalo bull which swam over from the opposite shore. . . . (He) . . . ran up the bank in full speed directly toward the fires, and was within 18 inches of the heads of some of the men who lay sleeping." Lewis credited his dog, Seaman, with causing the buffalo to change course, and disaster was averted. Lewis noted the only serious damage done was to a rifle trampled by the buffalo. The gun had been left in the ill-fated white pirogue, and Lewis wrote "it appears that the white pirogue, which contains our most valuable stores, is attended by some evil genie."

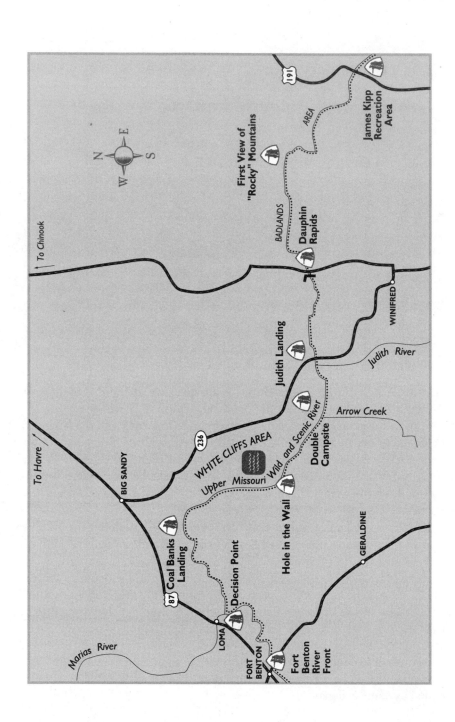

To Chinook

To Havre

Marias River

Judith River

Arrow Creek

BIG SANDY

WINIFRED

LOMA

GERALDINE

FORT BENTON

87

236

191

WHITE CLIFFS AREA

Upper Missouri Wild and Scenic River

BADLANDS

AREA

First View of "Rocky" Mountains

James Kipp Recreation Area

Dauphin Rapids

Judith Landing

Double River Campsite

Coal Banks Landing

Decision Point

Hole in the Wall

Fort Benton River Front

N W E S

Later that day, the explorers found huge mounds of rotting, stinking buffalo. They thought this was evidence of a buffalo jump, a ritual Lewis then described in detail in his journal, but no pishkun has ever been found in the immediate vicinity. Historians now believe the buffalo actually drowned and were washed up at the site on the river's backwater. Nevertheless, this river earned a most unromantic name: the Slaughter River.

Slaughter River is now known as Arrow Creek, an Indian name that actually predated the explorers' trip through the area. It got this moniker from a Blackfeet legend. A poor young man fell in love with a young woman, and they wanted to marry but were discouraged by the man's lack of property. Meanwhile, an evil warrior with many horses, lodges, and wives sought to add the young woman to his harem. Luckily, her father would not sell her to the rich warrior.

As the story goes, the young lovers took a walk up the creek. The evil warrior was waiting to ambush the unsuspecting pair when suddenly they heard a groan. When they investigated, the warrior had been shot with an arrow bearing feathers from a bird no one had ever seen and a projectile point unlike any other. The tribal elders figured the evil warrior must have been shot by the gods, thus paving the way for the young couple's marriage.

The Slaughter River/Arrow Creek campsite is the lone "double campsite" in Montana, that is, the only place the expedition camped on both its inbound and homeward journeys. The corps stayed here May 29, 1805, and the site was again visited by Lewis and his men on July 29, 1806.

On May 30–31, 1805, the explorers floated through an area now known as the White Cliffs of the Missouri. In one of the journals' most famous passages, Lewis wrote a lengthy description of these fantastic bluffs, noting how water had shaped the rich loam into "a thousand grotesque figures," pyramids, and "lofty freestone buildings . . . their parapets well stocked with statuary . . . so perfect indeed are those walls that I should have thought that nature had attempted here to rival the human art of masonry had I not recollected that she had first begun her work."

In a way, the Upper Missouri's "wild and scenic" designation may give people the wrong idea. The river is certainly scenic, but there are very few rapids. "Gentle and Scenic" would be a more apt description. This is a place where it's easy to kick back, daydream, read, ruminate, or do absolutely nothing at all. Modern floaters move downstream—not upstream as the Corps of Discovery did in 1805—making the Upper Missouri an easy paddle for even beginning canoeists and kayakers (see the accompanying do-it-yourself section). But travelers interested in a guided trip have ever-increasing options, with far more outfitters working this stretch of the Missouri than any other.

Among the newer companies on the Upper Missouri, River Odysseys West offers multi-day safari-style canoe expeditions. ROW uses 34-foot voyageur

Floating a section of the Wild and Scenic Upper Missouri in Montana.

canoes, similar in size to the pirogues used by Lewis and Clark. Several trips each year are accompanied by interpreters well-versed in Lewis and Clark lore, fur trade tales, and stories of the Nez Perce, who crossed the Missouri at Cow Island on their 1877 flight from the U.S. Army. But even when experts aren't present, ROW's guides pack along an extensive library that helps passengers learn as much as they like about the river's past and present.

ROW trip participants meet in Great Falls to tour the new Lewis and Clark National Historic Trail Interpretive Center. From there, a bus takes travelers to Fort Benton for lunch and a walk along the riverfront levee, then to the put-in at Coal Banks Landing. After an easy first half-day of paddling, participants arrive at camp, their tents already set up (one for every two people; singles get their own). There's time for a nap, a swim, or a hike before the first of many hearty meals. ROW serves up several choices—including a vegetarian entrée—at each dinner. Steak, shrimp, fajitas, pesto tortellini, catfish, chicken and dutch-oven lasagna were among the main courses on one recent trip. Creative breakfast fare is the rule, too; champagne or sparkling cider mimosas might accompany the final day's repast of eggs Benedict, asparagus, and sausage. Trips break for a simpler but tasty deli lunch each afternoon, and snacks and beverages (including kid-friendly fare) are abundantly available throughout the day. Travelers do have to work a bit for all this: all able-bodied participants are expected to help paddle, and everyone must take down his or her tent each morning. But ROW has luxury camping down pat, from the sleeping bags and sleeping pads provided for each participant to a portable, sheltered toilet and sun showers.

ROW offers mostly five-day trips on the Missouri, but it has a few three-day trips, too. On the second day of either itinerary, paddlers pass through the river's storied White Cliffs section, so romantically described by Meriwether Lewis. Optional shore hikes feature trips to such landmarks as the Hole in the Wall or explorations of abandoned homesteads in the bottomland. The five-day trip moves beyond Judith Landing into the Badlands area, taking out at Stafford Ferry. Along the way, ROW guides also keep a sharp eye out for river wildlife including bald eagles, great blue heron, beaver, and the occasional bighorn sheep.

For 2000, ROW's three-day Missouri River expeditions cost $675; the five-day version costs $1,065. Special prices are available for youth and children. Trips leave mid-June through mid-September. For more information, call ROW at (800) 451-6034, see the company's website at www.rowinc.com, or send e-mail to rowinc@aol.com.

Among other companies, Fort Benton–based Missouri River Outfitters ranks among the most experienced and best-known guides on the Upper Missouri, written about by such authors as Stephen Ambrose and Dayton Duncan. Larry and Bonnie Cook offer four- to seven-day outfitted canoe trips and canoe rentals for do-it-yourselfers. But they are probably best known for three- to five-day excursions on motorized, weatherized pontoon boats—the only craft of their kind on the Upper Missouri. The three-day trip takes out at Judith Landing, while the four- and five-day versions go all the way to James Kipp Recreation Area.

Both Cooks are Fort Benton–area natives and former teachers with a genuine love for the river, eager to share their wealth of stories of the Missouri's natural and human history. They wear traditional river clothing, and their boat flies a 15-star flag, the same style in use during the Lewis and Clark expedition.

The motorized trips travel downriver about 8 miles an hour. On board, passengers can browse books depicting sketches and paintings by Swiss artist Karl Bodmer, who traveled through the area with Prince Maximilian of Germany in 1833. It's remarkable to see how little the country has changed. Evening campfires often feature readings from the Lewis and Clark journals, along with lively discussions of expedition lore.

Most sights are on the river, but the Cooks also allow time for exploration along the banks. A hillside behind one favorite campsite still bears signs of Indian tepee rings and burial grounds. The trips are mostly outfitted; participants are asked to bring only a sleeping bag, clothing, and personal effects. The motorized trips easily accommodate people of all ages, and the Cooks try to vary each cruise's activities to suit the participants' interests and physical abilities. The food isn't necessarily gourmet, but it is good and plentiful. Breakfasts typically include such

Looking at tepee rings on the Missouri River Breaks, Montana.

fare as pancakes and sausage one morning, French toast and scrambled eggs the next. Dinner might be steak, corn, and muffins or pork chops and salad.

People interested in a river cruise should contact the Cooks in the fall of the year before they'd like to go; they start booking the trips in November, and they're often full within days. At least 10 people are needed for the motorized trips, although the Cooks can sometimes accommodate smaller groups on previously arranged cruises. Cost for 2000 is $200 per person per day with a three-day minimum. Prices are similar for the guided canoe trips. For more information, write Missouri River Outfitters, P.O. Box 762, Fort Benton, Montana 59442, or call (406) 622-3295. Their website is at www.mroutfitters.com.

Many of the outfitters floating the Missouri have headquarters elsewhere, but Canoe Montana/Montana River Expeditions has its office right on Fort Benton's Front Street. Owner Russell Young describes his offerings as "quiet adventures for discriminating explorers." Canoe Montana's adventures include sunset floats for $50, half-day trips from $60, and extended trips from $620. The company uses touring kayaks and canoes; it may also offer voyageur canoe trips in 2000 or beyond. Young is an outstanding photographer who takes photos of his guests on the river at no extra charge. Trips feature good food including many international cuisines. For more information, write Canoe Montana/ Montana River Expeditions (Russell Young), 1321 Front Street, P.O. Box 591, Fort Benton, Montana 59442; call (800) 500-4538; or see www.montanariver.com.

WILD AND SCENIC RIVER TRIPS

Interest in the Lewis and Clark Expedition has brought an explosion of activity to the Wild and Scenic Upper Missouri River. The Bureau of Land Management maintains a list of river permittees, and the roster may change from year to year. For a copy of the latest list, contact the BLM Lewistown District Office, Airport Road, Lewistown, Montana 59457. (The BLM is also a good source of information for do-it-yourself floaters; see the accompanying section for more details on rentals and shuttle service.) The following is a list of outfitters who were regularly guiding trips or renting gear on the Upper Missouri as of summer 1999:

- 3 Rivers Canoe Company (Bud Heidelbaugh), P.O. Box 125, Loma, Montana 59460, (406) 739-4220, www.3riverscanoes.com. Trips and rentals.

- Canoe Montana/Montana River Expeditions (see text). Trips and rentals.

- Glacier Sea Kayaking (Bobbie Gillmore), 390 Tally Lake Road, Whitefish, Montana 59937, (406) 862-9010, www.montanaweb.com/seakayak, seakayak@digisys.net. Trips.

- Hole in the Wall Adventures (Terry Selph), 731 West 4th St., Hardin, Montana 59034, (406) 665-3779. Trips.

- Lewis and Clark Canoe Expeditions (Jim Cummings), P.O. Box 728, Fort Benton, Montana 59442, (888) 595-9151, www.lewisandclarkguide.com, jcummings@montana.net. Trips and rentals.

- Lewis and Clark Trail Adventures (Wayne Fairchild), P.O. Box 9051, Missoula, Montana 59801, (406) 728-7609. Trips.

- M&M River Expeditions (Mike Nottingham), P.O. Box 201, Loma, Montana 59460, (800) 721-2133, www.classics.nu/mmre. Trips and rentals.

- Missouri Breaks River Company (Bill Marsik), 2409 4th Ave. N., Great Falls, Montana 59401, (406) 453-3035, www.missouribreaksriverco.com. As of 1999, the only outfitter leading jet-boat trips on the Missouri. Trips go at no-wake speeds on the Wild and Scenic portion from mile 51.5 to James Kipp Recreation Area.

- Missouri River Canoe Company (see text). Trips and rentals.

- Missouri River Outfitters (see text). Trips and rentals.

- Montana River Outfitters (Craig Madsen), 1401 Fifth Avenue South, Great Falls, Mpntana 59405, (406) 761-1677, craigm@montana.com. Trips and rentals.

- River Odysseys West (ROW Inc.) (see text). Trips.

- Starwest Adventures (Sid Napier), P.O. Box 227, Lewistown, Montana 59457, (877) 538-8670, www.tein.net/starwest, starwest@tein.net. Trips and rentals.

- Upper Missouri River Guides (Glenn Monahan), 315 West Fourth Street, Anaconda, Montana 59711, (406) 563-2770, www.uppermissouri.com. Trips and rentals.

- Wild Rockies Field Institute, P.O. Box 7071, Missoula, Montana 59807, (406) 549-4336, www.wildrockies.org/WRFI. Trips.▲

The Missouri River Canoe Company is another outfit deserving special mention. Don Sorensen and Jim Griffin operate out of Virgelle, just a mile upriver from Coal Banks Landing, the most popular put-in. They do everything from guided expeditions to canoe rentals to shuttle service, plus they offer rustic accommodations in cabins or an old-fashioned bed-and-breakfast. The company also has a "Paddles to Saddles" trip pairing a canoe journey with horseback riding along the Breaks. For more information, call (800) 426-2926 or (406) 378-3110, or see the website at www.canoemontana.com.

In addition to the water-based outfitters noted above, a few local entrepreneurs are offering trips along the river's banks and into the breaks backcountry. Gary Darlington's Missouri River Breaks Tours specialize in guided four-wheel-drive excursions across his land, which includes 9 miles of riverfront in the Eagle Creek area, where the corps camped May 31, 1805—the day they floated through the White Cliffs. Darlington's family has been in the area since the early twentieth century, and he takes visitors to many spectacular sights—including petroglyphs and rock formations—that cannot be seen from the river.

Darlington's land is accessed via a 20-mile gravel and dirt road drive from Big Sandy, or he can come to pick you up in Big Sandy if you choose. His tours run two to eight hours. Cost is a minimum of $80 for one person for two hours, with a second person half-price and a third person an extra $10 per hour. For a full-day tour, plan on $200 for the first person, $100 for the second, and $80 for the third. Lunch and snacks are included. Darlington may add cabins and back-

Floating the Wild and Scenic Upper Missouri.

Learning by immersion in the Wild and Scenic Upper Missouri, Montana.

packing access to his land in the future. For more information, write Missouri River Breaks Tours, HC 77-Box 811, Big Sandy, Montana 59520; call (406) 386-2486; or see it on the web at www.big-sandy.com/mrbtours/.

Meanwhile, Darlington's neighbor, Glenn Terry, has established Pilot Rock Trail Rides on the land his wife's family has worked since 1898. From horseback, visitors see some of the prettiest sections of the White Cliffs. Terry can take as many as eight people out for $20 per person per hour. Rides can range from a few hours to all day, but there's a four-hour minimum for groups of three or fewer. Terry also has a camp complete with a tepee that sleeps six to eight people. It rents for $50 a night. Many people float in for a horseback ride or overnight stay, but you can also drive in 18 miles from Big Sandy. For more information, contact Glenn Terry, P.O. Box 392, Big Sandy, Montana 59520 or call (406) 386-2455. It's best to give either Darlington or Terry at least a few days' advance notice for tours.

THE MARIAS RIVER AND FORT BENTON

When they reached what is now Loma, Montana, on June 2, 1805, the expedition saw a formidable river, one they'd had no warning of. "An interesting question was now to be determined," Lewis wrote the next day, "which of these rivers was the Missouri...what astonishes us a little is that the Indians who

FLOATING THE BREAKS ON YOUR OWN

During the 1999 season, about 5,200 people paddled the Upper Missouri—nearly double the number who made the trip in 1994. Most of the growth has been on guided trips, but plenty of people still paddle the Missouri on their own, either with their personal watercraft or with rentals from an outfitter.

The Upper Missouri is a gentle river, with no sizable rapids. It's an easy trip for even the most novice canoeist or kayaker. But it's a wild place, far from civilization, and paddlers must take care to prepare for their trip. Here are some pointers:

Get good local information: Start by obtaining the detailed, mile-by-mile river maps available from the Bureau of Land Management. They're published on two waterproof sheets. One includes maps 1 and 2, covering the river from Fort Benton to Slaughter River. The other, with maps 3 and 4, details Slaughter River to the final take-out at James Kipp Recreation Area. Maps may be purchased at the BLM's Upper Missouri Wild & Scenic Visitor Center at 1718 Front Street in Fort Benton or at any of the staffed river sites (see below). Or you can order them by mail (at $8 for the set) by sending a check payable to the BLM to the BLM Lewistown District Office, Airport Road, Lewistown, Montana 59457.

The BLM, which manages the river, has summer staff stationed at Fort Benton, Coal Banks Landing (the major put-in), Judith Landing (roughly the midway point), and James Kipp Recreation Area (terminus of the designated Wild and Scenic River). Check with them for information on current river conditions. The center in Fort Benton serves as a point of contact in the event of family emergencies. The number is (406) 622-5185. Although it's not mandatory, boaters are asked to register before any trip so BLM river rangers can find them if necessary. You can register at Fort Benton or any of the put-ins.

For detailed interpretive information, consider buying *Montana's Wild and Scenic Upper Missouri River*, an excellent mile-by-mile resource from Northern Rocky Mountains Books. It's available at many Montana bookstores or interpretive centers, or you can order it by sending a check for $13.95 plus $3.20 postage to the BLM Lewistown District Office, Airport Road, Lewistown, MT 59457. When ordering this book through the BLM, make checks payable to the Northwest Interpretive Association.

Be prepared: Aside from being another good information spot, Canoe Montana, 1312 Front Street in Fort Benton, is the best place to stock up on last-minute specialized gear for canoeing, kayaking, and wilderness camping. Coast-to-Coast Hardware at 1420 Front Street can help with more basic needs like coolers and flashlights.

Bring what you need, because—except for the small store at Judith Landing, usually open daily from 8 A.M. to 7 P.M., May to September—there are no services available along the way. Pay particular attention to drinking water (see below), sun protection, and insect repellent. (The bugs tend to get worse toward the lower end of the Upper Missouri, where the river slackens near Fort Peck Reservoir.)

Although weather during the prime Upper Missouri float trip season is usually quite good—hot and sunny during the day, comfortably cool in the evening—storms with heavy rain and hail sometimes occur. Bring good rain gear. Some people even advise taking along a helmet in case of hail! Even in fair weather, you'll encounter plenty of mud along the river banks, so bring proper footgear—river sandals or old tennis shoes are good for the boats, while a pair of lightweight hiking boots are best for camp time. (You'll see plenty of prickly pear cactus and perhaps a rattlesnake or two along the Missouri's banks.)

Watch where (and how) you camp: Camping conditions along the river are primitive and serene. There are several marked sites along the route; others have just evolved from word-of-mouth use. Little Sandy, Eagle Creek, Hole-in-the-Wall, Dark Butte, Slaughter River, Judith Landing, Stafford Ferry, and Lower Woodhawk are among the most popular and heavily used sites.

The BLM has erected shelters at Hole-in-the-Wall and Slaughter River. The three-sided log structures are basically just places for canoeists to get out of bad weather. They can sleep up to about a dozen people, if necessary.

As the Upper Missouri's popularity grows, it's becoming ever more important to tread lightly on this historic land. Take care to use established sites and fire rings, or use a fire pan. There is no garbage service along the route, so a pack-it-out policy is in effect. Check out the guidelines in the "How to Use This Book" chapter for more information on minimum-impact camping.

Nearly two-thirds of the land along the river is privately owned, and some landowners have posted no trespassing signs. But it's best to avoid even the land that isn't posted and to make camp on public land. Private land is designated on the official river maps.

Watch what you drink: Although water is available at several BLM sites along the river, it's not always safe to drink. And out here, you need plenty of drinking water—a gallon per person per day is a good guideline. The BLM recommends that floaters haul their own drinking water. If you rely on the river water sources, be sure to filter, boil, or chemically treat it before use.

The Judith Landing General Store at river mile 88 (from Fort Benton) is a good place to replenish your drinking-water supply, and they generally have plenty available for small canoe parties. But if you're traveling in a group of 10 or more, it's best to call ahead to reserve what you need. The number is (406) 386-2202.

For more information on floating the Upper Missouri, the BLM recommends you read a copy of its *Hazards and Highlights* brochures.▲

appeared to be so well acquainted with the geography of this country should not have mentioned this river on (the) right hand if it be not the Missouri." A small interpretive area off US 87 just south of town gives a commanding view of what's now called Decision Point.

From this hillside, it's easy to see why the explorers may have been confused, especially in late spring when both rivers were swollen with runoff. The north fork was whitish brown, very thick and turbid, looking much like the Missouri, while the south fork was transparent. But after exploring the north branch, Lewis was convinced it flowed in too much of a northern direction to be the right path to the Pacific. Further, he reasoned, if the river penetrated the mountains, it would be clearer.

Lewis had an experience here not unlike his adventure at the Tavern Cave way back in Missouri. On June 7, while exploring bluffs in the area, "I slipped at a narrow pass of about 30 yards in length and but for a quick and fortunate recovery by my espontoon I should have been precipitated into the river down a craggy precipice of about 90 feet." No sooner had Lewis regained his balance than he heard a voice crying for help. It was Private Richard Windsor, who—having slipped and fallen on the same narrow pass that tripped up Lewis—was hanging on for dear life. Lewis slowly talked Windsor down from the cliff, instructing him "to take the knife out of his belt behind him with his right hand and dig a hole with it in the face of the bank to receive his right foot, which he did, and then raise himself to his knees." That night, the captain was exhausted but happy to be alive. After a hearty meal of venison, "I now laid myself down on some willow boughs to a comfortable night's rest, and felt indeed as if I was fully repaid for the toil and pain of the day...."

The party spent nine days at this confluence, trying to figure out which way to go. Both leaders were convinced the south fork was the Missouri, but the rest of the men—including Pierre Cruzatte, probably the expedition's most experienced boatman—wanted to follow the northern fork. On June 11, 1805, Lewis and four others left to seek the Great Falls of the Missouri down the south fork. If they found the falls, they would know they were on the right path. The expedition's continued survival and success rested on making the correct choice. In the meantime, on June 8, Lewis took his turn at flattering womanhood, naming the mystery stream Marias River, in honor of his cousin, Maria Wood. "It is true that the hue of the waters of this turbulent and troubled stream but illy comport with the pure celestial virtues and amiable qualifications of that lovely fair one," he wrote. "But on the other hand it is a noble river; one destined to become in my opinion an object of contention between the two great powers of American and Great Britain with respect to the adjustment of the Northwesterly boundary of the former."

There were once plans for a town named Ophir at the mouth of the Marias. It was 22 miles downriver from Fort Benton, and planners felt that—in low

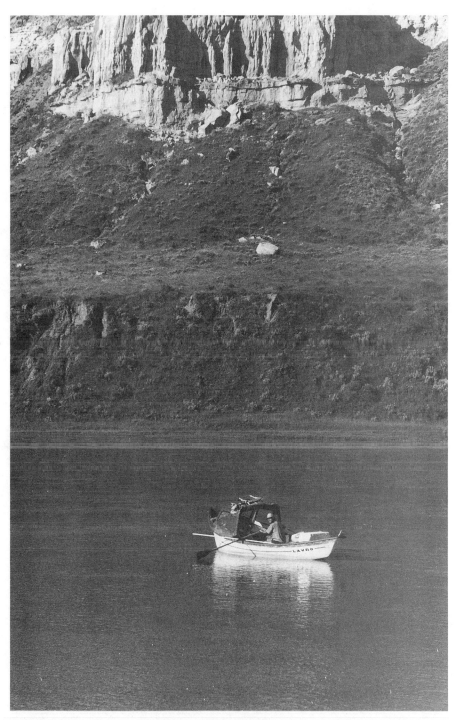

A drift boat on a section of the Wild and Scenic Upper Missouri, Montana.

water—if steamboats couldn't reach Fort Benton, they could possibly reach Ophir. There was also plentiful timber for building. Moreover, the town was the idea of men with high connections in Montana's territorial government. Ophir seemed destined for success.

Stock in the company was issued on March 24, 1864, and a charter was obtained 11 months later. All went well for a while: a field manager was hired to build the town, a sawmill was established, and 400 lots were laid out. But in May 1865, something went awry. One story goes that nine Blood Indians were killed on the streets of Fort Benton, and their bodies thrown into the river. The second story held that during the winter, Charlie Carson, cousin of Kit Carson, was trapping along the Missouri with two buddies when three Bloods stole their horses. Carson and his party pursued the Indians, caught and shot them, and regained their horses. Whatever really happened, a war party of 180 Indians was traveling to Fort Benton for vengeance when they encountered woodcutters building the town of Ophir. Ten whites were killed, and dreams of the town died with them. Nothing remains of the townsite; a few log cabins left over after the massacre eventually were used to feed the fires in steamboat boilers. Loma, however, has a smattering of visitor services and a museum specializing in geology.

Fort Benton has many claims to historical fame, but perhaps none so mighty as its reign during the steamboat era, when as many as 10 steamboats a day tied up at its waterfront. In its heyday, Fort Benton also boasted what was known as "the wildest block in the West," jam-packed with bars, dance halls, and brothels.

The upriver trip from St. Louis usually took 60 to 65 days. Passenger fare averaged $150. During the busy year of 1867, about 1,500 people traveled to Montana on the steamboats. The river route was faster and safer than overland routes, which frequently were closed down by Indians. The riverboats were also important to trade and shipping. The all-time peak of river traffic was in 1879, when 47 boats carried 9,444 tons of cargo up the river, but railroads started cutting into the riverboat shipping during the 1880s.

Fort Bentonites are proud their town is home to "Explorers at the Marias," the official Montana Lewis and Clark Monument. The riverfront statue was created by Bob Scriver to mark the U.S. Bicentennial in 1976. It depicts Sacagawea and her baby Jean Baptiste in addition to the captains. Scriver spent a year researching the expedition before starting his work on the statue, trying to ensure the accuracy of the equipment, clothing, body features, and faces. For example, the square compass in Clark's hand was modeled from the actual one he used, and Sacagawea is carrying her baby in a blanket because the packboard he rode in earlier was lost overboard a few days before the party's arrival at the mouth of the Marias River.

The finished product is of heroic proportions: one-sixth larger than life-size. The statue weighs 2.5 tons, is 21 feet high, and sits on an 85-ton granite base given as a gift from Tanner Brothers Quarry near Square Butte, Montana.

Statue of Lewis, Clark, Sacagawea, and Pomp at Fort Benton, Montana.

After its casting at the Modern Art Foundry in New York City, the statue was transported cross-country to Montana upright on the bed of a semitrailer, causing many a head to turn.

A four-block walking tour along Fort Benton's levee offers a good look at the town's history. Aside from the Lewis and Clark statue, you'll see a monument to the Whoop-Up Trail, a route to western Canada popular before the railroads; a replica of the *Mandan* keelboat, built for the film *The Big Sky*; the remains of the *Baby Rose* steamboat, mired in the Missouri mud below the Lewis and Clark statue; and a monument to the Mullan Road, another famous western route that traveled from Fort Benton to Walla Walla, Washington.

There's also a monument commemorating "Shep." This sheepherder's dog, made famous in "Ripley's Believe It Or Not," met every train into Fort Benton for five years after his master's body was taken away by rail. Eventually, Shep was run over by a train, and he was buried on a hillside overlooking the rail depot.

The riverfront tour ends at the Grand Union Hotel, once considered the finest between Minneapolis and Seattle. Long vacant, the hotel finally reopened in late 1999 after extensive remodeling by Montana natives Jim and Cheryl Gagnon. It now features 27 guest rooms and public areas done up in elegantly rustic style, with both Western and Victorian touches.

Fort Benton has more than its share of museums. The BLM visitor center at 1718 Front Street has exhibits including an oil painting by Todd Asay of the Eye of the Needle, the Missouri Breaks landmark that was damaged by vandalism in 1997. The visitor center is open from 8 A.M. to 6 P.M. daily, Memorial Day through Labor Day weekends. Admission is free.

Also on Front Street near the boat ramp, the Museum of the Upper Missouri features a wide range of artifacts from the area's past, notably the .44-caliber Winchester rifle Chief Joseph was said to be carrying when he surrendered to the U.S. Army in 1877, ending the Nez Perce War. The museum sits on the same site as old Fort Benton, which is now being reconstructed. Admission to the Museum of the Upper Missouri also includes entrance to the Museum of the Northern Great Plains. This facility focuses on the area's agricultural history, but it also is home to five splendid murals by noted Montana painter Robert Morgan. One, titled "Fortunate Meeting," depicts Lewis, Drouillard, and the Fields brothers arriving back on the Missouri River after their July 1806 encounter with Blackfeet Indians on the Two Medicine River.

The Museum of the Northern Great Plains also displays the Hornaday Buffalo. In 1886, when bison had nearly become extinct, taxidermist William Hornaday claimed this big bull—nearly 6 feet tall and more than 10 feet long—to show future generations what the great beasts looked like. It was displayed at the Smithsonian Institution in Washington, D.C., from 1887 through 1957, and it also served as a model for the buffalo nickel. It's seen here just as it was at the Smithsonian, with several other buffalo mounts. The Museums of the

Upper Missouri and the Northern Great Plains are open daily from 10 A.M. to 5 P.M. mid-May through September. Admission to both is $4 for adults and $1 for children.

Fort Benton has several motels, a bed-and-breakfast, and about half a dozen restaurants. For more information on Fort Benton, call (406) 622-3864. From here, it's an easy 35-mile drive to Great Falls.

HOMEWARD BOUND: CAMP DISAPPOINTMENT, THE TWO MEDICINE FIGHT SITE

As noted earlier, the Marias River had captivated and perplexed the explorers during the 1805 trip through Montana. On his way home in 1806, Lewis was eager to explore the river's upper reaches. His side trip into the area produced some of the most disappointing and dramatic passages of the entire expedition.

Lewis's main purpose in tracing the Marias River was to see if the river reached far enough north to satisfy the northern boundary agreement of the 1783 Paris Treaty between the United States and Great Britain, which ended the American Revolution. This treaty said a line drawn from the northwesternmost point of the Lake of the Woods to the Mississippi River would determine the northwestern boundary of the Northwestern Territory. It was later learned the Mississippi did not reach far enough north to satisfy that article of the treaty, so after the Louisiana Purchase, one of the purposes of the Lewis and Clark expedition was to find a tributary that would fulfill the treaty's requirements. Lewis found the Marias River didn't reach far enough north, either, and that's how he came to name Camp Disappointment.

The Camp Disappointment–Two Medicine region is still quite wild, and the major historic sites here, though marked, are not easy to find. Access is seasonal and dependent on farming operations and weather conditions. Moreover, the sites are on private land; permission must be obtained, and a four-wheel-drive vehicle is necessary to make the final approaches. For the latest information on access to both sites, visitors can stop by the Cut Bank Area Chamber of Commerce on US 2 or call (406) 873-4041. Guided tours to the Lewis and Clark route occasionally include access to the sites. If you're investigating a group tour, ask if Camp Disappointment and the Two Medicine Fight Site are on the itinerary.

Camp Disappointment was the farthest campsite north used by the expedition, although not the northernmost point reached by Lewis's party: they actually traveled about 2 miles farther north on their way to this site. The turnoff is located on US 2 just under 20 miles west of Cut Bank, Montana (and 15 miles east of Browning). Turn north just before reaching the Meriwether grain elevators and drive 3.2 miles north on Montana 444, also known as Meriwether

Participants of a Lewis and Clark Festival field trip at the Two Medicine Fight Site.

Road. Then turn left, or west, at a fence line just south of Willow Creek (which is in turn just south of the Cut Bank River). Camp Disappointment is located along a bend in the river a little more than 3 miles (by farm roads) northwest of the turnoff. A plaque marks the site.

Here, Lewis could see that the Cut Bank River was flowing directly from the mountains to the west, meaning—once again—the river did not meander far enough north to help America's claim. The site further earned its name because of the poor weather Lewis and his men experienced here. Beset by rain and clouds, Lewis was unable to complete the celestial observations he hoped would help pinpoint the camp's location.

Back on U.S. 2 a short distance west, there's a monument to the Lewis and Clark Expedition's farthest progress north, but it is badly defaced. Continue west to Browning, the center of the Blackfeet Indian Reservation and a gateway to Glacier National Park. (See more information below.) From Browning, head back toward Great Falls on U.S, Highway 89. About 10 miles to the southeast, the road crosses the Two Medicine River. Near here, the Lewis and Clark Expedition had its only armed—and fatal—encounter with Indians.

The Two Medicine Fight Site is even more difficult to find than Camp Disappointment, and a four-wheel-drive vehicle is recommended for the last approach. Near the Two Medicine River on US 89, look for a brown metal shed marked "Three Rivers Telephone Co-op" on the north side of the road. Turn north here. The road soon parallels a mile long pishkun (a buffalo jump) and the remnants of the Holy Family Mission, started in 1888 by the Jesuits. The mission was run by the Jesuits and Ursuline nuns until 1939. In the mid-1960s, 35 people were killed and the mission grounds inundated when spring floods swept through this area. Most of the bodies were never recovered. The facility no longer operates as a mission, but Catholic services are still held weekly.

This area also is the final resting place of James Willard Schultz. Born in Boonville, New York, in 1859, Schultz moved to Montana at age 17. He worked at Joe Kipp's trading post near what is now Conrad and married a Piegan woman. By living with the Blackfeet, Schultz had a ringside seat to the vanishing West— experiences and impressions he recorded in some three dozen books, including *My Life as an Indian*. Schultz died in 1947 and was buried near the irrigation canal beneath the buffalo jump.

The road eventually turns to gravel, then dead-ends at the paved Valier Road (Montana 358). Turn right here and drive south. The road crosses the Two Medicine River again. Another 1.8 miles south, turn right again onto another gravel road at the Stoltz Ranch. This road leads west past three irrigation ditches to a fork about 2.4 miles from the ranch turnoff. After proceeding through (and closing) the gate, bear left to the faint path leading up the ridge. Four-wheel-drive is advised for this ascent.

View of Camp Disappointment area near Cut Bank, Montana.

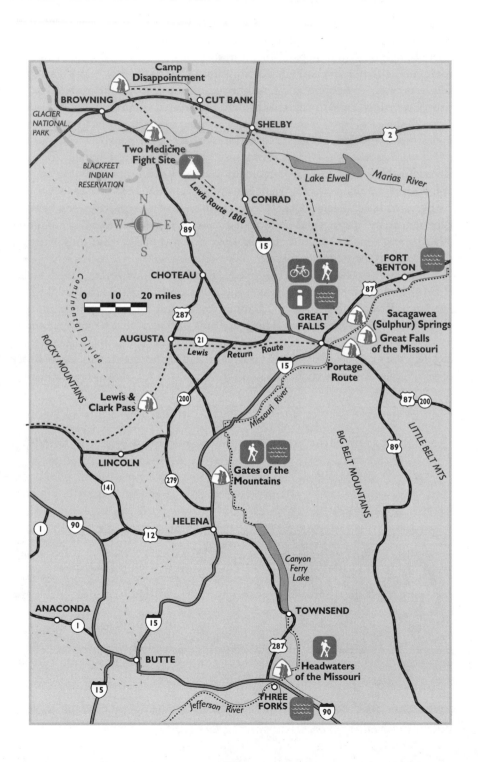

Once up on the ridge, look for a small rock cairn on the north side of the road. The rocks form an arrow that points directly to the Two Medicine Fight Site. (Look for the telltale clump of trees and a fence erected by area Boy Scouts.) Even if you cannot locate the cairn, the ridge affords an amazing 360-degree view of this wild, forlorn area and the badlands where dinosaurs once roamed.

The high ridge trail proceeds on past a group of tepee rings and another junction. The right fork is extremely rugged and descends into the badlands and a buffalo jump area; the left loops back to the gate. It's possible to hike to the fight site from the right fork; the site may also be approached by returning to the gate, then driving in a north-northwest direction toward the badlands, parking before the land drops off to the river, and walking the rest of the way.

Historians believe the fight occurred here based on descriptions in Lewis's journals. The hardy narrowleaf cottonwood tree within the fenced area may well be the very one on the site in 1806—or if not the tree, one of its descendants. (Several other cottonwoods mentioned fell to fire about 1980.)

Cuttings from the historic cottonwoods here have found their way to other sites around the country, including the Montana State Capitol grounds in Helena.

The site bears a historical plaque mentioning that Lewis and his party camped here July 26, 1806, with eight Blackfeet Indians with whom they'd nervously counciled that evening. They went to bed late and Lewis took the first guard, relieved later by Reuben Field, and then by Joseph Field. Carelessly, Joseph Field laid down his gun next to his brother's and fell asleep.

At daybreak, the Indians awoke first and, seeing the white men's guns unguarded, quickly made a plan of attack. Joseph Field woke up just in time to see an Indian seize the unattended guns. He hollered for his brother, and together they chased after the Blackfeet, "whom they overtook at the distance of 50 or 60 paces from the camp, seized their guns and wrested them from him, and Reuben Field as he seized his gun stabbed the Indian to the heart with his knife," Lewis wrote. "The fellow ran about 15 steps and fell dead." This was hearsay to Lewis, who was still asleep as the incident began.

In the meantime, Drouillard, too, was locked in a struggle for his gun. This finally awakened Lewis, who realized his own rifle was missing. Lewis reached for his pistol and chased after the Indian who had taken his gun, shouting for the brave to drop the weapon. Sensing failure, the Indian complied.

By this point, the expedition's horses and those of the Blackfeet were galloping away from the scene in two bunches. Drouillard and the Fields brothers chased one group, while Lewis followed the two Blackfeet pursuing the second—straight into a box canyon. Here, one of the Blackfeet jumped behind a pile of rocks; the other turned and took aim at Lewis, who was just 30 steps away. Lewis managed to fire first, striking the Blackfoot in the belly, but the Indian got off a shot, too. "Being bareheaded I felt the wind of his bullet very

GLACIER NATIONAL PARK

Meriwether Lewis didn't get to what is now Glacier National Park on his 1806 return trip, but modern travelers may find the park an irresistible detour from their historic travels. Glacier is justly famous for its high-mountain scenery, abundant wildlife, and wide variety of recreation.

From Browning, US 2 skims the park's south edge, while US 89 leads north to the Going-to-the-Sun Road and the heart of Glacier. If you have time for only a day in Glacier National Park, it is perhaps best spent driving at least part of this amazing 50-mile road, deservedly one of the world's most famous. Note, however, that Going-to-the-Sun Road is only open from mid-June to mid-October, and certain vehicle length and width restrictions apply.

Glacier is known as a hikers' park, with more than 700 miles of trails ready for exploration. Some of the most beloved include the Alpine Meadow Walk, which jumps off from Logan Pass on Going-to-the-Sun Road, and Avalanche Lake Trail, an easy path featuring scenic waterfalls. Other activities include backpacking, horseback riding, white-water rafting, open-air bus tours, fishing (get a free park permit), and bird watching.

Glacier visitors can choose from a wide range of accommodations, ranging from designated and backcountry campgrounds to European-inspired lodging at Many Glacier Hotel. For more information on Glacier National Park, call (406) 888-5441 or visit the park's website at http://www.nps.gov/glac/.▲

distinctly," Lewis later wrote. Knowing another Indian was hiding among the rocks, and that the others were still in the area, perhaps with reinforcements on the way, Lewis decided to give up his pursuit of the horses.

The party reclaimed enough of its own mounts—plus four owned by the Blackfeet—and beat a hasty retreat from the Two Medicine River. From there, they rode 120 miles in little more than 24 hours, stopping only to eat, catch catnaps, and let the horses graze. Amazingly, they arrived at the Missouri River just in time to find the parties led by Sergeant Gass, who had supervised the rest of the Lewis group around the Great Falls portage, and Sergeant Ordway, leading the group Clark sent down the Missouri from Three Forks.

The entire Lewis contingent, thus reunited, traveled down the Missouri, reaching the Yellowstone confluence within nine days of the Clark attachment—good progress, considering the adventure they'd had.

The Two Medicine Fight could have been a disaster for the expedition. Had Lewis and his men been killed, the journals and his accumulated knowledge of the exploration would have been lost forever. The deaths on the Two Medicine were the only casualties the Lewis and Clark expedition inflicted on the West's native peoples during the corps' 2.5-year journey. While it is sad anyone had to die, it is surely to the captains' credit that nearly all the Indian encounters resulted in friendship and cooperation, not animosity and violence.

Return to the Valier Road and drive south. From Valier, it is 15 miles east to Interstate 15 and about 70 miles to Great Falls.

GREAT FALLS

Lewis and Clark spent 32 days in the Great Falls area, more than any other place aside from their winter camps. At Great Falls, the explorers expected to encounter one cascade and a portage of no more than a half-mile, easily accomplished in a day. Instead, the corps found five formidable falls and wound up taking nearly two weeks to cover the distance they'd normally travel by water in a single day. The falls, in the order they were reached going up river, were the Great Falls, highest of the series at 89 feet; Horseshoe or Crooked Falls; Rainbow or Handsome Falls; Colter Falls, no longer visible, about a half-mile upriver from Rainbow Falls; and Black Eagle Falls, second highest with a drop of some 50 feet.

Because of the amount of time the Corps of Discovery spent here, Great Falls has evolved into a major center for modern Lewis and Clark buffs. Here you'll find the new Lewis and Clark National Historic Trail Interpretive Center on the bluffs of the Missouri River. Great Falls also is home to the Lewis and Clark Trail Heritage Foundation, and the foundation's local Portage Route chapter is among the nation's most active. For these reasons, the city is a treasure trove of expedition lore, well worth a stop.

The Great Falls of the Missouri are an apt place to begin any visit to the area. To get there, drive north on US 87 and follow the signs to Ryan Dam. The turnoff is about 2 miles north of the town of Black Eagle, just across the river from Great Falls. Remember that Lewis and several others had left the Marias River confluence, intent on making sure this south fork was indeed still the Missouri. Toward noon on June 13, 1805, Lewis and Private Silas Goodrich had walked about 2 miles toward the river when, Lewis wrote, "My ears were saluted with the agreeable sound of a fall of water and advancing a little farther I saw a spray arise above the plain like a column of smoke which would frequently disappear again and an instant caused I presume from the wind which was blowing pretty hard from the southwest. I did not however lose my direction to this point which soon began to make a roaring too tremendous to be mistaken for any cause short of the Great Falls of the Missouri." Today, the Ryan Dam day-use area includes several overlooks, picnic tables, and a shelter.

Lewis scrambled down a 200-foot bluff to witness what he called "the grandest sight" he had ever seen. He and his advance party had a good dinner of buffalo and trout and camped overnight at the site. The next day, Lewis sent

The Great Falls of the Missouri River.

Joseph Field down the river with word that the south fork was the true Missouri. Later, he walked upriver alone 5 miles and found a 19-foot high waterfall with an irregular rock shelf. He named this cascade Crooked Falls. In another half-mile he discovered what he called in his journal Beautiful or Handsome Falls, now known as Rainbow Falls. A quarter-mile farther, he spotted a small falls, Colter; and finally, two-and-one-half-miles more upriver, another large cascade. Nearby, he spied an eagle's nest—the very landmark Indians had mentioned the corps would see past the falls.

Meanwhile, as Lewis was exploring the Great Falls, Clark was attending to Sacagawea, who had been ill for about a week. He bled her and tried purges, poultices, and just about every other remedy in the corps' primitive medical repertoire, but nothing seemed to work. The situation was dire, for without Sacagawea, the expedition stood much less a chance of getting horses and proceeding peacefully to the coast.

When Lewis returned, he examined Sacagawea and sent for water from a sulphur spring he recalled seeing nearby. She felt better within hours. Today, the spring is still known as Sacagawea Springs. It is accessible on the north side of the Missouri via a 1-mile hike atop the bluffs north of the Morony Dam parking area. The unmarked trail isn't easy to find at first; to locate it, scramble up the hill to the left of the upper parking area and look for the path across the ravine. Continue following the path, now plain, until you see Belt Creek empty into the Missouri on the river's other side. Near here, a small creek begins flowing due north, smelling faintly of sulphur and leading to the clear springs a few hundred yards away. The area below Morony Dam is also a popular launching spot for river trips. From Sacagawea Springs, the Lower Portage Camp was about another mile downriver on the opposite shore.

If you have only a short time in Great Falls, spend it at the new Lewis and Clark National Historic Trail Interpretive Center on the Missouri River near Black Eagle Falls. Opened in 1998, this $6-million facility (with 5,500 square feet of exhibits) offers visitors one of the nation's most compelling and comprehensive looks at the expedition and its legacy.

The center's entrance resembles a coulee cutting into the hillside, similar to those the Corps of Discovery encountered on the Great Falls portage. Inside, the portage itself is recreated in a life-size diorama that shows the men struggling against the land and elements. ("The Explorers at Giant Springs 1805," Bob Scriver's last major sculpture before his death in 1999, sits near the base of the portage diorama.) Other exhibits upstairs set the stage for the trip by detailing Jefferson's instructions to the corps and Lewis's preparations for the trip, and by showing the status of the United States in 1803. Before going downstairs, take time to view the 30-minute film created especially for the center by noted documentary filmmakers Ken Burns and Dayton Duncan—essentially an abridged version of their acclaimed PBS documentary on the

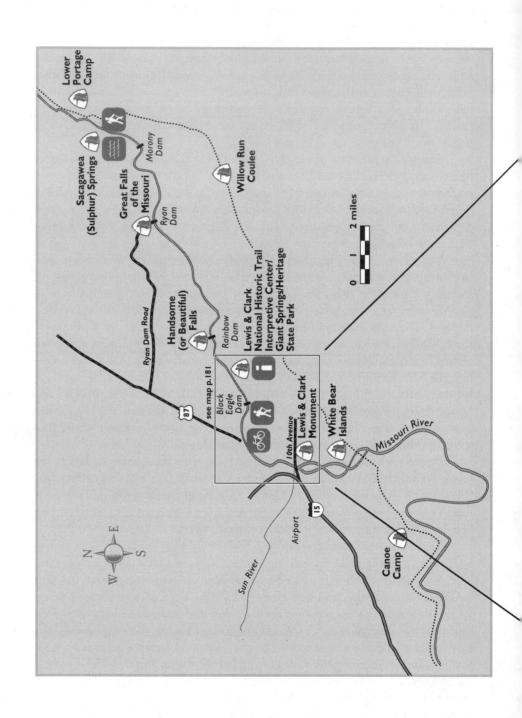

Lower
Portage
Camp

Sacagawea
(Sulphur) Springs

Great Falls
of the
Missouri

Morony
Dam

Willow Run
Coulee

Ryan
Dam

Ryan Dam Road

Handsome
(or Beautiful)
Falls

Rainbow
Dam

Lewis & Clark
National Historic Trail
Interpretive Center/
Giant Springs/Heritage
State Park

see map p.181

Black
Eagle
Dam

87

10th Avenue

Lewis & Clark
Monument

White Bear
Islands

Missouri River

Airport

15

Sun River

Canoe
Camp

N
W E
S

0   1   2 miles

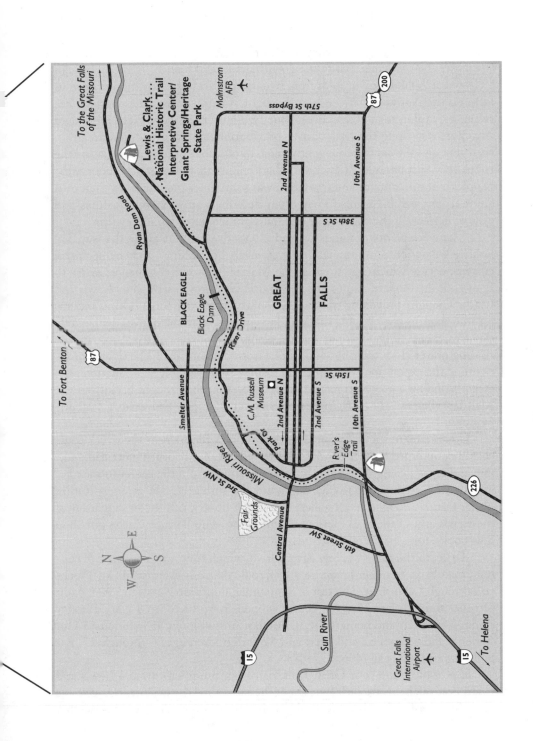

Corps of Discovery. The film briefly outlines the explorers' outgoing and return journeys; the array of native peoples the expedition met along the way; and the changing landscapes they saw from Camp Wood to the Pacific Ocean.

Once the film ends, exit to the downstairs level. Here, a "Journey Through a Crowded Wilderness" unfolds from two perspectives: the expedition's on your left and the Native Americans' on the right. Visitors learn how relations between the explorers and the natives ranged from warm to wary. Here, more than anywhere else along the trail, native contributions to the expedition are given their due, and the captains are gently taken to task for not fully appreciating the tribes they encountered. "Lewis and Clark's journals tell us much about these peoples, but the captains' interpretation was sometimes prejudiced by their own culture," one exhibit reads. "They often described only external features and events, neglecting the spiritual or cultural significance of what they saw."

There are plenty of hands-on and interactive exhibits along the way. Try lashing willow onto a boat; test your strength by "pulling" a canoe against a current; decide which way to go at the Marias-Missouri confluence; or try to figure out the modern names of some prairie creatures described by Lewis and Clark. Thought-provoking questions abound: When the corps saw no Indians for four months after leaving the Mandan villages, were the natives deliberately avoiding them? (The explorers did see plenty of evidence of tribal activity, including prayer cloth offerings and smoke from distant fires.) The final exhibits examine the expedition's outcome and display some notable reproduction artifacts, including a gorgeous recreation of a buffalo robe brought back from the Mandan villages. (The original is on view at Harvard University's Peabody Museum.)

Downstairs in the Jefferson Commons and outdoors near the river's edge, costumed interpreters give regular talks on such topics as bears, moccasin making, and tepee raising. The interpretive trail leading from the center to the river is delightful, with songbirds darting amid the lush riverside greenery. Other center features include an art gallery, a research library, and the headquarters of the Lewis and Clark Trail Heritage Foundation. The Portage Cache gift shop sells books, toys, gifts, and postcards.

To get to the center, follow River Drive, which runs north and east of central Great Falls. Summer hours are 9 A.M. to 8 P.M. daily, Memorial Day Weekend through Labor Day. The rest of September, hours are 9 A.M. to 5 P.M. daily. October through late May, the center is open from 9 A.M. to 5 P.M., Tuesday through Saturday and noon to 5 P.M. Sunday. Admission is $5 for adults, $4 for students and seniors 62 and over; and $2 for children ages 6 through 17. For more information, call (406) 727-8733.

If possible, time your Great Falls visit with the town's annual Lewis and Clark Festival, held late each June about the same time the explorers arrived. It's one of the best trail-related festivals, with activities including a living-history

The Corps of Discovery "At Lemhi," *oil on canvas by Robert F. Morgan.* Photo courtesy of the Montana Historical Society.

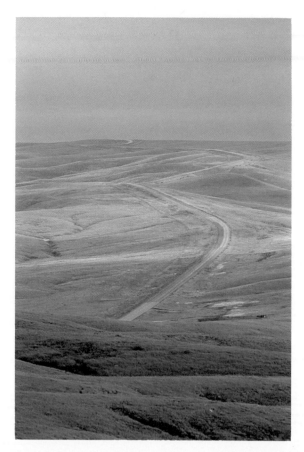

Rolling hills of South Dakota near Pierre (left). Photo courtesy of the South Dakota Department of Tourism.

Buffalo display in the W.H. Over State Museum Vermillion, South Dakota (below). Photo courtesy of the South Dakota Department of Tourism.

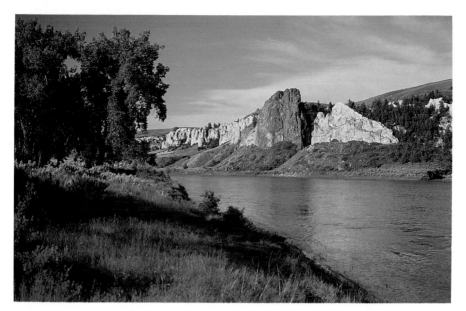

Wild and Scenic Missouri River, Montana. Photo by Michael S. Sample.

Square Butte near Ulm, Montana. Photo by John Reddy.

Rainbow over the Montana plains near the Rocky Mountain Front (left). Photo by Doug O'Looney.

Arrowleaf-balsamroot blooming near the Rocky Mountain Front northwest of Great Falls, Montana (below). Photo by John Reddy.

Gates of the Mountains tour boat (left). Photo by Darrin Schreder.

Lochsa River in Clearwater National Forest, Idaho (right). Photo by George Wuerthner.

Fall colors along the Missouri River (below). Photo by Michael S. Sample.

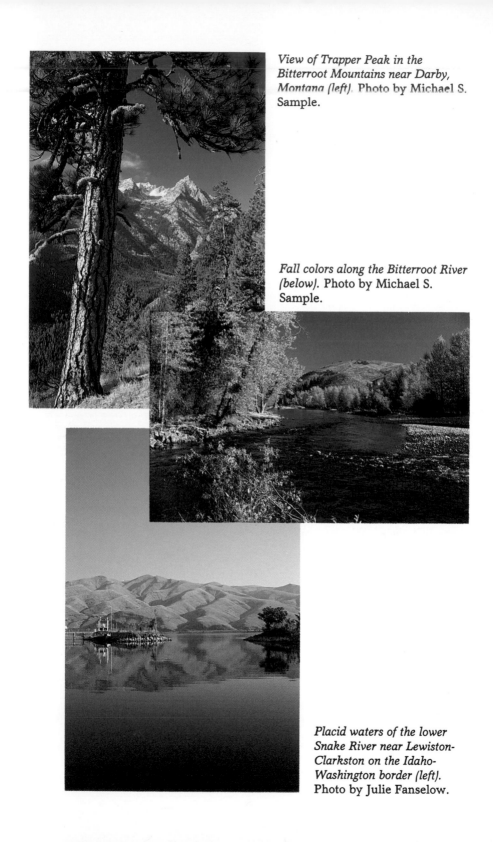

View of Trapper Peak in the Bitterroot Mountains near Darby, Montana (left). Photo by Michael S. Sample.

Fall colors along the Bitterroot River (below). Photo by Michael S. Sample.

Placid waters of the lower Snake River near Lewiston-Clarkston on the Idaho-Washington border (left). Photo by Julie Fanselow.

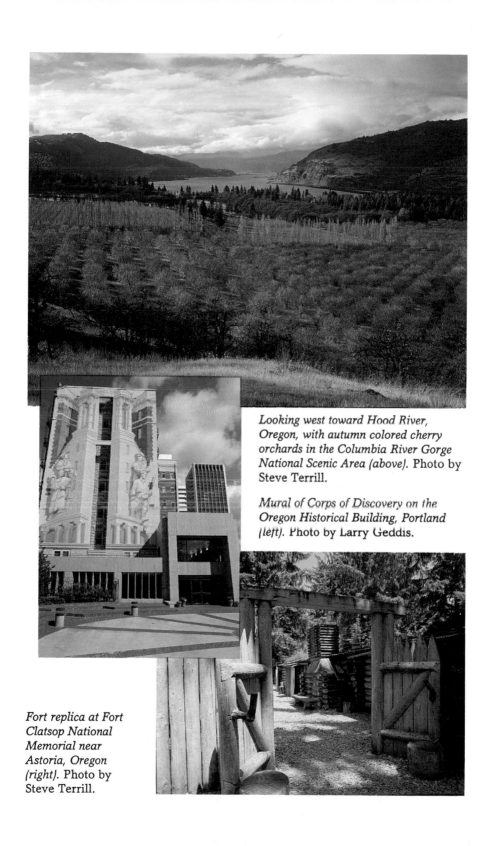

Looking west toward Hood River, Oregon, with autumn colored cherry orchards in the Columbia River Gorge National Scenic Area (above). Photo by Steve Terrill.

Mural of Corps of Discovery on the Oregon Historical Building, Portland (left). Photo by Larry Geddis.

Fort replica at Fort Clatsop National Memorial near Astoria, Oregon (right). Photo by Steve Terrill.

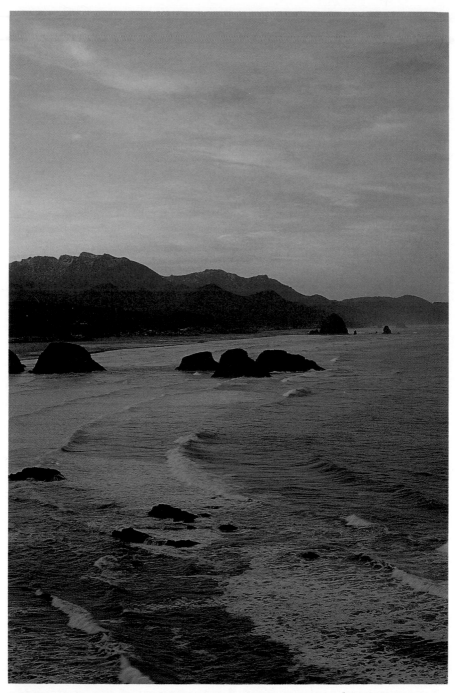

Sunrise over Cannon Beach and Haystack Rock near Ecola State Park, Oregon.
Photo by Larry Geddis.

Rainbow Falls at Great Falls, Montana.

encampment, noted speakers, float trips, and even a day camp for children. Registration is necessary for many events; contact the interpretive center for exact dates or more information.

Near the interpretive center, Giant Springs/Heritage State Park is also worth a stop. Clark discovered the spring on June 18, 1805, and Lewis later said it was the largest he'd ever seen, perhaps the largest in America. Indeed, Giant Springs lives up to its name with a flow of nearly 8,000,000 gallons per hour. The water comes from the Madison limestone formations lying beneath most of eastern and central Montana. Rainfall and melted snow soak into the limestone to the Great Falls area, where it flows upward about 700 feet through fractures before being pushed out at Giant Springs. This 38-mile trip takes hundreds of years, but the water gains momentum as it travels until it is pumped out at Giant Springs with a force of about 134,000 gallons per minute. The spring also forms the Roe River, the shortest in the world at just over 200 feet.

The springs are rich in calcium, magnesium, bicarbonate, and sulfate. These minerals are all excellent for nurturing trout, and a hatchery is located at the site. Visitors may buy fish food to feed the hatchlings—a great source of cheap entertainment! A playground, picnic tables, and big shade trees make this a very pleasant place to visit. Giant Springs/Heritage State Park is open from dawn to dusk, with the fish hatchery open daily from 8 A.M. to 4:30 P.M. For more information, call (406) 454-5840.

As the interpretive center shows, Great Falls had long been a key spot in Indian travels through the region. Because the confluence of the Missouri and Medicine (now Sun) rivers boasted the best fording spot for 40 miles in any direction, Indians frequently followed the Medicine River to its mouth here before crossing the Missouri and heading for elk and buffalo hunting grounds on the Plains. Today, this junction is overseen from Broadwater Overlook Park, off 10th Avenue South. The park's centerpiece is a heroic-sized bronze statue of Lewis and Clark sculpted by Bob Scriver to commemorate the Montana state centennial in 1989. In addition to the captains, it shows York and Lewis's dog, Seaman.

Lewis is pointing—but at what? After finding the remaining falls on June 14, Lewis discovered the Medicine River, which Indians at Fort Mandan had told him to expect. Elated, Lewis decided to kill a buffalo and make camp at the site. He picked his target, shot the beast, and stood watching it die, all the while neglecting to reload his rifle. Suddenly, he saw a grizzly bear walking toward him. Lewis headed off toward a tree where he intended to make camp, but the bear followed him. So Lewis switched directions, heading instead for the river, running in until he was waist-deep in water. He planted his feet, grasped his trusty espontoon, and held it menacingly toward the bear—an action that apparently startled the griz. Luckily for Lewis, the bear spun around and ran out of the river, out of sight. This same incident is depicted on a mural titled "The One That Got Away," painted by John Carlon on the side of the Army-Navy Store at Central Avenue and 8th Street North near downtown Great Falls.

Back east, Lewis had concocted the idea of a collapsible iron boat. He had the 90-pound frame fabricated at Harpers Ferry and felt that when the explorers needed to leave their dugout canoes behind when trekking overland, they could easily carry the portable boat. Constructed, the boat would be 36 feet long and carry at least 8,000 pounds—enough cargo space to replace the two pirogues.

At the upper portage camp at White Bear Islands, Lewis finally had the chance to test his invention. The boat was fitted with 28 elk skins and four buffalo hides, then launched into the river. It floated! But after about five hours, the boat started coming apart at the seams. Without pine trees to make pitch, the men had made do with beeswax, tallow, and charcoal, none of which worked as well. "I need not add this circumstance mortified me not a little," Lewis wrote. "I therefore relinquished all further hope of my favorite boat and ordered her to be sunk in the water…." Meanwhile, Clark took some men and proceeded upstream to find trees suitable for making new canoes of the time-tested dugout variety. The iron boat, whether submerged in the river or cached nearby, has never been found.

Lewis was dejected, but other words he wrote during the portage conveyed a good deal more hope. The captains had earlier toyed with the idea of sending a boatload of men back east from the Great Falls; they now decided not to do so.

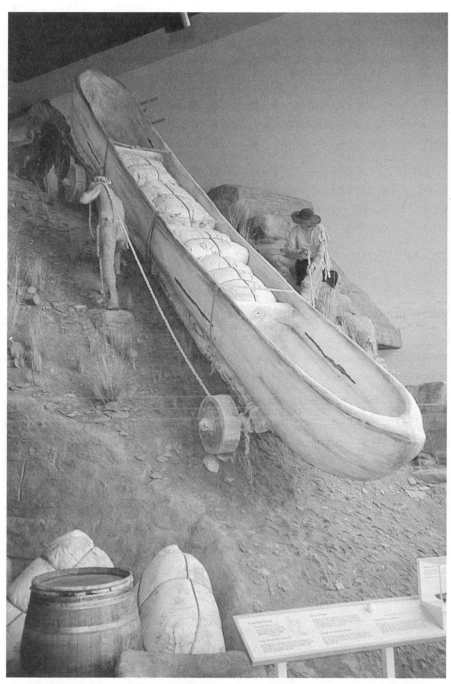

Diorama at the Lewis and Clark National Historic Trail Interpretive Center, Great Falls, Montana.

The party was still small enough, they reasoned, and all available hands might be needed to deal with the unknown ahead. "We have never hinted to anyone of the party that we had such a scheme in contemplation, and all appear perfectly to have made up their minds to succeed in the expedition or perish in the attempt," Lewis wrote. "We all believe that we are now about to enter the most perilous and difficult part of our voyage, yet I see no one repining. All appear ready to meet those difficulties which await us with resolution and becoming fortitude."

Aside from Lewis and Clark, Charlie Russell is Great Falls's major local hero. The famous Western artist lived much of his life in the area and is buried in Highland Cemetery. Russell's influence seems to loom everywhere—his

FOLLOWING THE PORTAGE

It's not well-marked, but visitors with time and inclination may want to try following the entire Lewis and Clark portage route across the southeast edge of Great Falls. The trek may still be traced with an excellent map available from the local Lewis and Clark Heritage Foundation chapter. Ask for the "Explorers at the Portage" brochure at the interpretive center, or write the Portage Route Chapter, P.O. Box 2424, Great Falls, Montana 59403, for a copy.

To outline it briefly, the portage began at what is now known as Belt Creek, located directly across the river from Sacagawea Springs. There, the corps built two truck frames with wooden wheels to haul their goods overland. From the creek, the trail wound up the coulee and on to the prairie bench. (A farm road now parallels the way.)

Hazards and inconveniences were many. Rattlesnakes were a constant threat all along the portage route, as were prickly pear cactus—the men's soft-soled moccasins were no match for these sharp-spined plants. The expedition's pace was also slowed by ruts gouged by the immense hoofprints of thousands of buffalo. The corps encountered several violent storms, with hail so fierce on one occasion it bloodied several men. Yet despite all the difficulties, Clark noted that "no man complains. All go cheerfully on."

The portage ended at the White Bear Islands, so named because they were teeming with grizzlies. There were three islands when Lewis and Clark camped here, and there are still three today—though not necessarily the same ones the expedition saw. The journals mention that the party drank the last of its spirits here on July 4, 1805. Paris Gibson, the founder of Great Falls, felt the event took place on a knoll north of what is now the Ayrshire Dairy, which overlooks the islands. Gibson commemorated the site with a brass plaque and city park. Both park and plaque are gone now, but the plaque's cement base still stands. ▲

GREAT FALLS TRAVEL TIPS

Great Falls International Airport (GTF) is served by Big Sky, Delta, Horizon, and Northwest airlines. Most major car rental companies have offices at the airport. The bus terminal is also at the airport, with service from Rimrock Stages and Intermountain Bus to most major Montana cities. If you travel to Great Falls by air, be sure to check out the mural by Robert Orduno above the main escalators at the airport. Measuring 10 feet by 35 feet, the painting shows the explorers making their portage.

Great Falls Transit runs several routes throughout the city, but none goes close to the Lewis and Clark Interpretive Center, except during the Lewis and Clark Festival each June. Buses typically run from 6:30 A.M. to about 7 P.M. Monday through Saturday. For updated schedule information, call (406) 727-0382.

The Great Falls Historic Trolley operates during the summer, with stops at all the major city visitor sites including the Lewis and Clark Interpretive Center and the C. M. Russell Museum. For rates and schedules, call (406) 771-1100.

For more information on Great Falls, call (800) 735-8535 or (406) 771-0885, or stop by the visitor center at Broadwater Overlook Park.

initials are even carved into a hillside by the Missouri riverbank—but the must-see attraction for Russell buffs is the C. M. Russell Museum Complex, located at 400 13th Street North. Here, visitors can see Russell's home, his original log cabin studio, and one of the largest collections of Russell art and personal effects in any one place. The C. M. Russell Auction of Original Western Art, held mid-March of every year, is one of Great Falls's biggest annual events.

Paris Gibson Square is another favorite with visitors. The square, at the corner of 14th Street and 1st Avenue North, includes the Center for Contemporary Arts and the Cascade County Museum, where changing exhibits and a permanent collection of more than 50,000 objects ensure there's always something new to see. The Museum Cafe here is also one of Great Falls's more interesting places to grab lunch.

 Great Falls's biggest recreational asset is the River's Edge Trail, which starts at the Missouri/Sun River confluence and will eventually go all the way out to the Great Falls and Sacagawea Springs. Walkers, strollers, joggers, cyclists, and skaters all enjoy the route, which is being built on a former railroad bed. The trail also passes the site of Lewis's grizzly bear encounter, which likely took place across the river from the tennis courts and horseshoe pits at a site now known as West Bank Park. Every July 4, Great Falls's annual Meriwether Lewis fun run is held to commemorate what must have been the West's fastest 50-yard dash. Sacagawea Island, a kind of nature preserve, is also visible in the river nearby.

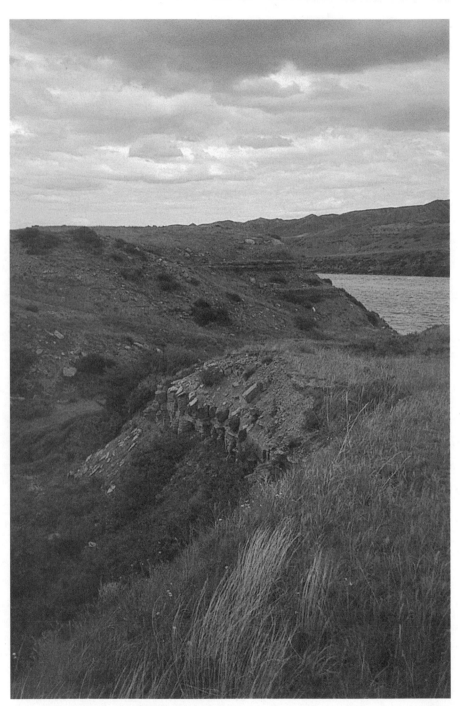

The Missouri River near Sacagawea Springs.

Cycle rentals ($12 for three hours, $19 for a full day) and riding information are available at Knicker Biker, 1123 Central Avenue.

If you didn't get a chance to float the Missouri from Fort Benton, it's not too late to sample it here. Montana River Outfitters offers several short boat trips in the Great Falls area. The Missouri Breaks float heads downriver from Morony Dam past Lewis and Clark's lower portage camp and through some nice whitewater. The Wolf Creek Canyon float travels along the Missouri south of Great Falls—an area of great beauty, fascinating geology, and lots of wildlife. Either trip can run a half day or whole day; prices start at $35 for adults for the half-day trips and run to $65 for a full-day float with a riverside steak dinner. For anyone really short on time, there's even a one-hour scenic float for just $15 for adults ($10 per child 12 and under). Montana River Outfitters also runs trips on the Upper Missouri, as well as Smith River fishing trips and horseback/float expeditions into the Bob Marshall Wilderness. For more information, call (800) 800-8218 or (406) 761-1677.

From Great Falls, it is possible to take scenic MT 200 directly to Missoula, a distance of 167 miles. Doing so will mean missing several key chapters in the Lewis and Clark story, but it will also save about 200 miles and a day or two of rugged travel. Montana 200 also takes the traveler close to the route Captain Lewis used on his return journey in 1806 (see the "Homeward bound: Lewis finds a shortcut" section later in this chapter for details). Travelers who want to continue following the corps' 1805 route should leave Great Falls south on Interstate 15. It's 76 miles from Great Falls to the Gates of the Mountains, our next major stop.

GATES OF THE MOUNTAINS

Driving south of Great Falls, it soon becomes apparent the Montana plains are ending and giving way to the lofty peaks that gave this state its name. ("Montana" is indeed the Spanish word for "mountain.") The ranges surrounding Great Falls—hardly visible in town but prominent once one leaves—are the Highwoods to the east, Little Belts to the southeast and the Big Belts to the southwest.

The area between Great Falls and Helena is sparsely settled, with the few towns along the way catering to tourism and outdoor activities. Near Ulm (Exit 270), the corps camped July 10–14, 1805, and built the dugout canoes needed to replace Lewis's iron boat. Ulm Pishkun State Park preserves a buffalo jump, pictographs, and prairie dog town. Cascade (Exit 256) has a free overnight camping park.

Although I-15 is one of the most scenic interstates found anywhere, the traveler can escape it by taking an even more pleasant recreation road that runs closer to the Missouri River. Access this scenic route at Hardy Creek (Exit 247).

From there, the route can be followed as far south as Spring Creek. Boat ramps and primitive camping areas are plentiful along the way.

Wolf Creek (Exits 226–228) is the access point to Holter Lake, the first of several popular lakes located just minutes from the interstate. Wolf Creek is also headquarters for several river and fly fishing guide services. But the canyon corridor's primary lure for Lewis and Clark buffs is the Gates of the Mountains boat trip. Even the name sounds inviting, a tribute to Meriwether Lewis's poetic imagination. To get there, take Exit 209 to Upper Holter Lake and follow the signs.

By the time Lewis and Clark arrived in this area in mid-July 1805, it had been months since they had seen any Indians (other than Sacagawea, of course). They were starting to get anxious, knowing the party would need horses to travel over the Continental Divide. Moreover, the captains figured they had to be getting close to Sacagawea's home country, the land of the Shoshones, or Snake Indians, as the white men called them. It was decided they would take turns traveling overland to increase the chances of meeting Indians. Clark and three other men left the canyon on the first expedition, with no clue of the river spectacle they were about to miss.

"This evening we entered the most remarkable cliffs that we have yet seen," Lewis wrote on July 19. "These cliffs rise from the water's edge on either side perpendicularly to the height of 1,200 feet . . . the towering and projecting rocks in many places seem ready to tumble in on us." Lewis also noted that, although it was getting dark, the men had to keep moving, for there was scarcely a spot on shore where "a man could rest the sole of his foot. . . It was late in the evening before I entered this place and was obliged to continue my route until sometime after dark before I found a place sufficiently large to encamp my small party. At length such a one occurred on the larboard side where we found plenty of light wood and pitch pine. This rock is a black granite below and appears to be of a much lighter color above . . . from the singular appearance of this place I called it the gates of the rocky mountains."

The boat tours here last nearly two hours and cover a distance of 6.5 miles on what is now Holter Lake. Guides offer a wealth of information on the canyon's natural and human history, while helping passengers scan the cliffs for bighorn sheep and mountain goats (most likely seen on the right-hand side going into the canyon and the left-hand side going out). Young bald eagles, osprey, cliff swallows, and barn swallows live here, too.

Also in evidence are pictographs, probably 200 to 300 years old and of Blackfeet origin. And the tours pass by Mann Gulch, where 12 men lost their lives in a wildfire August 1949. The fire spread from 30 acres to 2,000 acres in less than 10 minutes when the winds kicked up, and ended up burning 15,000 acres before it was through. The incident made national news and is detailed in

Gates of the Mountains boat tour.

Young Men and Fire, a book by Montana author Norman Maclean (best known for *A River Runs Through It*).

All trips stop at the Meriwether Picnic Area, believed to be where Lewis and his party found their small campsite. Although these stops are usually brief—just enough time to stretch one's legs and use the restroom—passengers have the option of catching a later boat back to the docks. Those who do so may want to pack a picnic or take the 1-mile trail to Coulter Campground, named after the expedition member but spelled differently for some reason. More ambitious backpackers could stay overnight—or longer—and trek into the Gates of the Mountains Wilderness. One popular destination, Refrigerator Canyon, is an 18-mile roundtrip from Coulter Campground.

Gates of the Mountains boat tours run Memorial Day Weekend through mid-September. Cruises are offered at 11 A.M., 1 P.M., and 3 P.M. weekdays and every hour on the hour from 10 A.M. to 4 P.M. on Saturdays, Sundays, and holidays during July and August. In June, weekday sailings are set for 11 A.M. and 2 P.M. with weekend and holiday cruises scheduled at 10 A.M., noon, 2 P.M., and 4 P.M. In September, tours are at 11 A.M. and 2 P.M. weekdays, and 11 A.M., 1 P.M., and 3 P.M. weekends.

Tickets cost $8.50 for adults, $7.50 for senior citizens (ages 60 and over), and $5.50 for kids 4 to 17. Children under 4 ride free. Plan to arrive about a half-hour early to buy tickets. Bring a jacket—even hot days can be breezy on the boat—and binoculars. For more information, call (406) 458-5241.

It's a 20-minute drive from Gates of the Mountains to Helena—Montana's charming capital city. A good way to get oriented here is with an hour-long ride on the Last Chance Tour Train, which departs from the Montana Historical Society on the corner of Roberts and 6th Avenue just east of the Capitol. The train—and Montana's downtown pedestrian mall, Last Chance Gulch—take their name from "the Georgians," four weary and despondent Southern gold prospectors who, arriving at what is now Helena in 1864, decided to make one more attempt at locating gold. They struck it rich, as did many others: by the late 1880s, there were more millionaires per capita in Helena than anywhere else in the United States.

Tour train guides point out important state buildings (including Montana's decidedly modest governor's residence), the elegant architectural gems on Last Chance Gulch, and the impressive west-side mansion district. Riders also learn that the Helena Masonic Temple has Meriwether Lewis's Masonic apron, and that a feisty local pilot once flew between the spires of the lovely Cathedral of St. Helena. In all, it's a very entertaining and informative trip. Trains depart at 10 A.M., 11 A.M., 1 P.M., 2 P.M., 3 P.M., 4 P.M., and 6 P.M. daily during July and August. From May 15 to May 30 and during September, trains leave at 11 A.M., 1 P.M., and 3 P.M. In June, departures are at 10 A.M., 11 A.M., 1 P.M., 2 P.M., and 3 P.M. Fare is $5 for adults and teens, $4.50 for seniors 65 and older, and $4 for kids ages 4 to 12. Call (406) 442-1023 for more information.

Before or after the train ride, stop in the Montana Historical Society. Highlights include the Mackay Gallery of Charlie Russell Art, including several paintings and drawings on the Lewis and Clark theme. "York," painted by Russell in 1908, is probably the most memorable rendering ever of the African American man who accompanied his master, Clark, on the expedition. The watercolor, set at the Mandan villages during the winter of 1804–1805, shows two Native Americans touching a towering, bare-chested York to see if he is painted. Others look on in wonder, as smoke from the lodge fire blends magically with light filtering in from above. The Montana Homeland exhibit also has a section on the expedition, featuring three large oil canvases by Robert Morgan: "White Bears and White Cliffs," "Decision," and "At Lemhi."

The Montana State Capitol, just across 6th Avenue, also honors Lewis and Clark with grand artworks, including Russell's "Lewis and Clark Meeting the Flathead Indians at Ross' Hole," at 12 feet by 25 feet his largest work. Other paintings by E. S. Paxson depict the explorers at the Three Forks and Lewis at Black Eagle Falls. The Capitol is closed for renovations through 2000, but regular tours will resume when it reopens. Until then, you can sometimes get a peek inside by inquiring at the Historical Society visitor desk.

Helena boasts an active cultural scene. On Wednesday evenings in summer,

Near Lewis and Clark Pass in the Helena National Forest.

downtown comes "Alive at 5," with a wide array of music in a variety of locations. Other hot spots include the Myrna Loy Center for the Performing Arts at 15 North Ewing and the Holter Museum of the Arts at 12 East Lawrence. In early 2000, the Myrna Loy Center closed temporarily; call ahead for information. (406) 443-0287. The city also has a full calendar of annual events including the Montana Traditional Jazz Festival in late June, the Last Chance Stampede in late July, and the Western Rendezvous of Art in mid-August. Like Billings, Great Falls, and Butte, Helena fields a Pioneer League baseball team, the Brewers.

Those yearning for more active sports need only look to Mount Helena, where an excellent network of trails offers hiking and mountain biking right out the city's back door. To get there, take Park Avenue to the Reeders Alley trailhead. Spring Meadow State Park, on the north side of town between Euclid Avenue and Country Club Drive, has good fishing, swimming, and bird watching. For more information on Helena, call (800) 743-5362 (out of state) or (406) 442-4120.

A bit out of town, but still close by, Frontier Town is an Old West theme village on the Continental Divide built almost entirely by one man, John Quigley. Aside from an outstanding view, Frontier Town offers a museum, a shop, and a restaurant—even a wedding chapel. Hiking trails thread through the nearby forest. Frontier Town is located 15 miles west of Helena on U.S. Highway 12.

From Helena, the Lewis and Clark Trail bends to the southeast, following

HOMEWARD BOUND:
LEWIS FINDS A SHORTCUT

When the expedition was on its way home in 1806, the captains split up at their Traveler's Rest camp at present-day Lolo, Montana (see chapter 7). From there, Clark explored the Big Hole Country and Lewis took the Indian road to the buffalo hunting grounds east of the divide. He crossed the Continental Divide at a point now called Lewis and Clark Pass, something of a misnomer since Clark never saw the place.

Lewis's route roughly parallels MT 200 from Missoula to Great Falls, a distance of about 170 miles. Lewis and Clark Pass may also be visited on a day trip from Helena, Great Falls, or Missoula. Helena is closest, so we'll explore the route from there.

Driving north from Helena, take Exit 200 (Lincoln Road) off I-15. Turn onto County Road 279 and head west. This road crests at Flesher Pass and a spectacular view before descending to MT 200.

Turn left on MT 200 and look for Forest Road 293 (Alice Creek) about 1 mile west. This is the turnoff, but it might be wise to drive 8 miles farther west to Lincoln for a stop at the Helena National Forest ranger station (open weekdays), where forest personnel can offer more detailed directions and a map to the site. The ranger station phone number is (406) 362-4265.

Return to FR 293 and head north. Five miles in, there's a historical sign that notes Lewis and his party stopped in the vicinity for dinner on July 7, 1806. From here, the Indian trail they followed closely parallels the forest road. Ten miles from MT 200, the traveler comes to a fork in the road. The right fork, now gated, is the way to the pass. A trail of about 1.5 miles leads in a northwesterly direction to the Continental Divide. Elevation at the pass is 6,421 feet.

Lewis and Clark Pass is rarely noted on Montana highway maps. Today, traffic is routed over the divide at Rogers Pass—elevation 5,610 feet—about 6 miles to the southeast. A sign on MT 200 notes that the coldest official temperature ever recorded in the continental United States occurred at a mining camp near Rogers Pass on January 20, 1954, when the mercury hit 70 degrees below zero.

Had Lewis and Clark known heading west what they learned at Traveler's Rest, they could have saved themselves many weeks of tough travel. It took the expedition about two months to cover the route between Great Falls and Traveler's Rest on the outbound trek in 1805; Lewis made the trip in just eight days using the shortcut the following summer, and Indians told the captains it could be done in as few as four days! But perhaps they would not have used the shortcut going westbound even if they'd known about it. After all, President Jefferson had instructed the corps to find the headwaters of the Missouri—a task they would not have accomplished had they followed the more direct route west from Great Falls.▲

U.S. Highway 12 to Townsend, then US 287 to Three Forks. En route, travelers may want to stop at Canyon Ferry Recreation Area, one of Montana's most popular. The original Canyon Ferry Dam was completed in 1898 to provide power to the booming town of Helena. The present dam, completed in 1954, is 225 feet high and impounds the 25-mile-long Canyon Ferry Lake.

Canyon Ferry Village has a visitor center that is open from noon to 4 P.M. Sunday, Monday, Wednesday, and Friday and noon to 8 P.M. on Saturday during the summer. If the center isn't open, you can still get information at a nearby shelter. Interpretive panels tell about the dam and describe an 85-mile auto tour through the nearby Helena National Forest.

There is scant Lewis and Clark interpretation. A picnic area on the lake's west shore is named for our heroes, but no camping is allowed. To get there from Canyon Ferry Village, take Montana 284 southeast, across the dam, and bear left at the Yacht Basin Marina area. The community of York near Canyon Ferry was named for New York City, not the York of Lewis and Clark fame.

Canyon Ferry's congested campgrounds seem better suited to RVers than tent campers, although a few decent tent sites may be found in the Court Sheriff area's back loop and at Hellgate. Showers are available at some of the nearby commercial establishments including Kim's Marina. Boats, windsurfing gear, and other water toys are available for rent at Yacht Basin Marina.

Canyon Ferry Lake's southern stretch reaches nearly to US 12 north of Townsend. The Indian Road Campground just north of town has a great little fishing pond designed for children under 12 and handicapped anglers. The Missouri River flows into the Canyon Ferry impoundment here, and a boat ramp is available. Townsend, 29 miles south of Helena, is an agricultural hub and tourist-oriented community. The Broadwater County Museum at 133 North Walnut Street has displays of pioneer artifacts and information on the area's mining history. From Townsend, it is 31 miles to Interstate 90 and the Missouri Headwaters.

THREE FORKS OF THE MISSOURI

As they moved up the Missouri past the Gates of the Mountains, Lewis and his party suddenly had reason to celebrate. Sacagawea recognized the land through which they were passing! "This piece of information has cheered the spirits of the party who . . . console themselves with the anticipation of shortly seeing the head of the Missouri yet unknown to the civilized world," Lewis wrote.

Clark and his contingent reached the Three Forks of the Missouri first, on July 25, and explored the surrounding area while waiting for Lewis. They looked everywhere for Indians, but there were still none to be seen. The rest of the party arrived July 27, and the expedition camped in the area through July 30, 1805,

Near the Three Forks of the Missouri River headwaters.

largely to allow time for rest. Clark in particular was well worn-out, his feet throbbing painfully from the many miles of overland travel over prickly pear cactus. More than ever, the expedition realized its need for horses. But again, Sacagawea offered reason for hope, recognizing this as the place of her kidnapping some five years earlier. She had been camped at the forks with her Shoshone family when the band was attacked by Hidatsa Indians, killing four men and taking a number of prisoners, "though I cannot discover that she shows any emotion of sorrow in recollecting this event, or of joy in being restored to her native country," Lewis wrote.

Here the captains had to decide which of the three forks would lead them toward the Continental Divide and the Pacific watershed. Although the streams were roughly similar in size, it wasn't an especially tough puzzle. They soon settled on the westernmost of the rivers, which they named the Jefferson in honor of "the author of our enterprise," as Lewis put it. The middle fork was named for then–Secretary of State James Madison, and the easternmost stream honored Albert Gallatin, Jefferson's Secretary of the Treasury (and a strong supporter of the Louisiana Purchase).

Missouri Headwaters State Park now commemorates the expedition's arrival, as well as the area's importance to Indians, trappers, traders, and settlers. The park is located 6 miles northeast of the town of Three Forks on Montana Secondary Route 285. Within the park, a short trail leads to the riverbank and a sign marking the headwaters.

An excellent interpretive display elsewhere in the park tells about the many aspects of Three Forks history. The visitor learns, for example, that the headwaters later served as the setting for a dramatic episode involving two former members of the expedition, John Colter and John Potts. In 1808, the two men were trapping on the Jefferson River. A band of Blackfeet, angered by previous encounters with whites, attacked both men.

Potts was killed right away, but Colter's fate seemed even worse: he was stripped and told to run for his life. Colter tore barefoot across the cactus-laden plains, outrunning all but one of his pursuers for about 6 miles. Despite his exhaustion, Colter turned on the Indian and killed him. He continued on into the Jefferson River and hid under a snag, eluding the other Blackfeet. Later, naked and weaponless, Colter headed for Manuel Lisa's fort on the Big Horn River. He made the 200-mile trip in seven days.

In 1810, Lisa, of the Missouri Fur Company, sent 32 trappers to establish a post at the headwaters. They found good beaver trapping, but grizzly bears and Blackfeet killed several of the frontiersmen, including George Drouillard, another Lewis and Clark alumnus. "Popular history has surrounded the mountain man with glory and adventure," one interpretive panel reads. "But reality was often short rations, bitter cold, boredom and even sudden death." The idea of a permanent post was soon abandoned, although trappers continued to work the headwaters region until the 1840s. By that time, the beaver had nearly become extinct, and silk had replaced fur as the hat material of choice.

As Sacagawea would attest, the Three Forks area had long been an important hunting ground for the region's Indians. An 1855 treaty between the natives and whites declared the headwaters region to be a common hunting ground for 99 years, supposedly guaranteeing all people "equal and uninterrupted privileges" in the area. But rapid settlement by the whites brought the treaty to its knees less than a decade later.

Native vegetation in the park remains much the same as when Lewis and Clark visited. Plants include buckwheat brush, big sagebrush, pincushion cactus, saltbrush, prickly pear cactus, and bluebunch wheatgrass. A short trail leads to an overlook that points out key features of the landscape in all directions, including the Tobacco Root, Madison, and Gallatin mountain ranges.

Missouri Headwaters State Park has a small but appealing campground, with a handful of choice secluded sites. There are no showers, but RVers will find a dump station available for use. Day-use visitors and campers alike enjoy facilities for picnicking, as well as fishing and boating access to the three rivers. Late each July, the park is the site of Three Forks' Weekend of Discovery, featuring Lewis and Clark lore and a mountain man encampment. The event transports visitors back to nineteenth-century ways with demonstrations on everything from black powder shooting to fishing techniques from the 1800s.

YELLOWSTONE NATIONAL PARK AND NEARBY ATTRACTIONS

Although only a sliver of Yellowstone National Park lies in Montana, the Treasure State claims three of the park's five entrances. The choices are West Yellowstone, south of Bozeman on US 191 or south of Three Forks via US 287; Gardiner, south of Livingston by way of US 89; and Cooke City/Silver Gate, reached by way of the famous Beartooth Highway, U.S. Highway 212, southwest from Laurel near Billings.

Yellowstone was the world's first national park, so declared by an act of Congress in 1872. Known for its geysers, waterfalls, and wildlife (not to mention the 1988 fires that burned more than a third of the park), Yellowstone is among the most frequently visited national parks, so it can be crowded. Still, Yellowstone is a big place, with more than a thousand miles of trails. Solitude is available for those who seek it out.

Yellowstone boasts so many spectacular sights that it's hard to know where to begin. Artist Point and Inspiration Point offer vistas of the Grand Canyon of the Yellowstone River and its famous falls. Old Faithful is but one example of the park's intense thermal activity, all triggered by an immense volcanic eruption 600,000 years ago. Norris Geyser Basin and the Fountain Paint Pots area offer the park's most concentrated displays of these steaming, gurgling natural features.

Sightseeing is definitely the main attraction at Yellowstone. But other opportunities available include fishing, backcountry camping and hiking, and canoeing (especially on Shoshone Lake). A permit is required to fish in Yellowstone, and there is a fee for anglers age 16 and up. Powerboaters are permitted on Yellowstone and Lewis lakes.

While at Yellowstone, don't forget its less famous but equally scenic sister park, Grand Teton National Park. Few people forget their first sight of the Tetons, which are among the youngest mountains in North America. These soaring, craggy peaks provide the setting for some of the greatest hiking in the world.

The Cascade Canyon Trail is among the most popular Teton treks, and the hikes to Hermitage Point or on the Paintbrush Trail often reward visitors with wildlife views. Mountain climbing instruction and guides are available. It's difficult to pull your gaze away from the mountains, but the lakes and the Snake River are lovely, too. Activities include scenic boat trips, boat rentals, sailboarding on Jackson Lake, and floats down the Snake. Horseback riding, fishing, and camping offer still more pleasures.

The town of Jackson sits south of Grand Teton National Park. Like other mountain resort towns, Jackson has gone through a lot of changes in recent decades. It no longer qualifies as a "typical" Western town, but it certainly is a fun place to visit. Jackson crackles with energy, from its creative restaurants to its lively nightlife (don't miss the famous Million Dollar Cowboy Bar on the main square downtown), superb shopping, and active arts scene.

Another northwest Wyoming town, Cody, is famous for the Buffalo Bill Historical Center, widely considered to be the best overall Western museum in the United States. The four-part complex includes the Buffalo Bill Museum, which documents Colonel William Cody's colorful life; the Whitney Gallery of Western Art, featuring original works by such famous names as Russell and Remington; the Plains Indian Museum, with extensive displays on the life and times of the region's great tribes; and the Cody Firearms Museum, which includes guns from throughout history. Cody is 80 miles east of the Fishing Bridge junction at Yellowstone National Park.

For more information, contact Grand Teton National Park at (307) 733-2880; Yellowstone National Park at (307) 344-7381 or www.nps.gov/yell; the Jackson Hole Area Chamber of Commerce at (307) 733-3316; or the Cody Country Chamber at (307) 587-2297.

For an off-the-beaten-path look at the Headwaters area, consider booking a tour with Northern Rockies Natural History. Guide Ken Sinay, a wildlife biologist by training, takes small parties of up to six people out on a stretch of the Jefferson River that runs far from the road. Reading from the Lewis and Clark journals and consulting the expedition's maps, Sinay strives to compare what we see today with what the expedition encountered 200 years ago. Then as now, antelope, sandhill cranes, bald eagles, and beaver are among the many species living along the river.

Sinay takes people out in a hard-bottomed boat outfitted with comfortable chairs. (He can even accommodate wheelchairs.) Cost for a full-day safari runs from $410 for one person to $720 for six, including lunch, snacks, and transportation. In the off-season (mid-September to mid-June), Sinay is often available to lead half-day tours of the Headwaters/Gallatin Canyon area for $75 per person. He's also known for his wildlife-viewing trips to and around Yellowstone National Park, and he'll custom-design itineraries elsewhere in Montana by request. For more information or to plan a trip, call (406) 586-1155, or see www.beyondyellowstone.com on the web.

Montana River Expeditions runs scenic canoe and kayak trips on both the Madison and Jefferson rivers; call (800) 500-4538 for information. Canoe rentals, shuttles, and fly-fishing trips also are available from the Canoeing House and Guide Service at (406) 285-3488.

Three Forks is an interesting little town in a picturesque setting. Visitors can shoot a round at the scenic Headwaters Public Golf Course or hire a river guide for a day of fly fishing or river running. The Headwaters Heritage Museum at the corner of Main and Cedar is an appealing small-town history museum with two full floors of fascinating exhibits. The most interesting thing on view from a Lewis and Clark perspective is an anvil dating to 1810, the

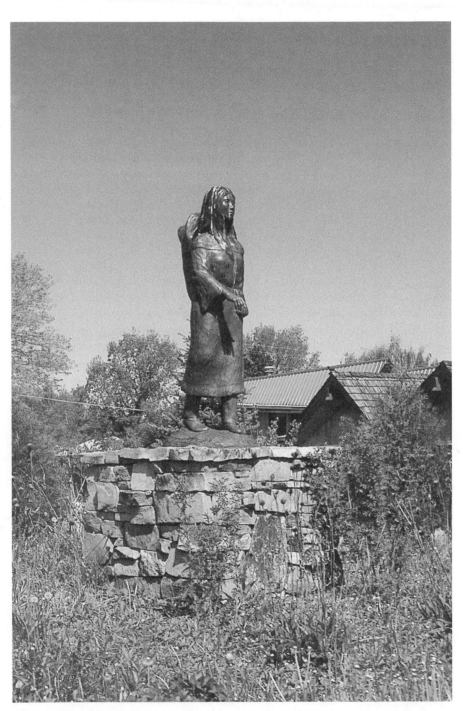

Statue of Sacagawea in Bozeman, Montana.

only artifact remaining from Manuel Lisa's short-lived Fort Three Forks. Though no one can be sure, John Colter and George Drouillard may have been among those using the anvil since both spent time at the fort that year. Travelers with young children may want them to watch a 30-minute video, "Song of Sacajawea," on a video player set up in the museum. Like the museum's scrapbook, the video promulgates several myths about the young Indian woman, but its spirit is true.

For more local information on Three Forks, stop by the caboose visitor center at the entrance to town. It's open from 10 A.M. to 5 P.M. Wednesday through Sunday in the summer. Or call the Three Forks Chamber of Commerce at (406) 285-4880.

From Three Forks, proceed west on Montana 2. Dillon is about 90 miles away via MT 2, Montana 55, and Montana 41.

LODGING

* Denotes town on Lewis's explorations of the Marias River region in 1806.

** Denotes town on Lewis's return route over the Continental Divide in 1806.

Rates are for double occupancy during summer season as of 1999 and are subject to change.

LOMA, MONTANA

Loma Motel, (406) 739-4400. $40.

Virgelle Mercantile, (800) 426-2926. Cabins and bed-and-breakfast accommodations. $60–$80.

FORT BENTON, MONTANA

Grand Union Hotel, (406) 622-1882, 1 Grand Union Sq. $80–$125.

Fort Motel, (406) 622-3312, 1809 St. Charles. $46.

Long's Landing Bed and Breakfast, (406) 622-3461, 1011 17th St. $50.

Pioneer Lodge, (406) 622-5441, 1700 Front St. $50.

*CONRAD, MONTANA

Conrad Motel, (406) 278-7544, 210 N. Main. $46–$56.

Conrad Super 8, (800) 442-4667, 215 N. Main. $52–$67.

*SHELBY, MONTANA

Crossroads Inn, (406) 434-5134, US 2. $58.

O'Haire Manor Motel, (800) 541-5809, 204 2nd St. S. $45.

*CUT BANK, MONTANA

Corner Motel, (406) 873-5588, 1201 E. Main St. $40–$45.

Glacier Gateway Inn, (406) 873-5544, 1121 E. Railroad St. $50–$55.

Northern Motor Inn, (406) 873-5662, 609 W. Main. $52.

*Browning, Montana

War Bonnet Lodge, (406) 338-7610. $60.

Western Motel, (406) 338-7572, 121 Central Ave. E. $60–$75.

Great Falls, Montana

Best Western Heritage Inn, (800) 548-0361, 1700 Fox Farm Rd. $60–$90.

Collins Mansion Bed & Breakfast, (877) 452-6798, 1003 2nd Ave. N.W. $65–$85.

Edelweiss Motor Inn, (406) 452-9503, 626 Central Ave. W. $40.

Fairfield Inn, (406) 454-3000, 1000 9th Ave. S. $60–$80.

Great Falls Inn, (800) 454-6010, 1400 28th St. S. $50–$60.

Holiday Inn, (406) 727-7200, 400 10th Ave. S. $75–$85.

Old Oak Inn, (888) 727-5782, 709 4th Ave. N. $55–$95.

Cascade, Montana

Badger Motel, (406) 468-9330, 132 1st St. N. $43–$48.

Fly Fishers' Inn, (406) 468-2529, 2629 Old Hwy. 91. Upscale lodge and guide service.

Wolf Creek, Montana

The Bungalow Bed & Breakfast, (888) 286-4250. 2020 US 287. $85–$90.

Frenchy's Motel, (406) 235-4251. $40.

Holter Lake Lodge, (888) 235-4331, 1350 Beartooth Rd. $40–$60.

Montana River Outfitters, (800) 800-4350, 515 Recreation Rd. Under $40.

Helena, Montana

Budget Inn Express, (800) 862-1334, 524 N. Last Chance Gulch. $40–$45.

Comfort Inn, (406) 443-1000, 750 N. Fee St. $65–$70.

Jorgenson's Holiday Motel, (800) 272-1770 (in state) or (800) 521-2743, 1714 11th Ave. $60–$100.

Knight's Rest Motel, (888) 442-6384, 1831 Euclid Ave. $45.

Shilo Inn, (406) 442-0320, 2020 Prospect Ave. $60–$90.

Park Plaza Hotel, (800) 332-2290 (in state) or (406) 443-2200, 22 N. Last Chance Gulch. $80–$85.

The Sanders—Helena's Bed & Breakfast, (406) 442-3309, 328 N. Ewing. $90–$105.

**Lincoln, Montana

Leepers Motel, (406) 362-4333, MT 200. $40–$45.

Townsend, Montana

Lake Townsend Motel, (406) 266-3461, 413 N. Pine. $38–$40.

Mustang Motel, (406) 266-3491, 412 N. Front. $36–$38.

THREE FORKS, MONTANA

Broken Spur Motel, (406) 285-3237, 124 W. Elm. $48–$52.
Bud Lilly's Anglers Retreat, (406) 285-6690, 16 W. Birch. $45–$165.
Fort Three Forks Motel, (406) 285-3233, I-90 at US 287. $52–$58.
Sacajawea Hotel, (800) 821-7326, 5 N. Main St. $75–$105.

CAMPING

BIG SANDY, MONTANA

Coalbanks Landing, 11 miles south on US 87, then south at sign for Upper Missouri Wild and Scenic River. Primitive sites.

Judith Landing, 44 miles southeast on Secondary Rte. 236, on the Upper Missouri Wild and Scenic River. Primitive sites.

FORT BENTON, MONTANA

Benton RV Park, (406) 622-5015, north side of town.

*CONRAD, MONTANA

Sunrise Trailer Court, (406) 278-5901, 4 blocks east of stoplight.

*SHELBY, MONTANA

Lake Shel-oole Campground, (406) 434-5222, 0.5 mile south on I-15 business bypass.
Lewis and Clark RV Park, (406) 434-2710, I-15 Exit 364, 131 9th Ave. N.

*CUT BANK, MONTANA

Shady Grove Campground, (406) 336-2475, 6 miles west on US 2.

*BROWNING, MONTANA

Sleeping Wolf Campground, (406) 338-7933, 0.5 mile west on US 89.

GREAT FALLS, MONTANA

Dick's RV Park, (406) 452-0333, I-15 Exit 278, west of river on 10th Ave. S.
Great Falls KOA, (406) 727-3191, 1500 51st St. S.

CASCADE, MONTANA

Atkinson Park, (406) 468-2808, adjacent to I-15 in town.

WOLF CREEK, MONTANA

Holter Lake, (406) 235-4314, I-15 Exit 226, left 3 miles to lake. Primitive sites.

HELENA, MONTANA

Buzz In RV Park & Campground, (406) 449-1291, 5 miles east on US 12/287.
Canyon Ferry Reservoir, (406) 444-4475, 10 miles east on US 12/287, then 12 miles north on County Rd. 284.
Helena Campground & RV Resort, (406) 458-4714, 5820 N. Montana Ave.

Kim's Marina and RV Resort, (406) 475-3723, 10 miles east on US 12/287, then 10 miles north on County Rd. 284.

**LINCOLN, MONTANA

Aspen Grove, (406) 362-4265, 7 miles east on MT 200. Primitive sites.

Spring Creek RV Park, (406) 362-4140, west edge of town on MT 200.

TOWNSEND, MONTANA

Indian Road, 1 mile north on US 12/287.

Silos RV Park, (406) 266-3100, 7 miles north on US 12/87, then east on Silos Rd.

THREE FORKS, MONTANA

Missouri Headwaters State Park, 6 miles northeast on Secondary Rd. 286. Primitive sites.

Three Forks KOA, (406) 285-3611, 1 mile south of I-90 Exit 274.

RESTAURANTS

LOMA, MONTANA

Ma's Loma Café, (406) 739-4000, US 87. Home cooking.

FORT BENTON, MONTANA

The Banque Club, (406) 622-5272, 1318 Front St. Popular steakhouse.

Bob's Riverfront Restaurant, (406) 622-3443, 1414 Front St. Good food, local gathering place.

*SHELBY, MONTANA

Retregea's, (406) 434-5932, 215 Main St. Wide menu.

*CUT BANK, MONTANA

Village Dining and Lounge, (406) 873-5005, Northern Village Shopping Center.

*BROWNING, MONTANA

Browning Cafe. (406) 338-7478, Burgers, soups, steaks. Open 24 hours.

GREAT FALLS, MONTANA

Baker Bob's Big Stack Bakery & Delicatessen/Back Alley Pub, (406) 727-5910, 110 Central Ave.

Bert and Ernie's Saloon and Eatery, (406) 453-0601, 300 1st Ave. S. Charbroiled burgers, big selection of imported draft beer. Also in Helena.

Eddie's Supper Club, (406) 453-1616, 3725 2nd Ave. N. Popular local steakhouse.

Jaker's Steak Ribs & Fish House, (406) 727-1033, 1500 10th Ave. S.

Mama Cassie's, (406) 454-3354, 319 1st Ave. N. Italian restaurant.

3D International, (406) 453-6561, 1825 Smelter Ave. (Black Eagle). Chinese-American-Mongolian fare overlooking Missouri River.

Penny's Gourmet to Go, (406) 453-7070, 815 Central Ave. Healthy food to eat in or take out.

Stir Crazy, (406) 727-5509, 1720 10th Ave S. Filipino food. Closed Sundays.

CASCADE, MONTANA

Badger Cafe, (406) 468-2777, 132 1st St. N. Homemade specialties.

Osterman's Missouri Inn, (406) 468-9884, 2474 Old Hwy. 91.

WOLF CREEK, MONTANA

Holter Lake Lodge, (406) 235-4331, on Holter Lake.

Oasis Bar and Cafe, (406) 235-9992.

HELENA, MONTANA

Benny's Restaurant, (406) 443-0105, 305 Fuller Ave. Breakfast, lunch, live music Friday evenings.

Country Harvest, (406) 443-7457, 2000 Prospect Ave. 24-hour family restaurant.

The Rialto, (406) 442-1890, 52 N. Last Chance Gulch. Famous burgers.

The Stonehouse Restaurant, (406) 449-2552, 120 Reeder's Alley. Wide, imaginative menu.

The Windbag Saloon, (406) 443-9669, 19 S. Last Chance Gulch. Burgers, steaks, and colorful atmosphere.

Yacht Basin Restaurant, (406) 475-3125, 7025 Canyon Ferry Rd. Overlooking Canyon Ferry Lake.

Yat Son Chinese Restaurant, (406) 442-5405, 2 S. Main St.

TOWNSEND, MONTANA

Fireside Restaurant, (406) 266-3516, US 12. Beef and seafood.

Rosario's Italian Restaurant and Pizzeria, (406) 266-3603, 316 N. Front St. Authentic Italian cuisine featuring veal, chicken, and pasta.

Yummies Cafe and Bakery, (406) 266-3210, 321 Broadway. Specialties include burgers and Saturday breakfast buffet.

THREE FORKS, MONTANA

Blue Willow Inn, (406) 285-6660, 6 miles south of town in Willow Creek.

Custer's Last Root Beer Stand, (406) 285-6713, 23 W. Date St.

Historic Headwaters Restaurant, (406) 285-4511, 105 S. Main St. Creative food. Open Wednesday–Sunday.

Sacajawea Hotel, (406) 285-6515, 5 N. Main St.

CHAPTER SEVEN

WESTERN MONTANA AND IDAHO

I have been wet and as cold in every part as I ever was in my life, indeed I was at one time fearful my feet would freeze in the thin moccasins I wore.

—William Clark, September 16, 1805, on the Lolo Trail in present-day Idaho.

THE JEFFERSON AND BEAVERHEAD VALLEYS

From the Three Forks area, follow Montana 2/U.S. Highway 287. When US 287 branches off south toward Yellowstone, stay on the Lewis and Clark Trail by continuing west on MT 2.

The entrance to Lewis and Clark Caverns State Park is just west of this junction. This was Montana's first state park, but before that it was a national monument, and President Theodore Roosevelt is credited with naming the park in honor of the captains. It's true the corps followed the Jefferson River right through this area, but there is no evidence the captains were aware of the caverns' existence.

A steep, winding, 3-mile road leading from the highway reaches the caverns, considered among the best in the Northwest. Trailers may be left in the lower parking lot at their owners' discretion, but park staff say all sorts of big rigs have made the drive with no trouble. Two-hour guided tours of the caverns are available May 1 through September 30. The visitor center has additional information and displays, and food and gifts are offered for sale during summer months. The scenic road also winds past two shady picnic areas and an overlook of the Jefferson River valley.

Aside from cavern connoisseurs, Lewis and Clark State Park draws its share of cyclists, anglers, hikers, canoeists, and wildlife watchers. Those who want to stay overnight have their choice of camping or cabins; the latter are available by reservation year-round. For more information, call (406) 287-3541.

From the park, continue west on MT 2. North of Three Forks, travelers will recall, the landscape was wide open with mountains in the distance. Here, the canyon is not much wider than the Jefferson River, with impressive cliffs towering on each side.

. . . .

After leaving Three Forks, Lewis and three other men set out in advance to resume the search for Sacagawea's people. On August 1, they came upon a herd of elk near what is now the tiny town of La Hood and killed two for lunch before moving on, leaving most of the meat for Clark and the rest of the party. The rear guard reached the site later in the day and made camp.

At Whitehall, which boasts several Lewis–and–Clark–themed murals, take Montana 55 south to its junction with Montana 41, which leads all the way into Dillon. About 10 miles south of Whitehall, MT 55 passes through three counties—Jefferson, Silver Bow, and Madison—within the space of about a mile.

At Twin Bridges, the Jefferson River splits into two forks, the right fork being the Big Hole River and the main stem becoming the Beaverhead (the Ruby River, meanwhile, branches off to the southeast a few more miles south). Concluding after a day's exploration that the main stem was still the correct route, Lewis left a note for Clark on a green willow pole and proceeded down the Beaverhead. This method of communication had worked before with no problem, but this time, a beaver gnawed down the willow and made off with the note. Confused, the Clark contingent set off down the Big Hole—a swift and dangerous stream. One canoe turned over and two others filled with water, resulting in the loss of some trade goods and gunpowder and an injury to Private Whitehouse. The party was finally turned back on the right course by Drouillard.

Twin Bridges is a good jumping-off spot for Virginia City and Nevada City, two famous Montana mining towns. Both are accessible via MT 287. Virginia City harbored 10,000 prospectors in the 1860s, and the town soon became a hotbed of lawlessness. A local group of vigilantes eventually took matters in their own hands, hanging the outlaws (along with the scofflaws' leader, the sheriff). Today, Virginia City has a population of only 150 or so, but it's still the seat of Madison County and a big hit with the tourists. Nevada City, 1 mile downriver, has nearly 100 buildings restored to preserve the air of an early mining camp. The Alder Gulch short-line steam railroad runs between the two towns.

Twin Bridges has a small riverside park. There's no camping, but a display board posts several large Forest Service maps. It's a good place to get your bearings and plot the rest of the day's travels. Twin Bridges is also home to the Madison County Fair each August, and to the R. L. Winston Rod Company, purveyors of top-notch fly-fishing gear. From here, continue south toward Dillon.

Seeing Beaverhead Rock from MT 41, the traveler's first thought is, "Boy, those Shoshone Indians must have had vivid imaginations." Supposedly, the rock resembles the head of a swimming beaver, and Sacagawea had no trouble recognizing the landmark when the corps arrived in the area. A historical marker about 0.5 mile south of the Beaverhead County line tells the tale: in August 1805, members of the expedition sighted what Clark called a "remarkable cliff" to the west. Both Lewis and Clark agreed on the resemblance and noted it in their journals, adding that Sacagawea said it meant her homeland was on a river just over the mountains to the southwest.

Area historians say Beaverhead Rock looks most like its namesake from the east, backlit by a setting sun. But there is some controversy in southwest Montana over which rock is the Beaverhead Rock. Most folks agree it is the one north of Dillon, but some feel it is an area otherwise referred to in the journals as Rattlesnake Cliffs—an area located south of Dillon at Interstate 15, Exit 56. From the modern highway angle, however, Rattlesnake Cliffs looks a lot like a buffalo, not a beaver's head. In its brochure, Dillon Flying Service promises passengers a look at "both Beaverhead Rocks—you decide which one Sacagawea identified as her tribe's landmark." Flights start at about $50 per person; to arrange one, call (406) 683-5242.

Beaverhead Rock is important because Sacagawea knew that near here, her people customarily crossed the Continental Divide. "The Indian woman recognized the point of a high plain to our right which she informed us was not very distant from the summer retreat of her nation on a river beyond the mountains which runs to the west," Lewis wrote on August 8, 1805. "She assures us that we shall either find her people on this river or the river immediately west of its source, which from its present size cannot be distant. As it is now all important with us to meet with those people as soon as possible, I determined to proceed tomorrow with a small party to the source of the principal stream of this river and pass the mountains to the Columbia, and down that river until I find the Indians." About 9 miles south of Beaverhead Rock, the expedition reached its 3,000-mile mark.

Dillon is a major trade center for southwest Montana, as well as the home of Western Montana College of the University of Montana. Stop by the 1909 Union Pacific Depot at 125 South Montana Street to load up on local travel information and see an impressive diorama depicting Lewis's departure for Lemhi Pass. Once featured in the Montana Historical Society Museum in Helena, the diorama sat in storage for many years before being reconstructed in Dillon. Next door, the Beaverhead County Museum has an extremely helpful staff and interesting exhibits from all aspects of life in early Dillon.

By now, you've probably noticed many Montana towns mark their communities by painting letters on a nearby hillside. In Dillon, the letter is "B," which might seem strange until you learn it can stand for either Beaverhead or the Bulldogs of Western Montana College. Dillon has an excellent variety of stores for a town its size. It's a good place to get fuel or stock up for a trip over Lemhi Pass or into the Big Hole country. This is also major fly-fishing country, with many outfitters available to guide a trip on the Big Hole or Beaverhead rivers.

Clark's Lookout, just northwest of Dillon, is locally known as Lover's Leap. Clark—again bringing up the rear after Lewis and party had gone on ahead—

reportedly ascended this bluff to survey the surrounding country and get his bearings before moving on. To get there, turn west at the sign for the Frontage Road/Old U.S. Highway 91 north. (It's at the big Town Pump truck stop on Dillon's north side.) After about 0.3 mile, the road goes underneath the overpass to the interstate. At 0.6 mile, it crosses the Beaverhead. After the bridge, turn left and cross a set of railroad tracks. Clark's Lookout is on the right.

The area is under the state parks department's jurisdiction, but it has not been developed. The only way to know you're in the right place is by the small sign on the log fence, noting that the site is property of the Montana Department of Fish, Wildlife and Parks. Perch atop the lookout for a picnic; then head for the interstate to continue following the explorers' trail.

County Road 278 (at Exit 59, Dillon) is the gateway to the Big Hole Valley, as well as a shortcut over the Divide for motorists unwilling to try Lemhi Pass. County Road 278 gives access to the ghost town of Bannack (Montana's first capital), the quintessentially Montanan ranching towns of Jackson and Wisdom, the Big Hole National Battlefield, and the Bitterroot Valley via Chief Joseph Pass. William Clark followed this route east on his trip home in 1806; highlights will be described in a separate section ("Homeward Bound: Clark Explores the Big Hole") later in this chapter.

CAMP FORTUNATE AND LEMHI PASS

Once back on I-15, drive south to Exit 44 (Clark Canyon Dam).

Camp Fortunate was inundated by the reservoir, but a lookout on the lake's west side offers an approximate view of this important site. It was here the expedition was assured of help in its passage across the Continental Divide, and here that Sacagawea's presence proved especially beneficial.

Lewis arrived in the area first, coming to a fork at the head of the Beaverhead River on August 10, 1805. After examining both forks, he and the advance party decided to follow the right stream, Horse Prairie Creek, although geographers later determined that the left fork—Red Rock River—led to the true Missouri River headwaters. Nevertheless, Lewis's instincts proved correct, as we shall soon see.

The next day, Lewis spotted a Shoshone on horseback—the first Indian the expedition had seen in the whole of what is now Montana. Thrilled, he moved toward the Indian, shouting "tab-ba-bone." Earlier, Lewis had asked Sacagawea the Shoshone word for "white man." She must have misunderstood, however, for the word "tab-ba-bone" actually meant "stranger." To make matters worse, John Shields continued moving toward the Indian, who—frightened by Lewis's calls and Shields's action—took off into the mountains, "and with him vanished all my hopes of obtaining horses for the present," Lewis wrote. "I now felt quite as much mortification and disappointment as I had pleasure and expectation at the first sight of this Indian." Lewis fixed an American flag to a pole as a symbol of peace, and his party spent the rest of the day trying to track the Indians, but to no avail.

On August 12, the party moved on up into the mountains, following what Lewis called a "large and plain Indian road. . . . I therefore did not despair of shortly finding a passage over the mountains and of tasting the waters of the great Columbia this evening." Another 4 miles on, Lewis and his men reached the head of Trail Creek, which Lewis dubbed "the most distant fountain of the mighty Missouri in search of which we have spent so many toilsome days and restless nights. Thus far I had accomplished one of those great objects on which my mind has been unalterably fixed for many years." With great gusto, Lewis drank the water. Meanwhile, Private Hugh McNeal "had exultingly stood with a foot on each side of this little rivulet and thanked his god that he had lived to bestride the mighty and heretofore deemed endless Missouri."

Plenty of excitement for one day, but there was more to come, and a bit of disappointment, too. "After refreshing ourselves we proceeded on to the top of the dividing ridge [Lemhi Pass] from which I discovered immense ranges of high mountains still to the West of us with their tops partially covered with snow," Lewis continued. "I now descended the mountain about three-quarters of a mile which I found much steeper than on the opposite side, to a handsome

Clark Canyon Reservoir, site of Camp Fortunate and the meeting with the Shoshone Indians.

bold running creek of cold clear water. Here I first tasted the water of the great Columbia River."

Lewis had crossed the divide, but the sight of those "immense ranges of mountains" made it clear there was still no easy way to the Columbia. It was already mid-August, and who knew how far they had to go? The men made their first camp in what is now Idaho, determined to contact the Shoshone the next day—which is exactly what happened.

On August 13, the advance party made its way into the valley and finally, about a mile ahead, saw two women, a man, and some dogs. Lewis and his men kept walking as the Shoshone stood still; when they came within a half-mile, Lewis asked the others to wait as he moved ahead, unfurling the flag and still calling out "tab-ba-bone." These Indians soon disappeared, but a mile down the road, the white men saw three more women. Giving them presents and painting their cheeks with vermillion, a sign of peace, Lewis asked them to alert their village that the white men came in peace. "We had marched on about two miles when we met a party of about 60 warriors mounted on excellent horses who came in nearly full speed," Lewis wrote. "The chief and two others who were a little in advance of the main body spoke to the women, and they informed them who we were and exultingly showed the presents which had been given them. These men then advanced and embraced me very affectionately . . . both parties now advanced and we were all caressed and besmeared with their grease and paint til I was heartily tired of the national hug. I now had the pipe lit and gave them smoke."

Lewis's next task was to convince the Shoshone to accompany him back over the divide. He told how Clark and the others were waiting over the mountains with their baggage, and that they needed horses to make the trip. At first, Lewis's pleas were met with resistance, for some of the Shoshone feared the white men might be in league with their enemies, the Pahkees. But Lewis finally convinced Cameahwait, the Shoshone chief, and a number of others to go with him. They arrived back at the forks of the Jefferson, with Clark nowhere to be found. Lewis feared the Indians, feeling tricked, would leave. But most stayed, and Clark and his contingent arrived the next day, August 17.

Nicholas Biddle, in his 1814 history of the expedition, related the meeting this way: "On setting out at 7 o'clock, Captain Clark with Charbonneau and his wife walked on shore, but they had not gone more than a mile before Clark saw Sacagawea, who was with her husband 100 yards ahead, begin to dance and show every mark of the most extravagant joy." As the parties drew closer, "a woman made her way through the crowd toward Sacagawea, and recognizing each other, they embraced with the most tender affection." The two women, it turned out, had been childhood friends. Sacagawea hadn't seen her since girlhood. The other child had slipped into the water to escape capture at Three Forks, which is how she got her name—Jumping Fish.

The captains and Indians exchanged greetings and made preparations for council. Sacagawea was set to help interpret the Shoshone message. "She came into the tent, sat down, and was beginning to interpret, when in the person of Cameahwait she recognized her brother," Biddle wrote. "She instantly jumped up, and ran and embraced him, throwing over him her blanket and weeping profusely. The chief was himself moved, though not in the same degree. After some conversation between them, she returned to her seat, and attempted to interpret, but her new situation seemed to overpower her, and she was frequently interrupted by tears."

Despite her emotion, Sacagawea was successful in helping the expedition negotiate for horses. Here at the newly named Camp Fortunate, the corps also cached canoes and supplies for the return trip, and prepared to begin their overland journey.

Today, just about any vehicle can travel over Lemhi Pass in the summertime, although the Idaho side (more steep and narrow than the Montana side, as Lewis noted) isn't recommended for large motor homes or vehicles towing trailers, with a maximum vehicle length of 26 feet. The turnoff for Lemhi Pass is 22 miles from Clark Canyon Dam and about 9 miles past the small settlement of Grant. Coming from Clark Canyon, turn right at the second of two Forest Service access signs. From the turn, it is 12 miles to the pass. The route is marked by a Lewis and Clark Trail sign. If you're traveling from southern Idaho, it's also

Horse Prairie Ranch near Lemhi Pass.

possible (and a bit faster) to get to the Lemhi Pass junction via Bannock Pass northeast of Leadore, Idaho. In that case, just watch for the turnoff on your left 12 miles from Bannock Pass.

The road passes through the Bar Double T ranch, and drivers may well encounter cattle on the road, so be alert. Past the ranch houses, the road can be a bit boggy and rutted, but still passable. A few miles farther, the road forks left to Frying Pan Road. Stay on the main way; it's just 3 miles to the pass.

Although the marker at Lemhi Pass lists its elevation at 7,339, most maps put it at 7,373 feet. In either case, this marked the high spot on the Lewis and

REAL WESTERN RANCH LIFE

Travelers looking for an authentic working ranch experience along the Lewis and Clark Trail will want to check into a stay at the Horse Prairie Ranch near Grant, Montana. It was on this very ground that Lewis first spotted the Shoshone boy on horseback. Today, ranch personnel can still point out such landmarks as the "elevated situation" where Lewis awaited further signs of Indians.

The HPR, in business under various names since the late nineteenth century, is a true cattle ranch that just happens to have some of Montana's most comfortable accommodations. Summertime guests stay for four or six nights, typically spending much of each day on horseback (though no previous riding experience is required; visitors go through a complete orientation at the beginning of their stay). When they're not helping wranglers move cattle, guests can take treks to such nearby historical sites as Lemhi Pass, the Big Hole National Battlefield, and Bannack. Other leisure activities include hay rides, fishing, line dancing, and campfires.

Horse Prairie Ranch does a great job of blending the ranch experience with fine amenities. The cabins—which sleep between one and eight people—feature modern furnishings, down comforters, and porches for enjoying the mountain views all around. There's no TV reception out here, but each cabin has a VCR, and guests can choose from a big library of tapes (by the Creekside Lodge's fireplace, beneath the Charlie Russell painting of "Lewis & Clark Meeting the Shoshones" on loan from the State Bank & Trust in Dillon). Mealtimes are a real highlight, with plenty of creative comfort food and lighter fare on each menu. Rates for a six-night stay start at $1,150 per person. (A minimum four-night stay is also available, with prices starting at about $775 per person.) For an authentic ranch adventure in an unbeatable historic location, Horse Prairie Ranch may well be Montana's last best place. For reservations or more information, call (406) 681-3155; write to Horse Prairie Guest Ranch, 3300 Bachelor Mountain Road, Dillon, Montana 59725; or go to http://guestranches.com/hpr/. ▲

Clark Trail. Today, it is a most splendid place to watch a sunset and perhaps spend the night. As dusk falls, the skies may turn purple, pink, or orange, shadows falling over one mountain ridge after another. A small primitive campground, Sacagawea Memorial Camp, rests just below the pass on the Montana side. This area is known as an elk calving ground, and lucky visitors may see elk or their tracks and other signs.

From Lemhi Pass, there are two ways to get down the mountain to Tendoy and Idaho 28; together, they make a loop known as the Lewis and Clark National Backcountry Byway and Adventure Road. (The actual route taken by the expedition lay mostly between the two present-day roads.) The route straight ahead, Agency Creek Road (marked on some maps as the Lewis and Clark Highway), is a sharp, steep descent with many tight curves. Via Agency Creek, it's 13 miles to Tendoy. The other route, on your right if you're facing into Idaho, is the Warm Springs Wood Road. It's exactly twice as long—26 miles—as the Agency Creek Road, but it's the better choice for larger vehicles up to 26 feet long or cars with minimal clearance. It's best to avoid both roads in bad weather.

We'll begin with a look at Agency Creek Road. At all times, be alert for oncoming traffic and remember that vehicles traveling uphill have the right of way. A sign a few miles down the road marks the corps' first Idaho campsite, which can be reached by hiking three-quarters of a mile from the road. Other signs explain later facets of area history. If you think modern vehicles have it tough, imagine what this route must have been like for the Red Rock Stage, which ran the 125 miles between Salmon, Idaho, and Red Rock, Montana, daily from 1866 until 1910. Several holdups occurred near Lemhi Pass, and it wasn't unusual for a stage to overturn on the treacherous road.

The area also saw some mining activity, most notably at the Copper Queen Mine, which operated sporadically from 1883 to 1940. There's another small campground about 7.5 miles from the summit. This one, a BLM site called Agency Creek, has a toilet and picnic tables.

Eleven miles west of Lemhi Pass, a sign on the left-hand side notes the nearby grave of Chief Tendoy, who was a well-respected and influential Indian leader. The site is sacred to Native Americans, and visitation by the general public is not considered appropriate. At 12 miles, the traveler comes to a "T" in the road. Turn right, then left to get to the hamlet of Tendoy.

The other route, the Warm Springs Wood Road, is also known as Forest Road 185. Almost immediately upon turning right from Lemhi Pass, motorists will encounter a fork in the road. Stay to the left. At 6 miles, the road intersects with the Continental Divide National Scenic Trail, which travels 3,100 miles from Canada to Mexico. A sign explains how hikers can follow the trail by following the dot-over-slash blazes on the trees to the east.

The first half of the Warm Springs Wood route travels mostly through

SALMON TRAVEL TIPS

Salmon is accessible via Salmon Air Taxi, which offers scheduled round-trip flights to and from Boise each Monday, Wednesday, and Friday. Round-trip cost from Boise is about $180 per person. Scenic chartered flights of the area also are available. For reservations, call (800) 448-3413 or (208) 756-6211. The nearest major airports are at Missoula (142 miles) and Idaho Falls (161 miles).

forested areas, but the terrain opens up about 14 miles from Lemhi Pass. Pull over at about the 16-mile mark (at the junction of Forest Road 186, Kenney Creek Road) for a tremendous view up and down the Lemhi Valley. Here, even more than at Lemhi Pass, it's possible to get a sense of what must have been going through the Corps' minds before they were certain they'd get horses. The entire western horizon is blocked by mountains, some covered by snow even in late summer.

From here, the Warm Springs Wood Road gets steeper and more winding, so be attentive and yield the right-of-way to any uphill traffic you encounter. Watch on your left for a large boulder commemorating Lewis's first display of the U.S. flag west of the Continental Divide on August 13, 1805, and on your right for a small interpretive kiosk heralding the homeland of Sacagawea (still steadfastly spelled and pronounced Sac-a-ja-WE-a in these parts). As the road enters Tendoy, several monuments and signs pay homage to Fort Lemhi, a Mormon outpost in the area from 1855 to 1858 and site of the first irrigation project in the Northwest.

The Tendoy Store on ID 28 sells gas, food, and a good selection of groceries and hardware. It's usually open daily from about 7 A.M. to 7 P.M. in summertime and 8 A.M. to 6 P.M. the rest of the year. Longtime owner Viola Anglin has all kinds of great stories about the wide range of Lewis and Clark buffs who inevitably stop in after traversing Lemhi Pass—including the man who rolled out his sleeping bag half in Montana, half in Idaho, to spend the night literally on the Continental Divide.

From Tendoy, it's a quick and scenic 22 miles north to Salmon, the major town in these parts. Idaho 28 parallels the Lemhi River through a valley that was Sacagawea's true homeland, the area in which she was born and grew up until that ill-fated trip to the Three Forks.

The Salmon National Forest office on U.S. Highway 93 south of Salmon has an interesting exhibit showing several researchers' opinions on the route Lewis and Clark took over Lost Trail Pass in September 1805. On an area topographic map, the known trail is traced through the September 2 campsite near Deep Creek north of Gibbonsville. From there, however, no one is sure of the exact route taken.

Salmon is a prime launching point for pack and float trips into the Central Idaho Rockies. The Lemhi County Historical Museum at 210 Main Street displays pioneer and Indian artifacts, along with antique treasures from the Far East. Stop by the visitor center at 200 Main Street for more information on the many recreational opportunities close to Salmon. The Salmon River, which originates in central Idaho not far from Sun Valley, is the longest American free-flowing and undammed river running entirely within one state. It parallels US 93 north and south of Salmon, and numerous fishing and recreation points dot the way.

Early each August, Salmon holds a Sacajawea Heritage Days festival. Events typically include a display of replica items from the Lewis and Clark Expedition; an appearance by the Shoshone-Bannock tribal dancers from Fort Hall, Idaho; a dutch-oven cookoff; concerts; and a hot-air-balloon rally. Salmon hopes to establish an interpretive center to honor Sacagawea sometime before the bicentennial. For the dates of this year's festival or an update on area activities, contact the Salmon Valley Chamber of Commerce at (208) 756-2100.

Near what is now North Fork, Idaho, Clark and an advance party—including his newly hired Shoshone guide, Toby—explored the Salmon River several miles downstream to see if it might provide the hoped-for route to the Pacific. It's possible to retrace their reconnaissance by motor vehicle along Forest Road 30 west of North Fork. Between 2 and 4 miles in, the party encountered what Sergeant Patrick Gass described as "dreadful narrows, where the rocks were in some places breast high, and no path or trail of any kind." The next day, Gass wrote that the river—by this point about 6 miles from North Fork—"is not confined by the mountains that it is not more than 20 yards wide, and very rapid. The mountains on the side are not less than 1,000 feet high and very steep." The party turned back between Spring Creek and Squaw Creek. Toby told Clark that no one from his tribe had ever ventured farther down the river. Clark, surveying the roiling, churning waters of Pine Creek Rapids, agreed they appeared entirely impassable.

The Salmon Wild and Scenic River—often called "the River of No Return"—is now a favorite among whitewater rafters. How can modern boaters go where Lewis and Clark and their Native American forerunners could not? For one thing, the Civilian Conservation Corps dynamited part of Pine Creek Rapids to build the road from North Fork. (Before the blasting, Pine Creek Rapids were almost certainly Class V.) For another, today's self-bailing whitewater rafts are technologically superior to the dugout canoes of Lewis and Clark's day.

North Fork is the jumping-off spot for float trips ranging from five hours to several days, making this an ideal place to fit some whitewater action into your travel plans. Kookaburra Guided Whitewater Trips offers a full-day trip including lunch for $75 per person. The adventures include Pine Creek Rapids and other Class III water, along with plenty of historical and natural interpretation

TOURING THE SALMON AREA

Salmon is one of the most remote places in the contiguous United States, but it's starting to emerge as a center of Lewis and Clark Trail tourism. Already, several local businesses are taking people on guided tours of the area. The excursions all are rooted in the idea that here in the high country, it's best to leave the driving to someone else.

Martin Capps's father homesteaded in the Salmon area in the early 1930s, and Capps—a licensed outfitter since 1954—has led trips into the nearby wilderness for many years. Recently, he's also been driving people over Lemhi Pass, either in their own vehicle or Capps's van. Cost is about $45 per person, with a four-person or $180 minimum. Lunch is extra. Capps also offers horseback riding trips to several locations (including the Continental Divide Trail); combination van and float trips down the Salmon River from North Fork; and working ranch vacations. Prices vary; call (208) 756-3954 or write Happy Hollow Vacation, HC 61 Box 14, Salmon, Idaho 83467 for details.

Two Salmon-area bed-and-breakfasts—one traditional, the other contemporary—offer optional guided Lewis and Clark tours to their guests. Greyhouse Inn Bed & Breakfast, 12 miles south of Salmon on US 93, is one of the nicest in central Idaho, with a scenic setting in the Salmon River Canyon and gracious hospitality from Sharon and David Osgood. Traveling across Bannock Pass to access Lemhi from the east—the way the expedition did—the Osgoods' tours stop for lunch at Sacagawea Memorial Camp before descending via the Agency Creek Road. Cost in 1999 was $45 per person. Overnight rates in the Greyhouse Inn's four cozy Victorian-style rooms run from $65 to $80 in the summer, including breakfast. The Osgoods' 100-year-old-plus house is itself historic; it was originally the hospital in Salmon before being moved upriver. For reservations or more information, call (800) 348-8097 or (208) 756-3968; write to HC-61, Box 16, Salmon, Idaho 83467; or see www.greyhouseinn.com.

Lewis and Clark tours also are possible from 100 Acre Wood Bed & Breakfast Resort, located 25 miles north of Salmon. This contemporary three-story log home has seven comfortable rooms priced from $55 to $115, including breakfast. Activities include fishing and boating, wildlife viewing, and dining at the resort's highly regarded restaurant. The resort's typical Corps of Discovery trek involves a full-day loop up Agency Creek to Lemhi Pass, returning via the Warm Springs Wood Road. The cost is $100, including lunch; package deals including lodging and dinner are available. The resort also sits within an easy stroll of Trail Gulch, terminus of the hiking trail that begins at Wagonhammer Springs south of North Fork. For more information or to book a room or tour, call Jon and Nancy Cummings at (208) 865-2165; write 100 Acre Wood, P.O. Box 202, North Fork, Idaho 83466; or send an e-mail to acrewood@ida.net. Solaas Bed & Breakfast hasn't gotten into the Lewis and Clark tour business, but it has a fine location right along ID 28 in the community of Baker, 9 miles south of Salmon. Roger and

Sharon Solaas's home started as a stage stop hotel. More recently, it served as the base of explorations for author William Least Heat-Moon, when he was in the area researching his best-selling book *River-Horse*. Solaas B&B has seven rooms available, priced at $45 to $50. For more information, write Solaas Bed & Breakfast, Box 59 RR1, Salmon, Idaho 83467, or call (208) 756-3903. ▲

and a gourmet lunch. Kookaburra also has two- and three-day trips geared especially to Lewis and Clark buffs, which include tours to Lemhi Pass and floats on the Salmon. Call (888) 654-4386 or see Kookaburra's website at www.raft4fun.com for reservations or information.

Many other outfitters run longer trips farther down the Salmon, beyond where Clark journeyed. These include Aggipah River Trips, (208) 756-4167; ARTA, (800) 323-2782; Echo: The Wilderness Company, (800) 652-3246; Idaho Adventures, (208) 756-2986; North Fork Guides, (208) 865-2534; Salmon River Outfitters, (208) 643-4426; and Wilderness River Outfitters, (208) 756-3959. For a complete list of outfitters, contact the Idaho Outfitters and Guides Association at (208) 342-1438. Plan on spending about $1,000 to $1,500 per person for a five- to six-day Main Salmon float.

The North Fork area also has a stretch of hiking trail where travelers can take the same path trod by Lewis and Clark. To get there, park at the Wagonhammer Springs area on the right side of US 93 northbound near milepost 324. Follow the 2-mile trail up Wagonhammer Creek to the mouth of Thompson Gulch. From there, take a left onto the marked trail that leads to Trail Gulch, which meets US 93 about 3 miles north of North Fork. Total trail distance is about 6 miles. This is a strenuous hike with many ups and downs. Be sure to carry water and wear sunscreen.

Once it became apparent the Salmon River was impassable, Clark sent Lewis a message outlining three possible options. The first involved obtaining one horse for each man and, using Toby as a guide, proceeding by land to a navigable river. The second plan would divide the men into two groups. One party would attempt to navigate the Salmon River, while the other would travel by horseback. The third idea also involved splitting the corps into two parties, with one going over the mountains to the north while the other returned to Great Falls for supplies that had been cached there before traveling, via the Sun River to the land of the Flatheads near present-day Missoula.

Clark recommended the first, noting that if the Indians and their women and children could make it, it would be a snap for his trail-hardened men. When Lewis received the message, however, he had learned the Shoshone didn't have enough horses to spare one for each of the white men. Lewis wrote back and asked Clark to come anyway, and get the 22 horses he had been able to buy. Clark negotiated for another two animals. Reunited, the parties started their ascent toward Lost Trail Pass.

HOMEWARD BOUND: CLARK EXPLORES THE BIG HOLE

On his return trip in 1806, Clark explored what is now one of Montana's most isolated and beautiful areas: the Big Hole. To follow his route today, head east on Montana 43 at Lost Trail Pass. Clark, coming from the north, actually traversed Gibbons Pass, also nearby. This way is navigable, but the road is not much better than the one Clark found almost 200 years ago. An interpretive marker between mileposts 12 and 13 on MT 43 mentions that Clark passed through the area in July 1806.

From the pass, Clark and his party traveled down into the Big Hole, southeast toward what is now Jackson, to Bannack, and to the Beaverhead River at what would become Armstead, a town now inundated by Clark Canyon Reservoir. From there, they followed the Beaverhead and Jefferson rivers to the Three Forks. Sacagawea, familiar with all this country, continued to help find the way.

Big Hole National Battlefield near Wisdom, Montana.

Big Hole National Battlefield, 10 miles west of Wisdom, is definitely worth a stop. Start in the visitor center, where a slide show is projected on a screen just above a panoramic window that looks out on the battlefield. The presentation explains just why and how the Nez Perce War of 1877 got started, while other exhibits tell of key Indian and white players in the battle. Many of the photos are accompanied by quotes.

Before the war, the Nez Perce prided themselves on never killing a white settler. In fact, the tribe was instrumental in helping Lewis and Clark complete their journey, as we shall see. By 1855, the Nez Perce were convinced to move onto a reservation, albeit one that preserved most of their original homelands. But with the discovery of gold on the reservation in 1860, whites wanted to redraw the boundaries to exclude the mining lands. In 1863, the U.S. government proposed a reservation just one-tenth the size originally agreed on. President Andrew Johnson signed the treaty in 1867, and the government started a campaign to get the Nez Perce onto the new reservation.

Some agreed to the move, but others did not. By 1877, the non-treaty Nez Perce were told they would be forcibly moved to the reservation if they did not go on their own. The major band of non-treaty Nez Perce lived in Oregon under Old Joseph—but Old Joseph's son, Young Joseph, wanted a peaceful solution and prepared to move the band to the reservation by the June 14 deadline. On June 13, however, three young Nez Perce men, angered by the forced move and seeking revenge for the murder of one of their fathers by a white man, killed four settlers. Over the next two days, the group—joined by 17 others—killed 14 or 15 whites. The Nez Perce War was on.

By the time they reached the Big Hole, Chief Joseph and the Nez Perce had fought several battles in Idaho—one, a crushing defeat of General Oliver O. Howard at White Bird Canyon, and others that proved inconclusive. Chief Joseph decided to take five non-treaty bands of some 800 people and 2,000 horses into Montana and on, they hoped, to refuge at the Canadian border. They arrived at the Big Hole August 7, sure they were far ahead of Howard and his troops. They did not know, however, that a second force led by Colonel John Gibbon had joined the chase and was closing in. The battle of August 9–10, 1877, resulted in the deaths of some 60 to 90 Nez Perce, only 30 of whom were warriors, the rest women and children, and 29 U.S. soldiers.

Three short hikes from a lower parking lot lead to key sites in the battle. The trails aren't long, but they are largely out in the open, so sunscreen and water are advised. It's 1.5 miles to the Nez Perce camp, 0.75 mile along a level trail to the siege area and 0.75 mile uphill to the howitzer site. (The original howitzer now sits inside the visitor center.) Picnic tables are available at the lower parking lot.

Memorial observances take place on the battlefield every year on the weekend closest to the battle anniversary. Once held separately, the white and Native American observances have now been combined. The public is welcome, but no picture taking is permitted.

Clark camped within a mile and a half of the battlefield, but no one is exactly sure where. Big Hole Battlefield itself has no campground, but May Creek Campground—about 8 miles east of Chief Joseph Pass—attracts many park visitors. Park service staff sometimes conduct interpretive campfire programs there on summer evenings.

Big Hole National Battlefield is open 8 A.M. to 8 P.M. late May through Labor Day and 8 A.M. to 5 P.M. the rest of the year. Admission is $2 per person or $4 per family during the summer and free otherwise. For more information, call (406) 689-3155.

The Big Hole is just as its name implies: wide 360-degree views rimmed everywhere you look by towering mountains. This is the haystack capital of the world—"valley of 10,000 haystacks," many call it. Wisdom and Jackson, 10 and 30 miles, respectively, east of Big Hole National Battlefield, are the area's two major towns (although each is actually quite tiny). Although it is home to just 175 people, Wisdom boasts the noted Wisdom River Gallery, specializing in Western and wildlife art. Jackson, meanwhile, is best known for its hot springs—Clark and company not only soaked their weary bones here in 1806, but they also cooked dinner in the water! These days, boiling meat is probably off-limits in the pools at Jackson Hot Springs Resort, but you can still get a home-cooked meal, along with a comfy cabin.

Bannack State Park commemorates another famous Montana ghost town (and seat of the first territorial capital). You can reach Bannack either from County Road 278 west of Dillon, or via 16 miles of good gravel road from Grant on the route to Lemhi Pass. Remains of several original buildings may be viewed, along with a visitor center that offers more information and photos on the nineteenth-century mining boom in Bannack.

LOST TRAIL PASS AND THE BITTERROOT VALLEY

The Corps of Discovery had one heck of a time getting over Lost Trail Pass—largely because their hapless guide, Toby, lost the trail to the pass. On September 2, 1805, Clark wrote: "We were obliged to cut a road over rock hillsides where our horses were in danger of slipping to their certain destruction." Several horses fell. One was crippled and two gave out.

Toby led the explorers over a trail more than a thousand feet higher than the current route, US 93, which generally follows the path of least resistance. A small visitor center at the pass offers information on attractions in both Montana and Idaho. From the pass, it is 31 miles to Darby, the first sizable town along US 93 in Montana's Bitterroot Valley.

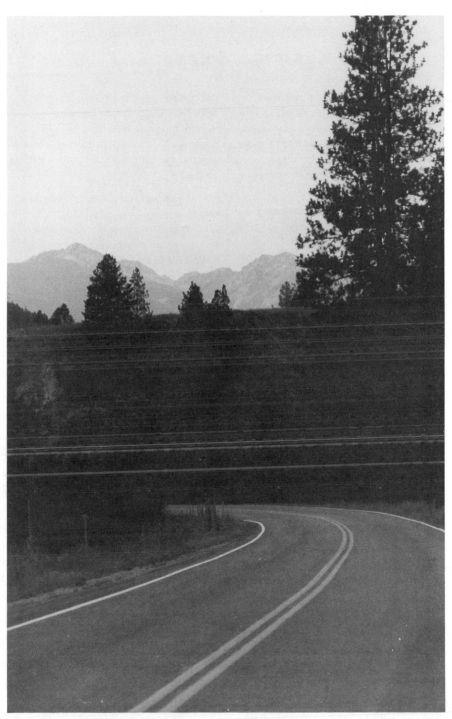

U.S. Highway 93 winds through the Bitterroot Mountains near Darby, Montana.

TOURING MISSOULA

Missoula, just 11 miles north from Traveler's Rest and Lolo, is indisputably one of the Rocky Mountain region's most interesting, lively towns. This city of about 45,000 people makes a fine place to overnight and re-supply before heading out over the Lolo Trail.

Five valleys converge in the Missoula area, so it's not surprising this has long been a way station for travelers. Lewis and party camped near the confluence of the Rattlesnake and Clark's Fork rivers on July 3, 1806, before leaving east on their shortcut across the Great Divide. Before that, Indians used the area as a thorough-fare to hunting grounds east of the mountains.

The valley floor here was once covered by glacial Lake Missoula to a depth of 2,000 feet, about 500 feet higher than the "M" above the University of Montana campus. Formed about 15,000 years ago during the most recent Ice Age, geologists estimate the lake filled and drained at least six times during its existence. The big valley makes for a fairly moderate climate (for Montana, at least), but the topography also tends to make Missoula suscep-tible to air inversions and pollution—again, at least by Big Sky standards.

The Historical Museum at Fort Missoula is the city's most interesting relic from the past. Federal troops arrived at the site in 1877, just in time to try stopping Chief Joseph and the Nez Perce from traveling down Lolo Creek. Failing that, they joined Colonel Gibbon at the Battle of the Big Hole. The fort's buildings were built soon after, and three of the original structures

still remain. Later, the fort was home to an unusual experiment in American military history: a bicycle corps. (Missoula remains a big cycling community, home of an extensive trails network and bike shops galore.)

The fort grounds are now home to a historical museum with permanent exhibits on Missoula history and changing displays on other aspects of early settlement in the area. Military reserve units and the U.S. Forest Service also have offices here. Don't miss climbing the fire lookout. Fort Missoula is open 10 A.M. to 5 P.M. Monday through Saturday and noon to 5 P.M. Sunday, Memorial Day through Labor Day. The rest of the year, the museum is open noon to 5 p.m. Tuesday through Sunday. Admission is $2 for adults and $1 for students and seniors. Children under 6 are free.

Missoula is perhaps best known as home of the University of Montana, not to mention as a primary cultural capital between Minneapolis and Seattle. In recent years, Missoula has become a real writers' and readers' center, with an abundance of fine bookstores and an active literary community. Don't miss the University bookstore, Fact and Fiction, or Garth's Books, among others. The city also has active theatrical and visual arts scenes, not to mention more than 20 movie screens. Needless to say, the recreation minded have it made in Missoula. Aside from the city's own network of riverside trails and the ever-popular hike to the "M" (a 1.5-mile round trip), residents and visitors can take their pick of the Rattle-snake National Recreation Area and

Wilderness to the north, Pattee Canyon Recreation Area to the southeast, and Blue Mountain Recreation Area to the southwest, all within a few miles from downtown.

Missoula has a full calendar of special events, especially during the summer. The city's big Fourth of July bash takes place out at Fort Missoula. In town, people go "Out to Lunch at Caras Park" on the riverfront every Wednesday June through August. Other regular events include an active farmers market (Tuesday evenings and Saturday mornings) and Wednesday-night band concerts at Bonner Park July through mid-August. For more information on Missoula, call (406) 543-6623 or stop by the visitors bureau office on the downtown side of the Van Buren Street footbridge.▲

Once they negotiated the mountains, the explorers had a relatively easy time of it in the Bitterroot Valley. Soon after descending, they came upon an area later known as Ross' Hole for Alexander Ross of the Hudson Bay Company, who ranged far and wide over these parts. He camped here with 55 Indian and white trappers, 89 women and children, and 392 horses in 1824 en route from Spokane to the Snake River. They spent nearly a month trying to break across the pass to the Big Hole, and Ross wound up naming the basin "the valley of troubles." For Lewis and Clark, however, this area brought their first meeting with the Flathead Indians and an opportunity to trade for more horses.

Montana's Bitterroot Valley is one of the nation's fastest-growing areas. The boom is most evident in the towns nearest Missoula, but even the smaller settlements have been converted from sleepy little timber towns to bustling burgs complete with espresso machines and offbeat shops. A taste of the past isn't impossible to find, however. The Sula Ranger Station rents out its historic East Fork Guard Station, 16 miles east of town, on a year-round basis. Stop by the ranger station weekdays or call (406) 821-3201 for more information. The village of Sula has a small store, campground, and cabins.

Lewis and Clark camped about 2 miles downstream from the present-day Spring Gulch Campground north of Sula, and everyone went to bed wet and hungry. Clark wrote: "It rained this evening. Nothing to eat but berries. Our flour out and but little corn. The hunters killed two pheasants only."

US 93 parallels the East Fork Bitterroot River, which runs along the highway from Sula to Conner, picking up the main stem there. The Bitterroot is noted for its rainbow and cutthroat trout. Several fishing access points are easily accessible near the road. Conner is also the turnoff point to Trapper Peak, at 10,157 feet the highest in the Bitterroots.

The Bitterroot National Forest ranger station in Darby doubles as a historic center offering displays and books. Five miles north of town, watch for the road to Lake Como. This popular and beautiful lake offers another great view of Trapper Peak, along with fishing, boating, camping, and hiking.

Hamilton—about halfway to Missoula from Lost Trail Pass—is the main trade center for the Bitterroot Valley. This was home to the Rocky Mountain Laboratory, which researched Rocky Mountain Spotted Fever, first detected here in 1873. "Neither cause nor cure was known and mortality was high," a historic marker reads. By 1906, scientists realized the disease was spread by a tick and were finally able to prevent and treat the fever via vaccinations and medicine. A modern federal laboratory has replaced the tents, log cabins, woodsheds, and abandoned schoolhouse that served the first researchers, and the center still studies infectious diseases.

At Hamilton, it's possible to get off the beaten path of US 93 and tool along on the Eastside Highway (also known as Montana 269). Simply turn east instead of west at the signs for Hamilton's city center. The famous Daly Mansion is the back road's first landmark. Marcus Daly came to America from Ireland as a poor immigrant. He liked mining and was soon attracted to camps of the West, where he quickly learned the trade. He rapidly grew rich and was a powerful force in Montana business and politics for many years.

A splendid Georgian Revival–style dwelling, also called Riverside, served as the summer home for the Daly family. Its 42 rooms are filled with exquisite furnishings. Privately held for many years, Riverside was acquired by the state in 1987 and is now open for tours. Cost is $5 for adults and $3 for students ages 5 through 14. Visitors may tour just the grounds for $1 per person. Hours are 11 A.M. to 4 P.M. daily.

The Lee Metcalf National Wildlife Refuge, north of Stevensville, offers a close-by oasis of calm in the increasingly urban Bitterroot Valley. The refuge is primarily a home for birds and waterfowl, including blue-winged teal, osprey, Canada geese, and many others. For another great hiking opportunity, try the Bass Creek Trail into the Bitterroot range. To get there, drive north from Stevensville on US 93 and watch for a sign on the west side of the road marking the turnoff to the Charles Waters Campground and Recreation Site. There's good fishing along the Bitterroot, too, although the stretch from Tucker Crossing to Florence Bridge is catch-and-release only. Look for other regulations posted near the many fishing access spots.

The Lewis and Clark expedition camped near the confluence of the Bitterroot River and Lolo Creek, at what is now the town of Lolo on September 9 and 10, 1805, and again on June 30 through July 2, 1806. The site they named Traveler's Rest was also a longtime Native American campsite. It's been on private property for many years, but local Lewis and Clark buffs and national historians have targeted it for preservation. As of 1999, no action had been taken to open the campsite area to interpretation, but that may change by the bicentennial observances of 2005–2006.

It was here the captains learned they could have taken a shortcut west from the Great Falls, rather than the arduous route they had just completed. That was disappointing news, especially now, with still more mountains to cross and winter quickly drawing nigh. There was little time to waste, and on September 11, the party started up the Lolo Trail—a march that would prove the most taxing part of the entire 28-month trip.

U.S. HIGHWAY 12

Lewis and Clark expected to cross one mountain range in the Bitterroots. Instead, they found ridge after ridge. By the time the expedition arrived in what is now northern Idaho, corps members were a hardened, gristled lot—mountain men, really. Still, nothing could have prepared them for what they encountered on the Lolo Trail.

Patrick Gass, who would survive longer than any other expedition member, called the Idaho Bitterroots "the most terrible mountains I ever beheld." For his part, Captain Clark—at 35 one of the oldest members of the corps—had long lived the military life, and wasn't one to complain. But over and over as his men crossed these mountains, he said he'd never been colder, never been wetter.

Today's travelers have a choice of routes across this rugged land. US 12 winds through the Lochsa-Clearwater canyon at the base of the Bitterroots. It's a good, paved scenic route officially marked as the Lewis and Clark Trail, but the corps followed only a portion of it. Most of the time, they were high on the ridge to the north: the real Lolo Trail, used for centuries beforehand by the Nez Perce and Salish peoples. The canyon below—which had to be extensively blasted just to make room for the two-lane US 12—was far too narrow in 1805–1806 to allow passage by land, and the rivers were unnavigable. US 12 itself wasn't even completed until 1962, which gives some indication of just how rough things were.

Which route to take? US 12 is the best route for enjoying the scenery and for making time, but the Lolo Motorway (Forest Road 500) gives the traveler a better firsthand feel for the hardships the expedition endured. If you have a low-clearance vehicle, or if you are concerned about breakdowns in remote areas, stick to US 12. If you're determined to travel the Lolo Motorway, consider taking a guided horseback, mountain bike, or van trip across the high country. See the Lolo Motorway section below for more details and plenty of cautions for drivers planning to tackle the route on their own.

Tank up with plenty of gasoline no matter which route you take. There's no fuel on US 12 west of Lolo for 50 miles, and only one gas station (at Powell) in the next 115 miles! Allow plenty of time, too: at least a half-day to travel US 12 between Lolo, Montana, and Lewiston, Idaho, and a full day at minimum if you

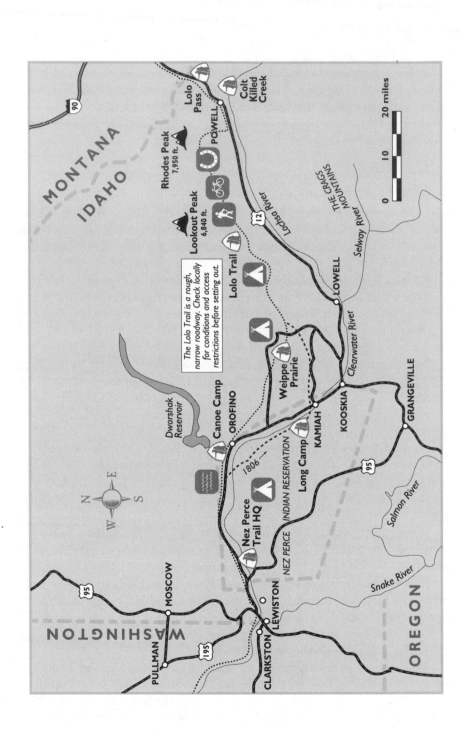

The Lolo Trail is a rough, narrow roadway. Check locally for conditions and access restrictions before setting out.

plan to take any part of the Lolo Motorway (two days if you intend to drive the whole route).

For now, we'll have a look at US 12, which follows Lolo Creek west out of Lolo. A few miles out of town, the traveler reaches Fort Fizzle, erected by the Army to try to prevent Chief Joseph and the Nez Perce from crossing Lolo Creek. It's now a Forest Service Historic Site.

The Forest Service has named a campground for our heroes on the south side of Lolo Creek, 15.5 miles west of Lolo. Interpretive panels on the bridge leading to the campsites explain the presence of tiny migratory songbirds that nest in bushes along the creek each summer. Birds to look for include Swainson's Thrush, Greenish Willow Flycatcher, and Yellow Warbler. Trails lead down to the creekbed on either side of this bridge. Altogether, Lewis and Clark Campground has 18 sites, a few of them pull-throughs. It's a pleasant and handy place to spend the night.

Alas, Lewis and Clark did not camp in the immediate vicinity. The corps kept mostly to the open, north side of the creek as it moved westward. Howard Creek Trail, accessed off the north side of US 12, is one place visitors still can follow closely in the steps of the expedition. It's a quick stroll of just about a half-mile round-trip, but parts are steep and rocky. A picnic area accompanies the trailhead.

US 12 continues its steady climb, soon arriving at Lolo Hot Springs Resort. "I tasted this water and found it hot and not bad tasting," Clark wrote. "I put my finger in the water and at first could not bear it for a second." Today, the resort offers a pool, restaurant, casino, campground, tepee rentals, and a hotel, all surrounded by intriguing rock formations. Visitors can also enjoy horseback trail rides, offered seven days a week every hour and a half starting at 9 A.M., or a trail ride and steak dinner held seven nights a week. For more information, call (406) 273-2290. By summer 2000, plans call for a Lewis and Clark exposition center featuring replica artifacts, artwork depicting the journey, and more. The best place to access information is on the Internet at www.fortlolohotsprings.com

A mile and a half past Lolo Hot Springs, another Forest Service campground, Lee Creek, serves as trailhead for a 5-mile path to Lolo Pass. Like the shorter trail at Howard Creek, Wagon Mountain Trail 300 parallels the route taken by Lewis and Clark. Lee Creek campers can also enjoy a 2.5-mile interpretive loop trail that traverses the immediate area. Day-use facilities at the campground include restrooms and picnic tables.

From Lolo Hot Springs, it is 7 miles to the Idaho border. West of the resort, a sign reads: "Winding road next 77 miles." More than any other highway along the trail since the hill country of Missouri, motorists need to be alert while traveling US 12. It's curvy, it's narrow, it's heavily used by logging and grain trucks, and it's one long deer-crossing zone.

The highway crosses the Montana-Idaho border and the Mountain-Pacific time zone line at Lolo Pass, elevation 5,233 feet. The former Mud Creek cabin that has stood here as a visitor center since 1979 will be closed in 2000 to make way for a larger facility set to open in 2002. The expedition crossed the Lolo divide about a mile east of the present pass and camped near Glade Creek. Packer Meadows near here are especially pretty in mid- to late June, when the fields turn purple with blooming camas.

As of 1999, the Glade Creek area had been transferred from the Plum Creek Timber Company to the Idaho Department of Parks and Recreation via the Idaho Heritage Trust, which raised $255,000 for the land acquisition. Still, there are no plans for major development at the site. Packer Meadows and the Lolo Pass area already are very popular with winter-sports enthusiasts, with more than 100 miles of marked snowmobile trails and more than 30 miles of cross-country ski trails, including some groomed paths.

A picnic area near milepost 165 on US 12 is of more than passing interest to avid Lewis and Clark buffs. This is the DeVoto Memorial Cedar Grove, a cool green cathedral named in honor of Bernard DeVoto, noted writer, historian, and editor of the Lewis and Clark journals. DeVoto used to camp here among the western red cedar while preparing his edition of the journals. Some say DeVoto's spirit still lingers in the area—his ashes were scattered over the grove after his death in 1955.

On September 14, the party reached what is now the Powell Ranger Station. Toby, their guide, had mistakenly left the main Lolo Trail and descended to the Lochsa—or Koos Koos Kee—River. By now, nearly all their food supplies were exhausted, and game was nowhere to be seen. Lewis broke out his food of last resort, an experimental "portable soup" he had obtained from the Army as emergency rations. It was barely edible, and the corps was forced to more extreme measures. "Here we were compelled to kill a colt for our men and selves to eat for the want of meat and we named the south fork Colt Killed Creek," Clark wrote. "The mountains which we passed today (were) much worse than yesterday . . . our men and horses much fatigued." By walking to the rear of the Powell Ranger Station complex, you can be sure you are standing near where the expedition camped, "opposite a small island at the mouth of a branch on the right side of the river which at this place is 80 yards wide, swift and stony," Clark wrote.

The Powell Ranger Station and nearby Lochsa Lodge are the last real outposts of civilization on US 12 until Lowell about 50 miles west. Aside from gasoline, Lochsa Lodge offers several cabins and motel-type rooms and a restaurant with a big fireplace. Nearby, the ranger station also serves as home to the local post office and the Powell Public Library—several cardboard boxes

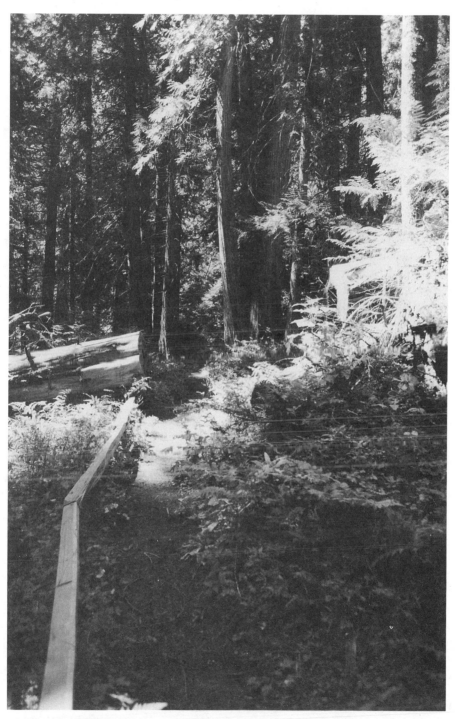

DeVoto Memorial Cedar Grove along U.S. Highway 12, Idaho.

filled with books. Self-guiding cassette tour tapes of US 12 are available at the ranger's office here. Pick one up and drop it off down the road at the Forest Service office in either Kooskia or Orofino.

For a nice hike with good fishing opportunities, take White Sand Trail 50, which begins 2 miles east of the ranger station, off of Beaver Meadows Road (Forest Road 368) near the White Sand Campground. Forest Road 569—Parachute Hill Road—is located on the north side of US 12 just east of the Powell Ranger Station road. This is probably the best access road to the eastern reaches of the Lolo Motorway.

On September 15, the corps trudged another 4 miles down the Lochsa River. Toby had finally figured out he had lost the trail, and he determined the party should climb a steep ridge to regain the route. So the party started up Wendover Ridge, located across US 12 from the present-day Wendover-Whitehouse campgrounds (the latter named for expedition member Joseph Whitehouse). It was no picnic, particularly for the horses. "Several horses slipped and rolled down steep hills which hurt them very much. The one which carried my desk and small trunk turned over and rolled down a mountain for 40 yards," Clark wrote. The field desk was smashed, but the horse managed to survive "and appeared but little hurt," according to Clark. After a rest of two hours, the party continued on to the Lolo Trail, where they found snow. There, the men supped on the portable soup, made a bit more palatable with some leftover colt. "From this mountain I could observe high rugged mountains in every direction as far as I could see," Clark added.

It's possible to hike part of the Wendover Ridge today, from US 12 to the Wendover-Badger Road. It takes a moderately fit person about 40 minutes to hike from the highway to the road, and about a half-hour to come back. From the Wendover-Badger Road, the trail continues, but it becomes faint and the air gets thin. The second leg goes to Wendover Ridge Rest Site, and the third to the Lolo Motorway at Snowbank Camp.

Colgate Licks and Jerry Johnson Hot Springs, both located not far west of the Wendover-Whitehouse campgrounds, are among the most popular stops along US 12. At Colgate Licks, deer, elk, and other animals are attracted to the springs by their salty content. A loop trail winds from the parking lot past the springs. The Jerry Johnson Hot Springs are accessed by a mile-long trail up Warm Springs Creek.

West of the hot springs, the traveler can make a little better time while enjoying the river canyon scenery. That's not to say the distractions fade completely, however: the Lochsa Historical Ranger Station has one of the West's best collections of Forest Service memorabilia. Forest Service retirees staff the ranger station, located across US 12 from the Wilderness Gateway campground, all summer. Forest Road 107—the Saddle Camp Road and another good access point to and from the Lolo Motorway—is located midway between Colgate Licks and the Lochsa Ranger Station. Wilderness Gateway Campground is a base of operations for several outfitters who lead horse-packing trips into the Selway-Bitterroot Wilderness south of US 12.

Twenty-five miles west of the historical station, US 12 finally reaches Lowell and, just beyond it, Syringa. Lowell serves as gateway to the Selway River; together, the Selway and Lochsa become the Clearwater River west of here. A 23-mile back road parallels the Selway, a river well-known to whitewater enthusiasts. In fact, the Lochsa, Selway, and Clearwater all present challenging rafting and kayaking opportunities. Area businesses can provide more information, as can the Idaho Outfitters and Guides Association at (208) 342-1438.

From Lowell, it's 23 miles to Kooskia (pronounced KOO-skee), a pretty little town surrounded by hills. Check out the Lewis and Clark mural on the side of Pankey's Grocery Store, depicting members of the Corps of Discovery on a hill near Nez Perce longhouses. The Kooskia National Fish Hatchery near the junction of US 12 and Idaho 13 raises more than one million salmon each year. Kamiah (KAM-ee-eye), a slightly larger town with good visitor services, is 7 miles north on US 12.

Heart of the Monster Nez Perce site near Kamiah, Idaho.

As we've already seen, the history of the Nez Perce people is closely inter-twined with that of the Lewis and Clark Trail, and we're now entering an area offering many opportunities to explore this tribe's history and present. The Nez Perce sites are well worth visiting, both because of the tribe's important contri-butions to the expedition and the Nez Perces' own proud past.

One such site is a basaltic formation on the outskirts of Kamiah that for centuries has been known as the "Heart of the Monster." According to Nez Perce legend, Coyote slew a great monster near here. The Nez Perce and other tribes sprang forth, each from where parts of the monster fell. The site is located across the road from the Lewis-Clark Resort RV park and motel just south of Kamiah on US 12.

On their return trip east in 1806, Lewis and Clark spent 27 days camped in the Kamiah area while waiting for snow to melt along the Lolo Trail. Here, the expedition members hunted, fished, and learned more about the Nez Perce, with whom the whites had become good friends. "Those people have shown much greater acts of hospitality than we have witnessed from any nation or tribe since we have passed the Rocky Mountains," Clark wrote. The site of the Long Camp, also sometimes called Camp Chopunnish, is noted with a state historical marker on US 12 not far from the Heart of the Monster.

Kamiah has a vaguely Victorian flavor and a full calendar of annual events. The Nez Perce celebrate Mata-Lyma, a root feast and powwow, the third week-end each May and Chief Looking Glass Days the third weekend in August. The local business community throws a free barbecue over Labor Day Weekend, complete with dances, games, and the crowning of the Barbecue Queen. Kamiah's Riverfront Park has a boat ramp and free RV camping for no more than 48 hours.

From Kamiah, it's 23 miles northwest on US 12 to Orofino, site of the expedition's Canoe Camp. But before we proceed, let's take a better look at the Lolo Motorway, the difficult but rewarding alternate route across the Bitterroot Mountains, and the Weippe Prairie, where the Corps of Discovery finally de-scended from the mountains in the fall of 1805. Kamiah is the western gateway to this route. If you decide to explore the motorway from here, be sure to stop by the local Clearwater National Forest office for more information and a map.

THE LOLO MOTORWAY

Indians, trappers, military men, and settlers have used what is now known as the Lolo Trail as the main way across northern Idaho. But the corps were almost certainly the first white men to travel the route. Much of their path is paralleled by present-day FR 500, the Lolo Motorway. The "motorway" designation may conjure up images of men in snappy driving caps and women in smart scarves breezing through the countryside in a convertible, but don't be misled: this

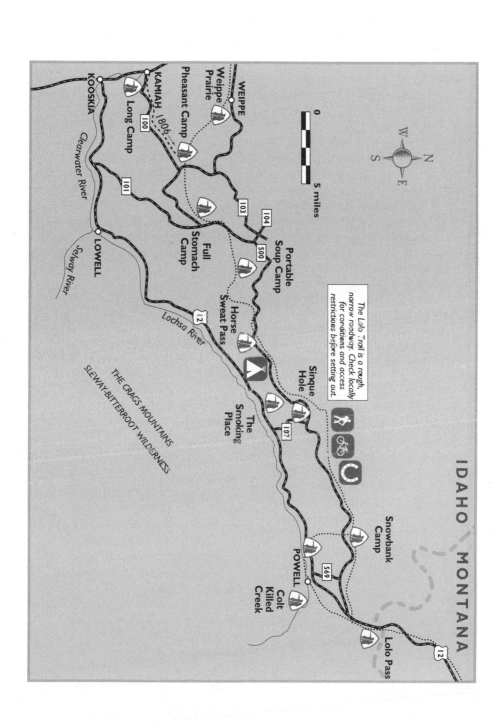

The Lolo Trail is a rough, narrow roadway. Check locally for conditions and access restrictions before setting out.

KOOSKIA

Clearwater River

KAMIAH 1806

Long Camp

Pheasant Camp

Weippe Prairie

WEIPPE

100

101

103

104

500

LOWELL

Selway River

Full Stomach Camp

Portable Soup Camp

Horse Sweat Pass

Lochsa River

12

Sinque Hole

The Smoking Place

107

THE CRAGS MOUNTAINS

SELWAY-BITTERROOT WILDERNESS

Snowbank Camp

POWELL

569

Colt Killed Creek

Lolo Pass

12

IDAHO

MONTANA

N
W   E
S

0   5 miles

GUIDED TRIPS ON THE LOLO TRAIL

Along with the Missouri Breaks of Central Montana, Idaho's Lolo Trail ranks as the most remote stretch of the Lewis and Clark Trail. And while it is possible to travel the Lolo on your own, it can be more fun—and safer—to take a guided trip.

 The Corps of Discovery spent most of their time up here on horseback, and you can do the same by booking a trip with Harlan and Barbara Opdahl of Triple "O" Outfitters. The Opdahls moved to Idaho from Minnesota in 1965, and they've been leading trips on the Lolo since the mid-1980s. Historian and author Stephen Ambrose is among their repeat customers. The most popular Triple O trip is a weeklong adventure that includes four days of riding in the backcountry.

The trips meet on designated summer Sundays in Lewiston, Idaho, and visit the Nez Perce Trail National Historic Park museum in Spalding and the Canoe Camp in Kamiah before spending the first night at Lochsa Lodge. Then it's on up to the Lolo Trail and stops at the Indian Post Office and the Sinque Hole. On Tuesday, the group mounts up for its first ride, including such sites as the Smoking Place and several Lewis and Clark camps. Wednesday, the group rides to Spirit Revival Ridge, where the explorers first caught sight of flat land. On Thursday, Triple O's trips continue west to the corps Jerusalem Artichoke Camp and Boundary Junction. Friday's itinerary includes Full Stomach Camp, Salmon Trout Camp, and the Lewis and Clark Grove. On Saturday, participants return to Lewiston. Some trips either begin or end with a stop at the Chief Looking Glass Days Powwow, held in Kamiah toward the end of each August. All include fun evenings around the campfire, often with storytellers or singers. The food is good and plentiful; it's not fancy, though you will get a taste of such wilderness fare as bear sausage and huckleberry pancakes.

Triple O charges $225 per person per day—or $1,575 in 2000—for their trips, which includes the guide service and horses, all meals, accommodations in two-person tents, and transportation to and from the Lolo Trail from Lewiston. A camp kitchen and portable toilets follow the horse caravan. Be prepared to rough it and to meet many of your own needs—you'll be setting up your own tent, for example. First-time riders are welcome, though novices would be wise to get some riding experience before tackling this area's steep slopes, even on a guided trip.

If a weeklong trip doesn't suit your needs or pocketbook, talk with the Opdahls about a shorter trip or a customized adventure. They've done horseback trips as short as two days, van-supported trips for hikers, and snowmobile excursions in winter. For a fee, they'll even help you plan a do-it-yourself adventure if you're determined to brave the Lolo on your own. For more information on current trip dates and rates, call (208) 464-2349 or (208) 464-2761; see www.tripleo-outfitters.com on the Internet; or write Triple "O" Outfitters, P.O. Box 217, Pierce, Idaho 83546.

If mountain biking is your passion, consider the three-day Lolo Trail trip offered by Lewis & Clark Trail Adventures. This 75-mile trek begins at 13 Mile Camp and ends at Canyon Junction, with a wide variety of terrain. The first day's ride includes 2,000 feet of elevation gain and loss, with a camp near Horseshoe Lake. The second day begins with a downhill ride to the Devil's Chair, followed by hiking to the Sinque Hole, Indian Grave, and the Smoking Place, then a bike ride to Dry Camp. The third day features the easiest riding and visits to Spirit Revival Ridge, Rocky Ridge Lake, and Full Stomach Camp. Riders can bring their own bike or one will be provided; there's also van support, in case you get tired of pedaling. Cost is $432 per person, which includes a shuttle to and from Lochsa Lodge and all meals. Expect high-carb, high-protein gourmet fare.

Lewis & Clark Trail Adventures also offers two Lolo trips that combine scenic driving in the van and hiking to the trail's high spots. One leaves Powell at 9 A.M. and returns by 5 P.M. the same day, costing $7 per person. The other is an overnight trip, which takes in a bit more terrain and costs $110. For the bicentennial, the outfitter has plans for several special Lewis and Clark–related events including an annual hike timed to coincide with the corps' September 15 climb up Wendover Ridge. Lewis & Clark Trail Adventures also runs river trips on the Missouri, Lochsa, and Salmon rivers. For more information on its offerings, call (406) 728-7609; see the website at www.trailadventures.com; or write Lewis & Clark Trail Adventures, P.O. Box 9051, Missoula, Montana 59801.

As of 1999, Triple O and Lewis & Clark Trail Adventures were the only two outfitters licensed to guide visitors along the Lolo Trail. But that may change as the bicentennial nears. For updated information, contact the Clearwater National Forest in Orofino (208-476-4541), Powell (208-942-3113), Kooskia (208-926-4274), or Kamiah (208-935-2513).

motorway is no joy ride. Moreover, it follows the Lewis and Clark Trail exactly only in a few places.

US 12 is open year-round, but the Lolo Motorway is typically accessible only from mid-July through mid-September. Four-wheel drive isn't essential, but good clearance is a must. Make sure tires, belts, and so on are in good shape (and carry full-size spare tires; small "donut" type spares are inadequate for this road). Needless to say, there are no services of any kind. The bottom line may be this warning from a recent Forest Service brochure: "Tow truck service can take days to arrange and can cost $250–$500."

Check with the Forest Service on current conditions before setting out. It's also wise to carry an axe (or chain saw) and shovel, since downed trees and isolated patches of snow aren't uncommon on the motorway even in high summer. If you camp overnight (there are no formal campgrounds along the way),

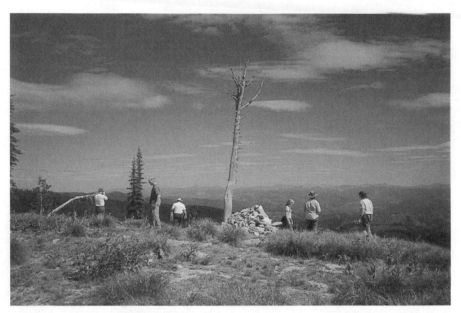

At the Smoking Place on the Lolo Trail, Idaho.

try to choose a site that has been used previously, and be sure to pack out your garbage. Finally, get a copy of the Clearwater National Forest map (available at the Lolo Pass visitor center or area ranger stations) before attempting exploration of the back roads.

Be sure to get the latest version of the map, which was to be available in 2000. The earlier edition, published in 1992, has one major Lolo Trail mistake; the junction labeled Pete Forks on the western reach of the trail is actually Boundary Junction. Pete Forks is a few miles north at the junction of FR 104 and 500.

Use caution and courtesy when driving the Lolo Motorway, or any of the roads that access it. Vehicles traveling uphill have the right-of-way; if you meet another vehicle while traveling downhill, you may need to back up as much as a quarter-mile to let the other vehicle pass. You may want to avoid driving shortly after sunrise (if you're heading east) or just before sunset (if you're driving west), because the sun's low rays—combined with road dust—wreak real havoc with visibility. Take special care to get your bearings at intersections. Many logging roads enter the motorway, often at odd angles, and it's easy to get turned around. With all these potential hazards and complications, there's a chance that the Forest Service may limit traffic on the Lolo Motorway during the years of the Lewis and Clark Bicentennial, 2004 through 2006. If you plan to travel the road at that time, be sure to check with a ranger station a few weeks beforehand to learn of any new restrictions or travel guidelines.

ROOMS WITH A VIEW

There are no motels along the Lolo Motorway, but four Forest Service rental cabins are within short (albeit bumpy) drives of the route. The best is Castle Butte, just 1 mile from the motorway. Castle Butte is a former working fire lookout about 15 feet square, perched on a stone foundation about 20 feet high. A catwalk extends around the lookout, and lightning rods at each corner give visitors a feeling of vulnerability and safety at the same time. Sweeping vistas are impressive in all directions, but especially to the south where the Selway-Bitterroot Wilderness—among the largest in the continental United States—lies sprawled beyond the Lochsa River. The river, for its part, may barely be seen, a slim and silvery ribbon far below your feet.

The lookout is furnished with a double bed, single cot, table with two chairs looking out toward the west (perfect for sunset dinners), propane stove, and several chests of drawers. A looseleaf-bound visitors' guide logs past renters' reactions, which range from deeply religious ("Thank you God for your marvelous creation") to anger at govern-ment policies that endanger the surround-ing wild country. ("It would be a shame to come back to Castle Butte in five years to be surrounded by clearcuts," one guest wrote in 1992.)

Castle Butte is a marvelous place to nap, write, paint, make music, learn to use the firefinder, or read: The visitors' book also contains a copy of *The Smokechaser*, a memoir by Carl A. Weholt, who tells of his days in the fire lookout and of the many colorful characters he met during his Forest Service career. It's also fun to rummage through items left by past occupants: an October 1965 Reader's Digest, a deck of cards, and a Western dime novel. For information on how to rent Castle Butte, contact the Clearwater National Forest's Lochsa Ranger District office, Route 1, Box 398, Kooskia, Idaho 83539, or call (208) 926-4275. It's typically available only mid-July through late September, at a cost of $30 per night with a two-night minimum.

Castle Butte may be the rental facility most convenient to the Lolo Motorway, but it's not the only one near the route. Not far to the west, Liz Butte Cabin is situated 3 miles off the motorway. Weitas Butte Lookout, about 3 miles north of Rocky Ridge Lake and Weitas Meadows, is perched on a 53-foot tower, making it unsuitable for families with small children. Austin Ridge, another high tower, lies 8 miles from the Lewis and Clark Trail, but it's available earlier in the season—usually by late June. For information on renting Liz Butte, Weitas Butte, or Austin Ridge, contact the Pierce Ranger District in Kamiah, Route 2, Box 191, Kamiah, Idaho 83536, or call (208) 935-2513. ▲

If you have any doubts about your vehicle's ability to handle the Lolo Motorway, it's best not to chance the trip. As an alternative, consider exploring the route's western end, accessible via Forest Road 100 from Kamiah. This is the least taxing part of the route, but it has several sites of interest to Lewis and Clark buffs. See the end of this section for details.

As you travel along the Lolo Motorway—or anywhere on the Lewis and Clark Trail, for that matter —it's important to remember that the historic route is seldom something you can follow precisely. The corps passed through only briefly and left scant evidence of its visit. Rather than dwelling on locating the exact campsites or precise trail tread, relax and enjoy the spirit of the place and the scenery.

After they climbed the Wendover Ridge and regained the Lolo Trail on September 15, Lewis, Clark, and company camped at what is now referred to as the Snowbank Camp. The next morning, they awoke to find their beds covered with four inches of fresh snow. All day, the snow kept falling, obscuring the trail and making everyone miserable. It was this day Clark pronounced he was "wet and as cold" as he'd ever been in his life. And on this night, camped at what's now called Lonesome Cove, the party had to kill yet another colt to keep from starving. Clark had tried to shoot a deer—one of very few the men saw in this area—but his gun apparently misfired.

A few miles west of the Snow Bank Camp sign, FR 500 comes to Cayuse Junction. Head less than a mile north from here on Forest Road 581 to reach Cayuse Creek. Once you cross the bridge over the creek, look to your right for some prime possible campsites along this lovely stream. Back on the motorway and another few miles west, the road nears the June 27, 1806, eastbound campsite, where Clark reported they ate bear's oil and boiled roots for dinner.

On September 17, the party probably passed—but did not mention—Indian Post Office, several rock cairns marking the highest point on the Lolo Trail at 7,033 feet. A short trail leads to the cairns; from there, walk a little way east along the ridge for one of the area's best sunset-viewing sites. This area has been important to the Nez Perce for many years, and it must be treated with the utmost respect.

Past Indian Post Office, the corps left the main ridge and followed a more northerly route for about 12 miles. The trails converge again past FR 107, also known as Saddle Camp Road, a good route back to US Highway 12. Within a few miles west of FR 107, FR 500 reaches the Sinque Hole camp of September 17, 1805, and the Smoking Place of June 27, 1806, where the returning expedition stopped to share a pipe with its Nez Perce guides. You can backtrack from here to FR 107, or proceed on the motorway—but be aware that west of here, you're committed to many more hours of rough travel.

The Dry Camp of September 18, 1805, marks the spot where Captain Clark moved ahead with six hunters to look for game. Left behind, Lewis and the rest

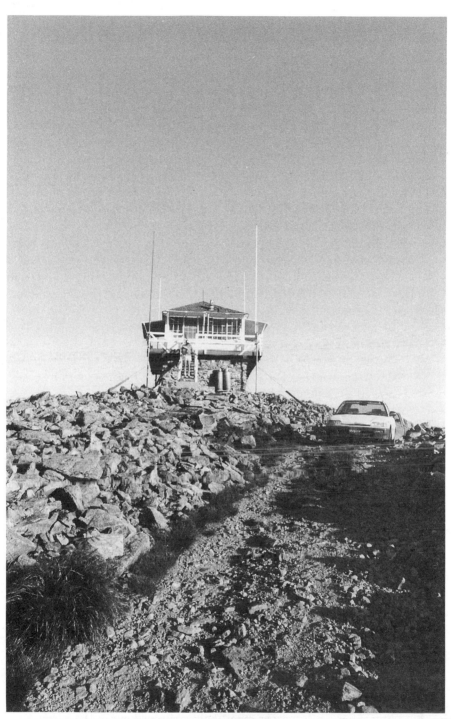

Castle Butte fire lookout on the Lolo Trail, Idaho.

suffered a particularly toilsome night. There was scant water, and supper consisted once again of leftover colt, portable soup, "a little bears oil and about 20 pounds of candles from our stock of provisions." Candles! Could matters possibly get worse?

From here, however, things finally looked up—literally. From nearby Sherman Peak, first Captain Clark and later Captain Lewis glimpsed prairies in the distance. True, the plains were still about 40 miles off, but the end of the mountains was finally in sight. The corps called this place Spirit Revival Ridge.

At Horse Sweat Pass, the Lewis and Clark Trail again leaves the main divide, regaining it 12 miles to the west. The motorway continues on due west, passing Rocky Ridge Lake and Weitas Meadows, a popular campsite and a good picnic stop with an actual pit toilet—a real luxury in these parts! Another few miles west, the motorway reaches Pete Forks Junction. You can jump off here, but if you've come this far, you may well want to stay on the motorway, which will soon be regaining the Lewis and Clark Trail a few miles to the south near Boundary Junction. Or if you've had enough, drive 1 mile west on Forest Road 104 from Pete Forks to reach Forest Road 103 at Beaver Dam Saddle. From here, it's 30 miles west to Weippe via FR 103 and FR 100.

The western reach of the Lolo Motorway near the Canyon Junction/ Mex Mountain area is a good gravel section of road, much more easily traveled than the rough dirt track to the east. This area also has the best, most accessible hiking along the remote route, with about 15 miles of continuous, easy-to-follow trail with moderate-to-steep grades. Taking off from the motorway between Boundary Junction and Canyon Junction, Trail 25 travels 5 miles to Salmon Trout Camp. From there, after crossing the Dollar Creek Bridge, the trail proceeds about 7 miles to Lewis and Clark Grove and another 3 miles to the trailhead at Lolo Campground.

Lewis and Clark Grove marks the spot where Clark and his advance party spent the night of September 19, 1805. It had been another rough day in which they'd traveled 22 miles over several mountains and through plenty of fallen timber. But it would be their last night on the Lolo Trail; from here, Clark and the advance guard would soon reach flat land. From the Lolo Campground, drivers can follow FR 100 either north to Weippe (via the gravel road at Petersons Corners) or south to Kamiah.

WEIPPE PRAIRIE

An Indian had told Lewis and Clark the Lolo Trail crossing could be made in five days. It had taken the corps twice that. But on September 20, 1805, Clark and his advance party of six other men finally stumbled out of the Bitterroots and onto the Weippe Prairie.

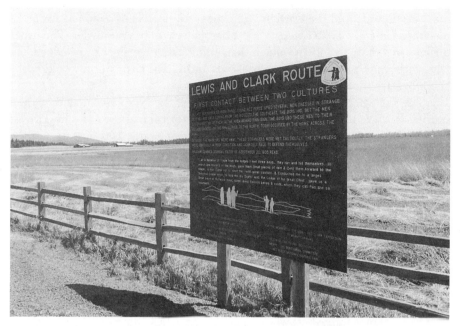

Weippe Prairie, Idaho, where the expedition first met the Nez Perce Indians.

As he and his men walked across the open plain, Clark saw three Nez Perce boys at a slight distance. Frightened, the boys hid in the grass as the white men approached. Clark found two of them and, after reassuring them, asked the boys to lead him and the others to their village.

Once again, many of the village leaders were away on a hunt. The nearest one, Twisted Hair, was at a fishing camp 20 miles down the Clearwater. Clark decided to go meet the chief the next day, but in the meantime bartered for some dried salmon, berries, and camas roots for his party and for the starving men still back in the mountains. He then dispatched Reuben Field and a Nez Perce guide to bring food back to Lewis and the others, who arrived at the Nez Perce camps on September 22.

Within a day, all the white men were sick as dogs. The reason, all thought, was the sudden change in diet from near-starvation rations to the rich salmon and camas roots. The Nez Perce could have easily taken advantage of this situation to kill the ailing explorers; in fact, tribal oral history indicates that the warriors who met Clark and his advance party intended to do just that. But providence intervened in the person of Watkuweis, a Nez Perce woman who had been kidnapped by Blackfeet several years before. Alone among the Nez Perce, Watkuweis knew of the whites; she had been sold to a white trader and lived among whites in Canada before returning to her homeland. "These are the people who helped me," Watkuweis told the warriors. "Do them no hurt." As Stephen Ambrose recounted in *Undaunted Courage*: "First Sacagawea, now Watkuweis. The expedition owed more to Indian women than either captain ever acknowledged." In fact, without these two women, the Lewis and Clark Expedition would probably not have succeeded at all.

The site where expedition members first met the Nez Perce may be viewed southeast of Weippe, about 3 miles from the historical marker on Idaho 11 west of Weippe. To get there, turn south on 4th Street South 100 (just east of the elementary school, but on the opposite side of the road). Drive south and turn left (or east) about 0.4 mile past the Weippe Cemetery. The site is another 0.4 mile east on the south side.

Weippe Prairie is a designated National Historic Landmark. A historical marker here notes that, "For the Nez Perce, this meeting meant the beginning of change for their way of life. For the members of the Lewis and Clark Expedition, it meant survival." Once again, native people had saved the Corps of Discovery from bitter defeat.

Weippe is a small town with minimal visitor services, but it does offer a great pizza parlor and a couple of places to buy gas. Mayor Norm Steadman is a major Lewis and Clark buff who sometimes provides commentary on trips offered by the Clearwater Canoe Company (see next section). From Weippe, head west on ID 11 to return to US 12 and the Clearwater corridor. En route, motorists are treated to dazzling views while descending a magnificent, winding grade. At US 12, turn right to proceed west toward Orofino.

THE CANOE CAMP AND THE CLEARWATER

After more than a month's search, Lewis and Clark had finally found a westward river to take them to the Pacific Ocean. Their next task was locating a campsite where they could make new canoes. They found the spot just west of what is now Orofino, Idaho. A roadside park along US 12 marks the approximate spot.

Interpretive panels at Canoe Camp recap the expedition's route through the Bitterroots and its meeting with the Nez Perce, as well as their labors at the Canoe Camp. They arrived in the area on September 26, 1805, and camped on the river's south side. Just days before, the men had been freezing in the mountains. Now, the weather was hot, and it sapped the men's already frail health. But by October 6, the party had built five new canoes to complete the run to the Pacific. The following day, the corps proceeded downriver with two new guides: Twisted Hair and Tetoharsky, both Nez Perce chieftains.

Look northeast across the river from Canoe Camp to see Dworshak Dam. This mighty structure is the highest straight-axis concrete dam in the West.

Completed in 1973, it rises 717 feet and backs up a popular 53-mile-long reservoir with some of Idaho's best steelhead fishing. Dworshak Reservoir is also known for its boat-accessed mini-camps: 80 scenic spots scattered along the shoreline that together provide 125 sites for camping and day use. To visit the dam or the town of Orofino proper, backtrack east from the Canoe Camp site and take the bridge across the Clearwater.

The Clearwater National Forest supervisor's office is just east of the Canoe Camp park, on the opposite side of US 12. Stop by for recreation information or a look at the displays, which include a wildlife diorama and an interesting relief map of the region.

Clearwater Canoe Company runs a variety of voyages along this stretch of river. Opportunities range from half-day paddles priced at $50 to overnight trips costing about $375. Clearwater Canoe Company uses the big voyageur-style craft that have become so popular along the rivers of Lewis and Clark. Although the trips run right along Highway 12 (with traffic nearly always in view), the company's big plus is its riverside tepee village, where trip participants can spend the night and learn primitive skills including fire making, basket weaving, archery, and hide tanning. The food is tasty, too, with such offerings as garlic and herb-basted chicken or buffalo burgers. Clearwater

Canoe Camp along the Clearwater River, Orofino, Idaho.

Canoe's offerings are fun for families, and they're a great choice for business team-building outings. The company also runs year-round drift-boat float and fishing trips. For more information, contact Jim Cook at Clearwater Canoe Company, 11330 Highway 12, Orofino, Idaho 83544, call (208) 476-9199, or see the website at www.clearwatertrips.com. Going upriver as they did east of the Rockies, Lewis and Clark frequently traveled as few as 15 miles a day. But now the current was with them, and it wasn't unusual to complete 30 or 40 miles in a day. In many places, however, the party encountered dangerous rapids—on October 8, Sergeant Gass's canoe struck a rock and sank, necessitating a day's stop for repairs.

US 12 hugs the Clearwater from Orofino all the way to Lewiston. On the way, watch the terrain change from forested river canyon to the grassy steppes of the Inland Northwest. For the next 200 miles, this arid landscape of velvety, undulating green-and-gold hills will be the dominant visual feature along the Lewis and Clark route.

This also remains the heart of the Nez Perce country, and a visitor center at Spalding serves as headquarters for the various units of Nez Perce National Park. The center is reached via a short jog south from US 12 on U.S. Highway 95. Lapwai, 3 miles south of Spalding, serves as Nez Perce tribal headquarters.

Spalding is named for the Presbyterian missionary Henry Spalding, who sincerely believed it was his duty to Christianize the Indians. "What is done for the poor Indians of this Western world must be done soon," he said. "The only thing that can save them from annihilation is the introduction of civilization."

The Nez Perce visitor center chronicles and exhibits many of the changes— good and bad—this philosophy brought to the Indians. A Book of Matthew printed in Nez Perce is among the items on display in the center. Other exhibits include a case full of beautiful beadwork, as well as a silk ribbon and silver friendship medal presented to the Nez Perce from Lewis and Clark. The center is also a good spot to find out about the Nez Perce of today. A scrapbook of news clippings has items ranging from the latest historical research on Chief Joseph to a profile of a Native American rap group.

The large factory on the south side of the Clearwater River near Lewiston is the Potlatch paper mill. Lewiston has its share of industry (and occasionally fragrant air to match), but it is also an educational center and major retail hub. The visitor center just north of the Clearwater River bridge has plenty of local information and an interactive Idaho tourism computer terminal.

Like most communities along the trail, Lewiston is busy making plans for better interpretation of its Lewis and Clark heritage. For now, your first stop should be the Lewis-Clark State College campus. Park at the corner of 9th Avenue and 6th Street and walk onto the campus's Centennial Mall, where artist Doug Hyde has created a beautiful collection of statues: Lewis and Clark conferring with Nez Perce chief Twisted Hair, a woman picking huckleberries,

Near the confluence of the Clearwater and Snake Rivers, Lewiston-Clarkston, Idaho-Washington.

and another woman showing a girl how to find camas roots. A replica dugout canoe is on view nearby, and the college library has a bronze relief of the expedition, as well as a good collection of books and publications related to Lewis and Clark.

Next, head for the interpretive shelter overlooking the confluence of the Clearwater and Snake rivers. To get there, park at the Lewiston Levee Parkways Center on the northwest side of downtown (on D Street) and walk over the footbridge. The center's entrance is graced with the sculpture "Tsceminicum," meaning "meeting of the waters" in Nez Perce. Designed by Nancy N. Dreher, the artwork depicts a variety of wildlife and the symbolic Earth Mother.

Displays in the shelter note that when Lewis and Clark arrived here, they thought they'd found the Columbia River. Six days later, after a difficult journey across the eastern Washington desert, they actually did reach the Columbia. While here, the corps camped on the north bank of what was then named Lewis's River—the Snake—on October 10, 1805.

Lewiston's historical center, the Luna House Museum, occasionally has exhibits of interest to Lewis and Clark buffs. It's located at 3rd and C streets and is usually open from 9 A.M. to 5 P.M. Tuesday through Saturday. Hours can vary, however, so call (208) 743-2535 before making a special trip. In addition to these sites, several local murals include Lewis and Clark themes, including those on the north side of the Lewis-Clark Center for Arts and History at 5th and Main streets downtown; the district health department building at 215 10th Street; and even the Lewis Clark Auto Superstore showroom, 1005 Warner Avenue in the Lewiston Orchards area on the plateau above downtown. There's also a new Lewis and Clark Discovery Garden on the north edge of town, just east of the Flying J truck stop.

Lewiston is blessed with a mild climate most of the year (although summer days can be scorchers). Because of that, local residents enjoy some recreational pursuits other Idahoans cannot: golfing 12 months a year, for example. Lewiston and its sister city, Clarkston, also have more than 15 miles of paths for joggers, cyclists, walkers, and strollers. Many of these trails are on the Lewiston Levee, which was constructed by the U.S. Army Corps of Engineers to protect Lewiston after the completion of Lower Granite Dam downriver.

Lewiston/Clarkston is also the unofficial headquarters for Hells Canyon, the deepest gorge in North America (deeper than the Grand Canyon because the Snake River runs smack-dab against Idaho's towering Seven Devils mountain range). The Hells Canyon National Recreation Area straddles the Snake River south of Lewiston and includes parts of the Wallowa Whitman National Forest in Oregon and the Nez Perce and Payette National Forests of Idaho.

When Congress created the recreation area in 1975, it saved some of the best whitewater rapids in the United States by protecting 67 miles of the Snake River. Congress also set aside 215,000 acres as the Hells Canyon Wilderness, with an outstanding network of trails open only to hikers and horseback riders.

Abundant in fish, wildlife, and geologic splendor, Hells Canyon is a sight to see. Sturgeon up to 12 feet long swim the depths of the Snake River. Elk, mule deer, bighorn sheep, cougar, bobcat, bear, and smaller mammals patrol the mountainsides. More than 30 outfitters offer float, jet boat, or whitewater trips through the canyon. For a list, contact the Hells Canyon National Recreation Area headquarters in Clarkston at (509) 758-0616. Private rafters and jet-boaters may also ply the area, but a Forest Service permit is required before launching.

From Lewiston, continue west on US 12 into Clarkston and Washington state. It's all downriver from here.

LODGING

*Denotes town on Clark's return route through the Big Hole, 1806.

Rates are for double occupancy during summer season as of 1999 and are subject to change.

WHITEHALL, MONTANA

Chief Motel, (406) 287-3921, 303 E. Legion. $40–$45.

Rice Motel, (406) 287-3895, 7 N.A St. $28–$38.

Super 8 Motel, (406) 287-5588, 515 N.Whitehall St. $42–$48.

TWIN BRIDGES, MONTANA

Hemingway's Lodge, (406) 684-5648, 409 N. Main St. $50–$75.

King's Motel, (800) 222-5510, 307 S. Main St. $40–$125.

DILLON, MONTANA

Best Western Paradise Inn, (406) 683-4214, 650 N. Montana St. $52–$68.

Centennial Inn Bed & Breakfast, (406) 683-4454, 122 S.Washington. $80.

Creston Motel, (406) 683-2341, 335 S.Atlantic. $40–$42.

Horse Prairie Guest Ranch, 3300 Bachelor Mountain Rd. (Guest ranch; minimum stay may apply.)

Horse Prairie Hilton Inn, (406) 681-3130. 12 miles west of I-15 on MT 324. $38–$100.

Sacajawea Motel, (406) 683-2381, 775 N. Montana. $32–$35.

Sundowner Motel, (800) 524-9746, 500 N. Montana. $35–$40.

SALMON, IDAHO

Greyhouse Inn Bed & Breakfast, (800) 348-8097, 12 miles south on US 93 $65–$80

Heritage Inn Bed & Breakfast, (208) 756-3174, 510 Lena St. $35–$45

Solaas Bed & Breakfast, (208) 756-3903, south of town on ID 28 in Baker. $45–$50.

Stagecoach Inn Motel, (208) 756-4251, 201 US 93 N. $50–$72.

Suncrest Motel, (208) 756-2294, 705 Challis St. $33–$40.

Wagons West Motel, (208) 756-4281, 503 US 93 N. $36–$60.

NORTH FORK, IDAHO

100 Acre Wood Bed & Breakfast Resort, (208) 865-2165, US 93. $55–$115.

North Fork Motel, (208) 865-2412, US 93. $36–$46.

River's Fork Inn, (208) 865-2301, US 93. $50–$55.

*WISDOM, MONTANA

Nez Perce Motel, (406) 689-3254. $46–$50.

Sandman Motel, (406) 689-3218. $35.

*JACKSON, MONTANA

Jackson Hot Springs Lodge, (406) 834-3151. $27–$70.

SULA, MONTANA

Broad Axe Lodge, (406) 821-3878, 1237 East Fork Rd. Cabins.

Camp Creek Inn Bed & Breakfast, (406) 821-3508. US 93. $60–$80.

Lost Trail Hot Springs Resort, (406) 821-3574, US 93 south of Sula. Cabins.

CONNER, MONTANA

Rocky Knob Lodge, (406) 821-3520, US 93. $42.

DARBY, MONTANA

Alta Meadow Ranch, (406) 349-2464, 9975 West Fork Rd. (Guest ranch; minimum stays may apply.)

Bud & Shirley's Motel, (406) 821-3401. $58.

Pepperbox Ranch, (406) 349-2920, 9959 West Fork Rd. (Guest ranch; minimum stays may apply.)

Wilderness Motel, (406) 821-3405, 308 S. Main St. $45–$55.

HAMILTON, MONTANA

Best Western Hamilton Inn, (800) 426-4586, 409 S. 1st St. (US 93). $58–$94.

Bitterroot Motel, (406) 363-1142, 408 S. 1st St. $38–$42.

Comfort Inn, (800) 442-4667, 1113 N. 1st St. $70–$90.

Deer Crossing Bed & Breakfast, (406) 363-2232, 396 Hayes Creek Rd. $75–$110.

LOLO, MONTANA

Days Inn, (406) 273-2121, 11225 US 93. $60–$80.

MISSOULA, MONTANA

BelAire Motel, (800) 543-3184, 300 E. Broadway. $40–$50.

City Center Motel, (406) 543-3193, 338 E. Broadway. $40.

4-B's Inn South, (800) 272-9500, 3803 Brooks St. $62.

Goldsmith's Inn Bed & Breakfast, (406) 721-6732, 809 E. Front St. $95–$130.

Holiday Inn–Missoula Parkside, (800) 399-0408, 200 S. Pattee St. $90.

Red Lion Inn, (406) 728-3300, 700 W. Broadway. $70–$90.

LOLO HOT SPRINGS, MONTANA

Fort Lolo Hot Springs Motel, (406) 273-2290, US 12. $75.

POWELL, IDAHO

Lochsa Lodge, (208) 942-3405, US 12. $35–$70

LOWELL, IDAHO

Ryan's Wilderness Inn, (208) 926-4706, US 12. $40–$45.

Three Rivers Resort, (208) 926-4430, US 12. $40–$100.

KOOSKIA, IDAHO

Bear Hollow Bed & Breakfast, (800) 831-3713, US 12. $55–$85.
Looking Glass Lodge Bed & Breakfast, (208) 926-0855, US 12. $65–$75.

KAMIAH, IDAHO

Clearwater 12 Motel, (208) 935-2671, US 12. $40–$50.
Lewis-Clark Resort, (208) 935-2556, US 12. $40–$60.

OROFINO, IDAHO

Konkolville Motel, (208) 476-5584, 2000 Konkolville Rd. $30–$46.
Riverside Motel, (208) 476-5711, 10560 US 12. $25.
White Pine Motel, (208) 476-7093, 222 Brown Ave. $35–$55.

LEWISTON, IDAHO

Carriage House Inn Bed & Breakfast, (208) 746-4506, 504 6th Ave. $75–$85.
El Rancho Motel, (208) 743-8517, 2240 3rd Ave. N. $30–$35.
Inn America, (800) 469-4667 or (208) 746-4600, 702 21st St. $42–$72.
Red Lion Hotel, (208) 799-1000, 621 21st St. $90–$100.
Sacajawea Select Inn, (800) 333-1393 or (208) 746-1393, 1824 Main St. $52–$58.
Super 8, (208) 743-8808, 3120 N. South Hwy. $45–$50.

CAMPING

THREE FORKS, MONTANA

Lewis & Clark Caverns State Park, (406) 287-3541, west on MT 2. Campground and cabins.

WHITEHALL, MONTANA

Pipestone Campground, (406) 287-5224, 41 Bluebird Lane (I-90 Exit 241, 6 miles west of town).

TWIN BRIDGES, MONTANA

Hemingway's RV Park, (406) 684-5648, 409 N. Main St.
Jefferson River Camp, (406) 684-5262, MT 41 between Silver Star and Twin Bridges.

DILLON, MONTANA

Armstead Campground, (406) 683-4199, I-15 Exit 44, at Clark Canyon Reservoir.
Clark Canyon Reservoir, I-15 Exit 44.
Dillon KOA, (406) 683-2749, 735 W. Park St.
Sacajawea Memorial Camp, at Lemhi Pass. Primitive sites.
Southside RV Park, (406) 683-2244, I-15 Exit 62, then right on Poindexter.

SALMON, IDAHO

Century II Campground, (208) 756-2063, US 93.

Salmon Meadows Campground, (208) 756-2640, US 93 at St. Charles St.

NORTH FORK, IDAHO

North Fork Campground, (208) 865-2412, US 93.

Wagonhammer Campground, (208) 865-2477, US 93.

GIBBONSVILLE, IDAHO

Broken Arrow Campground, (208) 865-2241, US 93.

Twin Creek, (208) 865-2383, US 93. Primitive sites.

*WISDOM, MONTANA

May Creek, (406) 689-2431, west of Big Hole National Battlefield on MT 43.

Trails Rest, (406) 689-3149, west of Big Hole National Battlefield.

*JACKSON, MONTANA

Jackson Hot Springs Lodge, (406) 834-3151, on County Rd. 278.

*BANNACK, MONTANA

Bannack State Park, (406) 834-3413, four miles south of County Rd. 278.

SULA, MONTANA

Lost Trail Hot Springs Resort, (406) 821-3574, US 93 south of Sula.

Moosehead Campground, (406) 821-3327, US 93.

Spring Gulch Campground, north of Sula on US 93. Primitive sites.

Sula Store & KOA, (406) 821-3364, US 93.

HAMILTON, MONTANA

Angler's Roost RV Park, (406) 363-1268, 4 miles south on US 93.

KOA–Bitterroot, (406) 363-2430, 9 miles south on US 93.

Lick Creek Campground, (406) 821-3840, 12 miles south on US 93.

Riverside RV Park, (406) 363-3744, 1.5 miles north on US 93.

LOLO, MONTANA

Bitterroot Gateway RV Park, (406) 273-6034, US 93.

Lee Creek, (406) 329-3750, 26 miles west on US 12. Primitive sites.

Lewis and Clark Campground, (406) 329-3750, 15 miles west on US 12. Primitive sites.

MISSOULA, MONTANA

El Mar KOA, (406) 549-0881, Reserve St. to Tina Ave.

Outpost Family Campground, (406) 549-2016, north of town on US 93.

LOLO HOT SPRINGS, MONTANA

Lolo Hot Springs RV Park & Campground, (406) 273-2290, US 12.

POWELL, IDAHO

Jerry Johnson, (208) 942-3113, west on US 12. Primitive sites.

Wendover-Whitehouse, (208) 942-3113, west on US 12. Primitive sites.

LOWELL, IDAHO

Apgar, (208) 926-4275, east on US 12. Primitive sites.

Knife Edge, (208) 926-4275, east on US 12. Primitive sites.

Three Rivers Resort, (208) 926-4430, US 12.

Wild Goose, (208) 926-4275, east on US 12. Primitive sites.

Wilderness Gateway, (208) 926-4275, east on US 12. Primitive sites.

KAMIAH, IDAHO

Lewis-Clark Resort RV Park, (208) 935-2556, US 12.

OROFINO, IDAHO

Canoe Camp RV Park, (208) 476-7530, 14224 US 12. Across from Nez Perce/Lewis and Clark Canoe Camp site.

LENORE, IDAHO

Dworshak State Park, (208) 476-5994, 1 mile north of town to Cavendish, then 10 miles east.

LEWISTON, IDAHO

Hells Gate State Park, (208) 743-2363, 4 miles south on Snake River Ave.

RESTAURANTS

WHITEHALL, MONTANA

Land of Magic Too Supper Club, (406) 287-5252, 27 W. Legion. Steaks and seafood.

TWIN BRIDGES, MONTANA

Blue Anchor Bar and Cafe, (406) 684-5655, 102 N. Main.

DILLON, MONTANA

Centennial Inn, (406) 683-4454, 122 S. Washington.

Crosswinds Restaurant, (406) 683-6370, 1008 S. Atlantic. Breakfast all day, prime rib on weekends.

Longhorn Saloon & Grill, (406) 683-6839, 8 N. Montana St. Breakfast, lunch, and dinner.

Papa T's, (406) 683-6432, 10 N. Montana. Family-oriented restaurant featuring burgers, pizza.

Western Wok, (406) 683-2356, 17 E. Bannack. Chinese and American food.

SALMON, IDAHO

Cabbage Patch Restaurant, (208) 756-3337, 206 Van Dreff St. Casual lunches, fine dining at night.

Granny's Steakhouse, (208) 756-2309, 1403 E. Main St. Burgers, pies, cinnamon rolls.

Salmon Valley Brewery, (208) 756-3391, 101 S. Andrews. Local microbrews and food.

Shady Nook Restaurant, (208) 756-4182, US 93. Specialties include prime rib and seafood.

NORTH FORK, IDAHO

100 Acre Wood, (208) 865-2165, north of town on US 93. Fine dining.

North Fork Cafe, (208) 865-2412, US 93. Hearty food popular with river rats.

River's Fork Inn, (208) 865-2301. Riverside dining featuring steaks and seafood.

GIBBONSVILLE, IDAHO

Broken Arrow, (208) 856-2241, US 93. Mexican food.

*WISDOM, MONTANA

Big Hole Crossing, (406) 689-3800. Home cooking.

Fetty's Bar & Cafe, (406) 689-3260. Specialties include shakes and burgers.

*JACKSON, MONTANA

Jackson Hot Springs Lodge, (406) 834-3151.

Rose's Cantina Cafe, (406) 834-3100. Breakfast, lunch, and dinner.

SULA, MONTANA

Lost Trail Hot Springs, (406) 821-3574, US 93. Steaks and more.

CONNER, MONTANA

Rocky Knob Restaurant, (406) 821-3520, between Sula and Conner on US 93. Hickory-smoked ribs.

DARBY, MONTANA

Outpost Restaurant, (406) 821-3388. Between Sula and Darby on US 93.

Trapper's Family Restaurant, (406) 821-4465, 561 Main.

HAMILTON, MONTANA

A Place to Ponder Bakery & Cafe, (406) 363-0080, 162 S. 2nd St. Baked goods, lunch specials.

Banque Club, (406) 363-1955, 225 W. Main. Steaks, chicken, ribs.

Coffee Cup Cafe, (406) 363-3822, 500 S. 1st. Popular for breakfast.

The Grubstake, (406) 363-3068, 1017 Grubstake Rd. Mountainside dining with a wide menu.

Stavers Tavern, (406) 363-4433, 163 S. 2nd. Steaks, seafood, fine beer, and ales on tap.

VICTOR, MONTANA

Cantina La Cocina, (406) 642-3192, US 93. Homemade Mexican food.

STEVENSVILLE, MONTANA

Fort Owen Inn, (406) 777-3483, US 93. Steaks and beef.
Marie's Italian Cafe, (406) 777-3681, US 93. Closed in winter.

FLORENCE, MONTANA

Glenn's Cafe, (406) 273-2534, US 93. Famous for pie.

LOLO, MONTANA

Guy's Lolo Creek Steakhouse, (406) 273-2622, US 12. Western-style steaks, chicken.
Lolo Trail Cafe, (406) 273-6580, US 93.
Wagon Wheel Pizza, (406) 273-0777, 6555 US 12.

MISSOULA, MONTANA

Black Dog Café, (406) 542-1138, 138 W. Broadway. Vegetarian and organic fare.
The Bridge, (406) 542-0638, 515 S. Higgins. Bistro fare, popular for pizza.
The Depot, (406) 728-7007, Railroad & Ryman. Steaks, salad bar, desserts.
McKay's On the River, (406) 728-0098, 1111 E. Broadway. Steaks, seafood, burgers.
Tipu's Tiger, (406) 542-0622, 531 S. Higgins. Indian, vegetarian, and vegan selections.
The Shack, (406) 549-9903, 222 W. Main. A breakfast favorite, patio dining.
Zimorino's, (406) 549-7434, 424 N. Higgins. Popular for pizza and pasta.

LOLO HOT SPRINGS, MONTANA

Lolo Hot Springs, (406) 273-2290, US 12.

POWELL, IDAHO

Lochsa Lodge, (208) 942-3405, US 12. Fireside dining.

LOWELL/SYRINGA, IDAHO

Middle Fork Café, US 12.
Three Rivers Resort, (208) 926-4430, US 12. Wide menu three meals a day.
Wilderness Inn, (208) 926-4706, US 12.

KOOSKIA, IDAHO

Idaho Backroads Café, (208) 926-4488, 118 S. Main.

KAMIAH, IDAHO

Jilinda's, (208) 935-0014, US 12. Family dining with great view of the
Clearwater River.
Kamiah Cafe, (208) 935-2563, 714 3rd St. Homemade food.
Syringa Lounge & Steak House, (208) 935-0960, 501 4th St. Steaks and salad bar.

WEIPPE, IDAHO

Weippe Pizza & Cafe, (208) 435-4823, 118 N. Main. Creative pizzas and more. Closed Mondays and Tuesdays.

OROFINO, IDAHO

Becky's Burgers, (208) 476-7361, 105 Michigan Ave.

Ponderosa Restaurant, (208) 476-4818, 220 Michigan Ave.

LEWISTON, IDAHO

The Helm Restaurant, (208) 746-9661, 1826 Main. Family dining.

Meriwether's Restaurant, (208) 799-1000, in the Red Lion Hotel. Fine dining.

Thai Taste, (208) 746-6192, 1410 21st St.

Waffles N' More, (208) 743-5189, 1421 Main. Popular for breakfast, close to motels.

Zany's, (208) 746-8131, 2006 19th Ave. Sandwiches and barbecue in fun atmosphere.

CHAPTER EIGHT

WASHINGTON AND OREGON

Men appear much satisfied with their trip, beholding with astonishment the high waves dashing against the rocks and this immense ocean.
—William Clark, November 18, 1805, on the Pacific coast.

THE SNAKE RIVER

*W*hen most travelers think of the Northwest, they think of evergreen forests, snow-capped Cascade peaks, and copious amounts of rain. All those qualities are true of western Washington and Oregon, but the Inland Northwest could not be more different. East of the Cascades, Washington is dominated by arid, rolling hills and bisected by deep river canyons. It was this land Lewis and Clark floated through during the week of October 10–16, 1805, on their way to the Columbia River.

Near Clarkston, Washington, the 300-foot Lewis and Clark Timeline details highlights of the expedition and reproductions of drawings from the journals. It can be viewed on the sidewalk outside Rooster's Landing Restaurant at Hells Canyon Resort, 1550 Port Drive. The resort also includes a marina and store. It's a nice place to watch a sunset.

The Snake River here is actually Lower Granite Lake, backed up by the Lower Granite Dam. Over the past few years, a debate has been raging in the Inland Northwest over whether to breach Lower Granite and three other dams on the lower Snake in an effort to help save declining wild salmon runs. A decision may be made by the time this book appears in print. If the dams are breached, the Snake will return to a state much closer to that seen by Lewis and Clark.

Chief Timothy State Park, 8 miles west of Clarkston on U.S. Highway 12, offers an excellent beach and pleasant camping. The park is also home to the Alpowai Interpretive Center, which includes a video and exhibits on the Lewis and Clark expedition. The center is usually open from 1 to 5 P.M. Wednesday through Sunday between Memorial Day and Labor Day. Visits by appointment are sometimes available at other times; to check, call (509) 758-9580.

Alpowai was a major Nez Perce settlement at the junction of Alpowa Creek and the Snake River. The town was led by Chief Timothy and Chief Red Wolf, who—like many Washingtonians after him—ran an apple orchard. In the 1860s, when the second treaty with the U.S. government drastically reduced the size of

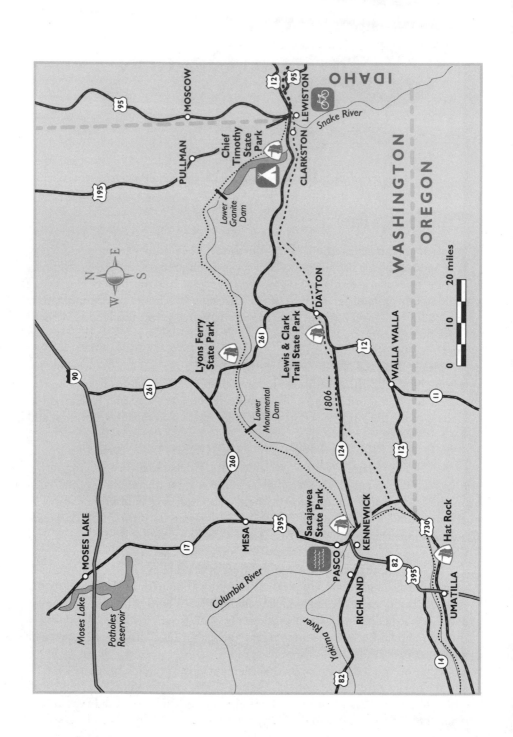

the Nez Perce reservation, Alpowai found itself outside the reservation boundaries. White settlers flowed into the area, and by the late 1880s the small town of Silcott overshadowed Alpowai, only to deteriorate by the 1920s and eventually disappear. In 1975, Lower Granite Dam's gates were closed, and water covered the Nez Perce village site.

After a steep climb up US 12, the panorama shifts again, this time to rolling fields of grain. This is the edge of the Palouse, one of the nation's most beautiful and productive wheat-growing areas. An interpretive sign mentions that on their way home May 3, 1806, the Lewis and Clark expedition camped at a grove of cottonwoods near the highway after a tedious 28-mile journey up Pataha Creek. Supper that night included scant rations of dried meat and dog. Throughout their travels in the Northwest, the party turned frequently to dog meat to help extend their rations—a phenomenon that had to unnerve Lewis's steadfast companion, Seaman, at least a little. The next morning, they followed a branch of the Indian trail they had followed up the creek. The trail can still be faintly seen on the north side of the highway across from the historic marker.

By now, today's traveler has lost the river Lewis and Clark worked so hard to find. Mayview Road, located past the rest areas east of Pataha, provides access to Lower Granite Dam and a back road that follows the Snake River and the Lewis and Clark route of 1805. US 12 runs parallel at a distance, following more closely the return route of 1806.

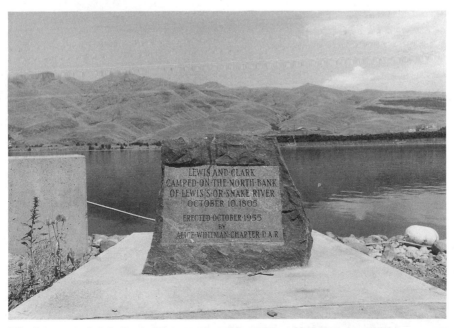

The Corps traveled the Snake River westward in 1805 and homeward in 1806.

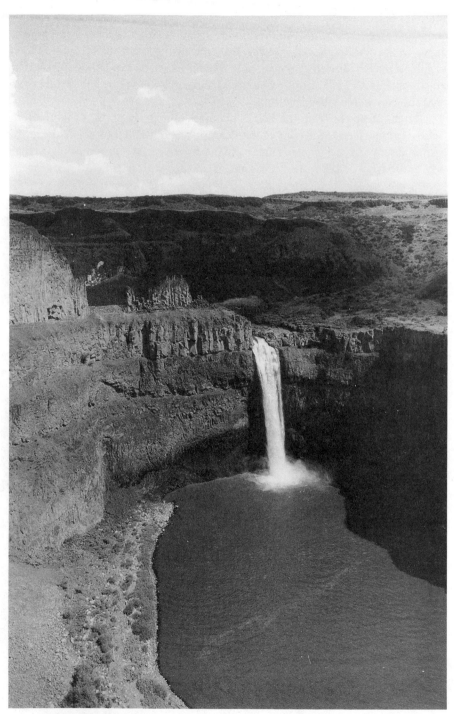

Palouse Falls, Washington.

Pomeroy is a major agricultural hub for Garfield County. The city park has a pool, lots of shade, and even a small golf course. Centennial Boulevard boasts a lovely garden, planted for the 100th anniversary of Washington's statehood.

Twenty-two miles west of Pomeroy, Washington 261 leads to Lyons Ferry State Park, nestled at the confluence of the Snake and Palouse rivers. The expedition had earlier named the Palouse River for George Drouillard, misspelling it as usual "Drewyer." Throughout the journals, Drouillard was praised as a hunter, scout, and interpreter. He was a good friend to Lewis and is considered one of the two or three most valuable enlisted members of the expedition.

Like Chief Timothy State Park, Lyons Ferry has a superb little beach area, perfect for cooling off on a blazing summer day. (Temperatures in eastern Washington frequently exceed 100 degrees F in the summer, so travelers should take advantage of any available means to keep cool.) Nearby Palouse Falls State Park is also worth the drive, largely because it seems entirely out of place in this denuded landscape. You're driving through a landscape with no water in sight when suddenly a gorge opens up and a 190-foot waterfall plunges majestically into a small pond. There's no easy way down to the pool, but some folks make the hike anyway. Camping is available at both parks. From Lyons Ferry/Palouse Falls, travelers can either follow back roads along the Snake River to the Tri-Cities (check a detailed state map to plot your route) or backtrack to US 12 to have a look at part of Lewis and Clark's homeward route via Dayton and Walla Walla, a route explained a bit later—albeit in reverse, the way the explorers encountered it.

Historical marker at Lyons Ferry State Park, Washington.

MEETING THE COLUMBIA

Travelers approaching the Tri-Cities on Washington 124 will find a wealth of camping opportunities along the lower reaches of the Snake River. These mostly come courtesy of the U.S. Army Corps of Engineers. Areas include Fishhook, Charbonneau, and Hood parks, each boasting a swimming beach, boat launch, and trailer dump station. As with other public campgrounds in eastern Washington, lawns at these parks are irrigated on a daily or nightly basis. Tenters should take care to make sure their shelter is placed far from sprinkler heads.

A Lewis and Clark interpretive sign at the intersection of Columbia Center Boulevard and Columbia Drive in Richland marks the farthest point upriver on the Columbia reached by the Corps of Discovery. But the main point of interest in the Tri-Cities is Sacajawea State Park and its fine, small interpretive center at the confluence of the Snake and Columbia. The center, built by the Work Projects Administration in 1939, will receive some upgrades before the Lewis and Clark bicentennial. It uses the spelling "Sacajawea," which, although considered inaccurate by many scholars, is definitely the most common spelling popularly used in the Northwest. A plaque notes that Sacagawea is now the preferred scholarly spelling, and that is the one used in most of the center's displays.

Sacagawea's contributions to the expedition are extensively and accurately explained. Other exhibits praise the pairing of Lewis and Clark. "Both men were experienced leaders and seasoned wilderness travelers. Lewis had commanded a frontier fort; Clark had dealt extensively with Indians. The skills one man lacked, the other possessed," one display reads. "In temperament, this was also true. Lewis was intellectual, speculative, and moody. Clark was pragmatic, extroverted, and even-tempered. Most important of all, Lewis and Clark worked together so harmoniously that it is difficult to believe the expedition actually had two individual leaders."

Viewed from the center, the Snake River is on the left and the Columbia River is on the right. The corps arrived in the area October 16, 1805, to a most hearty welcome from the Columbia River Indians—mostly Wanapums and Yakamas. Clark wrote: "After we had our camp fixed and fires made a chief came at the head of about 200 men singing and beating on their drums. They formed a half-circle around us and sung for some time. We gave them all smoke and spoke to their chief as well as we could by signs." By that night, the Corps of Discovery had logged 3,714 miles from Camp Wood.

The explorers had become used to the sight and taste of salmon long before this point, but they were astounded at the spectacle they met at the junction of the Snake and Columbia. They arrived at the height of fall chinook runs, and the men wrote of the immense quantities of salmon jumping from the rivers. Clark seemed frustrated at being unable to describe the sight. The corps was also confused by the vast numbers of dead salmon on the riverbanks. They didn't yet know that Pacific salmon, unlike Atlantic varieties, die after spawning, so they spurned the natives' offer of fish in favor of purchasing still more dogs.

The expedition camped at the confluence two nights, during which time the men made celestial observations, updated their journals, mended clothes, and bought at least 40 dogs. Clark also explored the Columbia several miles upstream, during which time he met with more Indians and was shown the mouth of the Yakima—or Tapteel—River. On October 18, a council was held and in the afternoon, the expedition at long last moved onto the Columbia River.

Sacajawea State Park is open April through September from 6:30 A.M. to dusk, and the interpretive center is generally open from 1 P.M. to 5 P.M. Friday through Tuesday, May through September. To get to the park from WA 124, turn right at the intersection for US 12. Immediately after crossing the Snake River, get into the left-hand lane. Signs point to the park, which is 2 miles from the intersection. For more information, call (509) 545-2361.

A colorful railroad town, Ainsworth, once occupied land near the confluence of the Snake and Columbia. The town was founded in 1879 when a railroad bridge was being built over the Snake River. A historical marker at the turnoff for Sacajawea State Park notes "it was a wild and lusty town, noted for brawls, gunfights, and hangings."

From the park, Lewis and Clark's route is most closely followed by taking US 12 south to Wallula, where the traveler picks up U.S. Highway 730 southwest to Umatilla, Oregon. This is the route we will follow next, but first you might want to pause awhile in the Tri-Cities, which together—with a population of about 130,000—make up the major urban center for southeastern Washington. The East Benton County Historical Museum at 205 Keewaydin in Kennewick has exhibits on the pioneers who followed Lewis and Clark to the region, while the Columbia River Exhibition of History, Science, and Technology at 95 Lee Boulevard in Richland sheds insight into the infamous Hanford Nuclear Reservation. For additional information on the Tri-Cities, call (800) 666-1929.

With three rivers at their disposal, Tri-Cities residents enjoy all kinds of water sports, from boating and fishing to swimming and waterskiing. Columbia River Journeys, with an office at the Columbia Park Marina, 1776 Columbia Drive S.E. in Richland, offers daily river cruises on the Columbia's free-flowing Hanford Reach. Trips run May through mid-October; in 1999, the cost was $36 for adults and $19 for children 4 through 11. For more information or reservations, call (509) 943-0231.

HOMEWARD BOUND: THE LAND ROUTE

On their way back east in the spring of 1806, Lewis and Clark decided to try an overland shortcut from the mouth of the Walla Walla River northeast to the confluence of the Clearwater and Snake and the land of the Nez Perce—a trek roughly followed by US 12 through Walla Walla, Waitsburg, and Dayton.

The jumping-off spot was present-day Wallula, a small town south of the Tri-Cities best known for the large Boise Cascade plant on the outskirts of town. Near here, the Corps of Discovery spent three days camped with the friendly Walla Walla Indians and their leader, Chief Yellept, whom they had met on the way west and promised to visit again. "He appeared much gratified at seeing us return, invited us to remain at his village three or four days, and assured us that we should be furnished with a plenty of such food as they had themselves, and some horses to assist us on our journey," Lewis wrote.

Madam Dorian Memorial Park is located just north of the junction of US 12 and US 730, with camping, picnicking, fishing access, and an RV dump station. The park is named for Marie Dorian, an Iowa Indian who—if it weren't for Sacagawea's amazing adventures—may have become the most famous Native American woman in history.

Dorian traveled west with the Wilson Price Hunt party of Astorians in 1811. The Astorians had left Missouri to establish trading posts along the Columbia and arrived at Wallula in January 1812. Later, members of the Dorian party trekked to the Snake River country to trap. There, the men were killed by Bannack Indians. Remarkably, Marie and her two young children survived the winter hiding in the Blue Mountains. She managed to get her children to safety in the spring, and lived the rest of her years in Walla Walla and the Willamette Valley.

From Wallula, it's a half-hour drive east on US 12 to the town so nice they named it twice. Walla Walla, meaning "many waters" or "small rapid stream," is worth a visit for several reasons, including Fort Walla Walla Museum and the Whitman Mission National Historic Site, both key outposts in the history of U.S. westward expansion.

Whitman Mission National Historic Site, 7 miles west of Walla Walla off US 12, tells one of the saddest tales from the saga of westward expansion. Marcus and Narcissa Whitman traveled west together in 1836 to found Waiilatpu, "Place of the Rye Grass," on the banks of the Walla Walla River. For the next decade, they would serve as missionaries, teachers, and friends to the Cayuse. Still, cultural differences remained and—with the coming of ever more whites—deepened. In 1847, emigrants brought a measles epidemic that spread rapidly among the Cayuse, who had no resistance to the disease. Soon, half the tribe was dead. When Dr. Whitman's medicine helped whites but not Indians, many Cayuse

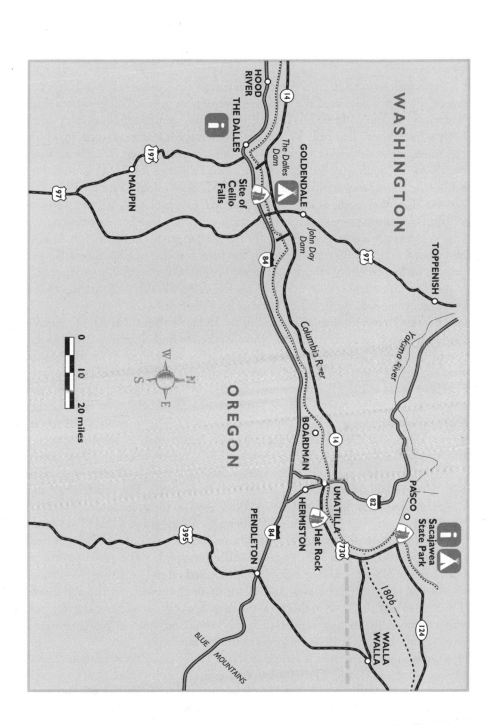

believed they were being poisoned to make way for the pioneers. On November 29, 1847, a band of Cayuse attacked the mission and killed the Whitmans and 11 others.

Through its exhibits, the Whitman Mission clearly shows the collision between the native people of the West and those who pursued religious zeal and America's "manifest destiny." A small interpretive center tells the story from both sides. Other sites at the Whitman Mission include a great grave in which the massacre victims were buried and an excavated area where early mission buildings are outlined. Visitors can get a good view of the entire grounds by taking the short, steep walk to the Whitman Memorial Shaft. From the top, you can see all of Waiilaptu, as well as the Blue Mountains. Living history demonstrations featuring pioneer and Indian crafts are given on summer weekends.

Whitman Mission is open daily from 8 A.M. to 6 P.M. June through August and from 8 A.M. to 4:30 P.M. the rest of the year. The cost of admission is $2 per person, or $4 per family group. Call (509) 522-6360 for more information.

A few miles farther east at 755 Myra Road, Fort Walla Walla Museum is a comprehensive facility focusing on every aspect of the area's history. A Lewis and Clark diorama on display in the hilltop Penner Exhibit Building features a "hide-and-seek" game for children, who are asked to find objects included in the scene. Kids will also be impressed with two early-twentieth-century playhouses that are among the collection of historical buildings moved to the site.

Fort Walla Walla Museum is open 10 A.M. to 5 P.M. Tuesday through Sunday, as well as on Monday holidays. Admission is $5 for adults, $4 for students and senior citizens, and $1 for children ages 6 to 12. The museum sponsors an annual Lewis and Clark Days event early each June, which includes interpretation not just of the Corps of Discovery but of the fur-trade era and area Native American lore. It's followed a few weeks later by a one-day Lewis and Clark Kids Camp for children entering grades four through six. The camp is open to the public, but slots fill quickly. Call (509) 525-7703 for more information.

US 12 continues east through Waitsburg to Lewis and Clark Trail State Park near the town of Dayton. The site's heavy woodsiness is in extreme contrast to many of southeastern Washington's other state parks. The preserve sits on both sides of US 12, with the campground located on the northwest side and a day-use picnic area (and Lewis and Clark marker) situated on the southeast. The marker explains how, in this area, the corps ate cow parsnip and dog for lack of better food. Again, they were on their way home, and camped west of present-day Dayton on May 1, 1806, and east of town May 2.

On summer weekends, Lewis and Clark Trail State Park often has special programs such as Ranger Gary Lentz's one-man show on the medical aspects of the expedition. Call (509) 337-6457 or see the park website at www.bmi.net/lctrail for information on upcoming events. Lewis and Clark Trail State Park was extensively flooded in 1996, but the rehabilitated campground will be open again by 2000—possibly with some new touches such as campsites identified not by numbers, but named for members of the Corps of Discovery.

THE COLUMBIA PLATEAU AND THE DALLES

U.S. Highway 730 starts its run alongside the Columbia River at the Wallula Gap just a few miles north of the Oregon state line. From here, the highway hugs the Columbia, offering splendid vistas. A turnout about 2 miles south of the US 12 junction tells the Cayuse legend of "Two Sisters," who may still be seen in rock on the cliffs above the road.

Lewis and Clark didn't mention the Two Sisters in their journals, but they did write of Hat Rock; Clark, in fact, is credited with giving the landmark its name. The Hat Rock State Park entrance is just west of the junction of US 730 and Oregon 37. The road that leads east at the Hat Rock State Park entrance

Looking south across the Columbia River with The Dalles and Mount Hood in the background.

View of the Columbia River near The Dalles, Oregon.

sign winds up in a private subdivision; instead, take the road to the left, which leads to an absolutely gorgeous little day-use park area with big shade trees, picnic tables, and a pond filled with ducks and geese eager for handouts.

The Lewis and Clark historical marker is located at the upper parking lot. It notes the captains passed and named this point on October 19, 1805. Clark climbed to the top of the landmark and said that, from its summit, a snow-covered mountain could be seen to the northwest. He first thought it was Mount Saint Helens, but it was really Mount Adams, Washington's second-highest peak at 12,307 feet. Homeward bound, the expedition passed Hat Rock again on April 27, 1806.

There is no camping in the park itself, but a private campground is located just outside the site boundaries. Other activities include swimming and boating. Climbing Hat Rock is no longer permitted.

From Hat Rock, continue west on US 730 to Umatilla, home of McNary Dam, the first of four on the Oregon-Washington border. A bit farther west, the Corps of Discovery camped October 19, 1805, on a now-submerged island not far from what is now the city park in Irrigon, Oregon. The park has interpretation of the encampment, and the communities of Irrigon and Boardman throw a party each year on the Sunday closest to October 19 to commemorate the occasion. Boardman and Irrigon will soon be linked by a recreational trail, too.

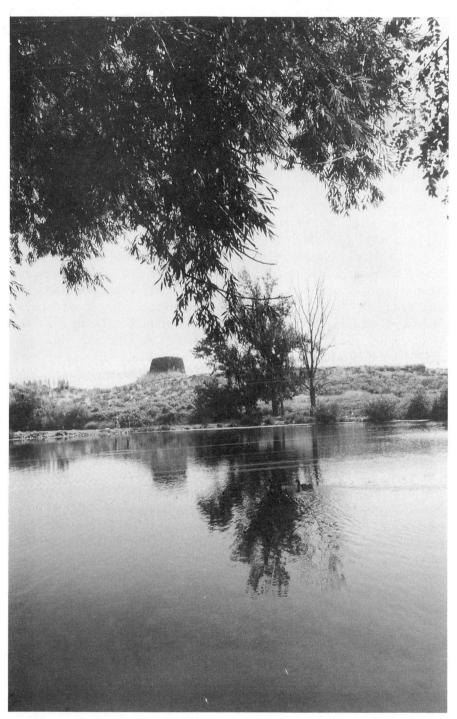

Hat Rock along the Columbia River near Umatilla, Oregon.

Two highways parallel the Columbia River the length of the Washington-Oregon border from Umatilla west. Washington 14 is a two-lane road that generally sits higher above the river with better views, while Interstate 84 (accessible via US 730 to Boardman) allows the traveler to really make some time.

Washington 14 has scant services between Interstate 82 and the junction with U.S. Highway 97 some 82 miles west, but camping is available in two places. Crow Butte State Park, on an island accessible by causeway, is near the Lewis and Clark campsites of October 20, 1805, and April 25, 1806. Maryhill State Park near the US 97 intersection is a popular oasis for camping and sailboarding.

Other landmarks near Maryhill State Park include the Maryhill Museum of Art and a replica of Britain's Stonehenge. The somewhat eccentric railroad magnate Sam Hill built both. He wanted Stonehenge to serve as a monument to peace. Maryhill Museum, meanwhile, is sometimes called the nation's most isolated art museum. Its priceless collection includes many Rodin sculptures, Indian artifacts, Russian icons, antique chess sets, and personal possessions donated by Queen Marie of Romania, all showcased in a lovely, lonely building overlooking the Gorge. On the east side of the grounds, a Lewis and Clark Overlook gives visitors a sweeping view of the Columbia River and several landmarks—including Miller Island and the Deschutes River—mentioned in the expedition journals. The museum also has a café, one of relatively few places to eat along this stretch of WA 14. Maryhill Museum is open daily from 9 A.M. to 5 P.M. March 15 through November 15, though a major renovations project may delay reopening in spring 2001, so call ahead to (509) 773-3733 for an update. Admission is $6.50 for adults, $6 for seniors, and $1.50 for children ages 6 to 12.

People traveling the Washington side may want to take a short side trip to the town of Goldendale, Washington, 11 miles up US 97, if for no other reason than to see the splendid mountain panorama on the plateau above the river gorge. If the weather is clear, the mountains may be "out," which is Pacific Northwest lingo for the peaks being visible. From south to north they are Mount Hood (elevation 11,235 feet), Mount Saint Helens (8,365 feet), Mount Adams (12,276 feet), and Mount Rainier (14,410 feet). Goldendale has the full range of visitor services, as well as the nation's largest telescope open to the general public at Goldendale Observatory State Park.

Horsethief Lake State Park is a satellite area of Maryhill State Park, and it is famous for its excellent Indian petroglyphs, including Tsagaglalal ("She Who Watches"), 10,000 years old and perhaps the most famous native drawing in the Northwest. Sadly, the rock art area was closed to the public after vandalism during the summer of 1993. Tours are still available by reservation on Friday and Saturday at 10 A.M. For information, contact the park staff or call (509) 767-1159.

On the Oregon side, the Columbia takes the starring role, even though it is little more than a lake. As have the Missouri and Snake rivers, the Columbia has

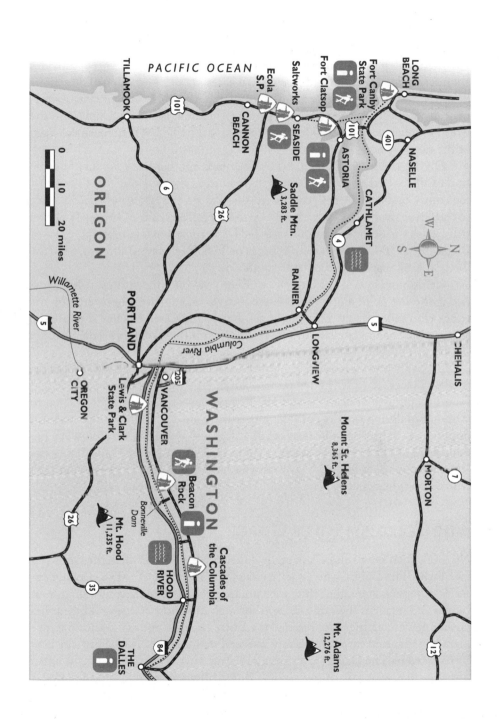

been greatly changed by the dams along its length. It's scarcely possible to imagine the raging, churning Columbia encountered by Lewis and Clark in 1805–1806. On the plus side, however, the U.S. Army Corps of Engineers provides abundant visitor facilities and recreational access at all its locations. The centers downriver at the Bonneville Dam are probably the most popular, but visitors may also want to visit the McNary Dam at Umatilla, John Day Dam (with the world's highest lock lift, 110 feet) at Rufus, and The Dalles Dam near the town of the same name.

On the Columbia Plateau, the traveler joins another historic route in addition to the one taken by Lewis and Clark. During the mid-nineteenth century, tens of thousands of Americans passed this way on the last leg of their journey to the fertile river valleys of western Oregon. Remnants of the Oregon Trail may still be seen in several locations near I-84, the most notable near the town of Biggs at Exit 104. Drive west from Biggs on U.S. Highway 30 and watch for the Oregon Trail marker on the road's south side.

Celilo, not far west of Maryhill and Biggs, was once the greatest fishing area and gathering point along the Columbia River and a place still revered by the tribes who called this river gorge home. Lewis and Clark reached a falls—the first of four major obstacles they encountered on the Columbia—on October 22, 1805, and spent two days negotiating the barrier.

At Celilo, the Columbia swept into several narrow channels and dropped a total of 38 feet. The men had to portage around the greatest drop of 20 feet, and found themselves besieged with fleas. "Every man of the party was obliged to strip naked during the time of taking over the canoes, that they might have an opportunity of brushing the fleas off their legs and bodies," Clark wrote. Celilo Falls were inundated by the waters of The Dalles Dam in 1957, changing the Indians' way of life forever. Travelers who have been proceeding west on I-84 will also get their first view of Mount Hood around this area.

THE COLUMBIA RIVER GORGE

No sooner had Lewis and Clark made it through Celilo Falls than the corps was faced with The Dalles, where the river again narrowed and spilled over a great series of rapids. Here, the white men amazed the local Indians by riding their canoes and much of the cargo straight through the Short Narrows. Three miles farther downriver, the party reached the Long Narrows and again shot the rapids. The exhausted corps then camped several nights at the "Rock Fort" site now surrounded by The Dalles's riverfront industrial area. To get there, take Webber Street on the west side of town north to 1st Street. Turn right and follow 1st Street to the site, which still bears much resemblance to Clark's description of "a high point of rocks." A mural at 401 East 2nd Street in The Dalles offers an artist's interpretation of the explorers' visit.

DUELING INTERPRETIVE CENTERS

The Columbia River Gorge has two major new interpretive centers, set about 45 miles and a river apart. Both are worth seeing—perhaps one on your way west and another coming home.

The Dalles is home to the Columbia Gorge Discovery Center. Its many kid-friendly exhibits make this a marvelous place for families, but even grownups will want to hang 10 on the see-yourself-sailboard exhibit or try draining the Gorge in the "river gallery," which shows how the area's dams changed the local landscape.

You can see a vintage newsreel about the creation of the Bonneville Dam or ask questions of local Native American artists who often spend weekends at the center, demonstrating their skills. The center also includes the Wasco County Historical Museum, which has an exhibit telling how in this area, Lewis witnessed an annual ritual known as the "first salmon" ceremony. When the natives caught the first salmon of the spring, "this fish was dressed and being divided into small pieces was given to each child in the village," Lewis wrote. In this way, the natives gave thanks for the fish and hoped to ensure the salmon would return each spring.

The Columbia Gorge Discovery Center is an impressive place, from its stunning entrance hall to its screened-in Basalt Rock Cafe and gift shop. Hours are 10 A.M. to 6 P.M. daily March 15 through November 15 and Thursday through Sunday the rest of the year. Admission is $6.50 for adults, $5.50 for senior citizens, and $3 for ages 6 to 16. (Children age 5 and under are admitted free.) For more information, call (541) 296-8600.

At Stevenson, Washington, the Columbia Gorge Interpretive Center is best recommended for its occasional appearances by storyteller Merna DeBolt, who portrays Meriwether Lewis's mother. DeBolt, a teacher by training, explains in entertaining style how Lucy Meriwether Marks taught her son the many uses of medicinal plants and herbs—knowledge he later put to use on the expedition. On a more moving note, she also shares Lucy's thoughts on whether Lewis's untimely death in 1809 was murder or suicide. Call ahead to find out when she will be performing.

Elsewhere in the center, a Lewis and Clark tapestry rug ranks among the most impressive exhibits. Created over 11 years by Gretchen Leiberg of Cheshire, Oregon, the rug includes 1.2 million stitches, including pieces from the suits of prominent Oregon state and U.S. officials. The tapestry is on indefinite loan from its owner, Bruce Meland of Bend, Oregon. Other exhibits at the center include a replica fish wheel (now illegal along the Columbia, for it was way too efficient in scooping up salmon) and a pit house similar to that used by the tribes Lewis and Clark encountered in the region. Take time for the impressive 12-minute slide show, which utilizes five projectors to tell the geological story of how the Gorge was formed. Center hours are 10 A.M. to 5 P.M. except New Year's Day, Thanksgiving, and Christmas. Admission is $6 for adults, $5 for students, and senior citizens, and $4 for children ages 6 to 12. Call (509) 427-8211 for more information. ▲

Once they passed the Short and Long Narrows of The Dalles, Lewis and Clark had just one major obstacle remaining: the Cascades of the Columbia. On the way there, the party enjoyed several days of relatively calm waters between The Dalles and Hood River. But although the water was placid, relations with the region's Indians were not; in fact, tensions rose higher here than in any place since the Teton Sioux country back in South Dakota.

Unlike the friendly bands at the confluence of the Snake and Columbia, many of the Indians farther downriver partook in thievery, deception, and begging, perhaps influenced by their past experiences with early white traders near the mouth of the Columbia. (It was in the mid-Columbia region that Lewis and Clark first saw wool clothing and blankets, powder flasks, and guns, all signs of other whites preceding them from the west.) Moreover, many of the Columbia River people were infested with fleas or lice, afflictions they passed on to the newcomers. As the corps moved through the Celilo-Dalles stretch, either Twisted Hair or Tetoharsky of the Nez Perce heard a rumor that one of the local tribes planned to massacre the white men. This story may have sprung from the Nez Perce's own mistrust of the Columbia River tribes—both men decided to leave the corps and return home after the passage through The Dalles—but the captains decided not to take any chances. With the local Indians watching, the men made a great show of examining their stores of weapons and ammunition, making sure all were in proper working order.

The Corps of Discovery successfully made it through the last water barrier, the Cascades of the Columbia, on November 1–2, 1805. The rapids here were known as the Upper and Lower Cascades; Clark came to call the upper rapids "the Great Chute." The baggage was portaged through this area, but the empty canoes once again made it through the rapids unscathed. Soon after the passage, Clark noted in his journal the presence of "a remarkable high rock . . . about 800 feet high and 400 yards round." He named it Beacon Rock, and it is indeed the world's second-largest freestanding rock monolith, second only to Gibraltar.

The Dalles area marks the traveler's entrance into the Columbia River Gorge National Scenic Area, the first region so designated in the United States. Quite simply, the Gorge is an area of sublime scenic splendor and recreational choices so abundant it would take weeks to exhaust the possibilities. Once again, the traveler has a choice of driving Oregon's I-84 or WA 14 through the Gorge (with the U.S. Highway 197 bridge at The Dalles offering the last free river crossing until the Portland-Vancouver metropolitan area). Both sides have plenty to offer. We'll look at I-84 first.

Hood River is unofficial Gorge headquarters, and a town that has changed dramatically with the influx of sailboarders, rock climbers, bungee jumpers, and other (mostly) youthful adventurers. Hood River plays host to some of the world's premier sailboarding competitions (notably the High Wind Classic in late June), as well as a full calendar of festivals such as the Apple Jam, a music festival held

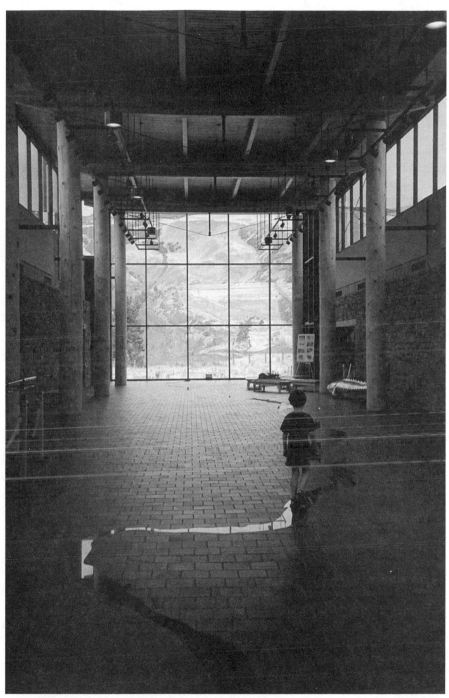

Columbia Gorge Discovery Center at The Dalles, Oregon.

in late August. Hood River also serves as a gateway to Mount Hood, with Oregon 35 south of town traversing the south shoulder of Oregon's highest peak.

Cascade Locks is home port for the sternwheeler *Columbia Gorge*, a pleasure boat that offers a narrated Lewis and Clark cruise every day during the summer. Another daily sailing focuses on the Oregon Trail. No matter what the topic, the sternwheeler is a good way to get to know the Gorge, or at least a small part of it. For more information on sailing times, call (503) 223-3928.

At one time, a natural bridge spanned the Columbia River near what is now Cascade Locks. Indian legend traces this "Bridge of the Gods" to Ka'nax, a chief who ruled the tribes on both sides of the Columbia. Ka'nax used the bridge to carry on love affairs with two different princesses: Wy'east (Mount Hood) and Pahto (Mount Adams). Ultimately, the gods of these two mountains destroyed the natural bridge, ending both the romances and Ka'nax's reign. Scientists explain it a bit differently, but with similar results. Around A.D. 1100, a massive landslide crumbled the bridge and created several sets of rapids within a 5-mile stretch of the Columbia River—the same rapids that slowed Lewis and Clark's passage in 1805.

If you visit only one dam on your Lewis and Clark journey, Bonneville Dam is a good choice. It has visitor facilities on both the Washington and Oregon sides, and each tells the important role hydropower plays in the Northwest economy. The Washington-side visitor center also has an exhibit explaining the archaeological dig of villages noted in the Lewis and Clark journals of October 1805. But the centers' most popular exhibits are doubtless the fish-viewing windows. Children especially enjoy watching salmon swim through the maze-like fish ladders that have been erected to help fish past the dams. Here, people employed as fish counters sit by a window all day and keep tabs on how many fish swim by. This close to the Pacific, the numbers are high. But the salmon have many more dams to pass before they reach their spawning grounds upriver. For wild salmon, life in the Columbia River is more than ever an uphill struggle for survival.

Just west of Bonneville, I-84 travelers have the opportunity to leave the freeway and drive the Columbia River Scenic Highway, a 22-mile masterpiece of engineering that provides close-up access to the famous Gorge waterfalls, as well as to Crown Point, a promontory 733 feet above the river.

Each set of falls has its own character and beauty. Horsetail Falls unfurls like a banner, while Wahkeena Falls cascades in a mass of curlicues. Multnomah Falls is world-famous and easily accessed from the interstate, as is Bridal Veil Falls. And that's just the start. Other falls can be reached by trails. The Gorge is a hiking paradise, with a multitude of paths snaking through shady side canyons and up mountain grades. For hiking information, stop by any Forest Service office or the Crown Point Visitor Center on the historic river route, where a computer is programmed to match trails with hikers' interests and abilities. A

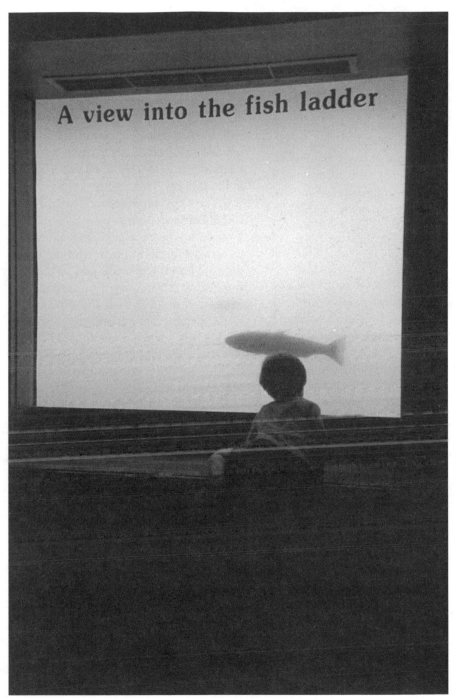

Watching salmon struggle upriver at Bonneville Dam.

PORTLAND TRAVEL TIPS

Portland International Airport (PDX) is served by Air BC, Alaska, America West, American, Canadian Regional, Delta, Continental, Harbor Air, Hawaiian Air, Horizon Air, Northwest, Reno Air, Skywest, Southwest, TWA, and United. All major auto rental companies have offices here, too. Amtrak serves Portland's Union Station at 800 N.W. 6th Avenue; Greyhound is at 550 N.W. 6th Avenue.

Portland has excellent public transportation via buses (Tri-Met) and light rail (MAX), with passengers riding free in "Fareless Square" (most of the downtown area) and for $1.10 to most other destinations. For schedules and other information, visit the Tri-Met office at Pioneer Courthouse Square, Portland's main downtown gathering place at Broadway and Yamhill, or call (503) 238-7433.

few favorites include the Eagle Creek Trail to Punch Bowl Falls (Exit 41); Dog Mountain Trail, a challenging hike that starts between Bingen and Stevenson on the Washington side; and the Oneonta Gorge. Rooster Rock State Park near Troutdale is popular with swimmers and windsurfers, with a separate nude sunbathing area designated about a mile to the east. Lewis and Clark named Rooster Rock and camped in the area on November 2, 1805.

The scenic route ends at Troutdale just east of Portland. Nearby is Lewis and Clark State Park, where a self-guiding nature trail showcases the local plants chronicled by the expedition. The small state park is near the Sandy River, where the expedition stopped November 3 on their final push to the Pacific. They found the river silty and shallow, and when Clark tried to wade across, he found the bottom like quicksand. So the captains named the waterway "Quicksand River" and explored along its shore for about a mile and a half before returning to make camp on Government Island in the Columbia. On the trip home, the corps again camped near the mouth of the Sandy and several men explored about 6 miles up the river. They learned from local Indians they had already passed the major tributary of the Columbia they had been seeking—the Willamette River—so Clark and several men backtracked to explore 10 miles up the Willamette from modern-day Portland.

On the Washington side, WA 14 remains an absolute delight, dominated by interesting little towns and stupendous views of Mount Hood. The Cascades are strikingly different from the Rocky Mountains, and they must have seemed strange to Lewis and Clark. The corps had grown used to the jagged, sawtooth contours of the Rockies, which frequently stretched out one ridge after another. The Cascade peaks, on the other hand, stand alone. These snowy sentinels seem to almost hover in midair, dwarfing everything around them. (Remember the average elevation in the valleys here is less than 100 feet above sea level, unlike

Horsetail Falls, Columbia River Gorge.

Native American fishing platforms along the Columbia River.

the high valleys of the Rockies where towns sit at 3,000 to 5,000 feet.) Mount Hood and its Cascade cousins are, of course, volcanic in nature, thus their conical shapes and isolated placement.

If the Columbia River Gorge is the nation's top sailboarding area, then Doug's Beach State Park east of Lyle, Washington, is the sport's epicenter. Hood River, the hip town downriver, may be where people work, eat, and sleep, but Doug's Beach is where they play. People interested in learning sailboarding will find several Gorge-area businesses eager to help. And although Doug's Beach is the place to see and be seen, many other less-crowded areas are better bets for novice sailboarders as well as for people who crave a more solitary sailing experience.

The twin towns of Bingen and White Salmon sit right across the river (and a toll bridge) from Hood River. Bingen has a winery, Mont Elise, with tours and tastings. The White Salmon River is popular for rafting, kayaking, and fishing. Both towns boast a number of German-style buildings, including the Glockenspiel Tower in White Salmon.

Carson is a gateway to Mount Saint Helens, as well as the site of Carson Hot Springs. Here, visitors are treated to hot mineral baths, massages, and towel wraps. Lodging, meals, and RV hookups are available, too. The best time to visit is on a weekday; folks from Portland and even Seattle crowd in on the weekends.

Bonneville Dam's Washington-side visitor center is situated between Stevenson and North Bonneville. The latter is a planned community in every sense of the word: the entire town was moved to its present location before construction began on Bonneville Dam's second powerhouse. The new town was dedicated in 1978.

Beacon Rock, just west of Bonneville Dam, is truly immense, to use one of the captains' favorite words. It was here Lewis and Clark first saw the effects of the tide as it rolled in from the Pacific. They didn't yet know they were still 142 river miles from the coast!

The remnants of a volcanic core, Beacon Rock is composed of basalt and has been eroded for years by the river. As the Oregon territory was settled, the 848-foot monolith was for years known as Castle Rock, but it has reclaimed its previous name. Interestingly enough, Henry J. Biddle, a descendant of Nicholas Biddle, early editor of the Lewis and Clark journals, once owned the rock. Biddle built the first trail to its top, completing it in 1918 after two years of work.

Today's trail is 4,500 feet long with a 15-percent grade and handrails lining most of the way. It's possible to hike to the top in about a half-hour, but the trek isn't recommended for people wary of heights. Advanced rock climbers are also welcome to try an ascent off the trail, but all climbers must register. Required equipment for climbers includes a hard hat, two 150-foot climbing ropes, clothes

Beacon Rock in the Columbia River Gorge.

TOURING PORTLAND AND VANCOUVER

Two great metropolitan areas anchor the Lewis and Clark Trail: St. Louis, Gateway to the West, and Portland, Gateway to the Pacific. Oregon's largest city is growing by leaps and bounds but still manages to preserve the Northwest outpost character that so endears it to residents and visitors alike.

Several Portland sights are of special interest to the Lewis and Clark aficionado. A striking statue of Sacagawea by sculptress Alice Cooper sits in the city's Washington Park. A *trompe l'oeil* mural at the Oregon History Center, corner of Park and Madison in downtown Portland, depicts an almost-lifelike Lewis, Clark, York, Sacagawea, Pomp, and Seaman. Inside the center, the Historical Society offers permanent and changing exhibits on Northwest history. Finally, the lobby of the Governor Hotel at 611 S.W. Tenth downtown features several murals honoring the Lewis and Clark Expedition.

Naturally, many Portlanders spend their free time fleeing town to the slopes of Mount Hood or the beaches of the windswept Oregon Coast. But anyone deciding to stay and explore the city itself has plenty of options from which to choose. Portland is a city of parks, with 4,700-acre Forest Park on the west side leading the way. This beauty spot boasts hiking trails and picnic grounds with spectacular views of the city. It is also close to Washington Park, home of the Metro Washington Park Zoo, the World Forestry Center, and an impressive Japanese Garden. Alder Creek Kayak & Canoe, right on the Columbia at 250 N.E. Tomahawk Island Drive, doesn't currently lead any Lewis and Clark–oriented trips, but the company rents gear and offers classes. Call (503) 285-0464 or see the website at www.aldercreek.com.

Weekends between March and December, the Portland Saturday Market beneath the Burnside Bridge offers wares from more than 250 artists, craftspeople, and fresh produce sellers. Food to eat on the premises and a wide array of entertainment are also available, and the market is open Sundays as well as Saturdays. Families flock to the acclaimed Oregon Museum of Science and Industry (OMSI) at 1945 S.E. Water Avenue for its interactive exhibits, planetarium presentations, and OMNIMAX Theater shows.

Special events in Portland include the Rose Festival, which takes place annually each June and lasts several weeks. Activities include parades, an air show, a hot air balloon festival, and more. Downtown Portland is known for its public gathering places and eclectic architecture. Northwest 23rd Avenue is another interesting area, full of shops and strolling people. For more information on Portland-area attractions, call the Portland/Oregon Visitors Association at (800) 345-3214 (or 503-222-2223 inside Oregon). The state also maintains an Oregon Welcome Center at Exit 308 off of Interstate 5 near the Oregon-Washington border.

Vancouver, the oldest city in Washington State, has a population of about 47,000. It sits right across the river from Portland, offering its residents what may be the best of both worlds: life in a large metropolitan area combined with

Vancouver's lingering small-town feel and easy access to recreation. Because of these attributes, Vancouver has twice been named an "All-American City." The Clark County Fair, held early each August, is one of the nation's 10 largest.

In the years following Lewis and Clark's explorations, Fort Vancouver became an important way station for trappers, traders, and emigrants on their way to the Oregon country. The fort was established by the Hudson's Bay Company in 1824, which hoped to secure Britain's claim to Oregon by moving its Northwest headquarters inland from the mouth of the Columbia. But by 1846, Britain's hopes of claiming Oregon were dashed when the Northwest Territory was divided along the 49th parallel (the current United States–Canada boundary), not the Columbia River, as the British had hoped.

Fort Vancouver is now a national historic site. Its stockade and several major buildings have been reconstructed on their original locations. Visitors are welcome from 9 A.M. to 5 P.M. daily Memorial Day through Labor Day and from 8 A.M. to 4 P.M. the rest of the year. Admission is $2 per person or $4 for a family. This is the site of a gala Fourth of July celebration often cited as one of the Northwest's best. For more information on Vancouver, contact the Vancouver/Clark County Visitor and Convention Bureau at (206) 693-1313.▲

for any change in the weather, a standard rack for fifth-class climbing, rappelling equipment, proper footwear, and a headlamp for the longer routes.

Beacon Rock State Park actually overlooks the rock from the north side of WA 14. It has a small campground and picnic facilities, as well as several hiking trailheads. The picnic area just down the road from the campground affords a good view of Beacon Rock, particularly at sunrise and sunset.

For more information on activities and attractions in the Columbia River Gorge, call (509) 427-8911 (Skamania County, Washington); (800) 366-3530 (Hood River); or (800) 255-3385 (The Dalles). From Beacon Rock, continue west on hilly and winding WA 14 or backtrack to Stevenson, cross the Bridge of the Gods, and proceed west via I-84 or the Columbia River Scenic Highway.

TO THE PACIFIC

From Vancouver or Portland, the traveler has three major options for getting to the Washington and Oregon coasts, the final westbound destination of our heroes. The fastest choice by far is U.S. Highway 26—the Sunset Highway—best accessed via the Interstate 405 beltway around downtown Portland. This route strays the farthest from Lewis and Clark's river route, but it is the best option if time is of the essence. U.S. Highway 30 out of northwest Portland stays close to the river on a two-lane crawl through heavy forests and small towns, winding up in Astoria. Washington 4 and 401 also take their time meandering along the river west from Longview/Kelso to the Long Beach Peninsula, although travelers choosing this option get a jump on things by taking I-5 north from Vancouver to Longview.

For travelers desiring a scenic approach or the closest route to that of Lewis and Clark, the best approach is probably a hybrid of the slower options: I-5 to Washington 432 (at Exit 36), then west to Washington 433 (Oregon Way), which crosses the Columbia to US 30 via the Lewis and Clark Bridge between Longview, Washington, and Rainier, Oregon. Kayakers and canoeists have yet another option: taking to the river along the Lewis and Clark Water Trail. This informal route follows the free-flowing Lower Columbia from Bonneville Dam to the coast (or at least as far as Gray's Bay, where the dangerous Columbia River bar looms and most small boaters bail out). Whichever way you choose, try to preserve historical order in your coastal explorations by starting on the Washington side, as the Corps of Discovery did.

As the Corps of Discovery pressed down the last stretch of the Columbia River, the captains noted more sightings of Indians who already possessed white men's trade goods. They also marveled at the natives' large, ornate, and high-prowed canoes, much more suited to the turbulent Columbia than the explorers' dugouts. But most of all, they spoke and wrote of unceasing rain—a phenomenon that would prove the hallmark of the corps' winter on the coast.

On November 7, 1805, the party camped near Pillar Rock, a site just east of the small modern-day town of Altoona, Washington. "Great joy in camp," Clark reported. "We are in view of the ocean, this great Pacific Ocean which we have been so long anxious to see, and the roaring or noise made by the waves breaking on the rocky shores (as I suppose) may be heard distinctly." Clark wasn't quite right. As historian David Lavender explained in *The Way to the Western Sea*, "Those waves were breaking on the steep shores of Gray's Bay, and the ocean was still about 20 direct-line miles away. And yet psychologically, Clark was right.

"Gray's Bay had been named for the American ship captain Robert Gray, who, on the bright spring morning of May 11, 1792, had entered the mouth of the Columbia and a little later had anchored in that bay, the first white man to do so. On entering that same bay from the east, the first whites to do so, the Corps of Discovery was finally tying the middle section of North America together."

Gray's Bay is the small boater's last best chance to experience the Lower Columbia before river conditions get increasingly dangerous toward the open sea. Veteran area paddlers say canoeists and kayakers need to avoid traveling the open waters of the Lower Columbia on their own unless they are experienced in self-rescue. Paddlers also must know how to be able to read

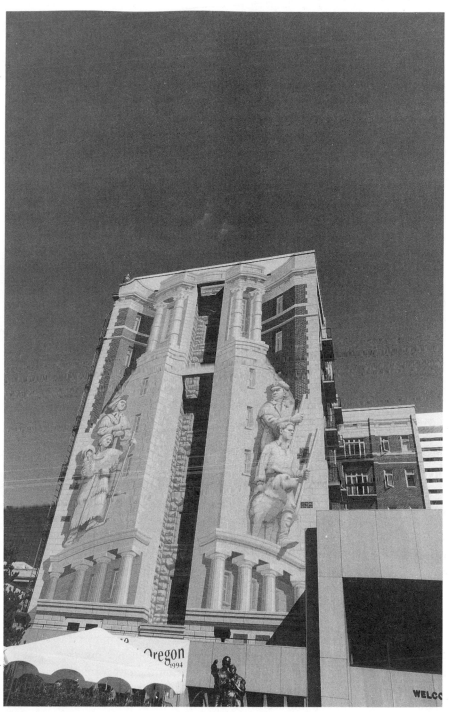

Lewis and Clark mural at the Oregon Historical Society in Portland.

water and navigational charts well enough to stay away from shipping traffic. Finally, unguided boaters should always wear a wet suit to prevent hypothermia in the event of a capsize.

Do-it-yourself boaters may be interested in the *Lewis & Clark Columbia River Water Trail Guide* by Keith Hay. A retired federal employee long involved with the trail, Hay has compiled a guidebook that includes sectional maps to the river, plus information on access points, navigational hazards, and services along the way. Publication was set for late spring 2000. For ordering information, contact the Oregon Historical Society Museum Store, 1200 S.W. Park Avenue, Portland, Oregon 97205-2483 or call (503) 306-5230.

The Skamokawa Paddle Center upriver from Gray's Bay via WA 4 has everything from sea kayak and canoe rentals starting at $15 for two hours to overnight tours along the Lewis and Clark route. Kayakers paddle past Sitka spruce dating back to the Corps of Discovery and explore Gray's Bay. Trips are offered regularly and are suitable for beginning kayakers. Cost is $199 per person for one person or $159 per person double occupancy, which includes kayak rental, equipment, and instruction, plus all meals and overnight accommodations in the Skamokawa Inn Bed & Breakfast. For more information, call (360) 795-8300 or (888) 920-2777, or see www.skamokawapaddle.com.

Skamokawa (pronounced Ska-MOCK-away) also is home to the River Life Interpretive Center in an 1894 building once used as a schoolhouse and fraternal lodge. It now has exhibits on the river's natural and human history, along with a great view of the Columbia from the bell tower. West of town Skamokawa Vista Park has camping and a great vantage point for seeing ships cross the Columbia River Bar.

From Gray's Bay, progress down the river was slow, no doubt much slower than the captains would have liked. On November 8, the corps pulled over to shore after finding the waves so high "that we thought it imprudent to proceed," Clark wrote. The next day, "monstrous trees" set afloat by a high afternoon tide nearly smashed the party's beached canoes. On November 10, the corps made all of 2 miles before high winds returned, compelling them to once again make camp. And so on. "We are all wet as usual and our situation is truly a disagreeable one," Clark wrote on November 11. On November 15, noting the 11th straight day of rain, Clark railed: "...the most disagreeable time I have ever experienced.... I can neither get out to hunt, return to a better situation, or proceed on."

Yet later that same day, the winds abated and the party pressed on. Again, the captains made but a few miles, but it was far enough. Now, there was no doubt: they had reached the Pacific Ocean. Noting the sweeping tide and immense waves, "I concluded to form a camp on the highest spot I could find in the marshy bottom, and proceed no further by water as the coast becomes very dangerous for crafts of the size of our canoes," Clark wrote, adding that "the ocean is immediately in front and gives us an extensive view of it from Cape Disappointment to Point Adams." Camp was made, and the corps stayed put November 15-24, 1805, while various parties went off to explore the coast.

This first coastal campsite is now marked at a roadside picnic area about 2 miles west of the bridge from Astoria, Oregon, on U.S. Highway 101. The area includes a historic marker and a large wooden statue of the captains looking out to sea. It's a fairly scruffy site for now, deserving some additional interpretation.

U.S. Highway 101 proceeds through the towns of Chinook and Ilwaco. At Ilwaco, Washington 103 heads up the Long Beach Peninsula, while a spur route provides access to Fort Canby State Park and its Lewis and Clark Interpretive Center on Cape Disappointment.

The center, slated for renovation sometime in the next few years, already does a good job detailing the entire expedition via photos, journals, and sketches. Especially informative displays include those on map-making techniques, weapons, frontier diplomacy, and members of the Corps of Discovery. One of the best is about Patrick Gass, including such items as his family Bible, expense account journal, metal flask, and a razor box believed to been carved and given to Gass by Sacagawea. The exhibits culminate at a picture-perfect, floor-to-ceiling window view of the Columbia River Bar and the Pacific Ocean beyond. It was likely near this spot that Clark stood with his men on November 10, 1805, and viewed with wonder "the high waves dashing against the rocks and this immense ocean." Lewis and a separate party explored the area earlier, and probably also saw this exact view.

The interpretive center is open from 10 A.M. to 5 P.M. daily from early May through September and 10 A.M. to 3 P.M. Saturdays and Sundays the rest of the year. Admission is free, though donations are welcome. For more information, call (360) 642-3029.

Following a visit to the center, be sure to explore more of the grounds. Cape Disappointment was named by British sea captain and fur trader John Meares, who visited the area in 1788 in an attempt to confirm the presence of a large river in the vicinity. Failing to do so, he named the promontory Cape Disappointment. Although others had speculated on the river's existence, it took Robert Gray, the American, four more years to cross the Columbia River Bar and explore nearly 100 miles upriver.

A trail leads to the Cape Disappointment Lighthouse, built in 1856 and the oldest one remaining in use along the West Coast. The lighthouse isn't generally open to the public, but it's easy to look in, and personnel on duty are happy to step out and answer visitors' questions. Ask about the treacherous Columbia Bar or the Coast Guard's Motor Lifeboat School, where students learn to conduct rescue operations on the world's most predictably rough surf. Another commonly asked question is: "Where does the river stop and the ocean begin?" The truth is, the river current is detected several miles out into the ocean at a spot the

Coast Guard calls Buoy 2, while brackish seawater is often found upriver all the way past Cathlamet, so pinpointing a precise dividing line is just about impossible.

The lighthouse vicinity also affords a good view of the rest of Cape Disappointment, including the bluff on which the visitor center sits and the Pacific Ocean beyond. It all makes a fine picture from this angle. The lighthouse trail also boasts a short, steep side trail leading to a scenic beach tucked in a tiny bay—a perfect place for a picnic.

Fort Canby State Park has a large campground with about 250 sites, but it is dwarfed by Fort Stevens State Park across the Columbia in Oregon, which has more than 600 sites. Despite these parks' gargantuan proportions, visitors can forget about just driving in and finding a site during summer. In fact, it's essential to make reservations for any state park campgrounds on the Pacific coast well before peak vacation season. Fort Stevens State Park has yurts available for rent, too, but these go especially fast, so call well ahead of time. For more information on reserving a campsite on the coast in either Washington or Oregon, call Reservations Northwest at (800) 452-5687. You can reserve a yurt or campsite up to 11 months ahead. Private campgrounds often are less crowded, but it's still wise to call and secure a spot in advance.

Washington's Long Beach Peninsula is heavily oriented to tourists. Visitors will find plenty of restaurant choices and legions of motels and campgrounds, although many will be full on summer weekends, especially during the kite festival in mid-August. The town of Long Beach has a pleasant beach area and boardwalk. The highway was once right on the beach, and freight moved by stagecoach. These days, some parts of the beach may be driven upon even in peak season; others are closed to vehicular traffic. Exhibits along the boardwalk explain the many shipwrecks that have occurred along the Columbia River Bar, where clouds, sandbars, and ceaseless drizzle all wreak havoc with navigation. In all, about 2,000 boats have been wrecked or sunk and some 700 lives lost.

Watching the ocean is almost like gazing into a campfire—simply mesmerizing. Waves roll, crash, and fall . . . roll, crash, and fall, doubling in on themselves. It's no place to swim, but other activities may be enjoyed including kite-flying, beachcombing, clam-digging, whale-watching, and simple strolling.

FORT CLATSOP NATIONAL MEMORIAL

By late November, it had become clear that the corps would not be able to stay on the Washington side of the coast. There was little game, and the explorers were sick of eating salmon and roots—goods they had to purchase from the local Indians at a high price. Moreover, there was the interminable rain and rotting clothing, bedding, and spirits.

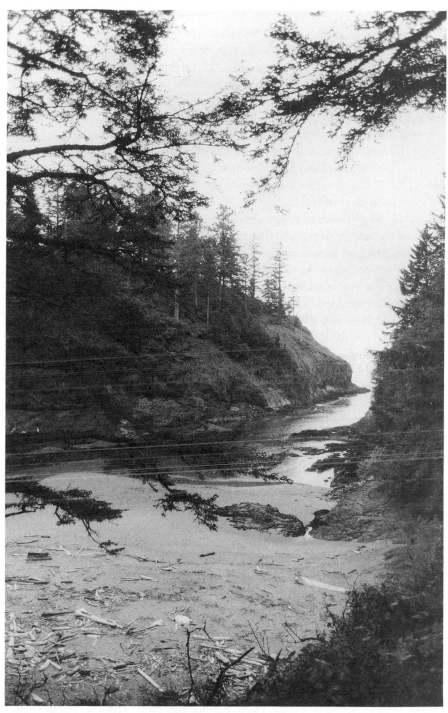

Secluded beach at Cape Disappointment, Fort Canby State Park, Washington.

Lewis and Clark had heard game was more plentiful on the south shore of the Columbia, and hoped that a suitable camp might be established close to both a freshwater river, which they'd had difficulty finding on the north side, and a seawater source from which they could make salt. Moreover, by staying close to the ocean, they increased their chances of meeting any trading ships that pulled into the Columbia harbors. Jefferson had instructed Lewis to send two men and a copy of his notes back by sea if a suitable vessel could be found.

Still, many members of the expedition had other ideas. Sick of the damp weather, they talked of moving back up the Columbia to spend the winter in a drier climate. Eager to reach a consensus before winter, the captains decided to put the matter to a vote on November 24, 1805, extending the franchise to York and Sacagawea as well as to the enlisted men. As Stephen Ambrose noted in *Undaunted Courage*: "It was the first time in American history that a black slave had voted, the first time a woman had voted." Based on scouting reports from Lewis, who'd gone over to examine the options, the party agreed to check out the south shore and stay there if enough game was available. The decision made, the party moved back to the vicinity of Pillar Rock and prepared to cross to the other side. Before they left, Clark carved his name in a tree, adding "December 3rd 1805. By Land. U. States in 1804-05."

Historic interpretive program at Fort Clatsop National Memorial near Astoria, Oregon.

The Corps of Discovery had a dangerous paddle across the Columbia to reach its new winter camp at the site of present-day Fort Clatsop National Memorial. Today, the trip is as easy as driving over the 4-mile-long bridge from Megler, Washington, to Astoria, Oregon. To get to Fort Clatsop from Astoria, follow the signs for Warrenton and Seaside. Both US 101 and the 101 business loop lead there, and both routes are marked. (Motorists taking US 101 should get into the left-hand turn lane as soon as possible after crossing Youngs Bay from Astoria to Warrenton.) Turn left onto Marlin Avenue, then left at the next stop sign.

Fort Clatsop is among the very best interpretive sites along the Lewis and Clark route. Exhibits, short hiking trails, and living history programs combine to give visitors a comprehensive picture of the expedition's winter on the Pacific coast. It's an especially interesting place for kids, who really delight in the summer living history programs (and are often invited to take part). Don't miss the fort replica, lovingly furnished in detail and staffed by National Park rangers who will answer any and all questions. The first Fort Clatsop rotted within 10 to 15 years of its occupancy, reclaimed by the soggy coastal climate. The wood in the replica is now treated every year to make sure the fort escapes the fate of its predecessor.

In 1901, the Oregon Historical Society started searching for the original fort site. But it wasn't until the expedition's 150th anniversary in 1955 that the replica was built, its construction based on floor plan drawings and descriptions from the expedition journals. Archaeologists (including, most recently, Ken Karsmizki of Montana's Museum of the Rockies) have not pinpointed the fort's exact location, but they are certain it was near the current replica.

During most of the journey, the captains and their corps shared very similar conditions. Here at Fort Clatsop, however, rank had its privileges. The fort measured about 50 feet square, with two rows of huts separated by a parade ground. One row had three small rooms, two of which measured 16 feet by 15 feet, with the other 15 feet by 18 feet. These were the enlisted men's quarters, each housing eight men. The other row held four rooms, the largest of which was the captains' quarters. Charbonneau, Sacagawea, and Pomp had another room for their own. An orderly room housed the sergeant of the guard and his three men, a rotating assignment. It's not known exactly where York lived, but he may have slept in the orderly room, too. The fourth room was used for smoking and storing meat.

There were also differences in the daily routine. After the voyage's original shakedown period, all the men generally pulled together, everyone more or less equal. But when they arrived at Fort Clatsop, the captains realized they would have to restore a level of military discipline. Sentries were always posted. Weapons were cleaned and inspected each day. Without some regimentation, the men

. . . .

Dugout canoe replica at Fort Clatsop.

may have started deserting to go live with the Indians after just a few weeks at their soggy outpost.

And it was rainy. In fact, it rained 94 days that winter, all but 12 days of their stay. Of the 106 days spent at the site, only six were sunny. The men spent their time in various ways: hunting, updating maps and journals (and plotting their return routes), and sewing elk-hide moccasins for the trip home. Each man made about 10 pairs of shoes during the winter's stay. That may sound like a lot of moccasins, but each pair typically only lasted 10 days before wearing out.

There was game, but it was of dubious quality. On Christmas Day 1805, Clark wrote: "We would have spent this day the nativity of Christ in feasting, had we anything either to raise our spirits or even gratify our appetites. Our dinner consisted of poor elk, so much spoiled that we ate it through mere necessity, some spoiled pounded fish, and a few roots." Dogs, too, remained part of the diet. The men were also plagued by fleas—all but Lewis. Sally Freeman, a ranger at Fort Clatsop, theorizes that Lewis's canine companion, Seaman, may have deflected the pests from his master.

All in all, it was a difficult winter. But again, the captains were able to gain information from the nearby Indians who, although reportedly prone to thievery, were friendly. And there were occasional diversions, such as the trip Clark and others made to see a beached whale on the ocean shore, and of other sorts, too: Lewis reported on January 27, "Goodrich has recovered from the Louis Veneri which he contracted from an amorous contact with a Chinook damsel. I cured him as I did Gibson last winter by the use of mercury." (Interestingly, since the men excreted the insoluble mercury, finding high mercury levels in the soil may help archaeologists pinpoint the location of the privy, if not Fort Clatsop itself.)

Fort Clatsop has several notable exhibits unlike those anywhere else. One right by the visitor center entrance describes exactly where the Corps of Discovery was in its voyage during any given day you might visit. Another explains in great detail the events leading up to the expedition, from early exploration of the Northwest coast to the Louisiana Purchase. Other features include a handsome sculpture called "The Arrival" by Stanley Wanlass, commissioned in 1980 to celebrate the expedition's 175th anniversary, and a slide show closed-captioned for the hearing-impaired.

One especially interesting display records the pay level of each expedition member, the roles each played in the mission, and comments from the captains on each. Drouillard was paid $833, Charbonneau earned $490, but Sacagawea received nothing. Most of the comments made about the men were complimentary, but Charbonneau proved an exception. "A man of no particular merit. Was useful as an interpreter only," Lewis wrote, perhaps remembering the near-disastrous episodes with the white pirogue on the Missouri River. Clark was more kind, saying: "You have conducted yourself in such a manner as to gain my friendship." Of Sacagawea, Clark added to Charbonneau, "Your woman on that long, dangerous, and fatiguing route deserved a better reward than we had in our power to give her." And of Pomp, he said, "As for your little son, my boy Pomp, you well know my fondness for him and my anxiety to take and raise him as my own child." Pomp was indeed adopted by Clark, educated in St. Louis and Europe, worked as a frontier interpreter and guide, and died in Oregon in 1866. He is buried in Eastern Oregon's Jordan Valley.

The corps originally planned to leave April 1, but hunting became difficult weeks earlier as the elk moved back to the mountains. Moreover, the warming temperatures gave the men a good case of spring fever, so they departed Fort Clatsop March 23, 1806. On that day, Clark wrote in his journal: "At this place we had wintered and remained from the 7th of December 1805 to this day and have lived as well as we had any right to expect."

Fort Clatsop is open daily from 8 A.M. to 6 P.M. mid-June through Labor Day and 8 A.M. to 5 P.M. daily the rest of the year. The park is closed on Christmas. Admission is $2 per person with a maximum of $4 per family. Admission tickets are good for a week. For more information, call (503) 861-2471.

Astoria is a fascinating, historic town worth a look either before or after Fort Clatsop. The Astoria Column atop Coxcomb Hill pays tribute to Lewis and Clark and others who led American westward expansion. A 164-step circular stairway leads to the top of the 125 foot column and great views of the area. The drive to Coxcomb Hill gives visitors a good glimpse of the Victorian architecture of Astoria, the first American settlement in the Northwest.

The Columbia River Maritime Museum is one of the best of its kind. In addition to seeing exhibits on seafaring history, visitors can tour the lightship *Columbia*, which not so long ago was the last seagoing lighthouse on the West Coast. Union soldiers at nearby Fort Stevens guarded the mouth of the Columbia during the Civil War, and in 1942, Fort Stevens became the only American military installation in the continental United States to be fired upon by foreigners since the War of 1812. A Japanese submarine fired 17 shells at the fort. There was no damage.

If you're caught in Astoria on a rainy day, consider spending some time at the city's Aquatic Center at 1997 Marine Drive. This year-round facility has everything from wading pools to water slides—even a river channel. (Betcha you can't float it just once.) If the weather's fine, head instead to Youngs River Falls, a 65-foot cascade found by one of the Corps of Discovery's hunting parties. The falls are along the Youngs River Loop Road south of US 101 between Astoria and Warrenton. Other outdoor highlights in the area include the Twilight Creek Eagle Sanctuary east of Astoria on US 30 and Sunset Beach on the Pacific Ocean south of Warrenton.

Pacific Wave Kayak at 21 US 101 in Warrenton rents kayaks and canoes and is a good source of information on local paddling. Although none of its standard tours is specifically related to Lewis and Clark, they do offer several excursions on the Lower Columbia and other nearby rivers. They can also outfit you for an easy trip up the Lewis & Clark River past Fort Clatsop. For more information, call (888) 223-9794 or see the website at www.pacwave.net

From Astoria or Fort Clatsop, continue south on US 101 to Seaside, home of the expedition's saltworks, and to the picturesque Oregon coastline of Cannon Beach.

SEASIDE AND ECOLA STATE PARK

By the time it reached the Pacific, the expedition had long since run out of salt for preserving and flavoring food, so shortly after the party's arrival at Fort Clatsop, Captain Lewis ordered that a salt cairn be established near the camp. After a search of five days, a suitable location was found in what is now the town of Seaside, about 14 miles south of Fort Clatsop.

The operation was established on January 2, 1806, by the expedition's three saltmakers: Joseph Field, William Bratton, and George Gibson. They remained on the site until February 20 and were able to produce about four bushels of salt by boiling sea water day and night, laboriously walking back and forth the 100 paces to and from the ocean. Sampling an early batch on January 5, Lewis pronounced it "excellent, fine, strong, and white. This was a great treat to myself and most of the party . . . I say most of the party for my friend Captain Clark declares it to be a mere matter of indifference with him whether he uses it or not; for myself I must confess I felt a considerable inconvenience from the want of it."

A replica of the Saltworks remains in its original location. To get there, take Avenue G west off US 101 to South Beach Drive and follow the signs. (Better yet, since parking is at a premium, walk down the South Prom from central Seaside and turn left on Lewis and Clark Way.) The monument sits between two private homes—a site determined in 1900 by the Oregon Historical Society, based on the testimony of a Seaside woman, Jenny Michel, whose Clatsop Indian father remembered the white men boiling water. He pointed out the spot to her when she was young. The site is now officially part of Fort Clatsop National Memorial.

Seaside is the most commercial town on the north Oregon coast, with lots of shopping, several good restaurants, and all kinds of entertainment ranging from an aquarium to carnival rides and lots of nightlife. Surprisingly, however, morning may be the best time to explore the coastal towns of Oregon and

Saltworks at Seaside, Oregon.

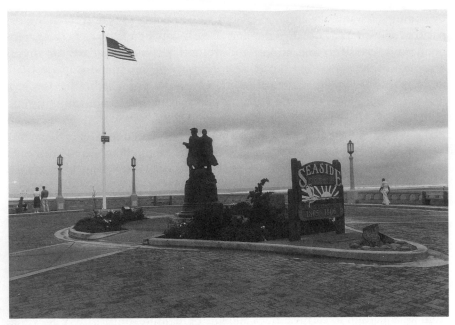

End-of-the-trail monument at Seaside, Oregon.

Washington. The beaches and boardwalks are nearly empty, allowing perfect conditions for a leisurely stroll. Moreover, almost every town has a great local bakery or coffee shop where you can pick up a cup of java and a snack for the trip.

Seaside's main commercial drag ends near the beach at what is called "the turnaround." A statue of Lewis and Clark shows the captains gazing off at the ocean, an exhausted Seaman lying at their feet. Other scenes from the expedition circle the monument's base. This statue, like the one at Fort Clatsop, is by former Astoria artist Stanley Wanlass.

In early January 1806, the corps heard of a great whale that had washed up on a nearby beach. Clark led a contingent of 15 people (including Sacagawea and Pomp) to seek the whale, which was pretty well picked over by the local Indians by the time the visitors arrived. Nevertheless, Clark succeeded in negotiating for the purchase of some 300 pounds of blubber and a few gallons of whale oil. "Small as this stock is I prize it highly; and thank providence for directing the whale to us; and think him much more kind to us than he was to Jonah, having sent this monster to be swallowed by us instead of swallowing of us as Jonah's did."

There are few places along the Lewis and Clark Trail where modern travelers can be certain they're hiking nearly the same route used by the explorers. Tillamook Head Trail is one of them. The trailhead is just south of Seaside; take Avenue U west from US 101, then south on Edgewood Drive and Sunset Boulevard. It's a moderately strenuous 6-mile trek one way to Indian Beach or 7 miles to Ecola Point, if you can arrange a shuttle. A 12- or 14-mile round trip would take the better part of a day to complete, but a hiker campsite is available for folks who want to make an overnight of it.

Experience Plus, a Colorado-based specialty tour company, includes Fort Clatsop and Tillamook Head in its week long Oregon Coast guided walking tour itinerary. For more information, check the website at www.xplus.com or call (800) 685-4565.

From Seaside, the trail climbs steadily for its first few miles before winding about the top of the headlands. Up there, it's mostly mud and thick rainforest-like vegetation, but at least there is a trail of sorts. Clark, describing his trek, wrote: ". . . at one place we were obligated to support and draw ourselves up by the bushes and roots for near 100 feet, and after about two hours labor and fatigue we reached the top of this high mountain, from the top of which I looked down with astonishment to behold the height which we had ascended." The area marked Clark's viewpoint is overgrown these days, but another spot just a bit farther on has a wide ocean vista.

Oregon Coast at Ecola State Park near Cannon Beach, Oregon.

At the 4-mile mark, the trail reaches a backcountry campsite outfitted with several picnic tables (one under a modest shelter), fire rings, and an outhouse. Nearby viewpoints afford hikers views of Tillamook Rock Light. The remaining stretch to Indian Beach descends gradually amid moss-draped trees and graceful ferns on a more open path. After a series of switchbacks near the 5-mile mark, look for a clearing that overlooks the Indian Beach area and Haystack Rock beyond. The trail winds up near the restrooms at Indian Beach.

If a long hike doesn't fit your schedule, simply drive to Ecola State Park, where short pathways lead to wonderful vistas of Haystack Rock and the rugged coastline. Just head south from Seaside on US 101 and watch for the Cannon Beach turn. (It's somewhat sudden on the right-hand side.) Follow the signs to Ecola State Park, and take care driving the winding entrance road. The park charges a small day-use fee, $3 in 1999. Bring exact change, because it may be necessary for the automatic permit-dispensing machine if the park entrance booth is not staffed.

Another Cannon Beach site, Les Shirley Park, offers further interpretation of the Lewis and Clark story. To get there, continue on the road into Cannon Beach instead of turning right toward Ecola State Park. The park, almost immediately on the left, has picnic grounds and another fine Haystack Rock view. Wherever you wind up, take time to savor the ocean sights and sounds and reflect on the journey of Lewis and Clark—one of the greatest adventures the world has ever known.

LODGING

*Denotes town on Lewis and Clark's homeward route, 1806.

Rates are for double occupancy during summer season as of 1999 and are subject to change.

CLARKSTON, WASHINGTON

Hacienda Lodge, (509) 758-5583, US 12. $40.

Highland House Bed & Breakfast, (509) 758-3126, 707 Highland. $55–$85.

Motel 6, (509) 758-1631, 222 Bridge St. $46.

Quality Inn, (509) 758-9500, 700 Port Dr. $70–$100.

POMEROY, WASHINGTON

Pioneer Motel, (509) 843-1559, 1201 Main. $43.

*DAYTON, WASHINGTON

Blue Mountain Motel, (509) 382-3040, 414 Main St. $40.

Dayton Motel, (509) 382-4503, 111 S. Pine St. $35–$65.

Weinhard Hotel, (509) 382-4032, 235 E. Main St. $70–$125.

TRI-CITIES, WASHINGTON

DoubleTree Hotel, (509) 547-0701, 2525 N. 20th Ave. (Pasco). $80.
Motel 6, (509) 546-2010, 1520 N. Oregon St. (Pasco). $38.
Ramada Inn Clover Island, (509) 586-0541, 435 Clover Island (Kennewick). $70–$100.
Super 8, (509) 736-6888, 626 Columbia Center Blvd. (Kennewick). $60.
Trimark Motel, (509) 547-7766, 720 W. Lewis St. (Pasco). $35.
Vineyard Inn, (509) 547-0791, 1800 W. Lewis St. (Pasco). $52–$57.

*WALLA WALLA, WASHINGTON

Capri Motel, (509) 525-1130, 2003 Melrose, $45.
Green Gables Inn Bed & Breakfast, (509) 525-5501, 922 Bonsella. $85–$160.
Vagabond Inn, (509) 529-4410, 305 N. 2nd Ave. $60–$75.
Walla Walla Travelodge, (509) 529-4940, 421 E. Main. $55–$60.

UMATILLA, OREGON

Desert River Inn, (541) 922-1000, 705 Willamette Ave. $67.
Tillicum Motor Inn, (541) 922-3236, 1481 6th St. $40–$45.

BOARDMAN, OREGON

Dodge City Inn, (541) 481-2451, 1st and Front St. $40–$45.
EconoLodge, (541) 481 2375, 105 Front St. S.W. $50.

THE DALLES, OREGON

Best Western Umatilla House, (541) 296-9107, 112 W. 2nd. $65–$85.
Lone Pine Motel, (541) 298-2800, I-84 Exit 87, $60–$110.
Shilo Inn, (541) 298-5502, 3223 Bret Clodfelter Way. $60–$110.
The Inn at The Dalles, (541) 296-1167, 3550 S.E. Frontage Rd. $35–$70.

HOOD RIVER, OREGON

Columbia Gorge Hotel, (541) 386-5566, 4000 Westcliff Dr. $150–$275.
Hood River Hotel, (541) 386-1900, 102 Oak. $50–$150.
Love's Riverview Lodge, (541) 386-8719, 1505 Oak. $65–$80.
Meredith Gorge Motel, (541) 386-1515, 4300 Westcliff Dr. $50–$80.
Panorama Lodge Bed & Breakfast, (541) 387-2687, 2290 Old Dalles Dr. $45–$85.
Vagabond Lodge, (541) 386-2992, 4070 Westcliff Dr. (I-84 Exit 62). $55–$75.

WHITE SALMON, WASHINGTON

Inn of the White Salmon Bed & Breakfast, (800) 972-5226. $100–$130.

STEVENSON, WASHINGTON

EconoLodge, (509) 427-5628, 40 N.E. 2nd St. $60–$65.
Skamania Lodge, (800) 221-7117, 1131 Skamania Lodge Dr. $135–$240.

CASCADE LOCKS, OREGON

Best Western Columbia River Inn, (541) 374-8777, 735 WaNaPa St. $90–$130.

Bridge of the Gods Motel, (541) 374-8628, US 30. $40–$60.

Econo Inn, (541) 374-8417, US 30. $45–$55.

PORTLAND, OREGON

Cameo Motel, (503) 288-5981, 4111 N.E. 82nd Ave. $36–$40.

Governor Hotel, (503) 224-3400, 611 S.W. 10th. $165 and up.

DoubleTree Hotel Columbia River, (503) 283-2111, 1401 N. Hayden Island Dr. $80–$120.

Holiday Inn–Downtown, (503) 235-2100, 1021 N.E. Grand Ave. $80–$115.

Hostelling International—Northwest Portland, (503) 241-2783, 1818 N.W. Glisan St.

Hostelling International—Portland, (503) 236-3380, 3031 Hawthorne Blvd. S.E.

Sauvie Island Bed & Breakfast, (503) 621-3214, 26504 N.W. Reeder Rd. $55–$80.

Sleep Inn, (503) 618-8400, I-84 Exit 13 (Gresham). $60–$90.

VANCOUVER, WASHINGTON

Best Western Ferryman's Inn, (360) 574-2151, 7901 N.E. 6th Ave. $60.

Fort Motel, (360) 694-3327, 500 E. 13th. $48.

Quality Inn, (360) 696-0516, 7001 N.E. Hwy. 99. $70–$85.

Salmon Creek Motel, (360) 573-0751, 11901 N.E. Hwy. 99. $50–$55.

LONGVIEW, WASHINGTON

Hudson Manor Inn, (360) 425-1100, 1616 Hudson St. $40–$46.

KELSO, WASHINGTON

Comfort Inn, (360) 425-4600, 440 Three Rivers Dr. $65 and up.

Kelso Budget Inn, (360) 636-4610, 505 N. Pacific. $42–$48.

ST. HELENS, OREGON

Village Inn, (503) 397-1490, 535 S. US 30. $45–$55.

RAINIER, OREGON

Rainier Budget Inn, (503) 556-4231. $40 and up.

CLATSKANIE, OREGON

Northwoods Inn, (503) 728-4311, 945 E. Columbia River Hwy. $35–$45.

CATHLAMET, WASHINGTON

Country Keeper Bed & Breakfast, (360) 795-3030, 61 Main St. $75–$95.

Nassa Point Motel, (360) 795-3941, 851 E. WA 4. $40.

Redfern Farm B&B, (360) 849-4108, on Puget Island. $55.

Skamokawa, Washington

Skamokawa Inn, (888) 920-2777, WA 4. $70–$190.

Naselle, Washington

Hunter's Inn, (360) 484-9215, WA 4. $50.
Naselle Village Inn Motel, (360) 484-3111, WA 4. $50.
Sleepy Hollow Motel, (360) 484-3232, WA 4. $40.

Chinook, Washington

Hostelling International—Fort Columbia State Park, (360) 777-8755.

Ilwaco, Washington

Heidi's Inn, (360) 642-2387, US 101. $48–$85.

Seaview, Washington

Shelburne Inn, (360) 642-2442, 4415 Pacific Way. $110–$170.
Sou'wester Lodge, (360) 642-2542, 38th Place. Bed and make-your-own breakfast. $40–$110.

Long Beach, Washington

Edgewater Inn, (360) 642-2311. $65–$90.
Shaman Motel, (360) 642-3714 or (800) 753-3750, 115 3rd St. N.W. $65–$85.
Super 8 Motel, (360) 642-8988, 500 Ocean Beach Blvd. $80–$100.

Astoria, Oregon

Astoria Dunes Motel, (503) 325-325-7111, 288 W. Marine Dr. $70–$90.
Astoria Inn Bed & Breakfast, (503) 325-8153, 3391 Irving Ave. $70–$85.
Bayshore Motor Inn, (503) 325-2205, 555 Hamburg. $65–$80.
Crest Motel, (503) 325-3141 or (800) 421-3141, 5366 Leif Erickson Dr. $55–$90.
Franklin Street Station Bed & Breakfast, (503) 325-4314, 1140 Franklin Ave. $80–$130.
Red Lion Inn, (503) 325-7373, 400 Industry St. $105–$125.

Warrenton, Oregon

Shilo Inn, (503) 861-2181, 1609 E. Harbor Dr. $85–$145.

Gearhart, Oregon

Gearhart Ocean Inn, (503) 738-7373, 67 N. Cottage St. $50–$95.

Seaside, Oregon

Best Western Ocean View Resort, (503) 738-3334 or (800) 234-8439, 414 N. Prom. $80–$245.
Ebb Tide Motel, (503) 738-8371 or (800) 468-6232, 300 N. Prom. $100–$115.
Hostelling International—Seaside, (503) 738-7911, 930 N. Holladay Dr.
Riverside Inn Bed & Breakfast, (503) 738-8254 or (800) 826-6151, 430 S. Holladay Dr. $50–$100.

Royale Motel, (503) 738-9541, 531 Ave. A. $50–$70.

CANNON BEACH, OREGON

Blue Gull Inn, (503) 436-2714 or (800) 507-2714, 487 S. Hemlock St. $65–$110.
Cannon Beach Hotel Lodgings, (503) 436-1392 or (800) 238-4107,
1116 S. Hemlock. $50–$170.
Hallmark Resort, (503) 436-1566 or (888) 448-4449, 1400 S. Hemlock. $100–$230.
McBee Motel Cottages, (503) 436-2569 or (800) 238-4107, 888 S. Hemlock.
$35–$135.

CAMPING

CLARKSTON, WASHINGTON

Chief Timothy State Park, (509) 758-9580, 8 miles west on US 12.

STARBUCK, WASHINGTON

Lyons Ferry State Park, (509) 646-3252, WA 261.
Palouse Falls State Park, (509) 646-3252, WA 261. Primitive sites.

*DAYTON, WASHINGTON

Lewis and Clark Trail State Park, (509) 337-6457, 4 miles east on US 12.

*WALLA WALLA, WASHINGTON

Fort Walla Walla Campground, (509) 527-3770, west of town at Fort Walla Walla
Museum complex.

TRI-CITIES, WASHINGTON

Arrowhead RV Park, (509) 545-8206, 3120 Commercial (Pasco).
Charbonneau Park, (509) 547-7781, off of WA 124 east of Pasco.
Columbia Park Campground, (509) 783-3711, 6601 S.E. Columbia Dr. (Kennewick).
Desert Gold Motel & RV Park, (509) 627-1000, Columbia Dr.
west of I-182 Exit 3 (Richland).
Fishhook Park, (509) 547-7781, off of WA 124 east of Pasco.
Hood Park, (509) 547-7781, 3 miles east of Pasco on Hwy 12E.

UMATILLA, OREGON

Hat Rock Campground, (541) 567-4188, east on US 730 opposite
Hat Rock State Park.
Umatilla Marina and RV Park, (541) 922-3939, north of US 730. No tents.

GOLDENDALE, WASHINGTON

Horsethief Lake State Park, (509) 767-1159, west on WA 14. Primitive sites.
Maryhill State Park, (509) 773-5007, near junction of US 97 and WA 14.
Peach Beach, (509) 773-4698, at Gunkel Orchards adjacent to Maryhill State Park.

THE DALLES, OREGON

Deschutes River Recreation Area, 17 miles east on I-84. Primitive sites.
Lone Pine Travel Park, (541) 296-9133, I-84 Exit 87.
Memaloose State Park, 11 miles west on I-84.

WHITE SALMON, WASHINGTON

Bridge RV Park, (509) 493-11111 or (888) 550-7275, 65271 WA 14.

HOOD RIVER, OREGON

Tucker Park, (541) 386-4477, 4 miles south on OR 281. Mostly tent sites.
Viento State Park, (541) 374-8811, 8 miles west on I-84.

CASCADE LOCKS, OREGON

Bridge of the Gods RV Park, (541) 374-8628, US 30.
Cascade Locks KOA, (541) 374-8668, US 30.

STEVENSON, WASHINGTON

Hidden Coves Campground, (509) 427-8098, WA 14.

NORTH BONNEVILLE, WASHINGTON

Beacon Rock RV & Trailer Park, (509) 427-8473, west on WA 14.
Beacon Rock State Park, (509) 427-8265, 3 miles west on WA 14.
Lewis and Clark Campground, (509) 427-5982, west on WA 14.

GRESHAM, OREGON

Oxbow Park, (503) 663-4708, 3010 S.E. Oxbow Pkwy.

PORTLAND, OREGON

Jantzen Beach RV Park, (503) 289-7626 or (800) 443-7248,
1503 N. Hayden Island Dr. No tents.
Reeder Beach Resort RV Park, (503) 621-3098, 26048 N.W. Reeder Rd.
on Sauvie Island. No tents.

RIDGEFIELD, WASHINGTON

Big Fir Campground & RV Park, (360) 887-8970 or (800) 532-4397, I-15 Exit 14.

WOODLAND, WASHINGTON

Columbia Riverfront RV Park, (360) 225-8051 or (800) 845-9842, I-5 Exit 22.
Lewis River RV Park, (360) 225-9556, I-5 Exit 21.
Paradise Point State Park, (360) 263-2350, south via I-5.

KALAMA, WASHINGTON

Camp Kalama RV Park, (360) 673-2456, I-5 Exit 32.

KELSO, WASHINGTON

Brook Hollow RV Park, (360) 577-6474, I-5 Exit 39.
The Cedars RV Park, (360) 274-5136, I-5 Exit 46.

CATHLAMET, WASHINGTON

County Line Park, East on WA 4 at the Cowlitz/Wahkiakum county line.

CHINOOK, WASHINGTON

Chinook County Park, (360) 777-8442, US 101.
Mauch's Sundown RV Park, (360) 777-8713, 4 miles east on US 101.
River's End Campground, (360) 777-8317, west of town on US 101.

ILWACO, WASHINGTON

Fort Canby State Park, (360) 642-3078, 2.5 miles southwest of US 101.
Ilwaco KOA, (360) 642-3292, 2 miles south on US 101.

LONG BEACH, WASHINGTON

Andersen's on the Ocean, (360) 642-2231, 1400 138th St.
Driftwood RV Park, (360) 642-2711, 1512 N. Pacific Way.
Pegg's Oceanside RV Park, (360) 642-2451, north on WA 103.
Pioneer RV Park, (360) 642-3990, WA 103 and Pioneer Rd.

ASTORIA, OREGON

Astoria-Warrenton-Seaside KOA, (503) 861-2606, 1100 N.W. Ridge Rd. (Hammond).
Fort Stevens State Park, (503) 861-1671, west on US 101.
Kampers West, (503) 861-1814, 1140 N.W. Warrenton Dr.
Sunset Lake Resort & RV Park, (503) 861-1760, 850 Lewis Ave.

SEASIDE, OREGON

Circle Creek RV Park & Campground, (503) 738-6070, US 101.

CANNON BEACH, OREGON

RV Resort at Cannon Beach, (503) 436-2231, Elk Creek Rd. No tents.

RESTAURANTS

CLARKSTON, WASHINGTON

Bamboo Gardens, (509) 758-8898, 907 6th St. Mandarin and Szechuan cuisine.
Bridge Street Connection, (509) 758-3141, US 12. Prime rib, daily specials.
Rooster's Landing, (509) 751-0155, 1550 Port Dr. Popular place on the river.

POMEROY, WASHINGTON

Donna's Drive-In, (509) 843-1510, 14th and Main.

*DAYTON, WASHINGTON

Panhandler's Pizza & Pasta, (509) 382-4160, 404 W. Main.

Patit Creek Restaurant, (509) 382-2625, 725 E. Main. French cuisine in an unlikely small-town setting.

Weinhard's Espresso Café, (509) 382-2091, 235 E. Main St. Breakfast and lunch.

*WAITSBURG, WASHINGTON

Farmer's Cafe, (509) 337-6845, 216 Main.

TRI-CITIES, WASHINGTON

Blackberry's Restaurant, (509) 735-7253, 329 N. Kellogg (Kennewick). Good breakfasts.

Captain's Table, (509) 586-0541, in the Ramada Inn Clover Island. Rooftop dining overlooking Columbia River.

Cedar's Pier 1, (509) 582-2143, 7 Clover Island (Kennewick). Steak and seafood with riverside seating.

Rattlesnake Mountain Brewing Company, (509) 783-5747, 1250 Columbia Center Blvd. (Richland). Riverside dining.

Roy's Western Smorgy, (509) 735-8539, 1300 Columbia Center Blvd (Richland). One-price buffet.

*WALLA WALLA, WASHINGTON

The Homestead Restaurant, (509) 522-0345, 1528 Isaacs. Lunch and dinner specials daily.

Jacobi's Cafe, (509) 525-2677, 416 N. 2nd. Wide menu, vegetarian dishes.

Pastime Cafe, (509) 525-0873, 215 W. Main. Italian and American food.

The Turf, (509) 522-9807, 10 N. 2nd. Sandwiches, Northwest microbrews.

THE DALLES, OREGON

Cousins, (541) 298-2771, at the Quality Inn. Ribs, pot roast, other home-style fare.

Lone Pine Restaurant, (541) 298-2800, I-84 at US 197. Family dining, breakfast all day.

Windseeker, (541) 298-7177, 1535 Bargeway Rd. Riverfront restaurant with deck seating.

HOOD RIVER, OREGON

Columbia Court Dining Room, (541) 387-5409, in the Columbia Gorge Hotel. Elegant dining and "famous farm breakfast."

The Mesquitery, (541) 386-2002, 1219 12th St. Gourmet grilling with mesquite wood.

6th Street Bistro & Loft, (541) 386-5737, 6th and Cascade. New American cuisine featuring local foods.

Sage's Café & Coffee House, (541) 386-9404, 202 Cascade St. Salads, sandwiches, baked goods.

Stonehedge Inn, (541) 386-3940, 3405 Cascade Dr. Elegant dining amid wooded surroundings.

LYLE, WASHINGTON

Country Cafe, (509) 365-3883, WA 14. Burgers, omelettes, homemade pie.

BINGEN, WASHINGTON

Fidel's, (509) 493-1017, 120 E. Steuben. Mexican food.

CASCADE LOCKS, OREGON

Charburger Restaurant, (541) 374-8477, 714 S.W. WaNaPa. Breakfast specialties, chili, chicken.

Sam Hill's River Room & Patio, (541) 374-8477, 745 WaNaPa. Northwest cuisine.

STEVENSON, WASHINGTON

Big River Grill, (509) 427-4888, WA 14. Tasty food in historic building.

Dee's Kich-Inn, (509) 427-4670, 10 N.W. 2nd St. Home cooking three meals a day.

Skamania Lodge, (509) 427-2508, in the Skamania Lodge. Sunday brunch.

TROUTDALE, OREGON

McMenamin's Edgefield Power Station, (503) 669-8610, just off I-84. Movie theater/bistro/B&B/hostel.

Tad's Chicken 'n Dumplins, (503) 666-5337, east on Crown Point Hwy. (Troutdale). Dining on the Sandy River.

PORTLAND, OREGON

Atwater's Restaurant & Bar, (503) 275-3600, 111 S.W. 5th Ave. Fine dining with a great view.

Avalon Restaurant, (503) 227-4630, 4630 S.W. Macadam Ave. French-Asian fusion fare.

Hamburger Mary's, (503) 223-0900, 239 S.W. Broadway. A funky local favorite.

Jake's Famous Crawfish, (503) 226-1419, 401 S.W. 12th St. Wide seafood menu.

Jake's Grill, (503) 220-1850, 611 S.W. 10th Ave. Steaks and more in the Governor Hotel.

Macheesmo Mouse, (503) 228-3491, 723 S.W. Salmon and other locations. Heart-smart Mexican fare.

Saigon Kitchen, (503) 281-1421, 835 N.E. Broadway. Locally popular Vietnamese restaurant.

Zell's: An American Cafe, (503) 239-0196, 1300 S.E. Morrison. Breakfast and lunch.

VANCOUVER, WASHINGTON

Juanita's Mexican Restaurant, (360) 834-5856, 231 3rd Ave. (Camas). Daily specials.

Sheldon's Café at the Grant House, (360) 699-1213. Historical setting at Fort Vancouver.

Peach Tree, (360) 693-6736, 6600 N.E. Hwy. 99. Family dining.

KALAMA, WASHINGTON

Columbia Inn Restaurant, (360) 673-2800, 698 N.E. Frontage.

LONGVIEW, WASHINGTON

Charlie's, (360) 636-5661, 1826 1st Ave. Family dining, wide menu.

Hart C's, (360) 425-6292, 3171 Ocean Beach Hwy. Thai and American cuisine.

The Masthead, (360) 577-7972, 1210 Ocean Beach Hwy. Seafood, burgers, chicken.

CATHLAMET, WASHINGTON

Ranch House Restaurant, (360) 795-8015, 3rd & Una.

SKAMOKAWA, WASHINGTON

The Duck Inn, (360) 795-3655, WA 4.

CHINOOK, WASHINGTON

Sanctuary Restaurant, (360) 777-8380, US 101. Seafood and more in turn-of-the-century church.

SEAVIEW, WASHINGTON

42nd Street Cafe, (360) 642-2323, 42nd St. and Pacific Hwy. Chicken, pot roast, seafood, steaks.

My Mom's Pie, (360) 642-2342, 4316 S Pacific Hwy. Pleasant atmosphere, Including outdoor tables.

Shoalwater Restaurant, (360) 642-4142, WA 103 at 45th St. Regional specialties.

LONG BEACH, WASHINGTON

Chuck's Restaurant, (360) 642-2721, WA 103. Chicken-fried steak, seafood, prime rib.

The Lightship Restaurant & Lounge (360) 642-3252. Casual ocean-view dining in the Edgewater Inn.

CLATSKANIE, OREGON

Northwoods Inn Restaurant, (503) 728-4311, 945 E. Columbia River Hwy.

ASTORIA, OREGON

Andrew & Steve's Restaurant, (503) 325-5762, 1196 Marine Dr. Greek specialties and seafood, open since 1916.

Cafe Uniontown, (503) 325-8708, 218 W. Marine Dr. Steaks, seafood, pasta.

Pig 'n Pancake, (503) 325-3144, 146 W. Bond. Breakfast anytime. Also in Seaside and Cannon Beach.

Shark Rock Café, (503) 325-7720, 1092 Marine Dr. Seafood, pasta, and more.

Ship Inn, (503) 325-0033, 2nd St. at Marine Dr. Fish and chips, other pub fare.

GEARHART, OREGON

Oceanside Restaurant, (503) 738-7789, 1200 N. Marion Dr. Casual gourmet dining with Pacific view.

Pacific City Bakery & Café, (503) 738-0245, 601 Pacific Way. Famous croissants, pasta, seafood.

Seaside, Oregon

Bell Buoy, (503) 738-2722, 1800 S. Holladay. Seafood since 1946.

Cisco's Grill, (503) 738-0171, 412 Broadway. Mexican and seafood specialties.

Dooger's Seafood Grill, (503) 738-3773, 505 Broadway. Clam chowder, steak, salads. Also in Cannon Beach and Long Beach.

Pudgy's, (503) 738-8330, 227 Broadway. Seafood and steaks with outdoor dining.

Sherry's On Broadway, (503) 738-5992, 604 Broadway. Award-winning clam chowder and good Italian food.

Cannon Beach, Oregon

Heather's Café, (503) 436-9356, 217 N. Hemlock. Soup, sandwiches, decadent desserts.

Ira's, (503) 436-1588, 3401 S. Hemlock. Creative Northwestern cuisine.

Wayfarer Restaurant & Lounge, (503) 436-1108, Ocean Front and Gower. Wide menu.

EPILOGUE

*I*t took Lewis and Clark 18 months to reach the Pacific Ocean on their outbound trip. But like any travelers eager to return home, they made much better time on the return-journey, arriving in St. Louis September 23, 1806, six months to the day after leaving Fort Clatsop. A newspaper account reporting the occasion read thus: "Mssrs. Lewis and Clark arrived here about one hour ago. Three cheers were fired. They really have the appearance of Robinson Crusoes, dressed entirely in buckskins."

In the years following the expedition, many of its members went on to fame and fortune. Even before the party arrived home, John Colter asked to be allowed to return west as a trapper. "We agreed to allow him the privilege provided no one of the party would ask or expect a similar permission," Clark wrote on August 16, 1806. Soon, Colter became known as the first white man to explore the area around what is now Yellowstone and Grand Teton national parks.

George Shannon, the enlisted party's youngest man, became a congressman from Kentucky. York was eventually freed by Clark, who helped get him started in a freight-hauling business. Patrick Gass, the first corps member to publish his journals, was a bit slower to establish his personal life. At age 60, he finally married Maria Hamilton, a woman one-third his age. He died shortly before his 99th birthday, outliving his young wife by more than a decade. He also lived longer than anyone else who had been on the expedition, including Sacagawea's son, Jean Baptiste.

As for Clark, he enjoyed a stellar post-expedition career. He was appointed Superintendent of Indian Affairs in 1807 and served in that role until his death in 1838. In 1813, he was also appointed governor of the newly established Missouri Territory and was reappointed three times, holding the office until Missouri became a state in 1821 (although he failed to win the post in the first state election). But it was in his position as Indian Superintendent that he won his greatest acclaim. "In this role, he broadened the base of goodwill the Lewis and Clark Expedition had established, and probably did more to help the Indians than any of his successors," wrote Roy E. Appleman in his National Park Service survey. "Their friend, protector, and advocate, who always tried to obtain as much justice as possible for them, he was fondly known as the 'Red-Headed Chief.'" Clark also had a happy personal life, marrying his sweetheart Julia Hancock in 1808. They had five children, naming the firstborn Meriwether Lewis Clark. Julia died in 1821, but Clark then married Harriet Kennerly

Radford, a widow with three children. Together, they went on to have two more sons.

And what of Lewis? Sadly, fate was not as kind. Despite his keen intellect and bright record of service, Lewis had difficulty establishing himself after the expedition, either professionally or personally. Things started well enough: Lewis was appointed governor of the Louisiana Territory and made plans for publication of the expedition's journals. But long given to brooding and mood swings, Lewis was not an especially adept politician. He also suffered financial problems, particularly after the U.S. War Department refused to honor drafts Lewis had signed to provide for the safe return of an Indian party that had accompanied the corps back east at Jefferson's request. Lewis was held personally responsible for the debt, and it appeared he would have to sell title to the 1,600 acres of land he was rewarded for his part in the expedition.

In the fall of 1809, Lewis set off for Washington to plead his case in person. On the night of October 9, two of his party's packhorses escaped, and Lewis dispatched his companion, Maj. James Neelly, to search for them. On October 11, Neelly found Lewis dead of two gunshot wounds. He was just 35 years old. To this day, no one has proven conclusively whether the captain's death was murder or suicide, but his memory is honored at a park along Tennessee's Natchez Trace. The park's centerpiece is a broken column that stands in mute testimony to Lewis's untimely death.

But even tragedy could not blunt the expedition's impact nor dull the sense something great had been accomplished. "The expedition of Mssrs. Lewis and Clark for exploring the River Missouri and the best communication from that to the Pacific Ocean has had all the success which could have been expected," Jefferson said in his report to Congress in December 1806. "They have traced the Missouri nearly to its source, descended the Columbia to the Pacific Ocean, ascertaining with accuracy the geography of that interesting communication across our continent, learned the character of the country, of its commerce and inhabitants, and it is but justice to say that Mssrs. Lewis and Clark and their brave companions have by this arduous service deserved well of their country." Long after their deaths, the legacy left by Lewis and Clark ensured the future of America as a world power and, even more important, as a nation that ever dares to dream—and to discover.

ANNUAL LEWIS AND CLARK EVENTS

Dates can change. Please call ahead to confirm.

Third weekend in May: *Lewis and Clark Rendezvous*, St. Charles, Missouri, (636) 947-3199.

Early June: *Lewis and Clark Days*, Washburn, North Dakota, (701) 462-8535.

Early June: *Lewis and Clark Days*, Fort Walla Walla Museum, Walla Walla, Washington, (509) 525-7703.

Late June: *Lewis and Clark Festival*, Great Falls, Montana, (406) 727-8733.

Third week of July: *Lewis and Clark Festival and White Catfish Camp*, Council Bluffs, Iowa, (712) 366-4900.

Third weekend of July: *Lewis and Clark Historic Festival*, Chamberlain, South Dakota, (605) 734-6542.

Fourth Sunday of July: *Clark's Day*, Pompey's Pillar near Billings, Montana. (406) 238-1540.

Late July: *Weekend of Discovery*, Three Forks, Montana. (406) 285-4880.

Early August: *Sacajawea Heritage Days Festival*, Salmon, Idaho. (208) 756-2100.

Fourth weekend of August: *Lewis & Clark Festival*, Lewis & Clark Visitor Center, Yankton, South Dakota. (402) 667-7873 ext. 3246.

Mid-October: *Lewis & Clark Days*, Clarkston, Washington. (800) 933-2128.

Third Sunday of October: *Lewis and Clark Heritage Day*, Irrigon, Oregon. (541) 481-3014.

INDEX

Bold numerals indicate maps.
Italic numerals indicate photographs.

ABOUT THE AUTHOR

Julie Fanselow was born in Illinois and grew up in Bethel Park, Pennsylvania. She earned a bachelor's degree in journalism at Ohio University.

After 10 years as a reporter and editor for daily newspapers in Ohio, Idaho, and Washington state, Fanselow became a full-time independent writer specializing in travel. Her other books include *Traveling the Oregon Trail* (Falcon), *Texas* (Lonely Planet), and *Idaho Off the Beaten Path* (Globe Pequot). She also has contributed to several volumes in the Discovery Travel Adventures guidebook series from The Discovery Channel/Insight Guides, and she writes regularly for *Sunset* magazine.

Fanselow is a founder of www.guidebookwriters.com, a website aimed at helping travelers connect directly with the world's top travel authors. She is a member of the Society of American Travel Writers, the American Society of Journalists and Authors, and the Lewis and Clark Trail Heritage Foundation. She now lives in Idaho with her family.

FALCONGUIDES® Leading the Way™

WILDLIFE VIEWING GUIDES

Alaska Wildlife Viewing Guide
Arizona Wildlife Viewing Guide
California Wildlife Viewing Guide
Colorado Wildlife Viewing Guide
Florida Wildlife Viewing Guide
Indiana Wildlife Vewing Guide
Iowa Wildlife Viewing Guide
Kentucky Wildlife Viewing Guide
Massachusetts Wildlife Viewing Guide
Montana Wildlife Viewing Guide
Nebraska Wildlife Viewing Guide
Nevada Wildlife Viewing Guide
New Hampshire Wildlife Viewing Guide
New Jersey Wildlife Viewing Guide
New Mexico Wildlife Viewing Guide
New York Wildlife Viewing Guide
North Carolina Wildlife Viewing Guide
North Dakota Wildlife Viewing Guide
Ohio Wildlife Viewing Guide
Oregon Wildlife Viewing Guide
Puerto Rico and the Virgin Islands WVG
Tennessee Wildlife Viewing Guide
Texas Wildlife Viewing Guide
Utah Wildlife Viewing Guide
Vermont Wildlife Viewing Guide
Virginia Wildlife Viewing Guide
Washington Wildlife Viewing Guide
West Virginia Wildlife Viewing Guide
Wisconsin Wildlife Viewing Guide

HISTORIC TRAIL GUIDES

Traveling California's Gold Rush Country
Traveling the Lewis & Clark Trail
Traveling the Oregon Trail
Traveler's Guide to the Pony Express Trail

SCENIC DRIVING GUIDES

Scenic Driving Alaska and the Yukon
Scenic Driving Arizona
Scenic Driving the Beartooth Highway
Scenic Driving California
Scenic Driving Colorado
Scenic Driving Florida
Scenic Driving Georgia
Scenic Driving Hawaii
Scenic Driving Idaho
Scenic Driving Indiana
Scenic Driving Kentucky
Scenic Driving Michigan
Scenic Driving Minnesota
Scenic Driving Montana
Scenic Driving New England
Scenic Driving New Mexico
Scenic Driving North Carolina
Scenic Driving Oregon
Scenic Driving the Ozarks including the
    Ouchita Mountains
Scenic Driving Pennsylvania
Scenic Driving Texas
Scenic Driving Utah
Scenic Driving Virginia
Scenic Driving Washington
Scenic Driving Wisconsin
Scenic Driving Wyoming
Scenic Driving Yellowstone & Grand Teton
    National Parks
Scenic Byways East & South
Scenic Byways Far West
Scenic Byways Rocky Mountains

■ *To order any of these books, check with your local bookseller*
or call FALCON ® *at* **1-800-582-2665**.
Visit us on the world wide web at:
www.Falcon.com

FALCON®

FALCON GUIDES ® Leading the way™

FalconGuides® are available for where-to-go hiking, mountain biking, rock climbing, walking, scenic driving, fishing, rockhounding, paddling, birding, wildlife viewing, and camping. We also have FalconGuides on essential outdoor skills and subjects and field identification. The following titles are currently available, but this list grows every year. For a free catalog with a complete list of titles, call FALCON toll-free at 1-800-582-2665.

BIRDING GUIDES

Birding Georgia
Birding Illinois
Birding Minnesota
Birding Montana
Birding Northern California
Birding Texas
Birding Utah

PADDLING GUIDES

Paddling Minnesota
Paddling Montana
Paddling Okefenokee
Paddling Oregon
Paddling Yellowstone & Grand
   Teton National Parks

WALKING

Walking Colorado Springs
Walking Denver
Walking Portland
Walking Seattle
Walking St. Louis
Walking San Francisco
Walking Virginia Beach

CAMPING GUIDES

Camping Arizona
Camping California's
   National Forests
Camping Colorado
Camping Oregon
Camping Southern California
Camping Washington
Recreation Guide to Washington
   National Forests

FIELD GUIDES

Bitterroot: Montana State Flower
Canyon Country Wildflowers
Central Rocky Mountain
   Wildflowers
Chihuahuan Desert Wildflowers
Great Lakes Berry Book
New England Berry Book
Ozark Wildflowers
Pacific Northwest Berry Book
Plants of Arizona
Rare Plants of Colorado
Rocky Mountain Berry Book
Scats & Tracks of the Pacific
   Coast States
Scats & Tracks of the Rocky Mtns.
Sierra Nevada Wildflowers
Southern Rocky Mountain
   Wildflowers
Tallgrass Prairie Wildflowers
Western Trees

ROCKHOUNDING GUIDES

Rockhounding Arizona
Rockhounding California
Rockhounding Colorado
Rockhounding Montana
Rockhounding Nevada
Rockhounding New Mexico
Rockhounding Texas
Rockhounding Utah
Rockhounding Wyoming

HOW-TO GUIDES

Avalanche Aware
Backpacking Tips
Bear Aware
Desert Hiking Tips
Hiking with Dogs
Hiking with Kids
Mountain Lion Alert
Reading Weather
Route Finding
Using GPS
Wild Country Companion
Wilderness First Aid
Wilderness Survival

MORE GUIDEBOOKS

Backcountry Horseman's
   Guide to Washington
Family Fun in Montana
Family Fun in Yellowstone
Exploring Canyonlands & Arches
   National Parks
Exploring Hawaii's Parklands
Exploring Mount Helena
Exploring Southern California
   Beaches
Hiking Hot Springs of the Pacific
   Northwest
Touring Arizona Hot Springs
Touring California & Nevada
   Hot Springs
Touring Colorado Hot Springs
Touring Montana and Wyoming
   Hot Springs
Trail Riding Western Montana
Wilderness Directory
Wild Montana
Wild Utah
Wild Virginia

■ *To order any of these books, check with your local bookseller*
*or call FALCON ® at **1-800-582-2665**.*
Visit us on the world wide web at:
www.Falcon.com

FALCON®

FALCON GUIDES ® Leading the Way™

HIKING GUIDES

Best Hikes Along the Continental Divide
Hiking Alaska
Hiking Arizona
Hiking Arizona's Cactus Country
Hiking the Beartooths
Hiking Big Bend National Park
Hiking the Bob Marshall Country
Hiking California
Hiking California's Desert Parks
Hiking Carlsbad Caverns
　and Guadalupe Mtns. National Parks
Hiking Colorado
Hiking Colorado, Vol. II
Hiking Colorado's Summits
Hiking Colorado's Weminuche Wilderness
Hiking the Columbia River Gorge
Hiking Florida
Hiking Georgia
Hiking Glacier & Waterton Lakes National Parks
Hiking Grand Canyon National Park
Hiking Grand Staircase-Escalante/Glen Canyon
Hiking Grand Teton National Park
Hiking Great Basin National Park
Hiking Hot Springs in the Pacific Northwest
Hiking Idaho
Hiking Indiana
Hiking Maine
Hiking Maryland and Delaware
Hiking Michigan
Hiking Minnesota
Hiking Montana
Hiking Mount Rainier National Park
Hiking Mount St. Helens
Hiking Nevada
Hiking New Hampshire
Hiking New Mexico
Hiking New Mexico's Gila Wilderness

Hiking New York
Hiking North Carolina
Hiking the North Cascades
Hiking Northern Arizona
Hiking Northern California
Hiking Olympic National Park
Hiking Oregon
Hiking Oregon's Eagle Cap Wilderness
Hiking Oregon's Mount Hood/Badger Creek
Hiking Oregon's Central Cascades
Hiking Pennsylvania
Hiking Ruins Seldom Seen
Hiking Shenandoah
Hiking the Sierra Nevada
Hiking South Carolina
Hiking South Dakota's Black Hills Country
Hiking Southern New England
Hiking Tennessee
Hiking Texas
Hiking Utah
Hiking Utah's Summits
Hiking Vermont
Hiking Virginia
Hiking Washington
Hiking Wisconsin
Hiking Wyoming
Hiking Wyoming's Cloud Peak Wilderness
Hiking Wyoming's Teton
　and Washakie Wilderness
Hiking Wyoming's Wind River Range
Hiking Yellowstone National Park
Hiking Yosemite National Park
Hiking Zion & Bryce Canyon National Parks
Wild Country Companion
Wild Montana
Wild Utah
Wild Virginia

■ *To order any of these books, check with your local bookseller*
*or call FALCON ® at **1-800-582-2665**.*
Visit us on the world wide web at:
www.Falcon.com

FALCON®

Discover the Thrill of Watching Wildlife.

 The Watchable Wildlife® Series

Published in cooperation with Defenders of Wildlife, these high-quality, full color guidebooks feature detailed descriptions, side trips, viewing tips, and easy-to-follow maps. Wildlife viewing guides for the following states are now available with more on the way.

Alaska	Nebraska	Puerto Rico &
Arizona	Nevada	Virgin Islands
California	New Hampshire	Tennessee
Colorado	New Jersey	Texas
Florida	New Mexico	Utah
Indiana	New York	Vermont
Iowa	North Carolina	Virginia
Kentucky	North Dakota	Washington
Massachusetts	Ohio	West Virginia
Montana	Oregon	Wisconsin

Watch for this sign along roadways. It's the official sign indicating wildlife viewing areas included in the Watchable Wildlife® Series.

■ *To order any of these books, check with your local bookseller or call FALCON® at*
1-800-582-2665.

www.falcon.com

FALCON®